International Review
of Health Psychology

Editorial Board

International Review of Health Psychology

VOLUME 3

Edited by
S. Maes
Leiden University, The Netherlands

H. Leventhal
Rutgers University, USA

and

M. Johnston
University of St Andrews, Scotland

JOHN WILEY & SONS
Chichester · New York · Brisbane · Toronto · Singapore

Copyright © 1994 by John Wiley & Sons Ltd,
Baffins Lane, Chichester,
West Sussex PO19 1UD, England

National Chichester (0243) 779777
International +44 243 779777

Other Wiley Editorial Offices

John Wiley & Sons, Inc., 605 Third Avenue,
New York, NY 10158–0012, USA

Jacaranda Wiley Ltd, 33 Park Road, Milton,
Queensland 4064, Australia

John Wiley & Sons (Canada) Ltd, 22 Worcester Road,
Rexdale, Ontario M9W 1L1, Canada

John Wiley & Sons (SEA) Pte Ltd, 37 Jalan Pemimpin # 05–04,
Block B, Union Industrial Building, Singapore 2057

British Library Cataloguing in Publication Data

A catalogue record for this book is available from the British Library

ISBN 0-471-94456-4

Typeset in 10/12pt Sabon by Acorn Bookwork, Salisbury
Printed and bound in Great Britain by Biddles Ltd, Guildford and King's Lynn

Contents

List of Contributors

Judith R. Anderson
Rutgers University, USA

A. Appels
State University of Limburg, The Netherlands

Padmini Banerjee
Kent State University, USA

Ron Borland
Centre for Behavioural Research in Cancer, Melbourne, Australia

Paula Britton
Kent State University, USA

Simon Chapman
University of Sydney, Australia

Richard Contrada
Rutgers University, USA

René F. W. Diekstra
University of Leiden, The Netherlands

P. Falger
State University of Limburg, The Netherlands

B. Golombeck
State University of Limburg, The Netherlands

David Hill
Centre for Behavioural Research in Cancer, Melbourne, Australia

Stevan E. Hobfoll
Kent State University, USA

Ad J. F. M. Kerkhof
University of Leiden, The Netherlands

W. Kop
State University of Limburg, The Netherlands

Elaine E. Leventhal
Rutgers University, USA

R. Markusse
State University of Limburg, The Netherlands

C. Meester
State University of Limburg, The Netherlands

Brian Oldenburg
University of Sydney, Australia

Neville Owen
University of Adelaide, Australia

Denise C. Park
University of Georgia, USA

Lothar R. Schmidt
University of Trier, Germany

Olar Vassend
Institute of Community Dentistry, Oslo, Norway

Preface

As explained in earlier volumes, it is our intention to publish, review-type chapters covering the following health psychology fields: (1) general concepts and methodology; (2) health behaviour and health promotion; (3) illness behaviour and health care and (4) professional and practical issues. This volume reflects once again the international dimension of the *Review*. Out of the nine chapters, four are written by Europeans, three come from the United States and two from Australia. The first three fields are well covered. In the first chapter (the general concepts and methodology domain) Lothar Schmidt, from the University of Trier, takes a critical look at public health psychology. Schmidt states that a psychological approach to public health problems is needed as the field would profit from the application of psychological models, assessment, intervention and evaluation strategies on condition that psychologists adopt a generally positive attitude about health on the individual and societal level from a lifespan perspective. In the second chapter Stevan E. Hobfoll, Padmini Banerjee and Paula Britton from Kent State University, present a conceptual analysis of the relation between stress resistance resources and health. The main issue of this chapter is to illustrate that the theory of conservation of resources, developed by the first author, may aid the study and understanding of this relationship. In the third chapter, Ad Appels and his colleagues from the State University of Limburg give an overview of research on the relationship between vital exhaustion and acute coronary syndromes. The chapter presents data from prospective studies and discusses relevant literature on the concept of vital exhaustion and related psychological correlates. The fourth chapter by Olav Vassend, who is affiliated with the University of Oslo, is concerned with the differential correlates of negative affectivity and objective health indicators. The author uses data from the Norwegian National Health Survey ($N = 7922$) to test crucial hypotheses, which are based on a brief review of the literature.

The next three chapters are concerned with health behaviour and health promotion. The fifth chapter by Brian Oldenburg from Sydney University on promotion of healthy lifestyles complements the first chapter by Schmidt as Oldenburg advocates that the clinical approach which has been used in the past to develop practitioner-delivered lifestyle interventions needs to be integrated into a broader public health approach. The author also stresses the importance of environmental factors which influence the development and change of health behaviour. The chapter concentrates, however, more on change strategies related to the stages of lifestyle change and an individual's preparedness to change. The sixth chapter by Rene Diekstra and Ad Kerkhof from Leiden University provides a critical review on the effectiveness of the prevention of suicidal behaviour. The authors discuss various types of prevention programmes and measures such as school-based-programmes, initiatives of suicide prevention centres, after-care for suicide attempters, therapy for persons with affective disorders and removal or obstruction of means to commit suicide. The authors reach to the conclusion that data is insufficient to prove the effectiveness of these preventive interventions. In the seventh chapter on regulatory innovations and behaviour change, Australians Ron Borland, Neville Owen, David Hill and Simon Chapman argue that health psychology research on disease prevention should focus more on the effects of large-scale social and regulatory innovations. They consider research on the impact of smoking restrictions and discuss the findings of a series of studies in Australia, both cross-sectional and longitudinal, on the impact of workplace smoking bans. Implications for the study of smoking cessation and for understanding some of the broader issues in the social regulation of health-related behaviours are discussed.

The third part, focussing on illness behaviour and health care, consists of two chapters. The cornerstone of both chapters is self-regulation theory. Chapter 8 by Denise Park, affiliated with the University of Georgia, is on self-regulation and the control of rheumatic disorders. The focus of the chapter is on understanding the cognitive representation of rheumatic illness by the individual and especially on mechanisms which underlie effective representations which lead to adaptive self-regulation of the disease. Coping strategies, medication adherence and the effect of interventions in relation to effective self-regulatory strategies are considered. Chapter 9 is a comprehensive review of psychological preparation for surgery by Richard Contrada, Elaine Leventhal and Judith Anderson from Rutgers University. The chapter provides a critical overview of research concerned with the evaluation of surgical preparation programmes. The authors use a combination of individual and interpersonal self-regulation constructs as a conceptual framework for the understanding and improvement of surgical outcomes and they discuss practical, methodological and data-analytic issues relevant to future research in the area.

As a chapter on health psychology in Latin America did not reach us in time we had no material for the part of the review on professional and practical issues. In order to ensure that this important field will be covered in the next volumes, we would like to encourage authors to send us short contributions of five to ten pages presenting and discussing case studies of relevant practical projects in their country, which could serve to develop or adapt models of health psychology practice in other countries. The scope of these contributions should not be primarily on the scientific evaluation of these projects, but rather on the theoretical or empirical base of the project, and should contain a well-illustrated description of the project and a critical evaluation, including suggestions for its implementation or practical use. Examples could be specific health promotion programmes in a community, worksite, school, clinical or leisure setting, psychological intervention programmes aiming at improving quality of life or enhancing secondary prevention and intervention in specific groups of patients and interventions in health care. In addition, all other short papers on professional issues such as training programmes in health psychology or related to the position of health psychologists in a specific country are also very welcome. Our open invitation to send us review (including meta-analysis) or documented opinion-type chapters on topics related to the other fields of the *Review* stands, of course, as before. We were thus able to publish in this third volume a few papers which were submitted spontaneously. It is, of course, always important to contact us with a suggested review topic at an early stage in order to prevent overlapping with existing chapters. As a result of our combined work it seems that the *International Review of Health Psychology* has established itself. We were glad to read and note the many constructive reviews from various parts of the world and we will continue to work and maintain a high standard and, last but not least, an international perspective.

I would like to thank my co-editors, Howard Leventhal and Marie Johnston, for their efforts in obtaining good chapters and for their constructive comments and all the work they have put into the production of this third volume. Special thanks also go to the many anonymous reviewers and the members of the editorial board who assisted us with valuable advice and, last but not least, my secretary Ellen Smelik who has put in a substantial amount of energy and work, including the many contacts with the authors, reviewers and the publisher as well as editorial assistance for the publication of Volumes 2 and 3. Although she rightly accepted a job at another level, I regret that she will no longer be my untiring partner for the forthcoming publications. In the meanwhile Jacqueline Dicke became the editorial assistant for the Review, a job which she is doing with dedication and competence.

Stan Maes
Leiden, 18 October 1993

Part I

GENERAL CONCEPTS AND METHODOLOGY

1 A Psychological Look at Public Health: Contents and Methodology

*University of Trier, Department of Psychology,
54286 Trier, Germany*

PUBLIC HEALTH PSYCHOLOGY: A NEW AREA?

As Holland and Fitzsimons (1991, p. 605) claim:

> There is a long-standing misapprehension that curative medicine is the most important component of maintenance of the health of the public. Populations, politicians, and even the public have been led to believe that the major advances in medicine, and thus in health, are provided through hospital services. Thus the potential of public health to implement its proposals and to have long-term influence on health status goes largely unrecognized.

A change of this view and a call for action against the political and health-related agencies is seen in the ideology of the WHO, especially "Health for All by the Year 2000".

Psychology should be restricted neither to the curative, clinical problems and motives of single individuals and small groups nor to mental health or the psychological aspects of illness. Instead, it should also promote prevention, community needs and the influences of the exosystem, thus including many topics of public health. As Lorion (1991, p. 516) stated: "Psychology as a scientific and applied discipline has a unique responsibility to participate in the pursuit of strategies that reduce the nation's health care needs."

Diekstra (1990) was one of the first psychologists to use the term "public health *psychology*".

> There are millions of people around the world who seek medical care for complaints or disorders that are caused or aggravated by their own behaviour or the behaviour of others. But one of the most important causes of their problems is nothing that a pathologist could see under a microscope and nothing that a doctor could change with a pill. In order to see it, to understand it, and to influence it, another approach is called for. That approach is the psychosocial or the behavioural one. (p. 29)

International Review of Health Psychology, Volume 3. Edited by S. Maes, H. Leventhal and M. Johnston
© 1994 John Wiley & Sons Ltd

Many of the handbooks of public health hardly refer explicitly to psychology as a science or as a profession at all. On the other hand, in the papers of psychologists such as Diekstra (1990) or Kiesler and Morton (1988), psychology is more or less postulated as important for public health, but its impact as a theoretical and an applied discipline in public health has not yet been convincingly demonstrated. The main aim of this chapter is to focus on the psychological aspects of public health, which lead to questions like the following: What is the psychological contribution to public health programs with regard to goals, contents and methodology? Which psychological models, diagnostical instruments and methods of intervention are usable in public health? Is there a professional and/or ethical limit to psychologists' participation in public health?

In order to deal with these issues, the scope of public health must first be briefly defined and analyzed. I do not feel competent to review the broad field of public health or the psychological contributions to it. My intention is the explication of some viewpoints in this realm. In an early stage of my work on the chapter, I thought about a more systematic analysis with regard to only a couple of public health areas. This approach bears at least two problems: (1) that mainly specialists of a certain field might be interested in it and (2) that one more or less concentrates on certain risks, prevention programs, etc. which are predominant in the given area and disregards others. I like to stimulate psychologists who do not work mainly in the field of public health to reflect upon the many political and societal influences of all our preventive and interventive work and to transfer their knowledge, theories and methods as much as possible to the realm of public health.

THE SCOPE OF PUBLIC HEALTH

As early as 1920, Winslow defined public health as:

> the science and the art of preventing disease, prolonging life, and promoting physical health and efficiency through organized community efforts for the sanitation of the environment, the control of communicable infections, the education of the individual in principles of personal hygiene, the organization of medical and nursing service for the early diagnosis and preventive treatment of disease, and the development of the social machinery which will ensure to every individual a standard of living adequate for the maintenance of health; organizing these benefits in such fashion as to enable every citizen to realize his birthrights of health and longevity. (p. 183)

This definition seems to be very much up to date, at least with regard to the medical part of public health and the main criterion of life expectation.

One of the classical examples of public health may be used for clarification. In the middle of the nineteenth century, Snow analyzed the distribution of cholera cases in London. The distribution showed a strong association of the cases with the use of a specific water pump. After removing the pump handle, the further spread of cholera in London was prevented.

Runyan et al. (1982) view Snow's methodology as being one prototype for public health intervention with current value. Key elements can be found in Table 1.1. Ingham and Bennett (1990) have derived additional psychological considerations in the traditional field of public health from a comparable set of assumptions.

However, even with regard to infectious disease, the behavior of the individual is often most important. This is not only true for sexually transmitted diseases but also for many infections, such as St Louis or tick-transmitted encephalitis.

The general importance and the scope of public health depend very much on the *definition of health* and disease. In an editorial, Abholz et al. (1992, p. 5) found the following three communalities in six definitions of public health: (a) delimitation of biomedical approaches, (b) an approach which is not oriented to the individual but to the population and the community and thus is political in nature and (c) a preventive orientation.

Seedhouse's (1990) discussions aim beyond such definitions. In his view, *health* and *disease* should not be located on a continuum but be thought of as *separate categories*. Accordingly, health itself is a continuum with "conditions of life which make it possible to do all that is desired" at one end and "conditions of life which are so disabling that nothing is possible" at the other (Seedhouse, 1990, p. 49).

According to Seeman (1989, p. 1107):

> health is comprehensive in scope and transactional in character. When we speak of health, we speak of organismic lawfulness and regulation in all parts of the human system. Furthermore, when we speak of health, we speak contextually, that is, we view the system as a whole and note the effects of regulation and disregulation in all relevant parts of the system. ... In a human-system model, we do not need to stand on the threshold of disease to understand or measure levels of health. This is not to say that disease is in any way less important to understand, but rather that it is not a necessary anchor to the definition of health.

Table 1.1.   Key elements of the public health approach (cf. Runyan et al., 1982)

1. Efforts are triggered by the identification of a *health problem* or concern.
2. The *population* is defined as the unit of interest instead of a specific individual.
3. The investigation of the problem and the choice of solution is derived through *empirical* means rather than by recourse to a theoretical model.
4. The intent is the *prevention* of the disease rather than the cure of the disease.
5. The appropriate intervention has a direct *implementation* without completely understanding the causal mechanisms.
6. It is a *regulatory action* at the environmental or community level without voluntary participation of the individuals at risk.

If one accepts such broad definitions of health, public health reaches far beyond the usual medical intervention.

Winett, King and Altman (1989) as well as Schwarzer (1992) contrast public health and health psychology as two poles of a continuum, with public health targeting the concerns of the society and health psychology targeting the concerns of the individual. Accordingly, Winett, King and Altman (1989) outlined four different levels of analysis: personal, interpersonal, organizational/environmental and institutional/societal. If a multitude of levels is regarded in analyses and interventions as well, it is not very important to debate too much about the boundaries of public health.

Figure 1.1 contains a general framework of public health in its broader view. The usual starting point is the registration and analysis of health risks (antecedent variables), illness-promoting factors and behaviors (intervening variables), or the first manifestation of illness. From those observations, a more or less causal interpretation is inferred with regard to macrosystemic and exosystemic conditions, objective and subjective stress, general or individual problems in settings, and the personality in its structure and its influences on concrete behavior. A change of stress and risk conditions or a strengthening of the individual in his or her competencies, capacities and protective factors should then lead to a state of better health.

One of the problems with modern-day risks is that some of the most dangerous ones are not directly perceptible by the individual, such as risks from exposure to radioactive substances or to many toxic substances. In addition, many substances take time to accrue to dangerous levels, be it in the human body, a local region or in the global community.

Descriptive epidemiological research is in principle a very important approach. Nevertheless, as methodologically oriented psychologists, we should not be overly confident in this type of research, which has many shortcomings with regard to the collection of information, and the interpretability of designs, often resulting in sources of confoundation and validity problems (see Greenland, 1991; Kramer, 1988; Netter, 1991; Palinkas, 1985).

In a very interesting analysis of many cross-sectional and prospective studies in Europe and the USA, Berger (1993), for example, has shown that, owing to misinterpretations of epidemiological studies, serum cholesterol is very much overestimated with regard to the etiology and prevention of cardiovascular disease. According to Berger, the augmentation of cardiovascular mortality in the Western industrial nations is mainly due to increased life expectancy. Especially in very old people (80 years and older), this is a predominant cause of death which cannot be regulated by primary prevention. Berger (1993) claims that intensive efforts to lower cholesterol levels are mainly due to wishful thinking, commercial interests and other motivations outside the scientific one, and that strong dietary

States of health or illness in the population or subpopulations
- higher risks
- body changes:
  old age, physical strains
- subjectively feeling ill
- beginning illness
- manifestation of illness

global factors
- ozone layer, tropical forests, war

macrosystem
- basic cultural conditions
- laws, regulations, political system, hospital care

exosystem
- local ecology:
  urban vs rural, chemical or other industry,
  earthquake or tornado region
- economy:
  general economy, poverty level
- specific living conditions:
  hygiene, sanitation, crime rate, traffic regulations, rate of unemployment
- social structure

social factors
- stressors
- risks
- support

settings
- family
- worksite
- school
- university

individual factors
- conditions of socialization during the lifespan
- personality structure
- dispositions
- resources, protective factors
- health (risk) behavior
  healthy or illness-prone lifestyles, risk taking, addiction

Figure 1.1. Framework of public health with states of health and illness and different (potential) etiological factors which can have an impact with different amounts of variance during the lifespan of the individual and during historical phases of societies. Intentionally, the different states and factors are not connected with arrows since in very complicated interrelationships regarding the different processes, there would be confusing numbers of connections. In addition, some of the factors can compensate for others in a given context. The framework does not contain all the psychological aspects which should be regarded in assessment and intervention. Some of these aspects will be outlined later in the chapter.

Table 1.2. Scope of public health programs and targets. The table contains rather conventional societal and medical approaches and more recent targets and problems. References are not quoted for the main domains of public health and areas (see Holland, Detels & Knox, 1991a, 1991b, 1991c; Winett, King & Altman 1989; Dlugosch & Schmidt, 1992).

- global and local ecological and environmental risks
  - ecological safety, e.g., environmental pollution control
  - dangerous regions (earthquakes, tornados, smog, chemical industry, nuclear reactors)
  - healthy cities, rejuvenation of ghetto areas
  - economic problems (poor regions, industrial changes)
  - environments that promote health (Stokols, 1992)
- hygiene, basic sanitation, water supply, food
- substitution of substances like fluoride or iodine
- infectious disease (general prevention, vaccination)
  - AIDS on very different levels with different main goals and target groups
- screening and prevention of most prevalent chronic diseases which are connected with risk behaviors or more prevalent in certain "risk groups"
  - cardiovascular disease
  - cancer, especially preventive screening
  - arthritis
- genetic risks
- oral hygiene and prevention
- injury prevention in general and with regard to certain risk groups
- lifestyle and risk-oriented regimens, behavior "pathogens"
  - broad scale with the intention to prevent various frequent diseases which have a strong influence on health and illness, nutritious eating habits, exercise, smoking, alcohol abuse, etc.
  - rather specific risk prevention, usually cardiovascular risks
  - laws or regulations against certain behaviors in public (e.g., no smoking areas; alcohol prohibition)
  - extreme stress in different settings
  - injuries, especially traffic injuries (e.g., seat belts, speed limits, helmets)
- lifespan-oriented prevention, optimal education (Brandtstädter & von Eye; 1982; Lohaus, 1993; Perrez, 1992; Röhrle, 1992; Schmidt & Dlugosch, 1992)
  - adolescence (Hurrelmann & Lösel, 1990; Jessor, 1993)
  - teenage pregnancy (Winett, King & Altman, 1989)
  - injuries in a broader sense than only traffic injuries and regarding children, adolescents and young adults (see Spielberger & Frank, 1992)
  - delinquency in children and adolescents
  - health problems of the elderly, including institutions
- strengthening of protective factors, behavioral "immunogens" and coping strategies
- underserved people, minorities, handicapped and disabled people, unemployment, poverty with regard to attempts to change living conditions and towards integration in the society
- secondary prevention in case of
  - natural disasters, catastrophes, wars
  - riot, e.g., the Los Angeles riots (Youngstrom, 1992a, 1992b)
- primary prevention against violence, racism, prejudice against immigrants and foreigners

---

changes in the elderly may be of more harm than of use. Even if his interpretation of these studies is correct, this would still not be an argument
against epidemiological research but for the very careful analysis and interpretation of research results, especially with regard to etiology.

The scope of public health and its potential implications for a public
health *psychology* may be specified in looking at concrete public health
topics and actions.

Table 1.2 contains a number of very different topics and treatments.
Some of them have a long tradition; others are more modern or more
formed by the interests of psychology and the social sciences. Many problems are associated with a rather technical approach (McGinnis et al.,
1991, p. 142): "The targets with the best prospects are probably those that
depend more on technical interventions and less on behavioural change,
those that offer the potential for greater economic returns or at least fewer
economic losses to industry or society, and those that appear to be most
socially neutral."

There is a strong tendency for psychological programs to include the
community and the more remote environment (Grob, 1991; Pawlik &
Stapf, 1992; Stark, 1989a; Stern, 1992; Winett, King & Altman, 1989). This
tendency reflects the fact that modern cultures exhibit problems that are
related to individual attitudes and behaviors as well as to complex ecological threats.

By intention, this chapter does not deal with aspects of relative health in
given institutions (rehabilitation, elderly), manifested severe illness, lifelong
or long-lasting handicaps, etc. Nevertheless, a comprehensive approach to
public health has to regard the psychological demands of these areas. In
addition, the special aspects of mental health and illness are only touched
upon from time to time (see Becker, 1992a; Sartorius et al., 1990).

PUBLIC HEALTH *PSYCHOLOGY*

Public health is a field which is increasingly interdisciplinary and which
has, during the last centuries, made many promising improvements, for
example, with regard to cardiovascular disease in many European countries
and the USA. Therefore, when I claim here, that this field should be structured using a psychological approach with regard to contents and methodology, my intention is not to criticize other approaches or scientific or
applied disciplines. Rather, I intend to stimulate psychologists to regard
health problems on different levels and to implement psychological approaches for the benefit of the health of individuals and the society.

In addition to presenting a broad overview, only a few selected areas
can be spotlighted here. First of all, it seems necessary to concentrate on
the psychological impact of all health related issues which are important
for the general population or specific subpopulations in space and time (see

also Stern, 1992; Stokols, 1992; Winett, King & Altman 1989). For any given individual problem, it seems optimal to reflect upon the importance of whole systems. For societal problems, it seems necessary to make sure that individuals or groups at high risk are reached and influenced. Often this can be accomplished using a sequential intervention strategy (see Perrez, 1991).

The whole repertoire of psychological methods, measurements and data analysis should be potentially included in public health endeavors as well as knowledge and theory from general and experimental psychology, social and communication psychology, developmental psychology and differential psychology (see Schmidt & Schwenkmezger, 1992). A joint effort of basic and applied research seems to be optimal (see Maes & van Veldhoven, 1989).

The proportion and importance of psychological knowledge and methods can be very different from topic to topic. However, even in cases where the problem and its solution are not connected with psychology, implied aspects of communication, persuasion or behavior change are.

ETHICAL CONSIDERATIONS

As psychologists, we should analyze and reflect the main goals and contents of public health and their ethical implications. It is amazing that the specific goals of public health are often not stated or even discussed. Especially in promoting early prevention, one should be careful not to sustain a further medicalization of the health system or a blaming of the victim in the society. The main effort should be the strengthening of health potentials and self-help whenever possible.

With regard to the main goal of public health medicine, a restructuring and reevaluation seems to be necessary. There, the main effort is the increase of life expectancy. The development of programs to ensure the quality and wellness as well as the possibilities for the compensation of handicaps becomes of major concern (see Abele & Becker, 1991; Kaplan, 1985; Kickbusch, 1988; Strack, Argyle & Schwarz, 1991). Ensuring life quality entails (especially among the elderly) the development of an upstanding and educated member of the community as equal partner in the systems of health and medicine.

Usually life quality is measured and evaluated for the single individual and/or his or her direct reference system. However, it also seems necessary to include the state of the whole society (see Kunzendorff, 1990). For example, the former German Democratic Republic fulfilled the health demands of the WHO in all respects and documented well-developed health education (Ludwig, Schmidt & Lämmel, 1988; World Health Organization, 1989). Nevertheless, large sections of this socialist society were sick; like a great prison, the socialist regime influenced the lives and life quality of most individuals to a considerable degree. As one of the reviewers of this chapter claims, this statement is of course very much dependent on the values that one brings to the problem: "Many would regard such a society as much less 'sick' than one which perpetuates massive gaps between rich and poor, which perpetuates slum conditions whilst the higher social classes sprinkle gold dust in their soup."

My point is that psychologists should include and reflect much more upon those political and societal factors than they have in their past preventive efforts. Today, even equations of health and illness which include terms of social development (e.g., Stark, 1989b) do not regard sufficiently these general societal influences (see Schmidt, 1991). However, it does not seem easy to define criteria with regard to politics, environment, education and other aspects for the state of health of whole societies.

As political and social developments in a historical context show, the same goals may in reality have very different underlying motives and implications (see Milles, 1991). Even the decrease of infant mortality or of major health risks can serve political motives (e.g., power- or war-related interests). The goals of physicians or psychologists in the health field can thus be at odds with those of the society. For many aspects of social policy, it is hard to find a scientific basis. How should one objectively evaluate for example, interventions with minorities and underserved people or the integration of asylum seekers?

THEORIES AND MODELS

Before presenting concrete models, two examples are chosen to show the use of basic psychological knowledge and theory.

Global environmental change is basically not a psychological domain. Indeed, no theorizing is possible at all without first obtaining results from natural science observations. However, even impressive results do not lead automatically to individual acceptance or behavior change (see Stewart, 1991). Halford and Sheehan (1991, p. 599) postulate that "global change is likely to be understood only to the extent that it impacts on everyday life."

Pawlik (1991, p. 559) has provided an excellent outline of the impact of psychological knowledge in this area. He claims that it is necessary

> to recognize some specific psychological processes involved in human response (or failures to respond) to global change. When examined within the theoretical framework of experimental psychology, these environmental changes can be described by five characteristics, which may suffice to account for slow or improper human response and which do deserve more systematic research in the future:
>
> • low signal-to-noise ratio of global change,
> • extreme masking and delay of cause–effect gradients,
> • psychophysics of low probability events,

- social distance between actors and victims of global change and
- low subjective cost-effectiveness of environment-conserving behaviour.

This example shows clearly that psychological analysis may yield very important hypotheses for interventions. Stern (1992), in an analysis of psychological aspects in global environmental change, discusses additional theoretical and applied psychological approaches in basic and policy-oriented research. While claiming the importance of psychology in this field on the one hand, he warns of being too optimistic on the other. He mentions the much longer time scale associated with this kind of research, which considers change effects over decades or even centuries.

Another example focuses on the use of developmentally oriented theories and models in adolescence, especially risk taking and invulnerability (see Dlugosch & Schmidt, 1990; Hurrelmann, 1989; Lösel, Kolip & Bender, 1992). Jessor (1993) sketches a comprehensive model of adolescent risk behavior, which includes risk and protective factors with regard to biology/genetics, social environment, perceived environment, personality and behavior. According to the model, these factors are in a reciprocal relation to each other and to risk behavior lifestyles, and thus to health/life-compromising outcomes.

The main purpose of this framework is the planning and integration of research in the paradigm of developmental behavioral science. Thus, an increasing number of "research questions are being drawn from the concrete reality of social life rather than from the abstract preoccupations of disciplinary tradition. ... How can we understand the process by which young people make it despite the adversity they face in terms of poverty, limited opportunity, and racial and ethnic discrimination?" (Jessor, 1993, p. 125)

There are a few general health models with a wider scope (see Antonovsky, 1979; Becker, 1992a), but most models are designed to account for the health behavior of the single individual (see "Health Belief Model", Becker et al., 1982; "REACT", Ajzen & Timko, 1986; Schwarzer, 1992). Those many valuable psychological models which often have an implicit applicability for public health topics are not reviewed here.

Only a few models which are directly usable in public health can be mentioned here. PRECEDE (Green, Kreuter, Deeds & Partridge, 1980) is a framework developed for Predisposing, Reinforcing, and Enabling Causes in Educational Diagnosis and Evaluation. It is a comprehensive and widely accepted planning model which starts with epidemiological and social diagnoses of health and non-health factors affecting the quality of life, and works through behavioral, educational and administrative diagnoses in order to identify the desired content of a program and how it should be delivered.

More recently, Ewart (1991) outlined a "social action theory", which incorporates individually centered self-regulation as well as societal influences in explaining individual health behavior (see Figure 1.2).

A social action view emphasizes social interdependence and interaction in personal control of health-endangering behavior and proposes mechanisms by which environmental structures influence cognitive action schemas, self-goals, and problem-solving activities critical to sustained behavioral change. Social action theory clarifies relationships between social and personal empowerment and helps explain stages of self-change. (Ewart, 1991, p. 931)

Principally, it is feasible and useful to combine different models of public health and individual health behavior in order to reflect the whole realm of interacting conditions and to plan comprehensive preventive and interventive actions.

Stokols (1992), for example, outlined an integrative model of healthy environments yielding different factors in the framework, reaching from the individual to the society. The same basic intention is shown by Seeman (1989) with his compensatory model of "positive health", which contains an analysis of intra-individual subsystems as well as of the interpersonal-ecological subsystem.

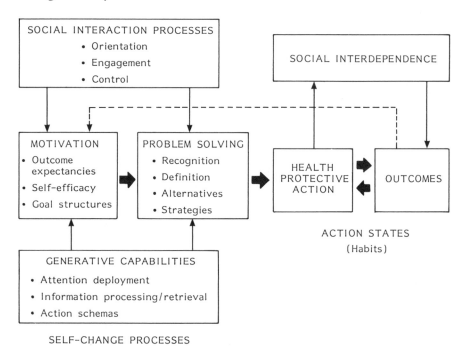

Figure 1.2. Process model representing self-regulation as a coordinated ensemble of interacting cognitive processes and capabilities (reproduced by permission from Ewart, 1991, p. 934)

To conclude, etiological models should be more comprehensive with regard to different conditions. Egger and Pieringer (1987), for example, proposed a model for coronary heart disease which allows for a greater diversity of public health targets and regulations than the usual risk models.

ASSESSMENT

In the field of health psychology, psychodiagnosis has not been well developed. It should have an important impact for epidemiological and evaluative purposes (Dana & Hoffmann, 1987; Karoly, 1985; Schmidt, 1990). In this article, three very different aspects of psychological assessment will be regarded. The first sketches epidemiology and a few psychological aspects of it. The second topic is related to differential aspects in assessment and its compatibility with public health approaches. Finally, a few psychological contents and measurements of health psychology, especially related to public health are listed and discussed briefly.

Epidemiology

In public health, epidemiology is generally the key diagnostical concern, with definite etiological implications. After providing several definitions, Detels (1991) concludes that it is most important to analyze the relationship between the agent (cause, risk), the host (individual) and the environment (cf. Winett, King & Altman, 1989). Samples usually come from different sections of the population (gender, social status, white or blue collar worker) or from different regional locations (urban vs rural areas; farmland vs industry; different climate zones, etc.).

Kramer (1988) classifies the methods of epidemiology by using three axes, namely, directionality (cohort, case-control, cross-sectional studies), sample selection (exposure, outcome, other criteria) and timing (historical, concurrent, mixed). The validity of the resulting types of studies is discussed under different aspects.

Jefferey (1989, p. 1194) has outlined very important distinctions with regard to the analysis of risk behavior from the different perspectives of the population and the individual. Relative risk is "the ratio of the chance of disease in individuals exposed to a risk factor compared to the risk of disease in individuals without exposure;" whereas population attributable risk "is the number of excess cases of disease in a population that can be attributed to a particular risk factor."

According to Kramer (1988) and Weyerer and Häfner (1992), these kinds of risk calculations lead to interesting results, for example, in comparing cigarette consumption with lung cancer and cardiovascular disease (see Table 1.3). Even with an extremely high relative risk for lung cancer, more heavy smokers are dying from cardiovascular disease.

Table 1.3. Mortality risk for lung cancer and cardiovascular disease for nonsmokers and heavy smokers (see Kramer, 1988; Weyerer & Häfner, 1992)

Cause of death	Mortality rate (per 1000, per year)		Relative risk	Attributable risk
	nonsmokers (1)	heavy smokers (2)	(2) : (1)	(2) − (1)
Lung cancer	0.07	2.27	32.43	2.20
Cardiovascular disease	7.32	9.93	1.36	2.61

A frequent shortcoming of epidemiological studies is their removal of problems from their natural context and thus the individually centered view of societal problems. Therefore, *social epidemiology* and social politics (Braun, Martini & Minger, 1989; Keupp 1992) become very important. These approaches treat general social problems like the change of family structure, the integration of foreigners or the life situation of handicapped people. They also offer a more holistic view; for example, underserved people are perceived with regard to the complex interrelations of poverty, educational chances, isolation, risks of injuries, unemployment and the access to health and social services.

Social epidemiology must be carried out with regard to societal as well as individual implications and needs. The unemployment rate, for example, can be used as one health indicator at the societal level and can be viewed in terms of general economical needs. Unemployment should be differentially viewed in a given society, depending on living regions, gender or age groups. The decline of iron and steel industry in Europe has led to mass unemployment with a cumulation of risks as well as to the opportunity of carrying out public health prevention activities. Finally, the subjective evaluation of the consequences of a single individual, his/her family, neighborhood, etc. must also be regarded. However, this should include the general context. For example, although unemployment is now very frequent in some regions of the former German Democratic Republic, it is in many cases much more harmful than in the old German Federal Republic. The socialist state did not allow unemployment; being denied work was a punishment and a form of exclusion from society. Hence unemployment today carries a particularly sharp social stigma.

Keeping the general methodological and contextual problems of epidemiology in mind, one should ask if psychological epidemiology should go beyond looking at the psychological aspects of risk factors. The health behavioral pathogens and immunogens as analyzed by Matarazzo (1984) are important for the change of unhealthy lifestyles, but they do not include many psychological aspects, and they do not address the search for meaning in life.

One might, for example, use measures of life quality and other subjective evaluations in epidemiological studies of different types and analyze whether such measures can make an important contribution. In addition, it seems both useful and necessary to include as counterpoise to the risk factors protective or compensatory health factors, which may lead to a greater invulnerability to disease or a faster recovery of healthy states (see Becker, 1992a, 1992b; Belz-Merk, Bengel & Strittmatter, 1992; Lösel, Kolip & Bender, 1992).

A psychological approach to epidemiology should not be static and cross-sectional; rather it should reflect aspects of the dynamic development of individuals during the whole life span (e.g., Lohaus, 1993, for epidemiological aspects of children and adolescents).

Differential perspective

Since applied psychology in diagnostic analyses as well as in prevention and intervention efforts is differential and individual in nature, one should also discuss whether public health should include differential requirements in order to be sufficiently effective for predominant health problems.

Depending on the health models, a differential approach needs to consider aspects such as the following: intra and interindividual differences with regard to different personality variables which may lead to positive or negative dispositions and conditions; objective risks and subjective risk perception of individuals from different subpopulations, at different points in the life span (different work sites; different age groups, e.g., adolescence) and with regard to the Zeitgeist or objective and perceived reinforcements and delays of gratification.

A few examples from the field of AIDS research demonstrate the importance of a differential approach. The first one concerns the differential effects of control beliefs. Lohaus, Gaidatzi & Hagenbrock (1988) reported results which confirm the assumption of specific control beliefs for HIV infection. They could show that internality is related to better information about HIV infection and a greater readiness to search for information and to perform preventive behavior. The fear of infection and the subjective probability of an infection risk are decreased. For external control beliefs, the results show the opposite direction.

Simon and Jäger (1989) have demonstrated in empirical studies that surface attitudes about AIDS may be similar for groups of persons with very different underlying mechanisms and dynamic aspects. They found that for the reception of preventive information, it is extremely important to know whether the personality type is open for problems or whether it is "anomic" (i.e., characterized by a closed, cyclic interpretation of everyday life events). Accordingly, information and instruction should only be successful if the peculiarities of AIDS problems for certain sections of the society are considered.

Pant and Kleiber (1993) differentially analyzed the sexual risk behavior and HIV status of intravenous drug users in Berlin. The condom use of about three-quarters of their sample was at best inconsistent and sometimes nonexistent. They found that drug addicts who know that they are infected are more willing to protect their partners and consequently more often follow rules of safer sex. Between groups with no information about the infection or with a negative test result, they found almost no difference in sexual behavior. They discuss the necessity to alter structural conditions like housing, worksite, educational chances and the legality of drug use in order to influence the health behavior of drug addicts positively.

With regard to female drug-users, they claim that a cynical view would lead to encouraging the addicts to prostitute themselves. This is inferred from the finding that drug-addicted prostitutes have learned to use condoms in order to avoid pregnancies and sexually transmittable disease.

Measurement contents and variables

At the beginning of this short overview, it should be recognized that useful psychological measurements—besides reaching sufficient reliability and validity—should be integrated in a network of psychological constructs that are known from other fields of psychology with a longer tradition. Unfortunately, this is almost never the case.

Figure 1.1 provides a structural outline of the following text. There are diagnostical instruments necessary which should be developed by psychologists or at least with psychological consideration with respect to contents and methodology. In the process of measurement development, the role of psychoepidemiology should be clarified. The comprehensive, classical book *Measurement Strategies in Health Psychology*, edited by Karoly (1985), contains a rich repertoire of methods and contents which are also important for public health. Westhoff (1993) has provided a collection of psychosocial measurements for health and illness.

The first task seems to be to develop devices to measure the states of health and health threats objectively and subjectively (i.e., being healthy as opposed to feeling healthy) in the population and relevant subpopulations. Screening variables as well as more differential measures for subpopulations and single individuals are needed (see Marteau, 1993).

One of the few reviews about health assessment instruments was provided by Dana and Hoffmann (1987), which includes health hazards, health status, holistic health, well-being and wellness. The review shows to what degree variables of health status and health hazards are interrelated. The latter are often used as indicators of unhealthy conditions, as predictors of the future health state or as predictors of life expectancy.

Measures of life quality in health and illness are urgently needed, as well as an analysis of conditions which influence the subjective evaluation of life quality (see Abel, 1991; Filipp & Ferring, 1992; Haisch & Haisch, 1990; Kaplan, 1985).

Using factor analysis, Frank (1991) described seven dimensions of physical well-being, which do not correspond in the least with missing symptoms on medical check lists: (1) satisfaction with bodily states, (2) feeling calm and relaxed, (3) vitality and life enjoyment, (4) stress reduction and agreeable fatigue, (5) healthy appetite for life, (6) concentration and motor precision (7) personal tidiness, freshness, physical comfortableness.

With regard to mental health, which is not the focus of this chapter, Becker (1989) has developed and factor analyzed a comprehensive questionnaire (Trierer Persönlichkeitsfragebogen, TPF). He describes the two super-factors of behavior control and mental health as well as different scales of mental/somatic well-being, self-actualization and self-esteem.

Looking at the right part of Figure 1.1 which contains the conditions of the states of health and illness, one can infer many measurement requirements. The global conditions do not seem at first glance to be related to psychological measurement. However, as mentioned above, psychologists should find out how individuals perceive global conditions, how willing they are to personally effect a behavioral change, and what kinds of environmental innovations might be applied. Grob (1991) developed questionnaires of this type and validated them using extreme groups of car drivers, who drove environmentally friendly cars vs vehicles which were more polluting. The willingness to engage in behavior for the protection of the quality of the air has been measured and predicted by Kals (1993).

Questionnaires dominate here, as they also do in related areas of health measurement. However, it seems necessary to validate them by the observation of behavior and the development of unobstrusive measures. Stern (1992), for example, mentions the interindividual or intergroup comparison of kilowatt-hours per month, energy costs per month and the implementation of solar heating systems.

The definition and measurement of indicators in the exosystem is mainly the domain of social scientists. At least with regard to the assessment of social structure variables and the subjective perception and interpretation of the environment (e.g., Jessor, 1993), psychology might have a stronger impact. The same seems to be the case for characterizations of the healthiness of different social conditions and settings. The research on social support and health is still advancing (e.g., Schwarzer & Leppin, 1989). Measurements in this area could help to establish intermediary-oriented public health programs (see Baumann, 1987).

For many conditions of health behavior and health, the perception of personal and population risks is a major source of variance. Several aspects and variables have been worked out by Belz-Merk, Bengel & Strittmatter

(1992), Bengel (1992) and Versteegen (1992) and, with regard to adolescence and young adults, by Hurrelmann and Lösel (1990) and Jessor (1993).

There is a rapid increase in the assessment of risks and protective effects of lifestyles, especially with regard to eating, drinking, exercise, sleeping, smoking, alcohol, and drugs (e.g. Schwarzer, 1992; Versteegen, 1988). In two comprehensive studies, the "Fragebogen zur Erfassung des Gesundheitsverhaltens" (FEG) (Krieger & Dlugosch, 1992) was used for the evaluation of short-term interventions of individuals with high risks or manifested illnesses visiting health resorts (Dlugosch, 1992). The questionnaire was also used as an indicator of the different health behaviors of white and blue collar workers and alternate shift workers (Rolinger, 1992). Besides the inclusion of some psychological aspects, such as motivation to change behavior and aspects of well-being, the lifestyle questionnaires are still very much related to traditional behavior "pathogens" and "immunogens".

While both, stress and risk factors or behaviors are regarded in almost all models and assessments, one misses rather often the measurement of protective, compensatory, and stabilizing variables, which may lead to relative "invulnerability" (see Jessor, 1993; Lösel, Kolip & Bender, 1992). In comprehensive reviews, Belz-Merk, Bengel and Strittmatter (1992; see also Haisch & Zeitler, 1991) have listed and discussed protective variables such as self-complexity, self-efficacy (see Schwarzer, 1993a), positive illusions, personal meaning in one's life, eustress, positive stress, uplifts and pick-me-ups (vs daily hassles), hardiness, optimism, sense of coherence, state of mental health, and psychological state of health. An important distinction with regard to the protective influence of optimism is made between defensive and functional optimism (see Schwarzer, 1993b).

There is a growing interest in the health concepts of lay people themselves, which are often quite different from those of professionals (e.g., Bibace, Schmidt & Walsh, 1994; Flick, 1991; Skelton & Croyle, 1991). It is obvious that health behavior and risk perception depend to a great extent on the cognitive concepts of health and illness. This is not only the case for children and adolescents but also for adults.

Coping with illness is still a leading area of research; it is not included in this review, however, since it is a subspecialty of medical rather than of health psychology. On the other hand, studying the coping of minor and major setbacks in life, be they real or imagined, and analyzing the differential aspects of these processes are very important for health psychology (see Weber, 1992).

There are of course very many personality variables which may have influences on the etiology and course of health and illness. Some important aspects of emotions for health and well-being have been outlined in the books and reviews of Friedman (1992), Janisse (1988) and Schwenkmezger (1991, 1992).

INTERVENTION

Targets and goals

The global review of the evaluation of the strategy for health for all by the year 2000 (World Health Organization, 1987) shows clearly that in the underdeveloped countries, the classical targets of public health are still predominant, namely, safe water, adequate sanitary facilities, immunization, pregnancy and childbirth. However, in the highly industrialized countries under present examination, the main targets have changed and urgently require the intensive participation of the citizens and, thus, of psychology.

Intervention in public health (usually primary or secondary prevention) may be oriented to very different aspects of the total set of conditions which are important for health and illness (see Figure 1.1 and Table 1.2 under pragmatic aspects):

- screening and influencing the global environment
- legislation in its social and ecological aspects, social policy
- structure and changes of the local, physical, or social environment, e.g., system for the disposal of garbage, locations of chemical industry, non-smoker areas or traffic-free zones
- specific actions in the environment in order to stop the spread of a disease, e.g., removal of the "pump handle", AIDS (e.g., mandatory documentation of the occurrence of infectious diseases in hospitals or at international borders)
- specific actions in order to reduce specific health risks, e.g., availability of condoms at universities or at discos
- health conserving or promoting actions in the community (healthy cities), parts of the community or in relevant formal and informal settings
- implementation of support systems in the social environment of a community and/or activation of given support systems of an individual by encouraging citizen participation
- change of structure and function of given institutions which do not fulfill the possibilities of maintaining optimal relative health
- changes of the individual's (subjective) motivation
- support of the competencies, resources, and the protective factors of the individual
- general empowerment and creation of self-help potentials

The relevant aspects of conditions and situations vary considerably and therefore, it is hard to represent them in a systematic order. For all psychological interventions, a potential connection must exist at the very least between the treatment and the individuals in the population (or defined parts of it).

The following classificatory aspects of psychological intervention in public health seem to be important. They are not presented in a strict, systematic order and are not without overlap:

- primary prevention without major risks vs secondary prevention with high risk groups vs crisis intervention (e.g., riots in Los Angeles, natural disasters) or intervention in institutions
- targets: population, defined subpopulations, settings vs individuals
- symptomatological or etiological oriented intervention
- specificity vs unspecificity
- external vs internal
- structural, technological vs individual (governmentally enforced, without (proper) information vs mature individual, informed consent, empowerment)
- passive or active individual
- directed to individual or to intermediary, e.g., parents, teacher, physician
- protection of people by measures against offenders, criminals, violence, etc.
- mass media vs personal counseling, individual psychotherapy.

As Roberts (1987) discusses, the traditional focus of health psychology is on lifestyle, whereas the traditional focus of public health is on rather passive and structural intervention. However, a maximum benefit "will come, not from a one-sided acceptance of the public health models by psychologists or vice versa, but from a mutual recognition that health problems cannot be solved in any other way than a multilevel one" (p. 147).

A most important principal question about preventive interventions is if one intends to concentrate on the passive individual with enforced governmental measures, or if one attempts to enable individuals to be generally more informed, competent and confident about their own possibilities to achieve healthy behavior, which means to facilitate their empowerment (Ingham and Bennett, 1990; Keupp, 1992; Kleiber, 1992). Arntson (1989, pp. 32) states that "Improving citizen's health competencies is a far better outcome of communication in health care contexts than increasing client's compliance or consumer's levels of satisfaction." Such a guideline should not disregard the fact that it can be necessary to change the world or at least some important conditions in which people live in order to enable as many people as possible to live a better life. A broad discussion of research and paradoxical results with regard to empowerment has been presented by Tolan et al. (1990).

It seems reasonable to follow Schwarzer (1992) in his view that a social technological intervention should take place only when it is unavoidable (i.e., after attempts to solve the problem while respecting the subject's individual freedom have failed).

A plausible interpretation of the procedure for deciding on the correct alternative has been outlined by McAlister et al. (1991, p. 15):

> The degree to which population behaviour can be modified will depend ultimately upon the perceived and experienced balance between forces. Behaviours with intermittently strong, short-term, positive consequences and only a chance of severe long-term penalties cannot be eliminated without the establishment of more immediate and certain penalties or a restructuring of incentives which decreases perceived need for immediate gratification, enhances perceived value of long-term consequences, or otherwise upsets the existing equilibrium of forces.

Thus, in Germany, it seemed necessary to legally enforce the use of seat belts in cars—doubly so, given the as yet unenforced speed limit on the German autobahn. In 1992 France introduced some very strong regulations against smoking in public, while Germany and many other countries still advocate interventions of more liberal and personal kinds.

In a special issue of behavioral medicine, Lichtenstein and Glasgow (1992) favor an integrative approach to smoking cessation:

> Rather than try to fit smoking cessation into our clinical paradigms, it is better to take a broader view and join the clinical and the health perspectives. This involves considering the broader environmental factors affecting smoking and involves bringing interventions to smokers and their environments. These interventions can still be rigorously evaluated, and the interventions can still be guided by psychological theory. (p. 525)

Maes and van Veldhoven (1989) state that programs for smoking cessation usually approach children and adolescents directly, disregarding that, aside from peer behavior, the tolerance of parents is the most powerful predictor of whether a child starts smoking. Therefore, the smoking attitudes and behavior of parents should be included in an intermediary approach.

While major changes of the global environment (see Pawlik, 1991; Stern, 1992) must take place on a structural level, many ecological attempts to intervene should use every possible level, from the society to the individual (see Table 1.4).

A major problem in ecological public health is the amount of information which is given to the government, the communities and the citizens. Most toxicologic accidents (burns, toxicologic substances in the air or the water) are trivialized by the factories and many officials. In a very extreme way, this happened at the nuclear disaster in Chernobyl in the former Soviet Union. Apart from the nuclear threat to the ecology, there is almost no agreement even between experts. In a German discussion, this is reflected in the dialectic formulation of the controversy: "Are all of us going to be poisoned by our environment or are we living in the cleanest state ever?" (Borgers & Karmaus, 1989). In a situation where information and communication is in such extreme dissonance, it seems almost impossible to motivate major parts of the population for ecological alertness and innovations.

This discussion is related to the orientation of public health on symptoms or on etiology. Classical public health did not concern itself very much with etiological, causal aspects which were often unknown. Of course, this view has changed dramatically for endeavors which are mainly oriented towards risk reduction. They face the problem of finding a consensus on the importance of certain risks (see Berger, 1993). Especially in the field of ecologically and environmentally oriented public health, it is often claimed that one has to fight the causes (e.g., Bonhoeffer, 1991). However, with regard to the causes or the threats of major global or local health risks, little agreement exists in many cases, and thus a causal intervention often seems inadequate (see Willems, 1974).

Because public health psychology, in comparison to medicine, has partly different goals and reaches beyond the medical field, it seems unhelpful to overemphasize their similarity. The danger results that projects like healthy cities are then dominated by medical screenings and information (e.g., blood pressure, diabetes) and do not contain enough psychological programs. An interesting alternative, showing all the psychosocial possibilities of healthy city actions, is given for Hamburg by Faltis et al. (1989).

The example of AIDS is used again to mention that the inclusion of differential aspects in prevention and intervention is necessary or at least helpful. Coates (1990) and Schwarzer (1992) have listed many differential aspects related to AIDS risk behavior, including demographical, cognitive and behavioral variables. According to data in diagnostic analyses, one can try to optimize the preventive actions with regard to personality types (Simon & Jäger, 1989) and subpopulations such as homosexuals, prostitutes, drug addicts, etc. (see Pant & Kleiber, 1993).

Methods and techniques

In comparison to the selection of the major targets and goals of intervention and their ethical implications, the choice of psychological methods and techniques of intervention seems to be of minor importance. For many public health problems, no clearcut prescription on the selection and adaptation of adequate methods of prevention and intervention for different targets even exists.

Holland, Detels & Knox (1991c) offer the following diverse list of intervention methods for public health in general: behavior modification, environmental applications, legislative applications, social applications and interventions, biological applications, and screening. Included in this very heterogeneous assembly of methods are of course many psychological methods and techniques.

In order to achieve the great diversity of goals and steps in public health and health prevention, one needs very different methods and techniques of psychological intervention. Of course, it is not necessary in this context to describe and discuss the psychological methods of intervention which are usually used for the single case or small groups.

Jefferey (1989) describes as possible interventions (excluding those which address the individual): (1) economic incentives, (2) environmental barriers (e.g., liquor store hours), and (3) controls on advertising. Even in forms of intervention not directed towards individuals, it is very helpful to regard psychological theories and practices, e.g., in communication and advertising (see Kisser, 1990). The examples chosen by Jefferey (1989) show clearly that in order to be effective, all forms of intervention must in the end reach the individual and thus need to include psychological aspects.

McAlister et al. (1991) list as the main types of social influence in behavior modification: education (empowering of thought and action), persuasion (imposing external values through communication and social reinforcement), motivation (through alteration of the consequences of behavior) and facilitation (through the manipulation of environments).

With regard to prevention in health psychology, Maes (1992) has discussed many important aspects of behavior change and its stepwise implementation with respect to settings, goals, behavioral advice, variation in programs, social networks, possibilities of choice, intrinsic values, independence and maintenance of behavior change.

In this chapter, the impact of the mass media should only be mentioned briefly because this is a special area of research. As Maes (1992) has discussed, the mass media probably do not produce direct effects in most individuals but rather create a certain climate with regard to health behavior and its changes. This implies, for example, that advertising spots for smoking or alcohol consumption should not be allowed. The legislation with regard to advertising are quite different in different countries.

Television broadcasts may have unintended strong, negative effects. This has been shown with regard to the types and frequencies of suicides occurring after certain movies in Germany and Austria (see Földy & Ringel, 1993). Földy and Ringel (1993) also discuss whether a steady information overload from TV might induce depression in major parts of the population. The question of whether violent TV movies create social violence is hotly debated and owing to problems of evaluation remains unresolved.

Multilevel and sequential strategies

When trying to change health attitudes and behavior, a multilevel and sequential strategy seems to be optimal. As can be inferred from the discussion above, a multilevel approach includes intervention at all levels, from societal to individual, and probably also employs multiple forms of

Table 1.4. Different strategies to prevent and control exposure to toxic substances (see Winett, King & Altman, 1989)

Society/institutions
- Guidelines and laws on acceptable and dangerous levels of exposure
- Epidemiological analyses of environmental risks
- Maintaining environmental hazard surveillance systems
- Technologies to prevent toxic exposure

Exosystem and organizational level
- Implementation of warning systems in factories and the community
- Education of the media on environmental hazards and their presentation
- Development of risk communication campaigns
- Development of policies to regulate exposure to toxins
- Procedures for cleaning up environmental hazards
- Development of emergency procedures and services for exposed individuals

Interpersonal level
- Communication between citizens, factory management and policymakers
- Establishing citizen action groups and self-help groups
- Participation in community organizations

Personal level
- Perception and understanding of environmental risks without panic
- Behavioral skills to protect oneself from exposure to toxins
- Behavioral skills in handling exposure to toxins
- Motivation to participate in community activities
- Better control of environmental risks

---

media. This is outlined in Table 1.4 in the prevention of exposure to toxic substances (see Winett, King & Altman 1989).

Different methods of communication, ranging from personal communication to mass communication, and the combination of different communication methods are analyzed by Farquhar et al. (1991) with regard to their influence on health behavior.

Authors such as Maes (1992), McAlister et al. (1991), Perrez (1992) or Winett, King & Altman (1989) claim the necessity of sequential strategies in public health efforts. These approaches may aim at different populations during the different steps (as in many AIDS campaigns) and may switch between specific and unspecific procedures (see Perrez, 1991). It is possible to use general campaigns in the mass media first and than to branch off to reach small groups (i.e., groups with high risks) or single individuals (e.g., with television information services). In the case of AIDS prevention, one could then approach the general population as a risk group, or alternately, address the supposed main risk groups (homosexuals, drug addicts, prostitutes) with different types of messages.

Maes (1992) favors macro- and micro-campaigns, especially with regard to the maintenance of behavior change effects, because behavior modification takes place in phases. Macro-campaigns could provide a certain health climate, which later will be used for specific attitude and behavior changes. There, it might be helpful if the individual perceives the persuasive situation as something desirable. This might entail a slowly developing empowerment of the individual using different approaches.

Limitations of preventive public health approaches

In prevention and public health, there is always the danger of doing too much and controlling too much (see Brandtstädter & von Eye, 1982; Keupp, 1992; Röhrle, 1992; Schwarzer, 1992). This position can become very problematic if we do not know enough about the risks which we want to prevent, or if expert evaluations and research results of one discipline or between disciplines are dissonant.

Willems (1974, p. 155), in a very interesting analysis of the different requirements of behavioral technology and behavioral ecology, comes to the conclusion that we should "be sensitive to 'other' effects of single-dimensional intrusions.... We know now that... feasibility and even intrinsic success are not sufficient grounds for immediate application.... One implication of this line of argument may well be a conservatism with regard to intervention in behavior-environment systems and the clear hint that the most adaptive form of action may sometimes be *in*action."

In a rejoinder to Willems, Baer (1974, p. 168) argues: "Some societies, waiting for a complete understanding of the modification programs they might be applying to their behaviorally dispossessed citizens, may find themselves burned down by those citizens, in the name of caution. Surely it is a basic tenet of ecology that there is no Santa Claus *anywhere* in an ecosystem."

Primary prevention is concerned with all attempts to foster optimal development during the lifespan (see Brandtstädter & von Eye, 1982; Hurrelmann, 1989; Lohaus, 1993; Perrez, 1992; Röhrle, 1992) and usually focuses on intermediary interventions with parents and teachers. One recent example is the review of Mulvey, Arthur and Reppucci (1993) on the prevention and treatment of juvenile delinquency. Most of the studies are concerned with family and school intervention aspects. According to those authors, most community approaches are not adequately evaluated. Zigler, Taussig and Black (1992) optimistically summarize an ecological approach to prevent juvenile delinquency, advocating treatments to promote overall social competence in early childhood.

Public health and health psychology must take care to avoid purism and dependence on dominating cultural and religious beliefs; they must regard the lifestyle and the life quality of whole cultures and subpopulations. Not all people and cultures want to live the spartan life, but rather want to enjoy their lives on different levels. With regard to the individual, many behaviors may not be healthy in a direct sense but can provide many people with the impression of living in a rather happy world. Ernst (1992) has discussed this in a book which states that healthy activities are first and foremost fun activities.

Since health is not a stable state but a complicated process, it is quite natural that it fluctuates (see Abele & Becker, 1991; Brandstätter, 1991). Thus, long-term campaigns of the same type can have reverse effects. In the USA for example, there are now "self-help" groups for overweight people who have slogans like "Bring something to eat!".

Even if living in the countryside may be healthier and make it easier to follow most health "prescriptions", more and more people prefer to live in or close to cities. One has to respect such far-reaching decisions, even if the direct health payoff may be below the optimal level. Similar decisions have to be accepted, for example, in cases of severe allergies. To confine oneself to one's home during the spring and summer may be most protective with regard to the allergy, but it is most restrictive with regard to individuals, who probably also have motives other than to protect themselves against an allergy.

EVALUATION

Maes and van Veldhoven (1989) state that more than 90% of all interventions in health psychology are not evaluated. If there is an evaluation, it is very often not convincing, owing to a lack of adequate control groups. Furthermore, they found that usually, only short-term effects are evaluated and that many studies have no precise goals which were formulated before the treatments took place. Neither the intervention nor the evaluation seem to meet the requirements of psychological theory and/or methodology.

A broad overview of the steps in evaluation is given in Table 1.5 (see Coates, 1990; Riemann, 1991). It seems urgent to work out precise designs for public health psychology (see Karoly, 1985). In the following, only a very few aspects will be sketched.

First of all, the base for public health research and its evaluation has to be as secure as possible. Therefore, in epidemiological studies using many variables, strict levels of significance must be reached and cross-validations must be carried out. If this is not carefully attended to, chance differences or differences in the selection and composition of samples may be overestimated with regard to subpopulations or living conditions. This is a major flaw of many major retrospective studies.

In any public health evaluation, one must recognize that the evaluation probably reaches more of the at-risk population than an individualized clinical approach. Therefore, rather small effects can be very important in absolute numbers. Lichtenstein and Glasgow (1992, p. 519) state concern-

Table 1.5. Steps in public health evaluations (see Coates, 1990; Lichtenstein & Glasgow, 1992; Perrez, 1992; Riemann, 1991)

Problem definition
    environmental, ecological risks, epidemiological results, etc.

Demand and priorities
    of citizens and experts, problems with higher priority

General design (see Karoly, 1985; Kramer, 1988)
    prospective or retrospective studies

Targets
    steps, subgoals, their importance and interrelation (e.g., information or direct attitude or behavior change)

Target groups
- population, high risk groups (identification of indicators)
- control groups, kind of control groups
- other groups as multipliers (e.g., family) or sponsors
- changing, as in some sequential strategies

Media in order to reach the groups
    one type of medium or changing in a multimedia approach

Setting(s)

Provider(s) of intervention
- status, professionals, VIPs
- changing with regard to media and target groups

Contents and steps of the intervention (see Coates, 1990)
- determination of factual information to be included
- provision of skills for risk reduction
- provision of motivators for risk reduction

Time schedule
- one intervention or many, sequential efforts
- time range of probable effects

Outcome
- specification of intended outcomes (cognitive, behavioral)
- objective and subjective indicators, criteria, measures
- time range

Cost-effectiveness
- effect strength
- comparison with other types of interventions
- reduced relative and population attributable risks, etc.

Use and publication of the results
- written summary regardless of the results for partners or the public
- publication for the scientific community

---

ing smoking cessation: "It can be seen that public health interventions are more population focused, are less intensive, and produce lower quit rates. Because they reach so many more smokers, they can produce much higher population quit rates, which will have larger public health consequences for reductions in morbidity and mortality."

However, in cost-effectiveness evaluations, the change criteria per individual must reach a critical amount in order to speak of change. For example, an average of one to three cigarettes less per day for a heavy smoker or a medium weight loss of 1.6 kilograms in a medical health education program (Bengel, 1989) does not seem enough to be considered a serious reduction.

Nevertheless, the goals of the programs can be very different. In some public health endeavors, the main goal is the distribution of information to the population or risk groups, illustrated by many AIDS and cardiovascular risk programs. This is not the final aim, but if this intermediary goal does not meet with at least partial success, no change in the attitudes and behaviors seems possible.

The degree to which one can change certain situations and behaviors of course varies. Some problems, like living in poverty or a ghetto in a major city, influence virtually all other health indicators and are at the same time virtually unalterable by psychological means (see Ingham & Bennett, 1990).

PROFESSIONAL REMARKS

Although I have discussed public health in this chapter with a focus on psychological contents and methodology and finally, on its professional implications, I do not mean to imply that other professions are evaluated as less important or should be seen mainly in a competitive relation.

Several psychologists (see Diekstra, 1990; Spurgeon et al., 1990) have outlined the professional aspects of public health psychology with different targets and strengths. Kiesler and Morton (1988, p. 999) claim that "psychologists have several advantages for use in the public interest: (a) an empirical orientation emphasizing outcomes, which can allow them to overcome professional biases; (b) expertise not traditionally allied with medicine and hospital care; (c) emphasis on both prevention and the concept of wellness; and (d) knowledge about the effect of the environment on behavior and well-being."

Statements of this kind make it very clear that psychology in public health should not be seen as just another technological or methodological approach but has the potential to make far-reaching insights as a science and a profession. This includes decisions at the societal (or political) level as well as in communities and with regard to settings and groups of individuals.

It seems not only necessary to implement psychological knowledge and methodology on many levels but to develop a general attitude which cannot of course, be prescribed to the whole profession. Clinical psychology and medical psychology are mainly oriented to symptoms and deficits and rather circumscribed interventions. This is doubtless an important, and successful approach; however, it has its limitations owing to restrictions in the health systems and the implementation of psychologists in them, as well as in its attitude towards the individual as a patient or client. Such psychological approaches often resemble curative medicine, regardless of attempts to show differences between the two.

In my opinion the main goal would be to advocate a *general positive attitude about health on the individual and societal level* and to understand its impact on situations throughout the lifespan. Being optimistic about health does not mean disregarding the problems with methods of prevention which have been sketched above. Nor does it suggest that one can live permanently in a state of total healthiness and fortune. Rather, it means that one should recognize the possibilities of relative, conditional health in all situations. Accordingly, the impact of health attitudes and behaviors should in any given situation and process in the lifespan be as great as possible. This is a fundamental attitude that can be found more and more in the subjective evaluation of handicaps and that may lead to efforts to socially integrate handicapped people as much as possible instead of programs to educate them separately. This argument applies not only to handicapped and disabled children but also to adults with organic handicaps and mental disease as well.

A better fundamental attitude should also help to implement psychology in the community, which was practically impossible for the disciplines of clinical and medical psychology (see Keupp, 1992; Spurgeon et al. 1990; Tolan et al., 1990). Again, the integration of underserved parts of our societies should thereby be facilitated.

On a more methodological level, the development of social epidemiology and especially of psychoepidemiology might help to collect more precise data about life quality and the aspirations of individuals in the population and relevant subpopulations. This could help to overcome concentrating narrowly on the aspects of physical or medical health risks and on the usual illnesses.

Special attention has to be given to the health care systems, which usually focus too narrowly on illness and its curative aspects. As a consequence, psychology has little or no part in the health systems and programs of many countries (see Schmidt & Dlugosch, 1991).

ACKNOWLEDGMENTS

I am grateful to David Motamedi for his proofreading and helpful discussions and to the two anonymous reviewers of this chapter for their valuable constructive and critical comments.

REFERENCES

Abel, T. (1991). Measuring health lifestyles in a comparative analysis: theoretical issues and empirical findings. *Social Science and Medicine*, 32, 899–908.
Abele, A. & Becker, P. (Eds). (1991). *Wohlbefinden, Theorie—Empirie—Diagnostik*. Weinheim: Juventa.
Abholz, H.-H., Borgers, D., Klosterhuis, H., Kühn, H., Reichelt, A., Rosenbrock, R., Scharfstedde, F. & Schagen, U. (1992). Editorial. *Jahrbuch für Kritische Medizin*, 18, 4–5.
Ajzen, I. & Timko, C. (1986). Correspondence between health attitudes and behavior. *Basic and Applied Social Psychology*, 7, 259–276.
Antonovsky, A. (1979). *Health, stress, and coping*. San Francisco: Jossey-Bass.
Arntson, P. (1989) Improving citizens' health competencies. *Health Communication*, 1, 29–34.
Baer, D.M. (1974). A note on the absence of a Santa Claus in any known ecosystem: a rejoinder to Willems. *Journal of Applied Behavior Analyses*, 7, 167–170.
Baumann, U. (Ed) (1987). Themenheft Soziale Netzwerke—Soziale Unterstützung. *Zeitschrift für Klinische Psychologie*, 16, 305–443.
Becker, M. H., Maimann, L. A., Kirscht, J. P., Haefner, D. P., Drachman, R. H. & Taylor, D. W. (1982). Wahrnehmungen des Patienten und Compliance: Neuere Untersuchungen zum "Health Belief Model". In R. B. Haynes, D. W. Taylor & D. L. Sackett (Eds), *Compliance Handbuch* (pp. 94–131). Munich: Oldenbourg.
Becker, P. (1989). *Der Trierer Persönlichkeitsfragebogen (TPF)*. Göttingen: Hogrefe.
Becker, P. (1992a). Seelische Gesundheit als protektive Persönlichkeitseigenschaft. *Zeitschrift für Klinische Psychologie*, 21, 64–75.
Becker, P. (1992b). Die Bedeutung integrativer Modelle von Gesundheit und Krankheit für die Prävention und Gesundheitsförderung—Anforderungen an allgemeine Modelle von Gesundheit. In P. Paulus (Ed), *Prävention und Gesundheitsförderung. Perspektiven für die psychosoziale Praxis* (pp. 91–107). Cologne: GwG-Verlag.
Belz-Merk, M., Bengel, J. & Strittmatter, R. (1992). Subjektive Gesundheitskonzepte und gesundheitliche Protektivfaktoren. *Zeitschrift für Medizinische Psychologie*, 1, 153–171.
Bengel, J. (1989). Ärztliche Gesundheitsberatung aus Sicht der Evaluation. In W. Schönpflug (Ed), *Bericht über den 36. Kongreß der Deutschen Gesellschaft für Psychologie* (pp. 121–130). Göttingen: Hogrefe.
Bengel, J. (1992). Gesundheit und Risiko. Untersuchungen zur gesundheitlichen Risikowahrnehmung und zu Determinanten des Vorsorgeverhaltens am Beispiel der HIV-Infektion. Unveröff. Habilitationsschrift, Universität Freiburg,
Berger, M. (1993). Die Cholesterin-Kontroverse in der Primär-Prävention der koronaren Herzkrankheit. *Jahrbuch für Kritische Medizin*, 19, 67–85.
Bibace, R., Schmidt, L. R. & Walsh, M. (1994). Children's perceptions of illness. In G. Penny, P. Bennett & M. Herbert (Eds), *Health psychology: A life span perspective* (pp. 13–30). London: Harwood.
Bonhoeffer, K. (1991). Prävention als politische Aufgabe (Interview mit W. Göpfert). *Psychomed*, 3, 32–34.
Borgers, D. & Karmaus, W. (1989). Werden wir alle vergiftet oder leben wir im saubersten Staat der Erde? *Jahrbuch für Kritische Medizin*, 14, 59–83.
Brandstätter, H. (1991). Alltagsereignisse und Wohlbefinden. In A. Abele & P. Becker (Eds), *Wohlbefinden, Theorie, Empirie, Diagnostik* (pp. 191–225). Weinheim: Juventa.
Brandtstädter, J. & Eye, A. v. (Ed). (1982). *Psychologische Prävention. Grundlagen, Programme, Methoden*. Berne: Huber.

Braun, H., Martini, H. & Minger, H. (1989). *Kommunale Sozialpolitik in den neunziger Jahren*. Cologne: Deutscher Gemeindeverlag.

Coates, T. J. (1990). Strategies for modifying sexual behavior for primary and secondary prevention of HIV disease. *Journal of Consulting and Clinical Psychology*, 58, 57–69.

Cramer, M. (1992). Prävention angesichts ökologischer Bedrohungen. In P. Paulus (Ed), *Prävention und Gesundheitsförderung. Perspektiven für die psychosoziale Praxis* (pp. 133–149). Cologne: GwG-Verlag.

Dana, R. H. & Hoffmann, T. A. (1987). Health assessment domains: credibility and legitimization. *Clinical Psychology Review*, 7, 539–555.

Detels, R. (1991). Epidemiology: the foundation of public health. In W. W. Holland, R. Detels & G. Knox (Eds), *Oxford textbook of public health*. Volume 2: *Methods of public health* (pp. 285–291). Oxford: Oxford University Press.

Diekstra, R. F. W. (1990). Public health psychology: On the role of psychology in health and health care in the 21st century. In P. J. D. Drenth, J. A. Sergeant & R. J. Takens (Eds), *European perspectives in psychology* (Vol. 2, pp. 19–37) Chichester: Wiley.

Dlugosch, G. E. (1992). *Gesundheitsverhalten und Wohlbefinden*. Unveröff. Dissertation, Universität Trier, Fachbereich I—Psychologie.

Dlugosch, G. E. & Schmidt, L. R. (1990). Problems and challenges in health education for young adults. In K. Hurrelmann & F. Lösel (Eds), *Health hazards in adolescence* (pp. 479–501). Berlin: de Gruyter.

Dlugosch, G. E. & Schmidt, L. R. (1992). Gesundheitspsychologie. In R. H. E. Bastine (Ed), *Klinische Psychologie* (Vol. 2, pp. 123–177). Stuttgart: Kohlhammer.

Egger, J. & Pieringer, W. (1987). Jenseits des Risikofaktorenkonzepts. *Das öffentliche Gesundheitswesen*, 49, 2–8.

Ernst, H. (1992). *Gesund ist, was Spaß macht*. Stuttgart: Kreuz.

Ewart, C. K. (1991). Social action theory for a public health psychology. *American Psychologist*, 46, 931–946.

Faltis, M., Trojan, A., Deneke, C. & Hildebrandt, H. (1989). Gesundheitsförderung im informellen Bereich. In W. Stark (Ed), *Lebensweltbezogene Prävention und Gesundheitsförderung—Konzepte und Strategien für die psychosoziale Praxis* (pp. 162–190). Freiburg: Lambertus.

Farquhar, J. W., Fortmann, S. P., Flora, J. A. & Maccoby, N. (1991). Methods of communication to influence behaviour. In W. W. Holland, R. Detels & G. Knox (Eds), *Oxford textbook of public health*. Volume 2: *Methods of public health* (pp. 331–344). Oxford: Oxford University Press.

Filipp, S.-H. & Ferring, D. (1992). Lebensqualität und das Problem ihrer Messung. *Veröffentlichungen der Joachim Jungius-Gesellschaft der Wissenschaften Hamburg*, 69, 89–109.

Flick, U. (Ed). (1991). *Alltagswissen über Gesundheit und Krankheit*. Heidelberg: Asanger.

Földy, R. & Ringel, E. (1993). *Machen uns die Medien krank? Depression durch Überinformation*. Munich: Universitas.

Frank, R. (1991). Körperliches Wohlbefinden. In A. Abele & P. Becker (Eds), *Wohlbefinden*. (pp. 71–95). Weinheim: Juventa.

Friedman, H.S. (Ed). (1992). *Hostility, coping and health*. Washington, DC: American Psychological Association.

Green, L. W., Kreuter, M. W., Deeds, S. G. & Partridge, K. B. (1980). *Health education planning—a diagnostic approach*. Palo Alto: Mayfield Publishing Company.

Greenland, S. (1991). Concepts of validity in epidemiological research. In W. W. Holland, R. Detels & G. Knox (Eds), *Oxford textbook of public health*. Volume 2: *Methods of public health* (pp. 253–270). Oxford: Oxford University Press.

Grob, A. (1991). *Meinung—Verhalten—Umwelt. Ein psychologisches Ursachennetz-Modell umweltgerechten Verhaltens.* Berne: Lang.

Haisch, J. & Haisch, I. (1990). Gesundheitspsychologie als Sozialpsychologie: Das Beispiel der Theorie sozialer Vergleichsprozesse. *Psychologische Rundschau,* **41,** 25–36.

Haisch, J. & Zeilter, H.-P. (Eds). (1991). *Gesundheitspsychologie. Zur Psychologie der Prävention und Krankheitsbewältigung.* Heidelberg: Asanger.

Halford, G. S. & Sheehan, P. W. (1991). Human response to environmental changes. *International Journal of Psychology,* **26,** 599–611.

Holland, W. W., Detels, R. & Knox, G. (Eds). (1991a). *Oxford textbook of public health.* Volume 1: *Influences of public health.* Oxford: Oxford University Press.

Holland, W. W., Detels, R. & Knox, G. (Eds). (1991b). *Oxford textbook of public health.* Volume 2: *Methods of public health.* Oxford: Oxford University Press.

Holland, W. W., Detels, R. & Knox, G. (Eds). (1991c). *Oxford textbook of public health.* Volume 3: *Applications in public health* Oxford: Oxford University Press.

Holland, W. W. & Fitzsimons, B. (1991). Public health—its critical requirements. In W. W. Holland, R. Detels & G. Knox (Eds), *Oxford textbook of public health.* Volume 3: *Applications in public health* (pp. 605–611). Oxford: Oxford University Press.

Hurrelmann, K. (1989). *Human development and health.* Berlin: Springer.

Hurrelmann, K. & Lösel, F. (Eds). (1990). *Health hazards in adolescence.* Berlin: de Gruyter.

Ingham, R. & Bennett, P. (1990). Health psychology in community settings: models and methods. In P. Bennett, J. Weinman & P. Spurgeon (Eds), *Current developments in health psychology* (pp. 35–61). Chur: Harwood.

Janisse, M. P. (Ed). (1988). *Individual differences, stress, and health psychology.* New York: Springer.

Jefferey, R. W. (1989). Risk behaviors and health. Contrasting individual and population perspectives. *American Psychologist,* **44,** 1194–1202.

Jessor, R. (1993). Successful adolescent development among youth in high-risk settings. *American Psychologist,* **48,** 117–126.

Kals, E. (1993). *Ökologisch relevante Verbotsforderungem.* Trier: Dissertation.

Kaplan, R. M. (1985). Quality-of-life measurement. In P. Karoly (Ed), *Measurement strategies in health psychology* (pp. 115–146). New York: Wiley.

Karoly, P. (Ed). (1985). *Measurement strategies in health psychology.* New York: Wiley.

Keupp, H. (1992). Gesundheitsförderung und psychische Gesundheit: Lebenssouveränität und Empowerment. *Psychomed,* **4,** 244–250.

Kickbusch, I. (1988). New perspectives for research in health behaviour. In R. Anderson, J. K. Davies, I. Kickbusch, D. v. McQueen & J. Turner (Eds), *Health behaviour research and health promotion* (pp. 237–243). Oxford: Oxford University Press.

Kiesler, C. A. & Morton, T. L. (1988). Psychology and public policy in the "health care revolution". *American Psychologist,* **43,** 993–1003.

Kisser, R. (1990). Psychologie in der Gesundheitserziehung. *Psychologie in Österreich,* **10,** 12–16.

Kleiber, D. (1992). Gesundheitsförderung: Hintergründe, Grundauffassungen, Konzepte und Probleme. *Psychomed,* **4,** 220–230.

Kramer, M. S. (1988). *Clinical epidemiology and biostatistics.* Berlin: Springer.

Krieger, W. & Dlugosch, G. E. (1992). Darstellung und erste Erprobung eines Fragebogens zur Erfassung des Gesundheitsverhaltens (FEG) (= Trierer Psychologische Berichte. Band 19, Heft 1). Trier: Universität Trier, Fachbereich I—Psychologie.

Kunzendorff, E. (1990). Psychische Gesundheit und soziale Bedingungen in einer gesellschaftlichen Krisensituation. *Psychomed,* **2,** 256–259.

Lichtenstein, E. & Glasgow, R. E. (1992). Smoking cessation: What have we learned over the past decade? *Journal of Consulting and Clinical Psychology*, 60, 518–527.

Lohaus, A. (1993). *Gesundheitsförderung und Krankheitsprävention im Kindes- und Jugendalter*. Göttingen: Hogrefe.

Lohaus, A., Gaidatzi, C. & Hagenbrock, M. (1988). Kontrollüberzeugungen und AIDS-Prophylaxe. *Zeitschrift für Klinische Psychologie*, 17, 106–118.

Lösel, F., Kolip, P. & Bender, D. (1992). Streß-Resistenz im Multiproblem-Milieu. Sind seelisch widerstandsfähige Jugendliche "Superkids"? *Zeitschrift für Klinische Psychologie*, 21, 48–63.

Lorion, R. P. (1991). Prevention and public health: psychology's response to the nation's health care crisis. *American Psychologist*, 46, 516–519.

Ludwig, W., Schmidt, W. & Lämmel, R. (1988). German Democratic Republic. In International Union for Health Education (Ed), *Health education in Europe—State of the art of health education in 28 European countries* (pp. 89–102). Utrecht: The Dutch Health Education Centre.

McAlister, A. L., Puska, P., Orlandi, M., Bye, L. L. & Zbylot, P. L. (1991). Behaviour modification: principles and illustrations. In W. W. Holland, R. Detels & G. Knox (Eds), *Oxford textbook of public health*. Volume 3: *Applications in public health* (pp. 3–16). Oxford: Oxford University Press.

McGinnis, J. M., Harrell, J. A., Artz, L. M. & Files, A. A. (1991). Objectives-based strategies for disease prevention. In W. W. Holland, R. Detels & G. Knox (Eds), *Oxford textbook of public health*. Volume 3: *Applications in public health* (pp. 127–144). Oxford: Oxford University Press.

Maes, S. (1992). Gesundheitspsychologie, Gesundheitsfürsorge und Krankheitspräven- tion. In H. Schröder & K. Reschke (Eds), *Psychosoziale Prävention und Gesundheits- förderung* (pp. 13–40). Regensburg: Roderer.

Maes, S. & van Veldhoven, M. (1989), Gesundheitspsychologie: Chancen und Kritik. In P. Jacobi (Ed), *Psychologie und Neurologie* (pp. 245–275). Berlin: Springer.

Marteau, T. M. (1993). Health-related screening: psychological predictors of uptake and impact. In S. Maes, H. Leventhal & M. Johnston (Eds), *International review of health psychology* (Vol. 2, pp. 149–174). Chichester: Wiley.

Matarazzo, J. D. (1984). Behavioral immunogens and pathogens in health and illness. In B. L. Hammonds & C. J. Scheirer (Eds), *Psychology and health* (pp. 9–43). Washington, DC: APA.

Milles, D. (1991) "Public Health"—Konzepte und Diskussionen in der deutschen Geschichte. In H.-U. Deppe, H. Friedrich & R. Müller (Eds), *Öffentliche Gesund- heit—Public Health* (pp. 38–59). Frankfurt: Campus.

Mulvey, E. P., Arthur, M. W. & Reppucci, N. D. (1993). The prevention and treatment of juvenile deliquency: A review of the research. *Clinical Psychology Review*, 13, 133–167.

Netter, P. (1991). Types of models in understanding and describing diseases. In L. R. Schmidt, P. Schwenkmezger, J. Weinman & S. Maes (Eds), *Psychological aspects of health psychology* (pp. 29–50) London: Harwood.

Noack, H. (1988). The role of socio-structural factors in health behaviour. In R. Anderson, J. K. Davies, I. Kickbusch, D. McQuenn & J. Turner (Eds), *Health behaviour research and health promotion* (pp. 53–68). Oxford: Oxford University Press.

Palinkas, L. A. (1985). Techniques of psychosocial epidemiology. In P. Karoly (Ed), *Measurement strategies in health psychology* (pp. 49–113). New York: Wiley.

Pant, A. & Kleiber, P. (1993). Heterosexuelles Risikoverhalten und HIV-1 Prävalenz bei intravenös applizierenden Drogenkonsumenten. *Zeitschrift für Gesundheitspsycholo- gie*, 1, 49–64.

Pawlik, K. (1991). The psychology of global environmental change: some basic data and an agenda for cooperative international research. *International Journal of Psychology*, 26, 547–563.

Pawlik, K. & Stapf, K. H. (Eds). (1992). *Umwelt und Verhalten*. Berne: Huber.

Perrez, M. (1991). Prävention, Gesundheits- und Entfaltungsförderung: Systematik und allgemeine Aspekte. In M. Perrez & U. Baumann (Eds), *Lehrbuch Klinische Psychologie*. Vol. 2: *Intervention* (pp. 80–98). Berne: Huber.

Perrez, M. (1992). *Präventive Interventionen im Bereich der Erziehung* (Forschungsbericht No. 90). Fribourg: Universität Fribourg, Psychologisches Institut.

Riemann, K. (1991). Hilfestellungen für praxisnahe Evaluation. In Bundesvereinigung für Gesundheitserziehung (Ed), *Praxisnahe Evaluation gesundheitsfördernder Maßnahmen* (pp. 27–36). Rheinbreitbach: Plump.

Roberts, M. C. (1987). Public health and health psychology: two cats of Kilkenny? *Professional Psychology*, 18, 145–149.

Röhrle, B. (1992). Prävention psychischer Störungen. In R. Bastine (Ed), *Klinische Psychologie* (Vol. 2, pp. 85–122). Stuttgart: Kohlhammer.

Rolinger, U. (1992). Zum Einfluß von Berufsstatus und Schichtarbeit auf das Gesundheitsverhalten. Unveröff. Dipl.Arbeit, Universität Trier, Fachbereich I—Psychologie.

Runyan, C. W., DeVellis, R. F., DeVellis, B. M. & Hochbaum, G. M. (1982). Health psychology and the public health perspective: in search of the pump handle. *Health Psychology*, 1, 169–180.

Sartorius, N., Goldberg, D., Girolamo, G. de, Silva, J. A. C., Lecrubier, Y. & Wittchen, H.-U. (1990). *Psychological disorders in general medical settings*. Toronto: Hogrefe & Huber.

Schmidt, L. R. (1990). Psychodiagnostik in der Gesundheitspsychologie. In R. Schwarzer (Ed), *Gesundheitspsychologie* (pp. 79–92). Göttingen: Hogrefe.

Schmidt, L. R. (1991). Public Health. Das Ringen um die öffentliche Gesundheitsförderung. *Psychomed*, 3, 12–16.

Schmidt, L. R. & Dlugosch, G. E. (1991). Health psychology within European health care systems. In M. A. Jansen & J. Weinman (Eds), *The international development of health psychology* (pp. 33–52). London: Harwood.

Schmidt, L. R. & Dlugosch, G. E. (1992). Entwicklungspsychologische Aspekte der Gesundheitspsychologie. *Zeitschrift für Klinische Psychologie*, 21, 36–47.

Schmidt, L. R. & Schwenkmezger, P. (Ed). (1992). Themenheft Gesundheitspsychologie. *Zeitschrift für Klinische Psychologie*, 21, 1–120.

Schwarzer, R. (1992). *Psychologie des Gesundheitsverhaltens*. Göttingen: Hogrefe.

Schwarzer, R. (1993a). *Measurement of perceived self-efficacy. Psychometric scales for cross-cultural research*. Berlin: Freie Universität.

Schwarzer, R. (1993b). Defensiver und funktionaler Optimismus als Bedingungen für Gesundheitsverhalten. *Zeitschrift für Gesundheitspsychologie*, 1, 7–31.

Schwarzer, R. & Leppin, A. (1989). *Sozialer Rückhalt und Gesundheit: Eine Meta-Analyse*. Göttingen: Hogrefe.

Schwenkmezger, P. (1991). Persönlichkeit und Wohlbefinden. In A. Abele & P. Becker (Eds), *Wohlbefinden. Theorie—Empirie—Diagnostik* (pp. 119–137). Weinheim: Juventa.

Schwenkmezger, P. (1992). Emotionen und Gesundheit. *Zeitschrift für Klinische Psychologie*, 21, 4–16.

Seedhouse, D. (1990). *Liberating medicine*. New York: Wiley.

Seeman, J. (1989). Toward a model of positive health. *American Psychologist*, 44, 1099–1109.

Simon, C. & Jäger, N. (1989). *AIDS. Einschätzungsmuster und Handlungskonzepte in der Bevölkerung der BRD*, Band 1. Mannheim: PENTA.

Skelton, J. A. & Croyle, R. T. (Eds). (1991). *Mental representation in health and illness.* New York: Springer.

Spielberger, C. D. & Frank, R. G. (1992). Injury control. A promising field for psychologists. *American Psychologist*, 47, 1029–1030.

Spurgeon, P., Broome, A., Earll, L. & Harris, B. (1990). Health psychology in a broader context. In P. Bennett, J. Weinman & P. Spurgeon (Eds), *Current developments in health psychology* (pp. 331–345). Chur: Harwood.

Stark, W. (Ed) (1989a). *Lebensweltbezogene Prävention und Gesundheitsförderung—Konzepte und Strategien für die psychosoziale Praxis.* Freiburg: Lambertus.

Stark, W. (1989b). Prävention als Gestaltung von Lebensräumen. Zur Veränderung und notwendigen Reformulierung eines Konzepts. In W. Stark (Ed), *Lebensweltbezogene Prävention und Gesundheitsförderung—Konzepte und Strategien für die psychosoziale Praxis* (pp. 11–37). Freiburg: Lambertus.

Stern, P. C. (1992). Psychological dimensions of global environmental change. *Annual Review of Psychology*, 43, 269–302.

Stewart, T. R. (1991). Scientist's uncertainty and disagreement about global climate change: a psychological perspective. *International Journal of Psychology*, 26, 565–573.

Stokols, D. (1992). Establishing and maintaining healthy environments. *American Psychologist*, 47, 6–22.

Strack, F., Argyle, M. & Schwarz, N. (Eds). (1991). *Subjective well-being. An interdisciplinary perspective.* Oxford: Pergamon.

Tolan, P., Keys, C., Chertok, F. & Jason, L. (Eds). (1990). *Researching community psychology. Issues of theory and methods.* Washington, DC: American Psychological Association.

Vaughan, E. (1993). Chronic exposure to an environmental hazard: risk perceptions and self-protective behavior. *Health Psychology*, 12, 74–85.

Versteegen, U. (1988). *Zur Bedeutung des Konzepts der "Lebensweisen" für die Gesundheitspsychologie. Eine empirische Untersuchung zu den Determinanten des Gesundheitsverhaltens 30–50jähriger Frauen.* Freiburg: Hektographie.

Versteegen, U. (1992). Risikowahrnehmung und Gesundheit. *Zeitschrift für Klinische Psychologie*, 21, 28–35.

Weber, H. (1992). Belastungsverarbeitung. *Zeitschrift für Klinische Psychologie*, 21, 17–27.

Westhoff, G. (1993). *Handbuch psychosozialer Meßinstrumente.* Göttingen: Hogrefe.

Weyerer, S. & Häfner, H. (1992). Epidemiologie psychischer Störungen. *Zeitschrift für Klinische Psychologie*, 21, 106–120.

Willems, E. P. (1974). Behavioral technology and behavioral ecology. *Journal of Applied Behavior Analyses*, 7, 151–165.

Winett, R. A., King, A. C. & Altman, D. G. (1989). *Health psychology and public health. An integrative approach.* New York: Pergamon.

Winslow, C. E. A. (1920). The untilled fields of public health. *Modern Medicine*, 2, 183–191.

World Health Organization (Ed). (1987). *Evaluation of the strategy for health for all by the year 2000. Seventh report on the world health situation.* Geneva: WHO.

World Health Organization (Ed). (1989). *Evaluation of the strategy for health for all by the year 2000. Part 2: Monitoring by country 1988/1989.* Copenhagen: WHO.

Youngstrom, N. (1992a). Psychology helps a shattered L.A. *APA Monitor*, 23, 1 and 12.

Youngstrom, N. (1992b). L.A. riots symbolize dysfunctional society. *APA Monitor*, 23, 12.

Zigler, E., Taussig, C. & Black, K. (1992). Early childhood intervention. A promising preventative for juvenile delinquency. *American Psychologist*, 47, 997–1006.

2 Stress Resistance Resources and Health: A Conceptual Analysis

STEVAN E. HOBFOLL, PADMINI BANERJEE, PAULA BRITTON
Applied Psychology Center, Kent State University, PO Box 5190, Kent, Ohio 44242-0001, USA

The relationship of psychological traits to health marks one of the building blocks of health psychology (Taylor, 1990). Another building block of health psychology is the link between stress and health. Combining how psychological traits interact with stress to affect health may yield even greater insights into the psychosocial dimension of health phenomena. In this chapter we provide a conceptual analysis of how the theory of Conservation of Resources (Hobfoll, 1988, 1989) may aid in the study and understanding of how stress resistance resources, one family of psychosocial traits, contribute to health. An integration of the manner in which resources interact to affect health and illness is critical to the future development of health psychology (Booth-Kewley & Friedman, 1987).

Prior to an interest in stress resistance resources and health, there was a surge of research on the relationship between stress and health. Most studies find that stress, especially severe or chronic stress, has a negative impact on health (Goldberger & Berznitz, 1993). Stress has been found to increase infectious disease through increasing vulnerability to infection and reactivation of latent viruses (Cohen & Williamson, 1991). Others have found that stress increases risk for coronary heart disease and hypertension (Krantz et al., 1988). A number of studies have found that rehabilitation, as well as years and quality of life following disease, are negatively affected by stress in the case of coronary patients cancer patients, dialysis patients, and numerous other patient groups (Fuerstein, Labbé & Kuczmierczyk, 1986).

Public health surveys also show a consistent relationship between stress and morbidity and mortality. Those who undergo greater stress are likely to show increased illness rates and shortened life expectancy (Taylor, 1990). These data reflect a wide array of health outcomes that affect morbidity and mortality, including stress's effects on accidents, suicide, poor health behavior, and development of a broad range of diseases.

International Review of Health Psychology, Volume 3. Edited by S. Maes, H. Leventhal and M. Johnston

However, the link between stress and illness is much stronger for some individuals than others. This led to the finding of a generally weak relationship between stress and health when averaged across individuals that, at first, dampened enthusiasm about the role of stress in affecting physical wellness. Rather than a weak link, however, investigators have come to realize that individual and group differences in susceptibility to stress's pathological effects can be attributed, in part, to differences in levels of psychosocial risk factors and differences in levels of psychosocial resources (Cohen & Syme, 1985; Taylor, 1990). This paper addresses the resource domain, in particular. An idea we will develop throughout this chapter is that those who possess greater resources, are less likely to be negatively impacted by stressful circumstances. For many individuals the link between stress and illness is weakened or interrupted. Further, these same resources are often directly linked to positive health in general, irrespective of stressful life circumstances.

In order to achieve our goals, conservation of resource (COR) theory will first be briefly explained. Following this explication, we review the health literature for a critical analysis of how COR theory may aid the understanding of the relationship between personal resources and health and illness. We will also evaluate the role played by social support in terms of its direct effects on health, its role as a stress buffer, and its interaction with personal resources. We focus, in particular, on studies that explore physical health and illness outcomes, and we will not directly address studies investigating the effects of resources on psychological outcomes. Therefore, when we use the term health, we mean physical health, unless we state otherwise. Demographic variables such as age, socioeconomic status, and occupation will not be addressed owing to space limitations, although surely they too are important. We hope to illustrate how COR theory may guide future research by providing a framework for hypothesis testing and further theory building.

CONSERVATION OF RESOURCE THEORY

Basic COR theory

COR theory begins with the premise that people have a basic motivation to obtain, retain, and protect that which they value. These things that people value, or that enable them to obtain or protect that which they value, are termed resources. Stress will occur therefore when any of three conditions occur: (1) environmental circumstances threaten resource loss, (2) environmental circumstances result in actual resource loss, or (3) individuals invest resources without receiving adequate return on their investment. It should be added that we are speaking of psychological stress; organisms may also be directly physical distressed (e.g., by physical trauma or a virus), but one does not need to rely on a theory of psychological stress to understand physical stress. This is sometimes forgotten when we confuse physical exhaustion with psychological stress as did Seyle (1951–56).

COR delineates four basic categories of resources: (1) objects (e.g., car, house), (2) conditions (e.g., tenure, marriage), (3) personal characteristics (e.g., social aplomb, high self-esteem), and (4) energies (e.g., credit, money, owed favors). Clearly there are many such resources that could be named. However, we found a group of 74 primary resources that people generally agree on as most critical (Hobfoll, Lilly & Jackson, 1992). This is not an exhaustive list, but can be viewed as comprehensive. Even within this list, there is probably a subgroup of resources that future research will identify as most critical.

Stress has typically been conceptualized as a state where personal coping ability is appraised as exceedingly taxed or outstripped by environmental or internal demands (Lazarus & Folkman, 1984). COR theory takes a somewhat different approach to stress. First, COR theory suggests that stress should focus on external not internal demands. Internal demands are important, but their study lies more in the realm of the study of neurotic processes. Stress has historically been linked to individuals' coping with external events that challenge them in some way. Adding internal processes clouds the picture, albeit a future area for investigation (i.e., neurosis and coping). Second, although COR theory considers appraisal to be important, idiographic or individualized appraisal is seen as less critical. As Lazarus and Folkman (1984) themselves acknowledge, for major stressors (and that includes chronic stressors), individual differences in appraisal plays a lesser role. To the extent the stressors that affect health are major or chronic in nature appraisal will be less critical because for these categories of stressors, appraisal is quite similar across persons (Hobfoll, 1988). Third, and perhaps most important, COR theory suggests that stress does not necessarily occur when demands tax resources or outstrip resources, as others suggest (Lazarus & Folkman, 1984). Indeed, demands are always taxing resources, but the result is not always stressful. Further, individuals' resources are seldom outstripped, except in the case of breakdown in very extreme circumstances.

The primacy of loss

An additional and critical principle central to COR theory is that individuals are biased to overestimate the weight of loss compared to gain. Cognitive psychologists have noted convincingly that humans have a bias to such overestimation of loss (Tversky & Kahneman, 1981). Given problems that have a loss facet and a gain facet of equal and opposite value, people do not make equal and opposite decisions. Rather, they "err" by overweighting the consequence of loss. In a simple example, they place a lower price on the purchase of a cup (gain) then they do the sale of the same cup (loss). In medical decisions, they are willing to grossly overinvest resources and take risks in order to avoid future regret (i.e., loss of some valued health state) (Tymstra, 1989).

In our own research we found that resource gain was not directly related to psychological distress (Hobfoll, Lilly & Jackson, 1992). In contrast, resource loss was strongly and directly related to distress. This is not to say that resource gain does not play a role, because it has a complex, important role. We found that resource gain becomes critical, over and above the effects of resource loss. This suggests that gain takes on added significance once loss cycles have been initiated and the system is attempting to counteract the loss or halt loss cycles by making resource gains.

The question immediately arises as to whether loss alone can account for psychological stress. Earlier research suggested that change, transitions, or even positive events can also engender stress. In a comprehensive literature review Thoits (1983) noted that undesirable events were most consistently related to psychological distress. In reviewing stressful life events surveys, it is clear that the undesirable events are not only loss events, but that loss is the only consistently negative theme about these events. The major life events that have been found to be critical to psychological stress are all profound loss events. These include loss of a loved one, loss of health, severe loss of income, loss of employment, loss of love, and loss of freedom.

Other events are more ambiguous. Moving and job change, for example, are such events. Studies that have examined ambiguous events have found that only when negative changes occur are the consequences stressful (Thoits, 1983). A move or job change that entails an enhancement of resources, such as better accommodation or increased status, do not have negative effects (Munton, 1990). Indeed, Cohen and Hoberman (1983) found that positive events contribute to improved stress buffering, limiting the deleterious effects of other negative events. This means that not only is positive change not stressful, it acts to help individuals combat negative events.

Transitions have also been conceived as stressful (Felner, Farber & Primavera, 1983). However, transitions may be better conceived as opportunities for coping. In such instances resources are called upon at a greater frequency and level of intensity. Consistent with the loss–stress relationship, if resources are not lost (e.g., loss of close personal ties), then negative sequelae do not seem to follow. Felner, Farber & Primavera's (1983) insight remains, however, in that transitions are times of extraordinary opportunity for preventive intervention. As they suggest, because adaptation calls on resources, negative changes are more likely than during stable periods and people's coping repertoires are likely to be called upon in ways in which they are less familiar than during everyday circumstances. Intervention that focuses on resources enhancement and better resource utilization are extremely valuable during such periods.

Key corollaries of COR theory

A number of key corollaries follow from COR theory, and may be helpful to an understanding of stress and health. The first corollary of COR theory is that *individuals must invest resources in order to limit loss of resources, protect resources, or gain resources.* Schönpflug (1985) has shown in insightful programmatic studies that coping with stressful challenges was accompanied by investment of other resources at the individual's disposal. In this way, people act by drawing on their resource reservoirs by taking certain risks and making certain resource investments in a strategic fashion.

Individuals have a limited supply of resources available to them. It is these resources that must be used in coping and adaptation. For example, time and energy must be expended in order to work on a problem. Similarly, money must be spent to purchase insurance or a needed vacation. How might more abstract personal resources, such as self-esteem, be invested, however? In order to confront stress, people risk their self-esteem by attempting, say, to problem-solve. Those who lack self-esteem, do not take this risk and instead may avoid challenges. High self-esteem individuals, nevertheless, are putting their self-esteem on the line, because if they fail in their coping attempts their self-esteem will likely suffer.

A second corollary of COR theory is that *those individuals with greater resources are less vulnerable to resource loss and more capable of resource gain.* In contrast, *those who lack resources, are more vulnerable to resource loss and less capable of resource gain.* For those with greater resources, challenging circumstances are less likely to cause resource loss because they can successfully mobilize their resources in the service of stress resistance, and in so doing prevent such loss. In more everyday circumstances, they can deploy resources in order to produce further resource gain. A pregnant woman who is challenged with stressful events who lacks resources, in contrast, might, for example, have to rely on resources that have a poor fit with the actual demand. A financial problem might lead to her having to work extra hours and cause a lack of proper sleep or health care. When stressors are not present, she might also not have the resources to invest toward resource gain. Indeed, the lack of resources may make even everyday stressors unmanageable.

A third corollary of interest here states that *those who lack strong resource pools are more likely to experience cycles of resource loss, while those who possess strong resource pools are more likely to experience cycles of resource gain.* This corollary follows because (1) stress is caused by resource loss, (2) it produces additional loss of resources through resource expenditure in coping, and (3) this process combines to leave the organism less resilient to the next loss.

Hence, loss and gain tend to follow in chains, with loss following loss and gain following gain. The enriched system has "fat" to expend on investing in repeated gain opportunities. The depleted resource system is increasingly vulnerable to stress, as each stressor sequence renders the system with less resources in the pool to offset the next challenge. Added to this, recent research suggests that chronic stressors are the most devastating (Goldberger & Breznitz, 1993). This means that the concept of "stressor event" actually should be unpacked to include the sequence of sub-events that are included in what has usually been called an event. Divorce, for instance, actually involves a complex sequence of losses that impinge on economics, time for childcare and household labor, companionship, social support, and social status. These complex sequences place long-term pressure on individuals' resources and the broader and deeper the array of resources the more likely that the individuals will be capable of affecting positive outcomes.

It is important to add that since loss is more highly weighted than gain, that loss cycles will have greater *intensity* and *velocity* than gain cycles. Intensity means that each loss in the cycle will have greater impact. Velocity means that the loss cycle will occur with greater speed than the gain cycle—loss will follow loss more rapidly than gain will follow gain.

STRESS RESISTANCE RESOURCES AND HEALTH

COR theory would suggest that when persons' resources are strained, their system becomes increasingly vulnerable, and they will be likely to experience distress. This distress can be related to health in at least three ways, as has been pointed out frequently by other health psychologists (Cohen & Syme, 1985; Krantz, Grunberg & Baum, 1985; Taylor, 1990), and as are predicted from most stress models. First, stress can directly affect the organism by negatively impacting physiological systems, as seen in marked increases in pulse, excess secretion of gastric substances, or increased blood pressure. These are responses to a taxed system. Secondly, the stress response may directly affect the immune system, and leave the organism more vulnerable to outside pathogens. Third, the stress response may result in psychological distress that, in turn, translates to poor health behaviors. This pathway is the least exotic, but probably most important. For example, individuals may become inattentive in traffic when anxious and have a car accident, or they may try to self-medicate their anxious emotions via drugs, alcohol, or smoking. These behaviors, in turn, lead to various illnesses, diseases, or accidents.

Hence, we argue that a possible contribution can be made to an understanding of the stress-health link to the extent we appreciate that both the original stressor and the sequence of stress-subsequent demands continue to drain resources and result in further resource loss. Because these deleterious effects are initially likely to occur in a resource-poor or weakened individual, loss cycles are also more likely to occur.

Combining the three corollaries presented earlier, stress will occur as a product of loss, threat of loss, or significant failure to gain resources. The organism will respond to initial loss with a mobilization of resources. Ongoing challenge will continue to call on and possibly deplete resources. Part of this challenge will emanate from the initial or outside stressor and part of the challenge will emanate from the resultant losses that follow as sequelae of the initial loss and stress response. For instance, a man may experience increased back pain following job loss. The back pain may make him more irritable and create further family tensions. Now, resources that are already depleted will need to address (1) job loss, (2) back pain, and (3) family problems. This spiral will quickly accelerate in intensity.

Thus far, we have presented the model and its hypothesized relationship to health. We have also highlighted key points in the model as they might relate to health. In the next section we will selectively review studies that explored the resource–health link and we will attempt to frame our discussion in the context of COR theory and other resource models.

RESOURCE CONCEPTS AND THEIR HEALTH EFFECTS

In order to discuss the COR model in relationship to the current resource literature, we conducted a review of the literature on studies involving resources and health. Our presentation is organized into studies addressing personal resources and social resources. Among personal resources, we examine control constructs, self-constructs, and ways individuals judge their environment. Among social resources, we focus on social support, which is best viewed as a metaconstruct that consists of social structure variables (e.g., network size and density), social condition variables (e.g., marriage, group membership), and social support interactions and their perception (Vaux, 1988). We attempt to integrate these diverse concepts within a theory of the common denominators of resource action—COR theory.

Personal resources

Control and health

By far the most work on personal resources has been done on concepts related to control. Control is broadly defined as the sense that one can affect one's environment with reasonable success. COR theory posits that control may be a central resource because it determines how other resources are managed. Those high in personal sense of control confidently use their resources to affect beneficial outcomes. This, in turn, creates a belief that resources can be used to contribute to successful adjustment in the face of life stressors. Such appraisals should not be confused with simple cognitive reframing. Rather, individuals are seen as actively manipulating their environment as a product of their approach. If individuals are not high in mastery or sense of control, there is no evidence to date to suggest that reframing the situation *as if* it is more controllable will positively affect their health.

There is reason to believe that control is, in fact, an important construct, hence that it deserves special attention. However, the dominance of research on control may also be related to its being introduced early with a convenient measure (Rotter, 1966), and the emphasis on control in our culture (Hobfoll, 1988). The prolific and multidisciplinary literature on the construct is evidenced by the multitude of names under which the general construct has been studied. For example, Pearlin et al., (1981) examined the concept of mastery; Bandura (1982) among others has studied self-efficacy; Rotter (1975) and Wallston and Wallston (1982) explored locus of control; Seligman (1975) investigated learned helplessness; Glass and Singer (1972) and Sherrod (1974) studied controllability; Burger (1985) looked at desire for control, and Kobasa (1982) examined hardiness. Each of these concepts relates to the notion that personal actions can enhance the likelihood of one's success.

These similar constructs span different phases of the coping process. Locus of control relates to individuals' belief in their control of outcomes and reinforcers. Self-efficacy relates rather to people's belief that their own behaviors can enable them to achieve certain outcomes (see Strecher et al., 1986). The two constructs have strong overlap, but do nevertheless appear to be separate conceptually and practically. Most researchers and theorists have, in fact, linked the two, proposing that the belief in control precedes the enactment of behaviors designed to create desired outcomes.

According to COR theory, control may be a critical construct because it is a *managerial resource*. In this way, those high in sense of control are likely to attempt to manipulate the resources in their environment toward effective problem solving. Those with an external locus of control or those with low efficacy are typically conceptualized as not enacting goal-directed behaviors; however, COR theory suggests that they either have poor resources to manage or manage their resources poorly.

There is good reason to believe that this sense of self-efficacy is not just in the mind (i.e., not just cognitive), but also translates to development and better use of more effective behaviors (Ozer & Bandura, 1990). Partridge and Johnston (1989) explored, for instance, whether a belief in personal control over recovery would be predictive of faster, more complete recovery from physical disability. They found that both stroke patients and patients suffering from wrist fractures adapted more successfully and had better health outcomes if they had greater sense of personal control, suggesting that they possessed and practiced the hehavioral repertoires necessary for rehabilitation.

Information is an important resource, but one that must be sought out and used. Such thinking is clearly consistent with theorizing of Wallston, Maides, and Wallston (1976) in their development of the health locus of control concept. Preserving health and combating illness requires the seeking out and exploiting of complex information from multiple sources. If one has the belief that one can affect one's own health, such information seeking and employment of knowledge is more likely. Involvement and adherence to medical advice has been found in this way to be higher in persons with greater sense of their own efficacy (Strickland, 1978; Wallston et al., 1987).

In studying hardiness and its relationship to health, both stress buffering (Kobasa, Maddi & Courington, 1981) and direct effects have been noted (Roth et al., 1989; Shepperd & Kashani, 1991). Hardiness was originally conceptualized as consisting of three components: control, commitment, and challenge. However, only the control and commitment aspects have been found to be of predictive value (Hull, Van Treuren & Virnelli, 1987). Kobasa and Puccetti (1983) found that hardy individuals have better health outcomes than those low in hardiness. Originally building her understanding of hardiness on managers whose company and jobs were threatened with loss, Kobasa saw hardy individuals as accepting this challenge and affecting their environment to their benefit. Consistent with COR theory, hardy managers sought potential resources in themselves and their environment and used these to overcome environmental challenge.

Study of explanatory style might provide insight in how sense of control, mastery, or efficacy might operate cognitively. Those high in sense of control tend to see events as things that they can influence, they see negative circumstances as changeable and not stable, and limit the extent to which they see these events affecting other areas of their lives (Abramson, Seligman & Teasdale, 1978). If individuals think they can affect the environment, if circumstances are changeable, and if they are not overwhelmed by seeing a negative turn of events as all-encompassing, it is more likely that the individual will rally resources to change events in their favor. They will rally resources for selfcare, self help, and in meeting life challenges (Kamen & Seligman, 1987). Kobasa's commitment dimension further suggests that one needs a determination to accept the challenge and be motivated toward problem-solving.

Control may also be related to health on a more direct physiological level. Kiecolt-Glaser et al. (1985) and Wiedenfeld et al. (1990) found that increasing sense of control and efficacy translated to increases in natural killer cell activity and immunological functioning. Repeated, control-depleting events similarly engendered suppressed immune functioning (Rodin, 1986). Such physiological responses may follow from cell-level reaction to negative emotions that follow unsuccessfully combatted stressful events. In this vein, those who possess greater sense of control may be better able to keep physiological integrity of immune function because they are less likely to experience depression, chronic anger and anxiety, and are more likely to sustain positive emotions (Kaplan, 1991). Those who are beset by these negative emotions, in comparison, are more susceptible to disease development. To the extent resources are available to stave off negative emotional reactions, healthy physiological functioning will be sustained.

Ways individuals view how they will be affected by their environment

Control relates to how individuals will affect their environment. Perhaps the flip-side of this are constructs related to how individuals sense that they will be affected by their environment. Antonovsky (1979) in his sense of coherence concept suggests that we place too much emphasis on personal control. He argues that many, perhaps a majority of people, have a perception of how they will be treated by external events that determines much of their behavior. Thoughts concerning will, forces of God, country, and fate are seen as more important than individual control of events.

COR theory suggests that when people view how the environment affects them, they are actually focusing on how their resources are affected. Health, self-esteem, wealth, and access to advancement are deeply affected by environmental circumstances. People, in turn, develop general outlooks toward the external conditions that contribute to these circumstances based on learned experiences (Allen & Britt, 1983). They also develop a sense of meaning to explain why these things occur in the way they do.

Optimism is a construct that reflects how positive individuals judge that events will affect them. Optimists have been found to have faster recovery from surgery than pessimists and demonstrated fewer signs of intraoperative complications (Scheier et al., 1986). Optimists do not necessarily believe that it is their acts that will or can affect the positive outcomes. Rather, they believe that a combination of fate and their own behavior will together lead to favorable ends.

Kamen and Seligman (1987) link pessimism with the kinds of behaviors others have associated with locus of control. They suggest that pessimists have poor health outcomes in large part because they are passive about self-care, life challenges, and mobilizing social support. Again, COR theory suggests that it is not that pessimists are passive, but rather that they either believe their resources to be inadequate or inadequately use their resources.

The latter process, at least, is not a passive one, and indeed may be quite active.

One of the themes central to readjustment is the search for meaning. Taylor, Lichtman & Wood (1984) found that among cancer patients, the types of attributions made as to the causes of cancer were related to better health outcomes and overall psychological adjustment. Taylor, Licht man & Wood maintain that much of this search for meaning and control is an illusion, but that those who construct positive illusions have improved responding to stress. Breznitz (1983) similarly suggested that a modicum of denial of the impact of severe stressors is a healthy approach. Individuals must have enough of a sense of how reality is challenging them to appropriately respond, but denying the full extent of the threat or loss prevents their being overwhelmed by negative emotions.

Research on search for meaning and realization of a meaningful world view is in its nascent stage. The constructs are theoretically appealing, however. Future research might work toward separating differences between hopelessness, pessimism, and failure to find meaning. Also, we wonder whether finding meaning is enough, or whether the meaning must contribute to optimism, control, or other beliefs that set certain health behaviors and internal health responses in motion.

The concept of self as a resource

Another important resource is a positive view of self. Self-esteem is a key concept here, denoted by a sense that the self is valued and considered to be deserving of positive regard from others. One of the most central resources depicted in COR theory is self-esteem (Hobfoll, 1988; Hobfoll & Freedy, 1990). Self-esteem is viewed as a robust resource that is slow to develop and robust in the face of adversity. In one sense, self-esteem denotes the feeling that one is deserving of resources, especially social and emotional approval. As a basic building block, self-esteem is pivotal for the establishment of other resources. Furthermore, as a basic resource, people will make supreme efforts to build and retain their self-esteem. DeLongis, Folkman & Lazarus (1988) found that individuals with low self-esteem had increased somatic problems both on and following stressful days. Curbow *et al.* (1990) reviewed this literature and noted that self-concept has been of particular interest in the oncology literature. However, in almost all studies, the interest was in the effects of self-concept on psychological and not physical health outcomes. Of importance here, nevertheless, is their conclusion that the self is often severely affected by cancer. A diminished sense of self has in other studies been found to be related to poorer health behavior and psychological distress might also affect the immune system as was discussed earlier.

Women with a poor self-concept are especially susceptible to eating disorders (Rosen, 1992). When seeing themselves as unattractive, some take extreme measures in eating and purging. Starving themselves, being followed by use of laxatives or vomiting are common reactions in this regard (Crowther et al., 1992). Similarly, poor self-concept has often been found to be related to alcohol and drug abuse (Jessor & Jessor, 1975; Kaplan, 1975). As with eating disorders those with poor self-concepts act in self-destructive manners in their use of chemicals.

Another view of the self is subsumed in the self-attention construct (Levanthal, Neranz & Strauss, 1980; Suls & Fletcher, 1985). Those who are more predisposed to focus on internal aspects of the self might be better able to attend to their psychologic and somatic reactions in the face of stressful events. By having such self-knowledge they would be better equipped to mobilize their resources and enact the required corrective behaviors available to them. Seemingly contradictory evidence is found, however, in work showing that high self-monitors, also attend to internal cues, but do so to their health detriments. The difference between high monitors and those high in self-attention, is that high monitoring has been construed as the tendency to monitor threatening information. This makes high self-monitors vigilant, but unlikely to feel that they can act to create a less threatening environment (Miller, Brody & Summerton, 1988). Those high in private self-consciousness monitor their internal states, but are believed then to adapt by using their resources in a more adaptive manner and in so doing to positively contribute to health (Suls & Fletcher, 1985).

How self-concept relates to use of resources may provide some insight in this process. Extreme eating behaviors and drug use do not go unnoticed by loved ones. Very often the behaviors themselves or their consequences are noted and loved ones respond. Those with good self-concepts have been found to positively translate social support to positive emotions (Hobfoll, Nadler & Leiberman, 1986) and to receipt of instrumental aid (Hobfoll, Shoham & Ritter, 1991). Those with poor self-concepts, in contrast, tend to diminish or misuse social resources. For example, despite feedback that they are thin, anorexic women do not alter their self-view and continue to see themselves as fat (Katzman & Wolchik, 1984; Worsley, 1981). Drug users associate with social networks that encourage their drug abuse (Hawkins & Fraser, 1989).

The research on self-concept and health, and especially how self-concept interacts with other resources to impact health, is deserving of much greater attention. In a way, the study of self-concept is not fashionable today, but it may prove to be a major resource, central to explaining how other resources are or are not utilized in service of health promotion, illness prevention, and eliminating the negative loss chains that follow initial psychological and health setbacks.

Overall, a number of personal resources appear to be related to health outcomes. There are, however, a few major concerns that should be considered. First, although names for resources are often different, the mechanisms for how different resources work are often overlapping. Control and pessimism may be quite different conceptually, but are often discussed as if they are the same. We do not have a firm understanding of the overlap between these concepts. Therefore, studies that investigate multiple resources and determine their relative contributions are called for. Second, theorists must better define how the mechanism for one resource should differ from the mechanism of action of another resource. Process analyses should then be undertaken to investigate whether those mechanisms actually occur. Third, application of general resource theories such as COR theory and that of Holohan and Moos (1991) might guide investigations of the interactive effects of multiple resources, as to how they combine to affect health outcomes.

Social resources

Personal resources are those resources contained within or possessed by individuals. Social resources are an important group of resources that exist outside individuals. They are one of the most critical external resources. Like other external resources, social resources must be available to individuals and individuals must either know how to use them or passively receive them (e.g., mother's love). In either case, they need to be mobilized to aid stress resistance and adaptation. Personal resources, in contrast, are carried by the individual and so are always there to be tapped at the time of need; mobilization time is instantaneous.

COR theory depicts social support as the principal vehicle for obtaining resources that are not possessed by the self (Hobfoll & Freedy, 1990). Social support is also of central importance because it is basic to the development of self-esteem and sense of identity. As Bowlby (1969) suggested, who we are is in large part a product of our early attachments and the provision of love and caring provided by those attachment figures. This sense of self is therefore inextricably tied with the lifetime involvement of supportive others in our lives. However, it is not only the resources they provide, but also the meaning of this provision which creates a sense of being loved, esteemed, and a part of a community of others.

The principal social resource that has received study is social support. Social support, however, is best depicted as a metaconstruct, or a broad family of social resources. For this reason, there is no one simple definition of social support. Rather, it is a higher-order theoretical construct comprised of several legitimate and distinguishable subconstructs (Vaux, 1988). Three major subconstructs of social support are: (1) support network resources, (2) supportive behavior, and (3) subjective appraisals of support. Most health research has focused on subjective support appraisals, and to a lesser extent on supportive behavior. Thus, social support, as it has been typically studied in the health literature, reflects "those social interactions or relationships that provide individuals with actual assistance or with a feeling of attachment to a person or group that is perceived as caring or loving" (Hobfoll & Stokes, 1988, p. 499).

Social support has long been linked with health and well-being. In fact, one of the initial stress moderator studies, concerned the role of social support in limiting the effects of stress on complications of pregnancy (Nucholls, Cassel & Kaplan, 1972). In this seminal investigation, women who received social support were found to have greatly reduced risk of pregnancy complications if they also had experienced high stress levels. Women who experienced high stress levels who were not well supported, in contrast, had greatly increased risk of pregnancy complications over what would have otherwise been expected. Although methodologically flawed, this study was essentially replicated in more careful examination (Norbeck & Tilden, 1983).

Two principal hypotheses have been set forth regarding the effects of social support. Although research confirms both paths, it is instructive to consider each separately because they outline different mechanisms of social support (Cohen & Syme, 1985). The first is the so-called direct effect of social support, defined as the main effect of social support on well-being, irrespective of stress levels. According to this model, social support will be related to better health, no matter how much stress is confronting individuals. Cohen and Syme (1985) suggest that social support might provide enhanced self-esteem and overall positive affect, which may influence susceptibility to illness by affecting neuroendocrine and immune system functioning (see also Jemmott & Locke, 1984), or through modification of health-promoting behavior and avoidance of risky health behavior. Social support might also directly affect health by providing opportunity for social interaction that sets the stage for adoption of appropriate roles and behavior (Cassel, 1976; Thoits, 1983). These roles might also affect physiological systems, and decrease the risk of encountering negative life events, which themselves could affect health. In terms of the COR model, support resources are likely to lead to other health-enhancing resources, and this constellation of resources contributes to health and limitation of illness.

The contrasting model is termed the stress buffering effect. The stress buffering model posits that social support will have an increasingly salutogenic effect, the higher the stress level. For individuals experiencing high levels of stress, social support would have a strong, positive effect. For those experiencing low levels of stress, social support would not have a marked effect (see Barrera, 1986). In this model, social support might limit emotional distress in response to stress. This lowered anxiety, anger, and depression and raised satisfaction and happiness could, in turn, affect neuroendocrine and immunological responding. Second, following stress and the resultant loss of resources, individuals are likely to engage in increasingly unhealthy means of coping. By limiting distress, however, they will be less likely to abuse alcohol and other chemicals, or overeat or undereat. Sleep patterns would be more likely to remain healthy, as well. COR theory suggests that resources lead to other resources. By finding a beneficial effect of social support, people would be more likely to continue to affiliate and receive other beneficial effects of support, precisely when they need them most.

The direct and stress buffering effect models were examined in a comprehensive meta-analysis by Schwarzer and Leppin (1989). This incisive report found modest evidence for the stress buffering effect of social support on health. A population effect size of -0.09 was found for stressed subjects compared to an effect size of -0.05 for non-stressed subjects. This suggests, as noted earlier by Cohen and Syme (1985) that both direct effects and stress-buffering effects of social support exist. It also suggests that the overall effect of social support on physical health may be modest. This modest effect may be due, in part, to the fact that stress has complex effects on physiological factors and these effects are hardly uniformly positive (Newberry, Jaikins-Madden & Gerstenberger, 1991).

In addition to testing the stress-buffering versus direct effect models, we are particularly interested in the overall strength of the relationship between social support and health. The strength of this relationship depends, as we would expect, on the kind of health variable studied (Schwarzer & Leppin, 1989). When global health status was used as the dependent variable, the population effect size was -0.11. When symptom indices were observed the effect size was -0.08. Similar levels of relationship were found for physiological measures such as blood pressure and heart rate (-0.07) and mortality (-0.08). Surprisingly, no significant relationship was found for the relationship between social support and heart disease or cancer.

Marked sex differences were noted in the effects of social support on health. As others have suggested, social support is a stronger ingredient in the stress-distress relationship for women than for men (Lowenthal & Haven, 1968; Hobfoll & Stokes, 1988). For females the overall social support–health relationship showed a population effect size of -0.09, whereas for men it was only -0.03. Further, women were more greatly affected by a supportive spouse (-0.08) and family support (-0.20) than were men $(-0.01$ and -0.07, respectively). This may indicate that men are not as likely to receive as much support (thus attenuating the effect of the relationship), or are not making as much use of the support. There is also a possible biological explanation, such that women are genetically conditioned to be more physiologically sensitive to familial–tribal variables than are men. There is, in fact, some indication that early man did not even live with the clan which included women, children, and elderly (Sahlins, 1970).

This sex separation may be responsible for promoting different social survival traits in the two sexes.

The differences in how social resources must be mobilized compared to personal resources also suggests that Schwarzer and Leppin's effect sizes may be underestimates (see also Schwarzer & Leppin, 1991). Meta-analysis combines many studies. In some studies, social support was assessed prior to health measures. However, in most studies, assessment was simultaneous. For this reason some investigations are actually focusing on the prospective effects of social support on health. Other studies, in contrast, are evaluating how health changes affect social support. Health setbacks will, in this way, result in an increase in social support, as the ill individuals act to mobilize their support systems. This will yield a positive relationship between social support and illness. Further, this effect will be strongest for those with most access to support and ability to activate that support. Hence, some studies are looking at the beneficial effects of social support on health outcomes, whereas other are examining how once troubled, those with available support, call on that help. This paradoxical dual-route of social support—limiting distress, yet increasing in response to distress—was illustrated in a study by Hobfoll and Lerman (1988).

Social support can thus be seen as having a general positive effect on health outcomes. However, much of the social support literature is surprisingly void of consideration of how support is used (Ritter, 1988). We know much more about support's effects than about how these effects are actualized. Nor do we have much information about how this valuable social commodity comes about. In the following sections we will attempt to arrive at a more contextual understanding of the role played by and the interplay with social support in the stress resistance process.

Social support in relation to personal resources

Social support and personal resources are related to each other in a number of ways. In an important theoretical article, Hansson, Jones and Carpenter (1984) exhorted other colleagues to attend to the fact that social support did not just occur for some individuals and not occur for others. Rather, drawing in part from research on shyness, they suggested that social support is the product of two personal resources, social skillfulness and self-confidence. Approaching others and asking for help potentially places the individual in an inferior position (Fisher, Nadler & Whitcher-Alagna, 1982). Those with poor self-esteem are likely to feel too vulnerable in many instances to place themselves in this position of relative inferiority. Those high in self-esteem might, in contrast, feel confident enough to take this risk. However, other research suggested that those high in self-esteem might find the help seeking position as too inconsistent with their self-view (Nadler & Mayeless, 1983). These differences have been found to be situationally dependent (Nadler & Mayeless, 1983), but in either case self-esteem is an important factor affecting the helping process.

Social skills are important personal resources, as well, and those who possess them should be better equipped to (1) build close social relationships, (2) build mutually beneficial support networks, and (3) call successfully on that support when the time is needed. Hobfoll and his colleagues examined Hansson et al.'s lead and confirmed these paths in a number of social support studies (Hobfoll, Nadler & Leiberman, 1986; Hobfoll & Lerman, 1989).

The team of Sarason and Sarason have suggested another way in which social support is related to personal resources. Specifically, they surmise that many of the aspects of social support are personal characteristics rather than environmental characteristics (Sarason, Sarason & Shearin, 1986). In support of their argument, it has been noted that the perception of support is only partially a reflection of environmental factors, and is fairly stable for individuals across situations. This may, in part, stem from the fact that people carry a sense of support that is developed over the lifespan, and is partially immune to temporal ups and downs. Another possibility is that individuals may have a belief in their ability to call on support should they need it. This is probably based on past experience, so it is environmental in one sense. Once this sense is developed, however, it can be said that the individual is relying not on social support, but on his or her ability to gain that valuable social commodity should it prove necessary.

Social support, even if environmentally based, needs to be activated in times of need. A particularly strong support system might be sensitive to individuals' requirements and act independently of individuals' behavior. Knowing that a friend looks depressed or has had an illness, it is easy to see how supporters might volunteer emotional or instrumental aid. However, those high in attributes that relate to social skillfulness and intimacy are more likely to both have good social support and to know how to effectively mobilize help when it is appropriate (Connel & D'Augelli, 1990).

Kobasa and Puccetti (1983) noted that those high in hardiness, also benefited more greatly from social support than those low in hardiness. They suggested that this might have occurred because they better utilized social support from stronger relationships. Hobfoll, Shoham and Ritter (1991) noted that greater social support for childcare tasks was received by women who were high in mastery. Indeed, Hobfoll and Leiberman (1987) actually found that low self-esteem individuals were negatively affected by social support. These interactive links between personal and social resources are suggestive of the positive and negative cycles suggested by COR theory. However, there are relatively few such interactive studies, and most of these assessed psychological outcomes rather than physical health outcomes.

ECOLOGICAL CONTEXT OF RESOURCES

The ecological context in which support operates is also critical to an understanding of the true effects of social support. Is support available, is the available support suitable, is it culturally acceptable to rely on support in this instance, and if so, for how long? Social contexts are extremely culturally sensitive and may limit or enhance the effects of social support.

Fit and Fitting of Resources

It has been stated that resources are only effective to the extent that they fit circumstantial demands (French, Caplan & Harrison, 1982). Theoretically a person may have adequate resources in general, but may be confronted with a specific set of demands for which he or she does not have the appropriate resource. *However*, research provides surprisingly little support for this well-accepted supposition. This has caused us to modify the person–situation fit hypothesis in a way that more closely reflects the data and is more consistent with COR theory.

COR theory posits that resources generate additional resources and allows access to other resources. This is an active process. The person–situation fit hypothesis is a passive one; it assumes that people either have or do not have the resource required to meet a particular set of demands. COR's active approach suggests otherwise; *when confronted with stressful events, individuals fit their resources to meet demands.* This process of *fitting* resources is dynamic. At first, individuals may rely on their own sense of mastery and enter into a problem-solving mode. When this resource begins to be depleted, they may turn to social support. If that support is not adequate they may shape the support through feedback as to what they need. In this way, persons with strong resource reservoirs, pick and choose among their resources and shape their resources to fit environmental contingencies.

Shaping of the situation also occurs. Reality is to some extent what we make of it, and those with strong personal and social resources seem to assess reality in a way that fits their strengths (Kobasa & Puccetti, 1983; Taylor, 1983). This reconstruction of reality is done in a manner that allows the available resources to have a better fit with demands. Breznitz (1983) theorized that individuals allow those aspects of the environment to titrate into their perceived reality at a pace consistent with their coping capabilities. Although earlier literature argued that such denial was unhealthy, Breznitz sees it as an aspect of healthy adaptation, as long as individuals continue their coping efforts.

People may also shape their situation to fit their resources by selecting certain aspects of their situation with which to cope and not others. Following myocardial infarct, a man may not have the resources to confront accompanying sexual fears, so he may choose to concentrate for a time on active return to work. After some success in this domain, he might then choose to enter a physical rehabilitation program to increase his stamina. Some challenges may even remain unanswered, and we would hypothesize that these will be in the domains where individuals perceive that their resources or the circumstances cannot be shaped or fitted to one another.

Those who cannot fit their resources to meet demands are especially susceptible to negative health outcomes. Work settings that exert high demands and where workers have low control over conditions or their status have been associated with a higher incidence of coronary heart disease (Krantz et al., 1988). However, in professions or situations where individuals can shape the nature of their work, high demand tends to have a less negative effect on health (Krantz et al., 1988; Siegrist et al., 1990). Lower status workers (e.g., blue-collar and female clerical workers) have limited opportunities to shape their environments or how they utilize their resources to approach work challenges, and have higher resultant risk for heart disease.

Mastery-related variables may be critical for this process of *resource management* (Hobfoll, 1988; Kobasa & Puccetti, 1983). The fitting and sorting of resources may indeed be the essential process of coping that such individuals do so well. Individuals are like chess players, but they play the game with different pieces as a reflection of their differing constellation of resources. Those high in mastery tend to have stronger resource armamentaria and use their resources more effectively to combat the challenges that confront them. Environments may play a large role here, as well, because many situations do not allow individuals to utilize their mastery to affect their environments as they choose, and in such circumstances mastery may even have a negative effect.

A MODEL FOR FUTURE RESEARCH

We would suggest a model for future research that has a number of facets. The more facets that are included in any given research project, the more likely that it will lead to valuable insights concerning the relationship of personal and social resources to health. At this time, most research has concentrated on how a single resource is linked to a single health outcome, mostly through self-report of both variables, and mostly in cross-sectional designs. Not all projects can, of course, be fully comprehensive, but by fitting together different investigations that develop different aspects of the model a fuller story will be told.

In Figure 2.1 we present our model. We begin with an overall cultural context. Too often this is either assumed to be understood or ignored, and health psychology has often, in our minds, been guilty of being too insensitive to cultural diversity and gender diversity.

Cultural context

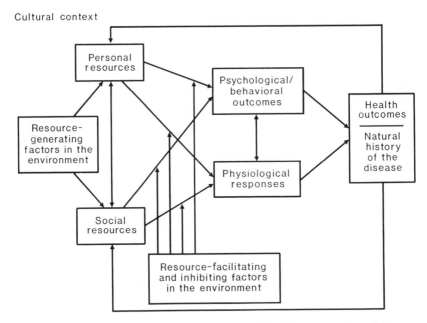

Figure 2.1   Stress resistance resources and health: a research model

Given the cultural context, we must study the link between resource-generating factors and resources. Socioeconomic status, favorable conditions in early life and then secondarily throughout the lifespan, age, and community resources all play a role here. From this wellspring we must learn more about how resources are generated and sustained (Hobfoll, 1988; Holohan & Moos, 1991).

Once resources are generated, they continue to act dynamically, interacting with one another. It is hard to imagine coping without this interplay between personal and social resource domains. Yet, researchers have typically separated the two domains artificially. COR theory and other health models (Becker & Maiman, 1975; Janis & Mann, 1977) include both aspects of the self and the self's social world, and an understanding of the true ecology of coping demands that we address both. Again, researchers will naturally need to choose limited numbers of personal and social resources in their investigations, but we argue that those that do will provide richer findings than those that ignore the personal–social interface.

Another area for research must attend to how resource-facilitating and inhibiting factors in the environment affect the contribution of resources on outcomes. Stress has generally been used as the single proxy for this general construct. However, even how we view stress has been modified, as investigators have noted marked differences in how people are affected by major life events, ongoing hassles, and chronic stressors (Lazarus & Folkman, 1984; Kaplan, 1990a, 1990b). Racism and sexism are two aspects of the environment that deserve special attention, as they appear to broadly shape the stress experience in an ongoing, comprehensive manner (Allen & Britt, 1983). Different work environments are important areas for study in this sense as well, and whether the environment makes meaningful work available may be the most important among these.

Physiological responses have been increasingly linked as following from psychological outcomes, and this is the next sequence in our chain. Johnson (1990) has shown, for instance, how anger and hostility may be closely tied with negative physiological responses that, in turn, may lead to or exacerbate illness. More research on in this vein is clearly warranted.

Health outcomes must be better developed and more broadly diversified. We must focus more on the natural history of the disease and address prevention at different times in the development of the disease. Others have also acknowledged through their work that disease and health are not static outcomes, but have sequences of development (Fuerstein, Labbé, & Kuczmierczyk, 1986). The more researchers address the development of disease along its natural continuum, the more likely that seemingly paradoxical findings will be understood. Factors, for instance, that may explain greater likelihood of hypertension, might also be related to greater adherence to treatment regimes.

Finally, many of the links are cyclical. By addressing research questions within longitudinal designs, these critical feedback loops can be delineated. Disease onset affects support systems in a way that will, in turn, affect the further development of the disease. Lane and Hobfoll (1992), for instance, found that increases in patients' anger in response to their illness acted to increase anger in supporters. This sequence is likely to alienate support that will be required for meeting ongoing instrumental and emotional needs of the patients.

Conservation of resource theory makes a number of specific suggestions as to the sequence of resource generation, resource interaction, resource mobilization, and resource modification. A number of specific hypotheses and research directions follow from COR theory. Among the most critical avenues for researching COR theory and its application to health are:

1. A focus on the prevention of loss of resources and interventions that might contribute to resource gain.
2. Further study of the primacy of resource loss compared to resource gain and how two interact to affect health.
3. Study of the intensity and duration of loss cycles in comparison to gain cycles, the former hypothesized to have greater intensity and duration than the latter.
4. The relationship of resource loss and gain to further loss and gain, the

cumulative effect being the believed underlier of negative health outcomes.

5. The suggestion that those low in personal resources are not passive, but rather view their resources as too weak to make a difference or act ineffectively in their use of resources.

6. Further examination of how coping itself depletes health resistance resources, making individuals increasingly vulnerable when confronting chronic stress conditions.

By moving to a more interactive, ecological context health research will more closely approximate the actual ecological interplay involved in coping and adaptation that is facilitated by resources. Basic insights have been gained in what might be called a first generation of research on personal and social resources and their effect on health that shows an association between the two, but does not identify the process by which outcomes occur. However, we expect that the direction in which this chapter hopes to catalyze research will yield even greater insights into the resource–health process.

ACKNOWLEDGEMENTS

Writing of this article was supported in part by grant 1 RO1 HD24901 from the National Institute of Child Heath and Human Development and by grant # 1 RO1 MH45669 from the National Institute of Mental Health.

REFERENCES

Abramson, L. Y., Seligman, M. E. P, & Teasdale, J. D. (1978). Learned helplessness in humans: critique and reformulation. *Journal of Abnormal Psychology*, **87**, 49–74.

Allen, L., & Britt. D. W. (1983). Social class, mental health, and mental illness: the impact of resources and feed back. In R. D. Felner, L. A. Jason, J. N. Moritsugu, & S. S. Farber (Eds), *Preventive psychology: theory, research and practice*. New York: Plenum Press.

Antonovsky, A. (1979). *Health, stress, and coping*. San Francisco: Jossey-Bass.

Bandura, A. (1982). Self-efficacy mechanism in human agency. *American Psychologist*, **37**, 122–47.

Barrera, M., Jr. (1986). Distinctions between social support concepts, measures and models. *American Journal of Community Psychology*, **14**, 413–445.

Becker, M. H., & Maiman, L. A. (1975). Sociohehavioral determinants of compliance with health and medical care recommendations. *Medical Care*, **13**(1), 10–24.

Booth-Kewley, S., & Friedman, H. S. (1987). Psychological predictors of heart disease: a quantitative review. *Psychological Bulletin*, **101**, 343–62.

Bowlby, J. (1969). *Attachment and loss*, vol. 1. *Attachment*. New York: Basic Books.

Breznitz, S. (1983). The seven kinds of denial. In S. Breznitz (Ed), *The denial of stress* (pp. 257–280). New York: International Universities Press.

Burger, J. M. (1985). Desire for control and achievement-related behaviors. *Journal of Personality and Social Psychology*, 48, 1520–1533.

Cassel, J. (1976). The contribution of the social environment to host resistance. *American Journal of Epidemiology*, 104, 107–123.

Cohen, S., & Hoberman, H. M. (1983). Positive events and social supports as buffers of life change stress. *Journal of Applied Social Psychology*, 13, 99–125.

Cohen, S., & Syme, L. S. (Eds). (1985). *Social support and health*. New York: Academic Press.

Cohen, S., & Williamson, G. M. (1991). Stress and infectious disease in humans. *Psychological Bulletin*, 109(1), 5–24.

Connel, C. M., & D'Augelli, A. R. (1990). The contribution of personality characteristics to the relationship between social support and perceived physical health. *Health Psychology*, 9, 192–207.

Crowther, J., Tennenbaum, D. L., Hobfoll, S. E., & Stephens, M. A. (Eds). (1992). *The etiology of bulimia nervosa: the individual and family context*. Washington, DC: Hemisphere.

Curbow, B., Sommerfield, M., Legro, M., & Sonnega, J. (1990). Self-concept and cancer in adults: theoretical and methodological issues. *Social Science and Medicine*, 31, 115–128.

DeLongis, A., Folkman, S., & Lazarus, R. S. (1988). The impact of daily stress on health and mood: psychological and social resources as mediators. *Journal of Personal and Social Psychology*, 54, 486–495.

Felner, R. D., Farber, S. S., & Primavera, J. (1983). Transitions and stressful life events: a model for primary intervention. In R. D. Felner, L. A. Jason, J. N. Moritsugu, & S. S. Farber (Eds), *Preventive psychology: theory, research and practice* (pp. 199–215). New York: Plenum Press.

Fisher, J. D., Nadler, A., & Whitcher-Alagna, S. (1982). Recipients' reactions to aid. *Psychological Bulletin*, 91, 27–54.

French, J. R. P., Jr., Caplan, R. D., & Harrison, R. V. (1982). *The mechanisms of job stress and strain*. Chichester: Wiley.

Fuerstein, M., Labbé, E. E., & Kuczmierczyk, A. R. (Eds). (1986). *Health psychology: a psychobiological perspective*. New York: Plenum Press.

Glass, D. C., & Singer, J. E. (1972). *Urban stress: Experiments on noise and social stressors*. New York: Academic Press.

Goldberger, L., & Breznitz, S. (1993). *Handbook of stress*, Vol. 2. New York: Springer.

Hansson, R. O., Jones, W. H., & Carpenter, B. N. (1984). Relational competence and social support. *Review of Personality and Social Psychology*, 5, 265–284.

Hawkins, J. D., & Fraser, M. W. (1989). The social networks of drug abusers before and after treatment. In S. Einstein (Ed), *Drug and alcohol use: issues and factors*. New York: Plenum Press.

Hobfoll, S. E. (1988). *The ecology of stress*. Washington, DC: Hemisphere.

Hohfoll, S. E. (1989). Conservation of resources: a new attempt at conceptualizing stress. *American Journal of Community Psychology*, 9, 159–172.

Hobfoll, S. E., & Freedy, J. R. (1990). The availability and effective use of social support. *Journal of Social and Clinical Psychology*, 9, 91–103.

Hobfoll, S. E., & Lerman, M. (1988). Personal relationships, personal attributes and stress resistance: mothers' reactions to their children's illness. *American Journal of Community Psychology*, 6, 565–589.

Hobfoll, S. E., & Lerman, M. (1989). Predicting receipt of social support: a longitudinal study of parents' reaction to their child's illness. *Health Psychology*, 8(1), 61–67.

Hobfoll, S. E., & Lieberman, Y. (1987). Personality and social resources in immediate and continued stress resistance among women. *Journal of Personality and Social Psychology*, 52, 18–26.

Hobfoll, S. E., Lilly, R. S., & Jackson, A. P. (1992). Conservation of social resources and the self. In H. O. F. Veiel, & U. Baumann (Eds), *The meaning and measurement of social support* (pp. 125–141). Washington, DC: Hemisphere.

Hobfoll, S. E., Nadler, A., & Lieberman, J. (1986). Satisfaction with social support during crisis: intimacy and self-esteem as critical determinants. *Journal of Personality and Social Psychology*, 296–304.

Hobfoll, S. E., Shoham, S. B., & Ritter, C. (1991). Womens' satisfaction with social support and their receipt of aid. *Journal of Personality and Social Psychology*, 61, 332–341.

Hobfoll, S. E., & Stokes, J. P. (1988). The process and mechanics of social support. In S. Duck (Ed), *Handbook of personal relationships: Theory, research. and interventions* (pp. 497–517). New York: Wiley

Holohan, C. J., & Moos, R. H. (1991). Life stressors, personal and social resources, and depression: a four-year structural model. *Journal of Abnormal Psychology*, 100, 31–38.

Hull, J. G., Van Treuren, R. R., & Virnelli, S. (1987). Hardiness and health: a critique and alternative approach. *Journal of Personality and Social Psychology*, 53, 518–530.

Janis, I. L., & Mann, L. (1977). *Decision making: a psychological analysis of conflict choice and commitment*. New York: Free Press.

Jemmott, J. B., & Locke, S. E. (1984). Psychosocial factors, immunologic mediation, and human susceptibility to infectious diseases: How much do we know? *Psychological Bulletin*, 91(1), 78–108.

Jessor, R., & Jessor, S. L. (1975). Adolescent development and the onset of drinking: a longitudinal study. *Journal of Studies on Alcohol*, 36, 27–51.

Johnson, E. H. (1990). *The deadly emotions*. New York: Praeger.

Kamen, L. P., & Seligman, M. E. (1987). Explanatory style and health. Special issue: Health Psychology. *Current Psychology Research and Reviews*, 6, 207–218.

Kaplan, H. B. (1975). *Self-attitudes and deviant behavior*. Pacific Palisades, CA: Goodyear Press.

Kaplan, H. B. (1990a). Measurement and the stress process: retrospect and prospect. *Stress Medicine*, 6, 249–255.

Kaplan, H. B. (1990b). Measurement problems in estimating theoretically informed models of stress: a sociological perspective. *Stress Medicine*, 6, 81–91.

Kaplan, H. B. (1991). Social psychology of the immune system: a conceptual framework and review of the literature. *Social Science and Medicine*, 33, 909–923.

Katzman, M., & Wolchik, S. (1984). Bulimia and binge eating in college women: a comparison of personality and behavioral characteristics. *Journal of Consulting and Clinical Psychology*, 52, 423–428.

Kiecolt-Glaser, J. K., Glaser, R., Williger, D., Messick, G., Sheppards, S., Ricker, D., Romisher, S. C., Briner, W., Bonnel, G., & Donnerberg, R. (1985). Psychosocial enhancement of immunocompetence in a geriatric population. *Health Psychology*, 4, 25–41.

Kobasa, S. C. (1982). Commitment and coping in stress resistance among lawyers. *Journal of Personality and Social Psychology*, 42, 707–717.

Kobasa, S. C., Maddi, S. R., & Courington, S. (1981). Personality and constitution as mediators in the stress–illness relationship. *Journal of Health and Social Behavior*, 22, 368–378.

Kobasa, S. C., & Puccetti, M. C. (1983). Personality and social resources in stress resistance. *Journal of Personality and Social Psychology*, 45, 839–850.

Krantz, D. S., Grunberg, N. E., & Baum, A. (1985). Health psychology. *Annual Review of Psychology*, 36, 349–383.

Krantz, D. S., Contrada, R. J., Hill, D. R., & Friedler, E. (1988). Environmental stress and biobehavioral antecedents of coronary heart disease. *Journal of Consulting and Clinical Psychology*, 56, 333–341.

Lane, C., & Hobfoll, S. E. (1992). How loss affects anger and alienates potential supporters. *Journal of Consulting and Clinical Psychology*, 60, 935–942

Lazarus, R. S., & Folkman, S. (1984). *Stress, appraisal, and coping.* New York: Springer.

Leventhal, H., Neranz, D. R., & Strauss, A. (1980). Self-regulation and the mechanisms for symptom appraisal. In D. Medhanic (Ed), *Psychosocial epidemiology.* New York: Neale Watson Academic Publications.

Lowenthal, M. J., & Haven, C. (1968). Interaction and adaptation: intimacy as a critical variable. *American Sociological Review*, 33, 20–30.

Miller, S. M., Brody, D. S., & Summerton, J. (1988). Styles of coping with threat: implications for health. *Journal of Personality and Social Psychology*, 54, 142–148.

Munton, A. G. (1990). Job relocation stress and the family. *Journal of Organizational Behavior*, 11, 401–406.

Nadler, A., & Mayeless, O. (1983). Recipient of self-esteem and reactions to help. In J. D. Fisher, A. Nadler, & B. M. DePaulo (Eds), *New directions in helping* (Vol. 1, pp. 167–188). New York: Academic Press.

Newberry, B. H., Jaikins-Madden, J. E., & Gerstenberger, P. J. (1991). *A holistic conceptualization of stress and disease.* New York: AMS Press.

Norbeck, J. S., & Tilden, V. P. (1983). Life stress, social support, and emotional disequilibrium in complications of pregnancy: a prospective multivariate study. *Journal of Health and Social Behavior*, 24, 30–46.

Nucholls, K. G., Cassel, J., & Kaplan, H. B. (1972). Psychosocial assets, life crisis and the prognosis of pregnancy. *American Journal of Epidemiology*, 95, 431–441.

Ozer, E. M., & Bandura, A. (1990). Mechanisms governing empowerment effects: a self efficacy analysis. *Journal of Personality and Social Psychology*, 58, 472–486.

Partridge, C., & Johnston, M. (1989). Perceived control of recovery from physical disability: measurement and prediction. *British Journal of Clinical Psychology*, 28, 53–59.

Pearlin, L. I., Lieberman, M. A., Menaghan, E. B., & Mullan, J. T. (1981). The stress process. *Journal of Health and Social Behavior*, 22, 337–356.

Ritter, C. (1988). Resources, behavior intentions, and drug use: a ten-year national panel analysis. *Social Psychology Quarterly*, 51, 250–264.

Rodin, J. (1986). Aging and health: effects of sense of control. *Science*, 233, 1271–1276.

Rosen, J. C. (1992). Body-image disorder: definition, development, and contribution to eating disorders. In J. H. Crowther, D. L. Tennenbaum, S. E. Hobfoll, & M. A. P. Stephens (Eds), *The etiology of bulimia nervosa* (pp. 157–177). Washington, DC: Hemisphere.

Roth, D. L., Wiebe, D. J., Fillingim, R. B., & Shady, K. A. (1989). Life events, fitness, hardiness and health: a simultaneous analysis of proposed stress-resistance effects. *Journal of Personality and Social Psychology*, 57, 136–142.

Rotter, J. B. (1966). Generalized expectancies for internal versus external control of reinforcement. *Psychological monographs*, 80, (1 Whole No. 609).

Rotter, J. B. (1975). Some problems and misconceptions related to the construct of internal versus external locus of control of reinforcement. *Journal of Consulting and Clinical Psychology*, 43, 56–67.

Sahlins, M. D. (1970). *Stone age economics.* Chicago: Adline.

Sarason, I. G., Sarason, B. R., & Shearin, E. N. (1986). Social support as an individual difference variable: its stability, origins and relational aspects. *Journal of Personality and Social Psychology*, 5, 845–855.

Scheier, M. F., Matthews, K. A., Owens, J., Abbot, A., Lebfevre, C., & Carver, C. S. (1986). Optimism and recovery from coronary artery and bypass surgery. Unpublished data.

Schönpflug, W. (1985). Goal directed behavior as a source of stress: psychological origins and consequences of inefficiency. In M. Frese, & J. Sabini (Eds.), *The concept of action in psychology* (pp. 172–188). Hillsdale, NJ: Erlbaum.

Schwarzer, R., & Leppin, A. (1989). Social support and health: a meta-analysis. *Psychology and Health*, 3, 1–15.

Schwarzer, R., & Leppin, A. (1991). Social support and health: a theoretical and empirical overview. *Journal of Social and Personal Relationships*, 8, 99–127.

Seligman, M. E. P. (1975). *Helplessness: on depression, development and death*. San Francisco: Freeman.

Selye, H. (1951–1956). *Annual report of stress*. New York: McGraw-Hill.

Shepperd, J. A., & Kashani, J. H. (1991). The relationship of hardiness and stress to health outcomes in adolescents. *Journal of Personality*, 59, 747–768.

Sherrod, D. R. (1974). Crowding, perceived control, and behavioral after effects. *Journal of Applied Social Psychology*, 4, 171–186.

Siegrist, J., Peter, R., Junge, A., Cremer, P., & Seidel, D. (1990). Low status control, high effort at work and ischemic heart disease: prospective evidence from men. *Social Science and Medicine*, 31, 1127–1134.

Strecher, V. J., DeVellis, B. M., Becker M. H., & Rosenstock, I. M. (1986). The role of self-efficacy in achieving health behavior change. *Health Education Quarterly*, 13, 73–91.

Strickland, B. R. (1978). Internal–external expectancies and health related behaviors, *Journal of Consulting and Clinical Psychology*, 46, 1192–1211.

Suls, J., & Fletcher, B. (1985). Self-attention, life stress, and illness: a prospective study. *Psychosomatic Medicine*, 47, 469–481.

Taylor, S. E. (1983). Adjustment of threatening events: a theory of cognitive adaptation. *American Psychologist*, 38, 1161–1173.

Taylor, S. E. (1990). Health psychology: the science and the field. *American Psychologist*, 45, 40–50.

Taylor, S. E., Lichtman, R. R., & Wood, J. V. (1984). Attributions, beliefs about control, and adjustment to breast cancer. *Journal of Personality and Social Psychology*, 46, 489–502.

Thoits, P. A. (1983). Multiple identities and psychological well-being: a reformulation and test of the social interaction hypothesis. *American Sociological Review*, 48, 174–187.

Tversky, A., & Kahneman, D. (1981). The framing decisions and the psychology of choice. *Science*, 24, 453–458.

Tymstra, T. (1989). The imperative character of medical technology and the meaning of "anticipated decision regret." *International Journal of Technology Assessment in Health Care*, 5, 207–213.

Vaux, A. (1988). *Social support: theory, research and intervention*. New York: Praeger.

Wallston, K. A., Maides, S., & Wallston, B. S. (1976). Health-related information seeking as a function of health-related locus of control and health value. *Journal of Research in Personality*, 10, 215–222.

Wallston, K. A., & Wallston, B. S. (1982). Who is responsible for your health? The construct of health locus of control. In G. Sanders, & J. Suls (Eds), *Social psychology of health and illness*. Hillsdale, NJ: Erlbaum.

Wallston, K. A., Wallston, B. S., Smith, S., & Dobbins, C. J. (1987). Perceived control and health. *Current Psychological Research and Reviews*, 6(1), 5–25.

Wiedenfeld, S. A., Bandura, A., Levine, S., O'Leary, A., Brown, S., & Raska, K. (1990). Impact of perceived self-efficacy in coping with stressors on components of the immune system. *Journal of Personality and Social Psychology*, 59, 1082–1094.

Worsley, A. (1981). In the eye of the beholder: social and personal characteristics of teenagers and their impressions of themselves and fat and slim people. *British Journal of Medical Psychology*, 54, 231–245.

3 Vital Exhaustion and the Acute Coronary Syndromes

A. APPELS, W. KOP, C. MEESTERS, R. MARKUSSE,
B. GOLOMBECK, P. FALGER

*Department of Medical Psychology, University of Limburg, Postbus
616, 6200 MD Maastricht, The Netherlands*

INTRODUCTION

Excess fatigue and feelings of general malaise have been found by many researchers to be the most prevalent precursors or premonitory symptoms of myocardial infarction (MI) and sudden cardiac death. Estimates of the percentage of people who experienced "undue fatigue" or "lack of energy" before a cardiac event range from 13% to 70% (Alonzo, Simon & Feinleit, 1975; Fraser, 1978; Kuller, Cooper & Perper, 1972; Rissanen, Romo & Siltanen, 1978; Gillum et al., 1976; Simon, Feinlieb & Thompson, 1972; Stowers and Short, 1970; Thiele, Simon & Thiele, 1985; Klaeboe et al., 1987). One of the reasons why this range is so broad is that there is no agreement about what phenomena coronary patients should be asked about.

In medicine, the clinic is the mother of science. Therefore, three case reports will be presented to illustrate the behaviors and feelings that we will write about in this paper. These case reports also illustrate the main questions to be discussed. Which feelings have a prodromal meaning? Do they reflect (sub)clinical heart disease or emotional tension due to stressful life events? Which physiological or biochemical mechanisms underlie the associations between these feelings and the acute coronary syndromes: unstable angina pectoris (AP), myocardial infarction (MI) and sudden cardiac death (SCD)?

Case 1

Mr P is 45 years old. At the age of 21 he began working in his own garage, where he worked 14 hours per day. After three years, he was forced to close down the garage because of low back pain. He became unemployed for six months. Thereafter, he started a cafeteria and worked 70 hours per week. Two years later the neighborhood was reconstructed and he lost a large number of customers. He asked the bank to give him a loan, but the bank refused and he had to close down the cafeteria. Becoming more and more disabled by his low back pain, he sought for an administrative job for two years and finally got a job as a high school custodian. This school consisted of three provisional buildings at different locations in town. After some years, the school received permission to build a new school, which meant that one of the three custodians had to leave his job. He does not have control over the decision as to which custodian will lose his job. He becomes tired, sleeps badly, and often wakes up during the night. He then goes down to the living room to smoke some cigarettes. He gets a feeling of hopelessness, becomes easily irritated, and does not feel well. Sometimes, he experiences unusual chest pain. When he watches the news on TV at 8.00 pm he often falls asleep so deeply that his wife cannot wake him. He feels ashamed because of this and chooses a straight chair from the kitchen to watch TV. During this period, his dog ate something that was poisoned from a nearby field. He accused some hunters of poisoning dogs in a local newspaper and asked the police to help him find them. The police responded that there was absolutely no proof and that he should take care to avoid a libel suit. After that response, he felt completely helpless. Five days later he suffers a heart attack.

Case 2

Mr V. is a 36-year-old former boxing champion, who works as a cook in a tourist hotel. During the season, he works 15–16 hours daily. Six years ago he became overworked and he once got so angry at a waiter who did not take the dishes out of the kitchen rapidly enough that he put him on the cooking-range for a full minute. For that reason, he was fired.

The following year he was again making long hours in another tourist restaurant. At the end of the third season, he became listless and tired. He avoided company and no longer joined his colleagues during coffee breaks. He wanted peace. He became silent and observed that he was often thinking about his father who had died a year and a half before. He began to read the obituaries in the local newspaper, something that he had never done before.

At home, he kept many animals, which he started to sell one after the other. When he had sold all of his birds, dogs, rabbits, and guinea pigs, he told his wife that he wanted a divorce. She then arranged a meeting with a psychiatrist. When the psychiatrist asked why he wanted a divorce Mr V. could not answer the question. He just wanted it. One week later he suffered a large MI.

Case 3

Mr P. is 62 years old. When asked about behavioral changes that he noticed in the months preceding his MI he answers: "The only change I noticed in the weeks preceding my coronary attack was a strange lack of energy. In my hobby room I have various instruments with which to make all kinds of things. I had promised my grandson to make him a wooden truck. I do not know why, but I could not raise the energy to go to my hobby room and keep my promise. I stood at the window for hours, doing nothing. My neighbor asked me what was going on. He had noticed that no sound had left my hobby room for weeks."

THE ORIGINS OF EXHAUSTION BEFORE MYOCARDIAL INFARCTION

Cardiological views

Fatigue is one of the most nonspecific of all symptoms in clinical medicine. Therefore, complaints of fatigue have diagnostic importance in relation to heart disease only when the details are known. In patients suffering from manifest heart disease, feelings of fatigue often reflect a failure of the left ventricle to augment the stroke volume when there is a need for higher cardiac output. This failure may be due to an impaired oxygen supply to the myocardium or to an impaired contractility of the left ventricle. Tiredness may also consitute a side effect of medication, especially diuretics and beta-blockers. "As a rule, the fatigue due to heart disease is related to effort, whereas the fatigue of anxiety or depression is constantly present" (Hurst et al., 1990).

The textbook by Brandenburg et al. makes a similar distinction: "When fatigue is chronic, is present on awakening and persists all day without change, the cause is most likely not cardiac. In such cases, anxiety or increased emotional tension and poor sleep are the main causes; anemia and other chronic disease states such as hypothyroidism should be considered. Conversely, if the symptom is new or of recent onset and tends to develop during the day to the point of physical exhaustion without any effort, a cardiac failure-related low output with subnormal increment with exercise is suggested" (Brandenburg et al., 1987).

Few cardiological studies have directly addressed the question of the origin of the excessive tiredness before MI or SCD. Kuller (1978) has related the prodromal symptomatology of sudden death to pathological changes observed at postmortem examinations. There did not appear to be relationship between any of the prodromal symptoms and the presence of acute pathological changes as manifested by coronary thrombosis. With regard to the feelings of fatigue he notes: "The basis of the fatigue syndrome has not been determined. No information is currently available describing the relationships of the fatigue syndrome to any specific pathophysiological changes. The most interesting hypothesis related to the fatigue syndrome suggests that fatigue is related to a decrease of left ventricular function, possibly secondary to increased myocardial damage.

An equally interesting and alternative hypothesis is that the fatigue represents a manifestation of depression" (Kuller, 1978). Freeman and Nixon
(1987) observed an association between some symptoms of exhaustion,
especially waking up unrefreshed from sleep, and poor energy levels and
the number of symptomatic episodes of ischemia during ambulatory monitoring. They note: "Even the shorter periods of ischemia which do not
cause infarction are still highly undesirable, because they can impair myo-
cellular function and cause what Braunwald has termed the stunned myocardium. This depresses left ventricular functions and may be the main
reason why many patients report a poor energy level when due inquiring is
made" (Freeman & Nixon, 1987).

Psychiatric views

Several psychiatrists have given a description of the mental precursors of
MI. Their descriptions of patients' experiences have much in common,
although they differ in the terminology used to summarize their findings.
The psychiatric labels that have been used, include "hidden withdrawal
and masked depression" (Fisher et al., 1964), "a combination of depression
and arousal effects" (Greene et al., 1972), and "pseudo-neurasthenic syndrome" (Polzien and Walter, 1971). This mental state reflects a breakdown
of the defense mechanisms, especially of compulsive striving for achievement and mastery (Arlow, 1945).

The first quantitative psychiatric study of the short-term precursors of
MI was published by Hahn (1971), who observed that coronary patients
were significantly more compulsive that is, involuntary counters of trivial
things like houses or trees, than controls were. This compulsive behavior
was interpreted as a defense mechanism directed against a depressive
ambivalence conflict. Upon decompensation of this defense through conflicts or stress, the underlying anxieties and depressive ways of coping with
conflicts manifest themselves. By means of a questionnaire, Hahn looked
into the ways in which this decompensation was experienced by coronary
patients. The vast majority reported to have experienced increasing irritability, strong mood changes, increased sweating, and a general feeling of
not being well (Hahn, 1971).

The first prospective psychiatric study on the mental precursors of MI
was published by Crisp, Queenan and D'Souza (1984). The database of
this study comprised patients aged 40–65 years who were registered with a
group general practice in London. Nearly all participants completed the
Crown–Crisp Experiental Index (CCEI). During the five-year follow-up
period, 26 men were admitted to a hospital with a confirmed diagnosis of
MI. Scores on the CCEI were compared with those of the remainder of the
male study population. Differences between groups in scores on the individual items of the CCEI were assessed, and a discriminant analysis was car-

ried out in order to devise the linear combination of variables that discriminated the groups most accurately. Twelve items were found to discriminate between individuals destined and those not destined for MI. The authors interpret this item subset as reflecting "a state of sadness, coupled with loss of libido and exhaustion" (Crisp Queenan & D'Souza, 1984). Although the study has advantages stemming from the longitudinal design, the results should be interpreted cautiously because chance fluctuations may strongly influence the results of a discriminant analysis.

In a new analysis of the same database, Haines, Imeson and Meade (1987) observed that the scale "obsessional neurosis", "depression", and "hysteria" were predictive of new ischemic heart disease. However, these scales lost their predictive power when they were controlled for phobic anxiety. This rather unique finding may indicate that only those symptoms of depression, which are also experienced by phobics, are predictive of MI.

Psychological views

During the last two decades, health psychology has directed much attention to the Type A behavior pattern (TABP). It is an overt behavior pattern that is composed of feelings of time pressure, competition, impatience, aggression, and easily provoked hostility. The Western Collaborative Group Study showed that healthy middle-aged men who were initially Type A were twice as likely to suffer an MI in the subsequent eight and half years than men not showing this behavior pattern (Rosenman et al., 1975).

On the basis of Type A theory, Glass (1977) developed a psychological model in which Type A individuals are supposed to pass through a state of frustration and exhaustion, a "prodromal depression", preceding MI. The basic assertion is that: "Type A individuals exert greater efforts than their Type B counterparts to control stressful events that are perceived as threats to their sense of control. These active coping attempts eventually extinguish, for without reward, the relentless striving of the Type A individual leads to frustration and psychic exhaustion, which culminates in a reduction of efforts at control" (Glass, 1977). Experimental studies give some support to this model (Krantz, Glass & Snyder, 1974). However, it has not yet been determined whether the interaction of TABP and helplessness is indeed prodromal to clinical coronary heart disease.

A somewhat different model has been suggested by Bruhn, McCrady and Plessis (1968). It merits quotation here because some of its elements have been found to be associated with coronary artery disease (CAD). Bruhn, McCrady and Plessis conceive MI as the endpoint of a history of "emotional drain".

Emotional drain is defined as a frustrating, longterm involvement of the individual's mental processes in his attempt to live with or cope with some life fact or conflict which involved some deeply ingrained aspect of the individual, such as his values, beliefs, self-concept, or interpersonal relationships ... Emotional drain implies a nearly constant state of mental preparedness on the part of the individual to cope with this conflict ... They drain the energy resources of the body to the point where the total organism is left in a state of physical and mental exhaustion ... The full impact of emotional drain comes to be realized as a personal burden. Thus, the life-long conflicts that are perceived as unsolvable to an individual whose mental resources are continuously mobilized as if he were attempting to solve them, may eventually leave him in a state of mental and physical exhaustion. It is this stage that may set the stage for myocardial infarction and sudden death. (Bruhn, McCrady & Plessis, 1968)

VITAL EXHAUSTION AS PRECURSOR OF MYOCARDIAL INFARCTION

When we initiated our research programme of the mental precursors of MI, we strongly felt that the most parsimonious strategy of selecting an established psychological test and testing its predictive power would have the disadvantage of a premature item selection, because the phenomenology of the mental state before MI was not well-documented. Instead, we interviewed a large number of coronary patients asking them about their feelings before their coronary events. Those responses were used to construct a scale, which was subsequently tested in two studies (Appels, 1980; Verhagen et al., 1980). Thirty-seven items were found to discriminate between coronary cases and a healthy control group. This scale was labelled form A of the Maastricht Questionnaire (MQ) in order to give the itempool a neutral name. At this stage of our "data-driven" approach, we could not yet decide which symptoms reflected (sub)clinical heart disease, a psychiatric syndrome, or a projection of current feelings into the past.

The first attempt to obtain more insight into the construct assessed by this scale was made in a study of about 50 busdrivers. Those who had elevated scores on form A of the MQ were interviewed by Dr M. Ceha, an experienced clinical psychologist, who was asked to give a general description of this group. She described the group as "vitally exhausted". This label fitted well with our experiences and had the additional advantage of avoiding a premature psychiatric label. Therefore, we labelled the construct assessed by this scale as "vital exhaustion" and defined it as a state characterized by: (1) feelings of excess fatigue and lack of energy; (2) increased irritability; and (3) feelings of demoralization.

Data from prospective studies

In 1979, the Municipal Health Authority of the city of Rotterdam (The Netherlands) started a health check-up of city employees. Between January 1979 and December 1980, 3877 male employees aged 39 to 65 years participated. The medical examination included measurements of blood pressure, serum cholesterol, glucose tolerance, relative weight, smoking, and an assessment of angina pectoris using the Rose Questionnaire. A resting electrocardiogram completed the cardiovascular screening. All subjects completed form A of the MQ. Twenty-one new items, derived from a new series of clinical interviews, were added to this scale.

The cohort was followed up for an average period of 4.2 years. Among those free of CHD at screening, 21 subjects died of MI, while well-documented non-fatal MI occurred in 38 subjects. The relative risk for a fatal or non-fatal MI associated with a score above the median of form A of the MQ, controlling for age, serum cholesterol, smoking and blood pressure, was 2.67 ($p < 0.01$). An analysis of the observed association against length of time-interval showed a sharp decrease in the relative risk for events occurring in the first, second, third or fourth year of follow-up. The age-adjusted risk for the first year of follow-up was 10.05, while the age-adjusted risks for the following years were 2.23, 3.04 and 0.68, respectively. These data suggest that exhaustion is a short-term risk indicator. No elevated scores at screening were observed among future cancer or gastrointestinal patients. This suggests that vital exhaustion is related to future CAD only.

An item analysis showed that the predictive power was based upon 16 items. Of the 21 items that had been added to the scale, eight were predictive. Based upon this item analysis, the final form of the MQ (form B) was constructed. Three items were omitted because of some doubts about their validity. Therefore, the final form consists of 21 items (Appels, Höppener & Mulder, 1987).

Given the paucity of prospective data about exhaustion as precursor of cardiac death, it was investigated whether a similar observation could be obtained using the data base of the Kaunas–Rotterdam Intervention Study. Between 1972 and 1974, 3365 males participated in a cardiovascular screening program in Rotterdam. This cohort was followed during an average period of 9.5 years. At screening all participants completed the Reeder Stress Scale, a nowadays outdated intrument to assess stress. It contains one item however, which is rather similar to the concept of exhaustion, namely: "I am completely exhausted mentally and physically at the end of the day". Before data-analysis, those persons with angina pectoris or with an electrocardiogram indicative of an old MI or of reversible ischemia were excluded from the study. Among those free of CHD at screening, 69 subjects died because of MI. The cumulative incidence of cardiac death was found to be 45/1000 in the exhausted group, 30/1000 in the intermediate group, and 26/1000 in the group which was not exhausted. Cox regression analysis showed a highly significant interaction between duration of follow-up and exhaustion upon the risk of cardiac death. Those who felt exhausted at screening were found to be at elevated risk during the beginning of the follow-up period. The hazard ratios for exhaustion were 8.96, 6.33, 4.47 and 3.16 for the first 10, 20, 30 and 40 months of follow-up, respectively. Thereafter, the association lost its statistical significance. These findings support the hypothesis that feelings of exhaustion increase the risk for cardiac death in men who are free of CHD. Surprisingly, this particular item was not predictive of future non-fatal MI. We suppose that this is due to the assessment of exhaustion by one item only. Single questions are rather unreliable, which limits their predictive power (Appels & Otten, 1992).

The major findings of these prospective studies were corroborated in a study by Siegrist et al. (1990), who followed 416 blue-collar workers, aged 25 to 55 years, for 6.5 years. It was found that a state of exhaustive coping, that reflected frustrated but continued efforts and associated negative feelings, such as disproportionate irritability and inability to withdraw from work obligations, increased the risk of myocardial infarction by more than 300 % when controlled for all classical risk factors (Siegrist et al., 1990).

Although not prospective in the classical sense of the word, a study by Ladwig (1989) should be mentioned in this context. It investigated how many contacts MI patients had had with their general practitioners during 180 days preceding their first MI, using the database of an insurance company. Only 9% of all patients did not contact their physicians within that period. A sharp increase was noted during the last weeks preceding hospitalization. During these visits, the practitioners were found to prescribe mainly psychopharmaca and nitroglycerin. Ladwig labels this stage as "an unorganized stage of the disease", since the vagueness of the clinical picture fosters false negatives (Ladwig, 1989).

Thus, these prospective studies show that feelings of exhaustion precede manifest heart disease in apparently healthy males. However, subclinical CAD cannot be ruled out as an explanation of the association between vital exhaustion and future CAD. Especially the finding that feelings of vital exhaustion are a relatively short-term risk indicator raises the question whether vital exhaustion reflects subclinical heart disease.

To gain insight into this important question, Kop investigated the association between vital exhaustion and the amount of atherosclerosis in angioplasty patients, the changes in exhaustion scores before and after angioplasty, and the clinical course after succesful angioplasty among exhausted and non-exhausted patients. Consecutive patients ($N = 127$; mean age 55.6 years) referred for angioplasty were evaluated with respect to vital exhaustion before coronary angioplasty and two weeks after discharge. The occurrence of new cardiac events was recorded during a 1.5 year follow-up. There was a significant relationship between the number of diseased vessels and MQ-scores both before and after angioplasty. However, the explained variance (R^2) was of low magnitude only (4%). This

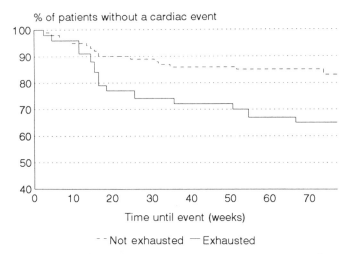

Figure 3.1. Vital exhaustion as related to the incidence of new cardiac events after PTCA

indicates that there is a relationship between severity of coronary disease and vital exhaustion, but also that atherosclerosis offers an insufficient explanation for exhaustion. No association was observed between vital exhaustion and left ventricular ejection fraction.

Angioplasty resulted in a decrease of feelings of exhaustion. However, when the MQ-scores of these patients were compared to the distribution of the MQ in the general population, it appeared that 74% of patients were exhausted before treatment and 60% were still exhausted after successful revascularization. This observation suggests that although restoration of perfusion diminishes feelings of tiredness, more than half of these patients continues to be exhausted. During follow-up, a new cardiac event (defined as either cardiac death, MI, coronary bypass surgery, repeated PTCA, restenosis of the dilated artery, or new angina with documented ischemia) occurred in 29 patients (23%). Vital exhaustion was significantly associated with new cardiac events after controlling for remaining stenoses after PTCA, the amount of vessel disease and other clinical characteristics (OR 2.40). Figure 3.1 presents the association between vital exhaustion and new cardiac events over time, as computed by a Kaplan–Meier analysis. The main conclusions from this study are that vital exhaustion is only modestly associated with the amount and extent of coronary vessel disease, is not associated with left ventricular ejection fraction, and influences the clinical course after successful PTCA independent of remaining stenoses (Kop et al., in press).

Data from case-control studies

The most extensive case-control study on the relation between vital exhaustion and first MI was carried out by Falger (1989). The study compared 133 male MI cases with 133 neighborhood controls and 192 hospital controls. The second control group was included in order to control for the effects of hospitalization on the recall of feelings of exhaustion.

The mean scores on the (retrospective form B of the) MQ were 18.0 (SD $\pm$ 10.8) in MI cases, 11.7 (SD $\pm$ 9.8) in hospital controls and 9.0 (SD $\pm$ 9.7) in neighborhood controls. By dividing cases and controls in two groups of exhausted and non-exhausted subjects according to a score above or below the median of the MQ (that is, eight or more affirmative replies to the 21 questions), Falger estimated the relative risk for first MI associated with exhaustion as 7.35 (95 % CI: 4.30–13.30) in the neighborhood series and as 2.90 (95% CI: 1.70–4.95) in the hospital series. All differences and odds ratios were statistically highly significant, confirming the belief that feelings of exhaustion are a risk indicator for MI. These data indicate that elevated exhaustion scores were also observed in other patient groups. Three interpretations of this finding were offered: vital exhaustion is a precursor of diseases other than CHD; other diseases are associated with one or more symptoms of exhaustion (e.g., sleep problems); or recent hospitalization may have caused some retrospective bias in both MI-cases and hospital controls (Falger, 1989). Later studies by de Vos and Verink have shown that the second interpretation is to be preferred. Painful ailments may cause somewhat elevated MQ scores.

Can these associations also be observed in females? This question was investigated in a study of 79 women who had been hospitalized because of a first MI (mean age 59.3; SD $\pm$ 9.1) and 90 women who had been hospitalized in the departments of general surgery and orthopedic surgery of the same hospitals (mean age 57.5; SD $\pm$ 9.4). The MI-cases reported significantly more symptoms of exhaustion than the controls. Their mean scores were 20.6 (SD $\pm$ 11.9) and 17.0 (SD $\pm$ 11.2) ($t = 2.02$; $p = 0.03$), respectively. Sixty-three percent of the cases and 39% of the controls were exhausted before admission (defined as a score above the median of the MQ) ($X^2 = 10.02$; $p = 0.001$). Non-anginal pain was strongly associated with vital exhaustion, the mean score of the group with pain being 26.3 and of the group without pain 16.2 ($t = 5.21$; $p < 0.001$). The estimated relative risk of exhaustion adjusted for age, hypertension, smoking, and non-anginal pain was 2.75 (95% CI: 1.28–5.87). This finding indicates that among women vital exhaustion is a risk indicator for MI as well (Appels, Schouten & Falger, in press).

A case-control study of a group of patients who had been admitted to the John Sealy Hospital, Galveston, Texas (USA), performed by Mendes de Leon, did, however, not observe a significant difference in mean exhaustion

scores between 79 patients admitted to the hospital for acute and/or worsening chest pain and 44 patients, admitted to the hospital for relative
acute conditions, most of whom were orthopedic patients. This negative
result might be due to the rather different formats of the questions and the
answering categories of the American version of the MQ used in this study
(Mendes de Leon, 1988).

Although the MQ proved to have predictive validity and to discriminate
well between coronary cases and controls in all except one study, it has
some shortcomings. Elevated scores often reflect a general tendency to
complain or longstanding mental or somatic problems, leading to a
number of false positives. The actual measurement cannot be corrected if a
subject misinterprets a question and does not leave room for the registration of idiosyncratic expressions. As a consequence, its use for the selection
of subjects for laboratory or clinical investigations is questionable. Therefore, we developed a structured interview to be employed in non-epidemio-
logical studies. The core of this 23-item interview is formed by questions
that were found to be associated with future heart disease in the prospective studies. Its content is illustrated in Table 3.1.

The interview was tested for its discriminating power in a case-control
study by Meesters. Subjects were 80 males who had been hospitalized
because of a first MI and 167 neighborhood controls, matched for age.
Table 3.2 shows that the interview scores discriminated significantly
between cases and controls. The table also shows a strong interaction
between exhaustion and age with respect to the risk of exhaustion. Mean
exhaustion scores did not differ between younger and older controls, but
the mean exhaustion score of younger cases was much higher than that of
the older ones. However, the difference between cases and controls remains
highly significant in the older group.

In order to obtain a more precise insight into the duration of exhaustion
before MI, Meesters added a question about its onset to each interview
item. He found that the duration of a state of exhaustion before MI was 3

Table 3.1.   Illustration of the exhaustion interview

Tiredness	— Do you feel weak all over or without energy?
	— Do you sometimes feel that your body is a battery that is losing its power?
	— Do you shrink from your regular work as if it were a mountain to climb?
Irritability	— Have you been irritated more easily lately than before?
	— Do you blow up more easily than before?
Demoralization	— Do you feel dejected?
	What makes you feel that way?
	— Do you feel defeated or disillusioned?

Table 3.2. Mean interview-defined exhaustion scores of younger and older MI-cases and healthy neighborhood controls

	N	Mean	SD	t	p
Age 38–55					
cases	34	10.3	5.9	5.70	0.00
controls	89	3.9	4.4		
Age 56–65					
cases	46	5.9	5.3	2.99	0.00
controls	78	3.2	3.6		

months in 20% of the patients, 6 months in 33%, one year in 26% and 1.5 years in 4%. In 17% of the cases, this state had lasted longer than 1.5 years. In this latter group, the complaints were often side effects of a chronic condition and did not reflect a decline in the total functioning which characterized most of the other patients (Meesters & Appels, in preparation). A case-control study by Sihm et al. (1991) about job characteristics as risk factor for MI gives and independent support to the case-control studies by Falger and Meesters. Recent studies of job stress as a risk factor for CAD indicate that a combination of high demands and low control increases the risk for CAD. Moreover, people who work in such conditions are at elevated risk to become exhausted (Karasek & Theorell, 1990). This model was corroborated by Sihm et al. in a study of young MI patients. Results showed that the best single expression of the influence of quantitative job demands on coronary morbidity was obtained with the parameter "exhaustion after work", which assessed the impact of work on the daily life of the individual rather than merely the time spent working (Sihm et al., 1991).

Case-control studies have a poor scientific reputation because they offer more opportunities for bias and mistaken inferences than other types of research. The major concern of the critics is that a search for meaning by the general public that is inclined to consider "stress" as the major cause of heart disease will result in attaching an inappropriate degree of importance to psychological risk factors. The information collected in case-control studies may be biased by hindsight, by the fallibility of human memory, and by a search for meaning (Contrada & Krantz, 1987).

In an attempt to gain some insight into the reliability of patients' reports of their feelings of exhaustion before MI, de Vos asked 48 infarction patients and their spouses to independently rate the level of vital exhaustion in the month preceding the coronary event on form B of the MQ. The mean score of the patients was 20.8 (SD ± 13.2) and the mean scores of their spouses was 19.7 (SD ± 14.4). The correlation coefficient was found to be 0.85. Although this high correspondence does not prove that the ratings are valid, it indicates that most of the behavioral changes of near-future coronary victims were also observed by others, at least in retrospect (de Vos, in preparation). In contrast to de Vos, Trijsburg et al. (1987) observed that MI patients rated their exhaustion before MI significantly lower than their spouses did. They concluded that MI patients are inclined to deny their fatigue before MI.

Did these case-control studies give a valid estimate of the strength of the association between exhaustion and MI? This question was investigated by computing the estimated relative risk of exhaustion adjusted for recall bias by using a "validity scale" consisting of those items which discriminated between MI patients and the neigborhood controls from the Falger study, but which did not have a predictive power in the prospective study of the Rotterdam civil servants. This method was proposed by Raphael (Raphael, 1987). It was possible to do so because the case-control study had started before the completion of the civil servants study and included the full item-pool. Logistic regressions were performed including age, smoking, and angina pectoris. Subjects were classified as exhausted, intermediate, or not exhausted, according to their scores in the third, second, or first tertile of the distribution of the MQ scores in the control group. Analyses began by computing the odds ratios adjusted for age, smoking, and angina pectoris. Thereafter, the same analysis was repeated including the validity scale. The relative risk of a score in the second tertile decreased from 3.13 to 2.97 when adjusted for recall bias. The estimated risk of a score in the third tertile decreased from 10.07 to 6.88 when adjusted for recall bias. Therefore, the excess risk for MI of a score in the second tertile was estimated to be 213% without and 197% with adjustment for recall bias. The differences between these estimates is (213−197/213) or 8% of the unadjusted estimate. Likewise, the risk of a score in the third tertile was overestimated by 40%. We therefore conclude that recall bias only leads to a modest overestimation of this premonitory symptom. This conclusion is in line with recent experimental research. Croyle and Sande (1988) have shown that students confronted with a "positive" test on a non-existing disease reported more of the risk behaviors that they had been told contributed, to the occurrence of the disease. Thus, confirmatory search resulted in a serious overestimation of the exposition to accepted risk factors. However, the recollection of any symptoms experienced in the months preceding the "discovery" of the disease was influenced to a moderate extent only. The search for meaning after the confrontation with a new disease may be less directed at premonitory symptoms but rather at risk behaviors supposed to be causal. That is the reason why more caution is needed with regard to reported life events as a possible cause of vital exhaustion. As far as exhaustion is concerned, the possible information bias of the case-control design does not seem to outweigh the operational and financial advantages of this design.

Table 3.3. Relative risk for myocardial infarction in (interview-defined) exhausted and non-exhausted Type As and Type Bs.

	Non-exhausted		Exhausted	
	B	A	B	A
Cases	22	18	9	31
Controls	62	78	11	16
SRR*	1.00	0.65	2.30	5.46

* SRR = standardized relative risk.

PSYCHOLOGICAL CORRELATES OF VITAL EXHAUSTION

Type A behavior

In the Falger study (1989), exhaustion was found to be positively associated with global Type A behavior as assessed by the Structured Interview. The mean exhaustion scores of Type A subjects were 13.3 (SD $\pm$ 10.2) and of Type B subjects 9.9 (SD $\pm$ 9.7) (t = 3.51; $p < 0.000$). The study by Meesters also showed a significant association between exhaustion and Type A behavior as assessed by the Structured Interview. These data also show a significant interaction between TABP and exhaustion, as predicted by Glass (1977). Table 3.3 shows the standardized relative risk when taking non-exhausted Type Bs as the reference group. Among non-exhausted subjects, Type A behavior does not increase the risk of MI. However, exhausted Type As have a five-fold risk compared to non-exhausted type Bs.

Life events

Falger observed strong associations between exhaustion and the following stressful life events over the lifespan: "Prolonged familial conflicts" and "prolonged financial problems" during childhood, "unemployment of the father", "serious conflicts with supervisors or subordinates", "prolonged overtime work", "serious educational problems with children", "serious marital conflicts", "serious illness or death of family members", "serious conflicts with family members", and "serious financial problems". Of these events, "prolonged overtime work" had the strongest association with exhaustion. This life event discriminated significantly between cases and controls. However, this association lost its discriminating power when vital exhaustion was controlled for. Thus, overwork is a risk factor for CAD when it leads to exhaustion. Moreover, this finding indicates that feelings of exhaustion are not only caused by uncontrollable events or other forms of mental stress, but may also be caused by more physical factors like having double jobs or too many working hours, which deprive people of sufficient time to relax (Falger & Schouten, 1992).

A similar pattern of associations was observed in the case-control study of female victims of MI. Feelings of vital exhaustion were found to be positively associated with a number of life events or more chronic adverse conditions such as "serious conflicts at work with supervisors", "serious conflicts with subordinates", "prolonged overtime work", "serious educational problems with children", "serious marital conflicts" and "prolonged financial problems".

Furthermore, positive associations were observed between exhaustion and lack of social support, adverse living conditions during youth (i.e., poverty, unemployment, and conflicts at home), longstanding marital or financial problems, unwanted childlessness, prolonged/serious educational problems with children, and ever been burned out or over-stressed. No association was found between exhaustion and number of children.

It is of importance to draw attention to the fact that "prolonged financial problems" was found to increase the risk for MI in both males and females. Ruberman et al. have reported that a major financial difficulty during the preceding year increases the risk for mortality after MI (Ruberman et al., 1984).

Hostility

During the last decade, much attention has been paid to hostility as a risk factor for MI. Hostility, which reflects a cynical mistrust of other people, is supposed to be the toxic component of Type A behavior (Williams, 1987). Meesters included an assessment of hostility by means of the Cook–

Table 3.4. Pearson correlations between hostility and interview-defined exhaustion in 80 MI cases and 166 healthy controls

	cases	controls
Cook–Medley	0.24*	0.33**
Buss–Durkee (total score)	0.42**	0.25**
assault	0.44**	0.18*
indirect hostility	0.37**	0.13
irritability	0.41**	0.30**
negativism	0.12	0.06
resentment	0.37**	0.39**
suspicion	0.09	0.17*
verbal hostility	0.17	−0.01
guilt	0.05	0.23**

*P < 0.05.
**P < 0.01.

Medley and Buss–Durkee scales in his case-control study. As shown in Table 3.4, the scores on both scales and on some subscales of the Buss–Durkee were positively associated with vital exhaustion. When exhaustion and the separate hostility indices were simultaneously included in multivariate analyses, all hostility (sub)scales, which discriminated between cases and controls at the univariate level, lost their discriminating power. This indicates that hostility is a risk factor for MI because it increases the risk to become exhausted, or because a cynical mistrust of other people after frustrating experiences is a consequence or concomitant of exhaustion (Meesters, in preparation).

Denial of fatigue

A psychological characteristic of at least a subgroup of coronary victims that may be related to exhaustion is formed by insensitivity to bodily symptoms. P. Nixon, a British cardiologist who has given some lively descriptions of pre-infarction fatigue, has noted that many MI patients are "colour blind" to exhaustion and to the somatic effects of arousal (Nixon, 1986). This statement is supported by the Carver, Coleman and Gluss (1976) observation that young Type A subjects spend more effort on a treadmill test than Type Bs do. Moreover, the fatigue ratings of Type As were lower than those of Type Bs. These results were discussed in terms of fatigue suppression as an instrumental response for attaining mastery over the environment. However, these findings could not be replicated in coronary patients (Schlegel et al., 1980; Siegel et al., 1990).

The under-reporting of fatigue may not so much reflect an instrumental response for attaining mastery but rather a genetic or early obtained decreased sensitivity with respect to bodily symptoms. Leitkin, Firestone and McGrath (1988) observed that Type A children (aged 5 to 14 years) reported significantly less clinical symptoms and pain after tonsillectomy and adenoid surgery than Type B children did. Their sick leaves were shorter after the intervention and they also reported less fatigue on a laboratory task. Droste and Roskam (1983) have shown that in silent ischemia it is not so much the ischemia that is silent but rather the patient by demonstrating that patients who do not experience ischemia are less sensitive to dental pain.

This insensitivity to bodily symptoms in coronary patients is an area that merits further exploration. It may partially explain why some people overtax their forces and do not experience fatigue unless they have reached the point of exhaustion.

"Burn-out"

During the clinical interviews that were designed for developing the MQ, many coronary patients reported that they had been "burned-out" once or more often in their lives. They usually reported that their mental state before admission had been almost similar to that earlier condition. For that reason, the item "have you ever been burned-out?" was added to the MQ, and used in the prospective study. A positive answer was found to be associated with an increased risk of MI, the age-adjusted relative risk being 1.31 (95% CI: 1.10–2.99). Moreover, a positive reply was strongly correlated with the MQ, suggesting not only that burnout and exhaustion share much common variance, but also that an earlier period of breakdown in adaptation to stress was associated with the current condition (Appels & Schouten, 1991a). This finding corroborates the observation of Paffenbarger et al. (1966) that students who said to have experienced a period of exhaustion were at increased risk for future CAD.

The concept of "burn-out" was first mentioned by Freudenberger (1974) to describe the job-related physical and mental state he observed among the enthusiastic, young volunteers who worked in a drug clinic. After one year many of them felt exhausted and easily irritated, and had developed a cynical attitude towards the clients and a tendency to avoid them. This cradle of the concept "burn-out" has strongly influenced the dynamic history of "burn-out" research. From the beginning, two contrasting tendencies existed. Many scientists remarked that "burn-out" symptoms can also be observed among those who do not have a job at all, while other scientists defended that "burn-out" occurs only among individuals who do "people work" of some kind. Maslach and Jackson (1986) belong to those who reserve this concept for persons who continuously work with other people. They define "burn-out" as: "a syndrome of emotional exhaustion, depersonalization and reduced personal accomplishment that can occur among individuals who do people work of some kind". Pines and Aronson (1988) on the other hand represent those who believe that symptoms of "burn-out" can also be observed in people who do not work in the welfare sector at all. They define "burn-out" as "a state of physical, emotional and mental exhaustion caused by longterm involvement in situations that are emotionally demanding".

In an attempt to answer the question whether "burn-out" is best represented by three dimensions or one, Shirom (1989) reviewed all validation studies. He concludes that of the three subscales of the Maslach Burnout Inventory (MBI), the emotional exhaustion scale correlates best with work-related variables and with observations made by spouses and superiors. Shirom concludes: "The major conclusion which may be drawn from the validation efforts is that the unique content of burnout has to do with a depletion of an individual's energetic resources". Consequently, Shirom defines "burn-out" as "a combination of physical fatigue, emotional exhaustion, and cognitive weariness" (Shirom, 1989).

It is evident that burn-out has much in common with the concept of vital exhaustion. In fact, six of the nine items that form the "emotional exhaustion" subscale of the MBI are part of the MQ. The major difference is that increased irritability is considered to be an element of vital exhaustion, while Maslach used peer ratings of a subject's irritability as an external criterion for the validation of the MBI.

Within this context, some new insights obtained from work psychology are worth mentioning. The classical theory of tiredness approaches "fatigue" as a change in the organism, which results in a decline of performance and feelings of fatigue. This theory is debated by a functionalistic approach, which conceives "fatigue" as an evaluative-motivational assessment of one's own psychophysiological state in relation to the demands of the task situation, resulting in a decision on the continuation of the activity (Meyman, 1991). This approach, therefore, suggests that the "decision" to slow down and to call oneself "tired" may form a goal-directed, health-protecting behavior. It might be that some characteristics of exhausted subjects, such as the tendency to avoid company, reflect this health-protecting behavior.

Depression

The MQ includes some known characteristics of depression, such as listlessness, fatigue, loss of libido, or waking up exhausted. In fact, nine out of the 23 questions of the exhaustion interview are identical to the questions that are used to assess depression according to the DSM-III-R criteria. This raises the question whether vital exhaustion is conceptually much different from depression.

Estimates of the prevalence of depression among MI patients range from between 35% to 45%. About half of these depressions existed before MI, while the other half is considered to be mainly reactive (Lloyd & Cawley, 1983; Schleifer et al., 1989). Major depressive disorders assessed by the Diagnostic Interview Schedule according to DSM-III-R criteria have been found to predict cardiac events in patients with coronary heart disease, after controlling for degree of stenosis, left ventricular ejection fraction, and smoking (Carney et al., 1988). MI patients who are depressed have a poorer prognosis (i.e., SCD, cardiac arrest and re-infarction) than MI patients who are not depressed (Silverstone, 1987; Ladwig et al., 1991). Shekelle and Ostfeld (1965) found in a prospective study that non-survivors of MI had a higher score on the MMPI-depression scale than survivors did. A meta-analysis of these and other studies made Booth-Kewley and Friedman (1987) conclude that depression is reliably associated with CHD. However, this conclusion was questioned by Matthews, who did not accept case-control studies to be included in meta-analysis (Matthews, 1988).

There are two indications that vital exhaustion differs from depression. Items asking for a lowered self-esteem or guilt feelings were not predictive of MI in the civil servants study. Moreover, self-reproach is rare among coronary victims. Typically coronary patients blame others for the occurrence of negative events, although they confirm that the event made them feel helpless when it occurred (Byrne, 1980). Consequently, the core elements of depression, as described by cognitive psychologists such as: "I am the cause of my misfortune"; "I shall always be a failure or have misfortune"; "Whatever I do is unsuccesful", are rarely heard among coronary victims.

The strongest argument to distinguish exhaustion from depression is given by van Diest and Appels (1991). They used the Profile of Mood States (POMS) to monitor feelings of a depressed mood, vigour and fatigue in 12 interview-defined exhausted and 10 non-exhausted healthy males during three weeks. Current affective, cognitive, motivational and somatic symptoms of depression were further assessed by the Beck Depression Inventory (BDI). Significant differences were observed with regard to loss of vigour and excessive fatigue. A depressed mood, the key symptom of depressive disorders, was hardly mentioned by the exhausted subjects during the three weeks of observation. Both groups differed significantly with regard to their mean BDI-scores. However, a detailed analysis of the symptoms which caused this difference showed that it could be exclusively attributed to the BDI-symptoms "fatigability", "work inhibition", "sleep disturbances", and "loss of libido". Only one exhausted subject reported a depressed mood, and no-one reported weight loss, loss of appetite, suicidal ideation, self-accusation, or sense of punishment (van Diest & Appels, 1991). Studies that used the POMS to register the mood states of coronary patients underscore the importance of distinguishing a depressed–sad mood from feelings of fatigue and lack of vigour. Shephard, Kavanash and Klavora (1985) observed that coronary patients had significantly lower POMS-vigour scores compared to a control group. The mean POMS-depression scores did not differ between both groups. Dimsdale et al. (1981) observed that fatigue, and not depression, as assessed by the POMS predicted substantial cardiac morbidity events (i.e., hospitalization, MI, cardiac resuscitation, or death) in the year after catheterization.

As was mentioned before, nine items of the interview to assess vital exhaustion are identical to questions used for DSM III-R classifications. This strong association raises the possibility that exhaustion confounds the association between depression and the acute coronary syndromes. If exhaustion reflects subclinical heart disease depression might be predictive of future heart disease because of its association with exhaustion.

The answer to the question whether vital exhaustion is distinct from depression depends at least partially on the relative weight given to the vital components, compared to the mood disturbances in the assessment of depression. Loss of interest or pleasure is common, but a depressed mood is rare among exhausted subjects. Almost all depressed subjects are exhausted, while about half of the exhausted subjects are depressed. We do not object to those who say that our data indicate that a depressive episode often precedes the onset of the acute coronary syndromes. However, we would like to add that this statement is rather crude, because it incorrectly suggests that feelings of sadness belong to the precursors of MI and it does not stress the importance of mental and emotional exhaustion.

Sleep problems

During the last decade, several studies have indicated that sleep problems might belong to the risk indicators for CAD (Partinen et al., 1982; Koskenvuo et al., 1988). A detailed analysis of the follow-up data of the civil servants study showed that especially being exhausted at waking up was predictive of future MI (RR = 2.1). Interestingly, the relative risk of waking up exhausted increased by 50 % when those with problems falling or staying asleep were excluded from these analyses. This makes it rather unlikely that early-morning tiredness, caused by problems falling or staying asleep has any predictive power (Appels & Schouten, 1991b). In passing, it is of interest to note that Koskenvuo et al. (1988) observed a positive association between hostility and morning fatigue.

Van Diest has conducted a series of studies about the associations between sleep complaints and sleep disorders on the one hand and vital exhaustion at the other hand. It was observed that nearly all sleep complaints were more prevalent among exhausted subjects. Of major importance are the results of his sleep physiological study. It was shown that the sleep latency and the sleep duration of exhausted and non-exhausted subjects were only marginally different. Exhausted subjects probably attribute their tiredness to having problems with falling or staying asleep. The major difference was formed by a significantly reduced delta sleep among the exhausted subjects. Most normal recovery processes are supposed to take place during the delta or deep sleep phase (van Diest, in press).

These studies do not answer the question of the relevance of a reduced slow wave sleep (SWS) with respect to cardiovascular control during sleep. In normal subjects heart rate and blood pressure and the variability of heart rate and blood pressure reach their lowest level during SWS. This is due to an increased parasympathetic activity. One might expect that these decreases do not occur, or to a less extent in exhausted subjects, rendering them more vulnerable to arrhythmias and ischemic events.

Somatic risk factors

Tiredness and fatigue may have numerous causes. The strongest association between vital exhaustion and any of the somatic risk factors is the association between smoking and vital exhaustion. Especially heavy smokers have elevated MQ-scores. No negative associations, or only very weak ones, have been observed between blood pressure and exhaustion. Elevated scores were also observed among those treated for hypertension. This may reflect a side effect of drugs, a higher detection rate of hypertension among exhausted subjects, or both. Elevated MQ scores are also observed among those suffering from diabetes and among physically inactive subjects. In general, there appears to be no association between serum cholesterol and exhaustion.

Finally, the relation between age and exhaustion differed between the quoted studies. Correlation coefficients ranged between -0.30 and 0.15.

We do not yet have information about changes in lifestyles before the onset of MI. According to our clinical impressions those who were exhausted before MI smoked less in the months preceding their coronary events and drank less alcohol and coffee. However, some patients reported an increased consumption of tobacco, alcohol, or coffee. These behavioral changes merit further exploration.

POSSIBLE MECHANISMS RELATING VITAL EXHAUSTION TO THE ACUTE CORONARY SYNDROMES

The association between a state of exhaustion and near future manifest CHD in apparently healthy individuals raises the question of which physiological or biochemical mechanisms may explain this association.

Recently, Fuster et al. (1992) have summarized the current views on the pathophysiology of CAD and the acute coronary syndromes. They proposed a pathophysiological classification of vascular damage that is divided into three types, representing stages of increasing severity (see Figure 3.2). Type I consists of functional alterations of endothelial cells without substantial morphological changes; Type II consists of endothelial denudation and intimal damage with intact internal elastic lamina; and Type III consists of endothelial denudation with damage both to the intima and media. Type I injuries are promoted by several factors including, among others, hypercholesterolemia, circulating vasoactive amines, infections, and chemical irritants in tobacco smoke. Type I injury leads to the accumulation of lipids and macrophages. The release of toxic products by macrophages presumably leads to Type II damage, characterized by the adhesion of platelets and the proliferation of smooth muscle cells, a process that may contribute to the formation of an intimal lesion. A lipid lesion surrounded by a thin capsule may be disrupted, leading to Type III damage with thrombus formation. When thrombi are small they may get organized and contribute to the growth of the atherosclerotic plaque. When thrombi are large and occlusive, they can contribute to acute coronary syndromes.

It is believed that recurrent episodes of disruption of atherosclerotic plaques, resulting in intraluminal thrombosis, leads gradually to coronary occlusions (see Figure 3.3). This process is dynamic and repetitive. In some

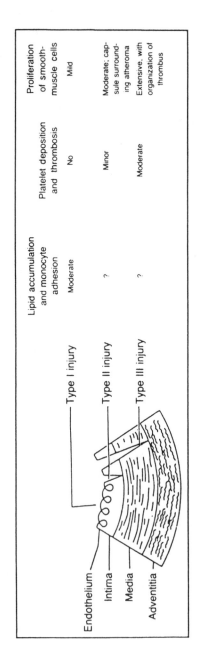

Figure 3.2. Classification of vascular injury or damage and vascular response. (Adapted from Fuster et al., 1992; copyright 1992 *NEJM*)

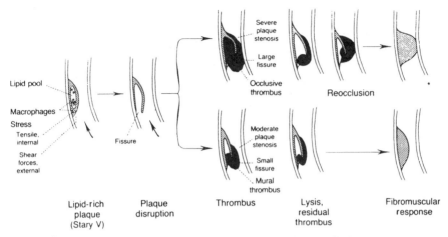

Figure 3.3. Typical dynamic evolution of a complicated disrupted plaque (From Fuster et al., 1992; copyright 1992 *NEJM*)

patients with unstable angina, plaque disruption may lead to intermittent or transient vessel occlusion and ischemia by a labile thrombus. In others, more severe vascular damage in the form of a large ulcer may lead to the formation of a fixed thrombus and a more chronic occlusion, resulting in acute MI. The disruption of small plaques is important in the pathogenesis of acute MI, whereas longstanding severe stenoses more commonly result in total vessel occlusion, with a small or silent infarction or no infarction at all, perhaps because of the presence of well-developed collateral vessels.

Several factors contribute to the disruption of plaques, among them are sudden changes in coronary tone. Local factors, such as the degree of plaque disruption, and systemic factors, such as a thrombogenic state of the circulation, can favor local thrombosis. Platelet aggregation and the generation of thrombin may be activated by circulating catecholamines. This mechanism, and cathecholamine-dependent vasoconstriction, may be of major importance in humans because it could link emotional stress, circadian variation, and catecholamine effects, to the development of arterial thrombosis and vasoconstriction (Fuster et al., 1992).

The dynamic and repetitive pattern of coronary occlusion preceding acute coronary syndromes coincides with feelings of exhaustion. Are these a marker of this pathogenic process or do they contribute to the process? The model by Fuster et al. gives numerous indications that the neurohormonal system, and consequently, the state that we have labeled vital exhaustion, can be involved in the pathogenesis of the acute coronary syndromes.

Animal studies have shown that the brain can be involved in the pathogenesis of Type I and Type II injuries. Electrical stimulation of the lateral hypothalamus in conscious unrestrained animals on normal diets induces severe endothelial damage and denudation in the coronary arteries. Continued stimulation results in intimal lesions with features of atherosclerotic plaques (Gutstein, 1988). It is not impossible that a state of exhaustion increases the risk for Type I or Type II lesions. Van Doornen (1988) observed a significant correlation between the MQ and increases in serum cholesterol and adrenaline between rest and exposure to a real life stressor in young, healthy males.

Thrombus formation plays a major role in Type III damage. There are two major components of the blood-clotting process: coagulation and fibrinolysis. The former process refers to the formation of the blood clot, while the latter refers to the removal of the clot. Under normal conditions, both processes are equilibrated. This equilibrium seems to be disturbed during a state of exhaustion. Lulofs (1990) compared platelet activity of exhausted and non-exhausted Type A and Type B subjects during rest and during a laboratory task. Platelet aggregation was measured according to a method developed by Brown. Contrary to the hypothesis, maximal aggregation increased during the task in all groups, except in the exhausted Type As who showed a decrease. It was speculated that in exhausted Type As platelets are already more sensitive during baseline conditions. The experiment was repeated using a method to measure in vivo platelet activation. However, no significant main effects or interactions were found (Lulofs, 1990). In a different study, Kop investigated three coagulation factors (i.e., factor VII, VIII, and fibrinogen) and one fibrinolytic factor (Plasminogen Activator Inhibitor) in eight exhausted and seven non-exhausted males during rest. Blood samples were collected twice and the averaged values were used. No differences were observed with regard to coagulation factors. However, the mean PAI-values were significantly higher in the exhausted males on both occasions, indicating reduced fibrinolytic activity (Kop, Hamulyak & Appels, submitted). Although still tentative, these data suggest an imbalance in the formation and removal of thrombi in exhausted subjects.

Mental factors may influence the process leading to Type III injuries in several other ways. Mental stress may cause vasoconstriction of the smooth muscles in coronary patients and is probably the main cause of so called "spontaneous ischemia" observed during ambulatory monitoring (Rozanski et al., 1988; Bairey, Krantz & Rozanski, 1990; Deanfield et al., 1984). Hyperventilation, a well-known symptom of psychological tension, has such strong association with vasoconstriction that hyperventilation-testing has been proposed as a valuable and safe alternative to ergonovine for the diagnosis of coronary spasms. This probably explains why hyperventilation-induced abnormal coronary vasoconstriction predicts the risk of restenosis after successful coronary angioplasty (Ardissino et al., 1991).

Perhaps the threshold for myocardial ischemia or electrical instability is especially low among those who have become exhausted because of prolonged tension. Low heart rate variability, which reflects sympathovagal imbalance, and a prolonged QT interval increase the risk of cardiac mortality by about 300% (Schwartz, Periti & Malliani, 1975; Algra, 1990; Odemuyima et al., 1991). Both variables have been found to be associated with feelings of dejection and being overwhelmed (Huang, Ebey & Wolf, 1989; Zotti et al., 1991).

The temporal parallelism of the development of the acute coronary syndromes and vital exhaustion probably refers to a complex interaction between a mental state and some elements of the pathogenic process. Inflammation of the intima can cause feelings of fatigue. Angina may influence sleep adversely and evoke or strengthen existing dysthymic feelings. Long-lasting mental stress may affect the immune-system, rendering a coronary artery more vulnerable to infection, strengthening or reinforcing feelings of fatigue. The simultaneous presence of ischemic episodes and the feeling of waking up unrefreshed, as observed earlier by Freeman and Nixon (1987), may also refer to an interaction. Because of these mutually reinforcing processes, there is no "chicken-or egg" problem but rather a problem of unravelling vicious circles. These are complex and dynamic interactions. For example, mental stress leads to abnormal constriction in irregular and stenosed vessels segments, but not in intact segments. Moreover, the same stressor leads to vasodilatation in normal vessels, but to vasoconstriction in segments with local endothelial dysfunction (Yeung et al., 1991).

CONCLUSION AND PERSPECTIVES

Feelings of loss of energy and unusual tiredness are the most prevalent premonitory symptoms of MI and SCD. Thus, there is a phenomenon to be explained. The previous paragraphs reported the attempts to describe and measure this premonitory signal. We now can hear but, yet, cannot explain it.

In our "data-driven" approach we were able to show that vital exhaustion precedes CHD in apparently healthy individuals. The reports of MI-patients (and, consequently, the discriminating power of vital exhaustion as observed in cases-control studies) are not seriously invalidated by retrospective bias. A follow-up study of PTCA-patients showed that the association between exhaustion and new coronary events is probably independent of the amount and extent of atherosclerosis. Is exhaustion, then, the end of a stress process? The concept of vital exhaustion has a considerable overlap with "burn-out" and depression. This raised the questions whether vital exhaustion is synonymous with depression, or whether depression is a risk factor for CAD, because of its overlap with exhaustion. Therefore, the nomological network of vital exhaustion still needs further investigation. The sparse data collected strongly suggest that Type A subjects tend to exhaust themselves, maybe because they are less sensitive to fatigue. The life events or biographical characteristics most strongly associated with exhaustion are prolonged overtime work and financial problems. This suggests that people may exhaust themselves and/ or that long-lasting and uncontrollable conditions may result in a state of exhaustion. In this state, normal healing seems to be impaired.

The three major questions with regard to vital exhaustion as precursor of MI and SCD remain. Does exhaustion reflect subclinical heart disease? Is vital exhaustion synonymous with depression? Which mechanisms underlie the association between exhaustion and MI? The answers are simple: we do not know. As long as it is impossible to control for some elements in the development of the acute coronary syndromes, one cannot rule out the possibility that the pre-infarction exhaustion is a marker of subclinical heart disease. For example, the lack of energy experienced by the otherwise healthy and happy third patient whom we described at the beginning of this chapter, may be caused by an inflammatory process in the coronary arteries. There is no final criterion to decide whether vital exhaustion is conceptually different from depression. Nearly all depressed patients are exhausted, but only about half of the exhausted subjects are depressed. Maybe the first patient met the criteria for depression, but the second one certainly did not. Research on the underlying mechanisms has just recently begun. Independent replications are still lacking.

Despite these uncertainties, the total picture is gradually becoming more clear. As indicated by Fuster et al. (1992), it is believed that recurrent episodes of disruption of atherosclerotic plaques, resulting in intraluminal thrombosis, leads gradually to coronary occlusion. There is no doubt that this process often coincides with feelings of intense fatigue in most patients. In fact, of all associations observed, exhaustion correlates best with unstable angina (Appels & Mulder, 1989). It seems that in near-future coronary patients normal healing is impaired. This also seems to characterize exhausted subjects. Some characteristics or correlates of their behavior, such as the tendency to avoid company, could express this protopathic behavior and can be understood as an attempt to protect the organism against further stimulation, as a cry for rest. (The functionalistic approach of tiredness says that fatigue is not only a reflection of a somatic deterioration, but also serves a goal!) Exhausted subjects seem to have lost some adaptive responses. They lose most of their delta sleep, during which recovery takes place, and are probably less able to remove a thrombus. They seem to have lost some otherwise healthy reactions. Lulofs' finding of decreased platelet activation during stress in exhausted Type As may sound less paradoxical if one considers a slight increase in platelet activity during stress as a health-protecting reaction and, furthermore, if one realizes that exhaustion is the end stage of a longstanding stress process. Original hyper-reactivity may turn into hypo-reactivity after longstanding exposure to stress. Future research would probably be most fruitful when directed at the question which adaptive mechanisms are impaired or lost in exhausted subjects.

The same principle may be applied to investigating the contribution of exhaustion to the spiralling down to coronary occlusion. Given the limitations of epidemiological studies in healthy populations, follow-up studies of MI-patients and PTCA-patients in particular offer an efficient alternative. In these studies, one could not only investigate which impaired recovery processes increase the risk of a new cardiac event after PTCA, but also whether psychological interventions, directed at regaining the sympatho-vagal balance, will strengthen normal healing (in some people by learning to experience normal fatigue!) and may result in a decrease of new coronary events.

REFERENCES

Alonzo, A, Simon, A. & Feinleib, M. (1975). Prodromata of myocardial infarction and sudden death. *Circulation*, **52**, 1056–1062.

Algra, A. (1990). Electrocardiographic riskfactors for sudden death. Ph.D. dissertation, Rotterdam.

Appels, A. (1980). Psychological prodromata of myocardial infarction and sudden death. *Psychoth. Psychosom.*, **34**, 187–195.

Appels, A. Höppener, P. & Mulder, P. (1987). A questionnaire to assess premonitory symptoms of myocardial infarction. *Int.J.Cardiol.*, **17**, 15–24.

Appels, A. & Mulder, P. (1988). Excess fatigue as a precursor of myocardial infarction. *Europ. Heart J.*, **9**, 758–764.

Appels, A. & Mulder, P. (1989). Fatigue and heart disease. The association between vital exhaustion and past, present and future heart disease. *J.Psychosom.Res.*, **33**, 727–738.

Appels, A. & Otten, F. (1992). Exhaustion as precursor of cardiac death. *Birt.J.Clinical Psychol.*, **31**, 351–356.

Appels, A. & Schouten, E. (1991a). Burnout as a risk factor for coronary heart disease. *Beh. Med.*, **3**, 53–58.

Appels, A. & Schouten, E. (1991b). Waking up exhausted as risk indicator of myocardial infarction. *Am.J.Cardiol.*, **68**, 395–398.

Appels, A. & Schouten, E. & Falger, P. (in press). Vital exhaustion as precursor of myocardial infarction in women. *J.Psychosom Res*.

Ardissino, D. Barberis, P., De Servi, S., Merlini, P. A., Brammucci, E., Falcone, C. & Specchia, G. (1991). Abnormal coronary vasoconstriction as a predictor of restenosis after successful coronary angioplasty in patients with unstable angina pectoris. *New Eng. J. Med.* **325**, 1053–1057.

Arlow, J. (1945). Identification mechanisms in coronary occlusion. *J. Psychosomatic Res.*, **7**, 195–209.

Bairey, C. N., Krantz, D. S. & Rozanski, A. (1990). Mental stress as an acute trigger of ischemic left ventricular dysfunction and bloodpressure elevation in coronary artery disease. *Am.J.Cardiol.*, **66**, 28G–31G.

Booth-Kewley, S. & Friedman, H. (1987). Psychological predictors of heart disease: a quantitative review. *Psychol. Bull.*, **101**, 343–362.

Brandenburg, R. O., Fuster, V., Giuliani, E. R. & McGoon, D. C. (Eds) (1987). *Cardiology: fundamentals and practice.* Chicago: Yearbook Medical publishers.

Bruhn, J. G., McCrady, K. E. & Plessis, A. (1968). Evidence of emotional drain preceding death from myocardial infarction. *Psychiatry Digest,* 29, 34–40.

Byrne, D. G. (1980). Attributed responsibility for life events in survivors of myocardial infarction. *Psychotherapy and Psychosomatics,* 33, 7–13.

Carney, R., Rich, M., Freedland, K., Saini, J., te Velde, A., Simeone, C. & Clark, K. (1988). Major depressive disorder predicts cardiac events in patients with coronary heart disease. *Psychosom. Med.,* 50, 627–633.

Carver, Ch., Coleman, A. & Glass, D. C. (1976). The coronary prone behavior pattern and the suppression of fatigue on a treadmill test. *J. Pers. Social Psychol.,* 33, 460–466.

Contrada, R. J. & Krantz, D. S. (1987). Measurement bias in health psychology research designs. In: Kasl, S. V. and Cooper, C. L. (Eds), *Stress and health: issues in research methodology.* Chichester: Wiley.

Crisp, A., Queenan, M. & D'Souza, M. F. (1984). Myocardial infarction and the emotional climate. *Lancet i,* 616–619.

Croyle, R. T. & Sande, G. N. (1988). Denial and confirmatory search: paradoxical consequences of medical diagnosis. *J. Appl. Social Psychol.,* 18, 473–490.

Deanfield, J., Kensett, M., Wilson, R., Shea, M., Horlock, P., de Landsheere, C. & Selwyn, A. (1984) Silent myocardial ischeamia due to mental stress. *The Lancet,* 3 November, 1001–1005.

Diest, R. van (in press). A sleep physiological study of exhausted and non-exhausted males. *Psychosom. Med.*

Diest, R. van & Appels, A. (1991). Vital exhaustion and depression: a conceptual study. *J. Psychosom. Res.,* 35, 535–544.

Dimsdale, J., Gilbert, J., Hutter, A., Hackett, Th. & Block, P. (1981). Predicting cardiac morbidity based on risk factors and coronary angiographic findings. *Am. J. Cardiol.,* 47, 73–76.

Dixhoorn, J. van, Duivenvoorde, H., Staal, J., Pool, J. & Verhage, F. (1987). Cardiac events after myocardial infarction: possible effects of relaxation therapy. *Europ. Heart. J.,* 8, 1210–1214.

Doornen, L. van (1988). Physiological stress reactivity. Its relationship to behavioral style, mood, sex and aerobic fitness. Ph.D. thesis, Free University of Amsterdam.

Droste, C. & Roskam, H. (1983). Experimental pain measurement in patients with asymptomatic myocardial ischaemia. *J. Am. Coll. Cardiol.,* 1, 940–945.

Falger, P. (1989). Life-span development and myocardial infarction: an epidemiological study. Ph.D. dissertation, Maastricht.

Falger, P. & Schouten, E. (1992). Exhaustion, psychological stressors in the work environment, and acute myocardial infarction in adult men. *J. Psychosom Res.,* 36, 777–786.

Fisher, H. K., Dlin, B., Winters, W. L., Hagner, S. B., Russel, G. W. & Weiss, E. (1964). Emotional factors in coronary occlusion. *Psychosomatics,* 5, 280–291.

Fraser, G. E. (1978). Sudden death in Auckland. *Austr. NZ J. Med.,* 8, 490–499.

Freeman, L. & Nixon, P. (1987). Time to rethink the clinical syndrome of angina pectoris? Implications for ambulatory ST monitory. *Quarterly Journal of Medicine,* 62, 25–32.

Freudenberger H. J. (1974). Staff Burnout. *J. Soc. Issues,* 30, 159–165.

Fuster, V., Badimon, L. Badimon, J. & Chesebro, J. (1992). The pathogenesis of coronary artery disease and the acute coronary syndromes. *New Eng. J. Med.,* 326, 242–250; 310–318.

Guillum, R, Feinleib, M, Margolis, JR, Fabsitz, R. & Brasch, R. (1976). The prehospital phase of acute myocardial infarction and sudden death. *Preventive Medicine*, 5, 408–413.

Glass, D. C. (1977). *Behavior pattern, stress and coronary disease*. Hillsdale: NJ Erlbaum.

Greene, W. A., Goldstein, S. & Moss, A. J. (1972). Psychosocial aspects of sudden death. *Arch. Int. Med.*, 129, 725–731.

Gutstein, W. H. (1988). The central nervous system and atherogenesis: endothelial injury. *Atherosclerosis*, 70, 145–154.

Hahn, P. (1971). *Der Herzinfarkt in psychosomatischer Sicht*. Gottingen: Verlag fur medizinische Psychologie im Verlag Van den Hoeck und Ruprecht.

Haines, A. P., Imeson, J. D. & Meade, T. (1987). Phobic anxiety and ischaemic heart disease. *Brit. Med. J.*, 295, 297–299.

Huang, M. H., Ebey, J. & Wolf, S. (1989). Reponses of the QT interval of the electrocardiogram during emotional stress. *Psychosom. Med.*, 51, 419–427.

Hurst, J. W., Schlant, R. C., Rackley, C. E., Sonnenblick, E. H. & Wenger, N. K. (Eds) (1990). *The heart arteries and veins*. New York: McGraw-Hill.

Karasek, R. & Theorell, T. (1990). *Healthy work*. New York: Basic Books.

Kinlen, L. J. (1973). Incidence and presentation of myocardial infarction in an English community. *Br. Heart J.*, 35, 616–622.

Klaeboe, G, Otterstad, J. E., Winsnes, T. & Espeland, N. (1987). Predictive value of prodromal symptoms in myocardial infarction. *Acta Med. Scand.*, 222, 27–30.

Kop, W, Appels, A, Bar, F, Mendes de Leon, C. & de Swart, H. (in press) VE as risk indicator of new coronary events in PTCA patients. *Psychosom. Med.*.

Kop, W., Hamulyak, C & Appels, A. (submitted) Vital exhaustion and the blood-clotting process.

Koskenvuo, M, Kaprio, J, Rose, R, Kesaniemi, A, Sarna, S, Heikklia, K & Langinvainio, H. (1988). Hostility as a riskfactor for mortality and ischaemic heart disease in men. *Psychosom. Med.*, 50, 330–340.

Krantz, D. S., Glass, D. C. & Snyder, M. L. (1974) Helplessness, stresslevel and the coronary prone behavior pattern. *J. Exp. Soc. Psychol.*, 10, 284–300.

Kuller, L. H. (1978). Prodromata of sudden death and myocardial infarction. *Adv.Cardiol.*, 25, 61–72

Kuller, L, Cooper, M & Perper, J. (1972). Epidemiology of sudden death. *Arch.Int.Med.*, 129, 714–719.

Ladwig, K. (1989). Patient- und Artzreaktionen auf spezifische und unspezifische Warnsignale in der Vorphase eines akuten Myokardinfarktes. *Verhaltensmodifikation und Verhaltensmedizin*, 10, 181–195.

Ladwig, K. H, Kieser, M, Konog, J, Breithardt, G, & Borggrefe, M. (1991). Affective disorders and survival after acute myocardial infarction. Results from the postinfarction late-potential study. *European Heart J.*, 12, 959–964.

Leiktin, L, Firestone, Ph & McGrath, J. (1988), Physical symptom reporting in type A and type B children. *J. Cons. and Clin. Psychol.*, 56, 721–726.

Lloyd, G. G. & Cawley, R. H. (1983). Distress or illness? A study of psychological symptoms after myocardial infarction. *Brit. J. Psychiatry*, 142, 120–125.

Lulofs, R. (1990). Stress reactivity. Type A behavior and vital exhaustion. Ph.D, Dissertation, Maastricht.

Maslach, C. & Jackson, S. E. (1986), *Maslach Burnout Inventory*. Palo Alto: Consulting Psychologists Press.

Matthews, K. (1988). Coronary heart disease and type A behaviour: update on and alternative to the Booth-Kewley and Friedman (1987) quantitative review. *Psychol. Bull.*, 104, 373–380.

Meesters, C. & Appels, A. (in preparation). An interview to assess vital Exhaustion.

Mendes de Leon, C. F. (1988). Behavioral and emotional precursors of acute heart disease. Ph.D. thesis, University of Texas Medical Branch, Galveston, Texas.

Meyman, F. F. (1991). *Over Vermoeidheid.* Amsterdam: Studiecentrum Arbeid en Gezondheid.

Nixon, P. (1986). Exhaustion: cardiac rehabilitation's starting point. *Physiotherapy*, 72, 224–228.

Odemuyima, O, Malik, M. Farell, T, Bashir, Y, Poloniecki, J. & Camm, J. (1991). Comparison of the predictive characteristics of heart rate variability index and left ventricular ejection fraction for all-causes mortality, arrhythmic events and sudden death after acute myocardial infarction. *Am. J. Cardiol.*, 68, 434–439.

Paffenbarger, R. S., Wolff, P. A., Notkin, J. & Thorne, M. C. (1966). Chronic disease in former college students. I: Early precursors of fatal coronary heart disease. *Am. J. Epidemiol.*, 83, 314–328.

Partinen, M., Putkonen, P., Kaprio, J., Koskenvuo, M & Hilakivi I. (1982) Sleep disorders in relation to coronary heart disease. *Act. Med. Scand. (Suppl)*, 660, 69–83.

Pines, A & Aronson, E. (1988). *Career burnout: causes and cures.* New York: The Free Press.

Polzien, P. & Walter, J. (1971). Das pseudoneurasthenische syndrom im Frühstadium der Koronarsklerose. *Münchener Med. Wochenschr.*, 44, 1453–1456.

Raphael, K. (1987). Recall bias: a proposal for assessment and control. *Int. J. Epidemiology*, 16, 167–170.

Rissanen, V, Romo, M, & Siltanen, P. (1978). Premonitrory symptoms and stress factors preceding sudden death from ischaemic heart disease. *Act. Med. Scand.*, 204, 389–396.

Rosenman, R., Brand R., Jenkins, C. et al. (1975). Coronary heart disease in the Western Collaborative Group Study: final follow-up experience of 8½ years. *JAMA*, 233, 872–877.

Rozanski, A., Nairey, C., Krantz, D., Friedman, J., Resser, K., Merell, M., Hilton-Chaften, S., Hestrin, L., Bietendorf, J., & Berman, D. (1988). Mental stress and the induction of silent myocardial ischaemia in patients with coronary artery disease. *N. Engl. J. Med.*, 318, 1005–1012.

Ruberman, W., Weinblatt, E., Goldberg, J. & Chaudhary, B. (1984). Psychosocial influences on mortality after myocardial infarction. *New Engl. J. Med.*, 311, 552–559.

Schlegel, R., Wellwood, J., Copps, B., Gruchow, W. & Sharrath, M. (1980). The relationship between perceived challenges and daily symptomreporting in type A vs Type B postinfarct subjects. *J. Beh. Med.*, 3, 191–204.

Schleifer, S., Macari-Hinson, M., Coyle, D., Slater, W., Kahn, M., Gorlin, R. & Zucker, H. (1989). The nature and course of depression following myocardial infarction. *Arch. Int. Med.*, 149, 1785–1789.

Schwartz, P., Periti, M. & Malliani, A. (1975). The long Q-T syndrome. *Am. Heart J.*, 89, 378–390.

Shekelle, R.B. & Ostfeld, A.M. (1965). Psychometric evaluations in cardiovascular epidemiology. *Annals NY Acad. Sci.* 126, 696–705.

Shephard, R., Kavanagh, T. & Klavora, P. (1985). Mood states during postcoronary cardiac rehabilitation. *J. Cardiopulmonary Rehab.*, 5, 480–484.

Shirom, A. (1989). Burnout in work organizations. In: C.L. Cooper and I, Robertson (Eds), *International review of industrial and organizational psychology.* New York: Wiley,

Siegel, W., Hlatky, M., Mark, D., Barefoot, J., Harell, F., Pryor, D. & Williams, R. (1990). Effect of type A behavior on exercise test outcome in coronary artery disease. *Am. J. Cardiol.*, 66, 179–182.

Siegrist J. (1987). Sleep disturbances and cardiovascular risk. In:J. Peter, T. Podszus and P. von Weicher (Eds), *Sleep related disorders and internal diseases*. Berlin: Springer,

Siegrist, J., Peter, R., Junge, A., Cremer, P. & Seidel, D. (1990). Low status control, high effort at work and ischaemic heart disease: prospective evidence from blue collar men. *Soc. Sci. Med.*, **31**, 1127–1134.

Sihm, I., Dehlholm, G., Hansen, E., Gerdes, L., & Faergeman, O. (1991). The psychological work environment of younger men surviving acute myocardial infarction. *Eur. Heart J.*, **12**, 203–209.

Silverstone, P. (1987). Depression and outcome in acute myocardial infarction. *Brit. Med. J.*, **294**. 219–220.

Simon, A., Feinlieb, M.& Thompson, H. (1972). Components of delay in the prehospital phase of acute myocardial infarction. *Am. J. Cardiol.*, **30**, 476–481.

Stowers, M. & Short, D. (1970) Warning symptoms before myocardial infarction. *Brit. Heart J.*, **32**, 833–838.

Thiele, R., Simon, H. & Thiele, G. (1985). Stressfactoren bei Herzinfarktpatienten vor Eintritt des Herzinfarktes. *Zeitschr Gesamte Inn Med.*, **40**, 483–488.

Trijsburg, R., Erdman, R., Duivenvoorde, H., Thiel, J., & Verhage, F. (1987). Denial and overcompensation in male patients with myocardial infarction. *Psychoth. Psychosom.*, **47**, 22–28.

Verhagen, F., Nass, C., Appels, A., van den Bastelaer, A., & Winnubst, J. (1980). Cross validation of the A/B typology in The Netherlands. *Psychoth. Psychosom.*, **34**, 178–186.

Verink, H. (in preparation). Psychosocial riskfactors for CAD in women.

Vos, de Y. (in preparation). Sleep problems preceding myocardial infarction.

Williams, R. (1987). Refining the type A hypothesis: emergence of the hostility complex. *Am. J. Cardiol.*, **60**, 27–32j.

Wolf, S. (1969). Psychosocial forces in myocardial infarction and sudden death. *Circulation*, **40**, 74–83.

Yeung, A., Vekshtein, V., Krantz, D., Vita, J., Ryan, Th., Ganz, P. & Selwyn, A. (1991). The effect of atherosclerosis on the vasomotor response of coronary arteries to mental stress. *New Engl. J. Med.*, **325**, 1551–1556.

Zotti, M., Bettinardi, O., Soffiantino, F., Tavazzi, L. & Steptoe, A. (1991). Psychophysiological stress testing in postinfarction patients. *Circulation*, **83** [suppl II], II-25-II-35.

4 Negative Affectivity, Subjective Somatic Complaints, and Objective Health Indicators. Mind and Body Still Separated?

OLAV VASSEND

Institute of Community Dentistry, University of Oslo, PO Box 1052, Blindern, 0316 Oslo, Norway

This chapter is concerned with the role of negative affectivity (NA) in health psychology research, and in particular the differential correlates of NA on the one hand and subjective health indicators (e.g. somatic complaints) and objective health measures (e.g. health behavior, blood pressure, presence of illness) on the other. The first section provides a brief introduction to NA-research as applied to stress and health-related topics. A comprehensive review of the vast literature possibly relevant to this research field, e.g. studies of anxiety and autonomic responses in the psychophysiological tradition, is beyond the scope of the present article. Instead, greater weight has been given to more recent research within the "NA-tradition" (Watson & Pennebaker, 1989; Watson & Clark, 1984).

In the second and third sections, the complexities involved in disentangling the relationship between NA and somatic health/illness related variables are illustrated and elucidated on the basis of two comprehensive empirical investigations. In the fourth section the major findings are discussed and related to three general types of theories of the NA-somatic complaints relationship; the psychosomatic hypothesis, the disability hypothesis, and the symptom perception hypothesis.

NEGATIVE AFFECTIVITY, STRESS AND HEALTH

Extensive evidence has demonstrated that two broad mood factors, which Tellegen (1985) has termed negative affectivity (NA) and positive affectivity (PA), are the dominant dimensions in self-reported mood (Watson & Tellegen, 1985).

NA is a general factor of subjective distress, and subsumes a broad

International Review of Health Psychology, Volume 3. Edited by S. Maes, H. Leventhal and M. Johnston
© 1994 John Wiley & Sons Ltd

range of negative mood states, including fear, anxiety, hostility and aspects of depression, e.g. sadness and loneliness. In contrast, PA is a dimension reflecting one's level of pleasurable engagement, e.g. interest and joy, with the environment. Both NA and PA can be measured either as a state (i.e. transient fluctuations in mood) or as a trait (i.e. stable individual differences in general affective tone).

Watson, Clark and Carey (1988) have demonstrated that NA is broadly correlated with symptoms and diagnosis of both anxiety and depression, whereas PA is consistently related only to symptoms and diagnosis of depression. Moreover, extensive research has shown that NA, but *not* PA, is closely connected with the perception and reporting of somatic complaints (Costa & McCrae, 1987; Watson & Pennebaker, 1989; Vassend, 1989).

However, in a thorough review of relevant studies, Watson and Pennebaker (1989) claim that although NA is correlated with subjective health complaints, much research indicates that this personality dimension is virtually unrelated—at least directly—to actual, long-term disease outcomes (e.g. mortality, cardiac disease and cancer), and only weakly related or completely unrelated to biological indicators or risk factors (e.g. blood pressure, immune system functioning) as well as health-related behaviors (e.g. physician visits, health-related absences from work or studies). For example, it is well documented that both experimentally induced stress as well as naturally occurring stressful situations—i.e. situations that ordinarily cause increases in state NA—are associated with changes in hormonal levels and immune responses (for reviews, see Zuckerman (1991) and Kiecolt-Glaser and Glaser (1991). However, studies of immune system or endocrine system functioning and trait NA measures have yielded inconsistent results, although the majority suggests that in normal individuals activity in these physiological systems is largely unrelated to NA (Watson & Pennebaker, 1989; Zuckerman, 1991). On the other hand, chronic physiological aberrations have been observed in some psychiatric disorders; for example several studies have demonstrated that severe depression or depressed affect is linked with impaired cellular and/or humoral immune functioning and elevated plasma cortisol levels (Stein, Miller & Trestman, 1991). Moreover, studies have shown that NA is related to health through a variety of maladaptive behaviors, for example alcoholism and suicide (Costa & McCrae, 1987); and a large body of psychophysiological research has demonstrated a relationship between anxiety and heightened autonomic activation (Zahn, 1986), at least at the state level.

Thus, the nature of the association between NA on the one hand, and self-reported complaints, health behavior and objective health/illness indicators on the other, is profoundly complex and requires a detailed consideration of the evidence. An outline of some of the main issues in this research field and a more detailed rationale for the empirical studies reported in the next two sections are given below.

One important question immediately arising concerns the strength of the NA–somatic complaints correlation when relevant extraneous variables, such as demographic characteristics and health condition, as well as health-related habits and lifestyle, have been controlled for. In most studies, only a very limited set of control variables is included, or simple (zero-order) correlations are presented as the sole data. In addition, the samples that have been investigated are as a rule selected from particular subpopulations (e.g. college students, elderly people), precluding the estimation of parameters that are valid for the general population. Recent Norwegian studies have shown that both NA and self-reported somatic complaints are correlated with sex, age, somatic health status, and social background variables (Moum, et al., 1991; Lavik & Uhde, 1988). Common risk factors, in particular smoking, overweight, lack of physical exercise, and use of alchohol are implicated in a number of health problems and should consequently be included as control variables in studies of NA–health connections (for a review of the role of these variables in the context of health psychology research, see Sarafino (1990). Thus, replications and extentions of previous findings concerning NA and health indicators, using relevant control variables and samples drawn from the general population, are needed.

As accumulated research has shown (Watson & Clark, 1984), the NA trait represents a diffuse, nonspecific measure of negative emotion. Obviously, studies of the relationship between particular components of NA (e.g. hostility, anxiety, and depression) and specific health complaints merits study. In Watson and Pennebaker's (1989) study, for example, sum scores of subjective somatic complaints were consistently used in the correlation analyses. Hence, the relative strength of the associations between NA components and specific symptoms or symptom clusters disappears. Studies (Vassend, 1989) have shown that cognitive anxiety (e.g. worry, ruminations, disturbing thought) was more strongly related to somatic complaints than behavioral (social avoidance) components of anxiety. Moreover, diffuse and widespread symptoms (e.g. weakness, fatigue) were more strongly associated with NA than more specific and localized symptoms. In the present study, investigations of the differential somatic correlates of NA will be pursued further.

Results from existing studies on the relationship between NA and health/illness behavior are conflicting. For example, Watson and Pennebaker (1989) found no systematic relationship between NA and health-related behaviors such as physician visits, health-related absences and frequency of exercise. Other studies (e.g. Vassend, 1989; Tessler, Mechanic & Dimond, 1976; Mechanic, 1980) have reported significant, albeit low, correlations between measures of NA and number of sick days or health visits. This issue is an important one, related as it is to the relationship between the individual's perception and reporting of bodily signs and symptoms on the one hand, and practical consequences in terms of health behavior and use of the health care services on the other. In the study reported on in section two, data pertaining to the NA–health behavior relationship will be presented.

The relationship between NA, physiological dysfunction and disease outcome remains obscure. Costa and McCrae (1985a) argue that neuroticism-related complaints are best viewed as exaggerations of bodily concerns rather than as signs of organic disease. For example, NA is related to the reporting of chest pain (a symptom of angina pectoris), but it is unrelated to objective indices of cardiac health, including risk factors for heart disease and heart-related mortality (Costa & McCrae, 1987; Watson & Pennebaker, 1989). However, a few studies of cardiac patients have ascertained an association of higher NA levels during hospitalization with poorer psychosocial and medical outcome at follow-up (Diederiks et al., 1983; Shaw et al., 1986). Moreover, a 35-year prospective study of 126 former college students demonstrated that the emotion of "severe anxiety" expressed in one or more of the original laboratory stress experiments, appeared to be a reliable marker for increased susceptibility not only to coronary heart disease but to overall future illness (Russek et al., 1990). Certainly, the experience of severe anxiety in particular situations is not necessarily a consequence of high-NA trait level. Still, several uncertainties remain regarding the impact of NA on actual health status. In section three results from a study of associations between NA-facets and objective health indicators are described.

In the area of stress research, several studies indicate that the relationship between reported life events and well-being (including measures of somatic complaints) may be far weaker than previously thought (Brett et al., 1990; Schroeder & Costa, 1984; Depue & Monroe, 1986). NA not only contaminates the reporting of life events but is associated with various self-reports of well-being, including somatic complaints. Furthermore, measures of social support (e.g. Sarason's Social Support Questionnaire, see Sarason, Sarason and Pierce (1988) appear to correlate with facets of NA.

In the first of the two empirical studies, data from the Norwegian National Health Survey performed in 1985 are presented. The main purpose of the study was to estimate the (statistical) effect of NA-related variables on self-reported somatic complaints, when controlling for a number of relevant extraneous variables. Effects of NA on satisfaction with own health and use of health services, again controlling for relevant extraneous variables, were also analyzed.

Thus, emphasis is given to the problem of characterizing the relationship between the dependent and independent variables by determining the extent, direction and strength of the association. A list of control variables was constructed based on prior knowledge and theoretical assumptions about the relationship of the dependent variable to each covariate under consideration (Kleinbaum, Kupper & Muller, 1988). In accordance with research discussed in the present review, the following categories of variables were selected: demographic characteristics, indicators of health condition (e.g. acute or chronic illness, physical disability), health-related behaviors and lifestyle (e.g. physician visits, smoking, physical exercise), and finally, social network indicators.

In the second study, further analyses of the NA–physical complaints association were performed. This study, originally designed to investigate effects of air pollution on somatic health, includes, in addition to the NA and complaints measures, results from medical examinations and clinical laboratory tests (e.g. blood pressure, lung function tests). In the statistical analyses, these medical variables were first included as control variables. In a separate regression analysis, the combined effect of NA, health-related behaviors and medical variables on systolic blood pressure was then analyzed. The investigation also included a group of patients with chronic pulmonary disease (which comprises asthma, chronic bronchitis and emphysema). NA and somatic symptom reporting in this clinical group were compared with the corresponding measures in the non-clinical part of the sample.

Several general predictions can be made. (1) Different NA-facets are related to various types of somatic complaints, but the strength of the associations (in terms of correlation or regression coefficients) are uncertain when relevant control variables are included in the analyses. (2) Weak positive or zero correlations between NA and measures of health-related behavior are expected. Again, the strength of the relationship is uncertain when control variables (e.g. presence of illness episodes) are included. Moreover, the relationship between NA and measures of more subjective health evaluations (i.e. satisfaction with own health, a variable not necessarily connected with actual behavior) is not clear. (3) Finally, a lack of relationship, or at most a weak relationship, between NA and objective health indicators (e.g. medical tests, presence of illness) is predicted.

STUDY 1

Method

Sample

The sample for the Norwegian National Health Survey 1985 was randomly drawn in a 2-step-wise manner from stratified sample areas (Central Bureau of Statistics, 1987). In interview surveys a certain non-response is inevitable owing to refusals, absence from home during the interview period, etc. The non-response of the Health Survey 1985 was 21.3% of the gross sample of 13 438 persons. Analyses of the distributions of select variables in the gross sample and in the net sample indicated that possible effects of sample bias were quite small (Central Bureau of Statistics, 1987). Data were collected by home interviews and structured questionnaires. In the present study, data for persons 16 years and over, comprising a total of 7922 individuals (4099 women and 3823 men, mean age 45 years) were used. In the statistical analyses the exact number of subjects varies somewhat, depending on the amount of missing information.

NA and somatic complaints

The subjects were asked 30 questions about emotional and physical troubles. Questions on anxiety and depression were borrowed from the Hopkins Symptom Checklist (Derogatis, Lipman & Covi, 1973). Each item is rated on a 4-point scale (1, not troubled; 2, a little troubled; 3, quite a bit troubled; and 4, very much troubled). The subjects were asked to select the numbered descriptors that best described how much discomfort or trouble the given problem had caused during the past 14 days. Using factor analysis (principal components analysis followed by varimax rotation) two factors were extracted; Anxiety and Depression. This common scale construction strategy was used to provide maximum discrimination between distinct facets within the broader NA-domain. The items comprising the anxiety scale were: (1) nervousness or shakiness inside; (2) suddenly scared for no reason; (3) worrying too much about things; (4) feeling fearful or anxious; (5) feeling tense or keyed up; and (6) attacks of panic or anxiety. The items included in the depression scale were: (1) feeling low in energy; (2) feeling lonely; (3) feeling blue; (4) feeling no interest in things; (5) feeling hopeless about the future; (6) feeling everything is an effort; and (7) feelings of uselessness. Cronbach's alpha was 0.82 for the Anxiety scale and 0.79 for the Depression scale. Nearly all the items comprising the two scales are included in the Symptom Checklist 90 (Revised, SCL-90R) (Derogatis, 1983), a well-known and thoroughly studied psychometric instrument. In an ongoing study (Vassend, Lian & Andersen, 1992) of personality and subjective physical and emotional complaints, the SCL-90R scales Anxiety and Depression correlated in the range of 0.50–0.60 with facets of the Neuroticism scale of the NEO Personality Inventory (Costa & McCrae, 1985b, 1989).

As can be seen from the item list, the scales are uncontaminated by overlap with somatic symptoms. Items with a pronounced diffuse or mixed somatic–psychological content (e.g. sleeping problems), were excluded from the analyses. Somatic complaints were assessed by 13 questions covering rather common pains and other discomforting bodily symptoms and sensations (see Table 4.2). Thus, 26 of the total of 30 items originally presented to the participants were used in the present analyses. A factor analysis of all 26 items revealed three factors roughly corresponding to anxiety, depression, and somatic complaints. The 13 somatic complaints items were analyzed individually, or a simple sum score was used. Cronbach's alpha for the total somatic complaints score was 0.71. A subscale comprising the most common symptoms of musculo-skeletal origin (i.e. pain in shoulders, neck and arms, back pain, and pain in hips or legs) was also constructed (Cronbach's alpha = 0.65).

Health behavior variables

The variables reflecting health-related behaviors were selected from the large number of questions on health/illness employed in the Health Survey. The following measures were chosen (items, scoring criteria, etc. are described in the report from the Central Bureau of Statistics (1987) and in Bjørnøy, 1987).

1. Number of contacts with the health services in the survey period (last 14 days). The scoring of this variable was based on several specific questions where the terms "contacts" and "health services" were strictly defined.
2. Time since last physician visit.
3. Number of days with reduced activity or partly in bed due to illness or disability in the survey period.
4. Presence of chronic disease or injury (scored 1, Yes, or 2, No).
5. Presence of physical disability not classified as chronic illness or injury (scored 1, Yes, or 2, No).
6. Satisfaction with own health (scored on a 5-point scale ranging from 1, very good, to 5, very bad). To ease comprehension of correlations, results based on the reversed scoring (1, very bad; 5, very good) are reported in the results section.
7. Smoking scored 1, regular smoker (on a daily basis); 2, previous regular smoker; and 3, never smoked).
8. Consumption of alcohol (rated on a 7-point scale ranging from 0, no alcohol the last 12 months, to 6, drinks almost every day).
9. Frequency of exercise (rated on a 5-point scale ranging from 0, no physical exercise, to 4, exercise 5–7 days per week).

Background variables and social network indicators

A detailed study of the respondents' social network and available social support was not attempted in the Health Survey. Still, two useful indicators of amount of social contact were employed:

1. Contact with family and friends (rated on a 6-point scale ranging from 1, has no friend/family, to 6, almost daily contact.)
2. Leisure time activities during the last 12 months. The value on this vari-

able (1, no activities, to 5, very high activity) is a derived score based on three specific questions pertaining to participation in organized activities (e.g. political or religious meetings, playing in an orchestra, organized sport or games) and other activities like going to the cinema, the theater, or exhibitions.

Finally, the background variables sex (coded 1, men, and 2, women), age and family income (in Norwegian kroner) were included in the analyses.

Results

Descriptive statistics for somatic complaints, anxiety and depression scores are shown in Table 4.1. As expected, musculo-skeletal problems were the most prevalent type of somatic complaints reported in the general population, the proportion of high scorers (i.e. mean scores between 3 and 4) being much higher than high-scorers of anxiety, depression or total somatic complaints.

Correlations among the somatic complaints score, anxiety and depression are displayed in the first part of Table 4.2. As can be seen, somatic complaints correlate significantly with both NA indicators (anxiety and depression). In addition, anxiety and depression are related to a very broad array of somatic symptoms and sensations as shown in Table 4.3. Although all the coefficients are significant, some of the correlations (particularly between NA and items referring to gastro-intestinal complaints and allergy) are quite low.

Correlations between somatic complaints, anxiety and depression on the one hand, and selected lifestyle variables, health behaviors and background variables on the other, are presented in the second and third parts of Table 4.2. Both the NA variables and somatic complaints scores are significantly

Table 4.1. Mean, standard deviation (SD) and proportion of respondents falling in different scoring categories on NA and somatic complaints scales. $N = 7673$

| | Mean | SD | Scoring categories (Proportions of respondents in percent) | | | |
			1.0	>1 <2	≥2 <3	≥3
Total somatic complaints score	1.2	0.3	24.3	73.2	2.4	0.1
Musculo-skeletal complaints	1.5	0.6	42.9	36.5	15.9	4.7
Anxiety	1.1	0.3	68.1	29.1	2.1	0.7
Depression	1.1	0.3	69.5	28.4	1.7	0.4

Table 4.2. Correlations (Pearson's r) between anxiety, depression and somatic complaints on the one hand, and demographic variables, health behaviors and lifestyle variables on the other. All coefficients are significant (one-tailed) at the 5% level owing to the large sample size (N between 7300 and 7900)

	Somatic complaints: total score	Musculo-skeletal complaints	Anxiety	Depression
Somatic complaints (total score)	—	0.81	0.48	0.49
Musculo-skeletal complaints	—	—	0.31	0.34
Anxiety	—	—	—	0.67
Sex	0.16	0.12	0.13	0.12
Age	0.24	0.26	0.08	0.17
Family income	−0.19	−0.17	−0.10	−0.18
Chronic disease	−0.19	−0.18	−0.09	−0.09
Physical disability	−0.15	−0.15	−0.08	−0.10
Time since last physician visit	−0.31	−0.26	−0.18	−0.20
Number of contacts with health services	0.25	0.23	0.19	0.19
Number of days with reduced activity	0.38	0.36	0.22	0.29
Satisfaction with own health	−0.55	−0.51	−0.33	−0.41
Frequency of exercise	−0.09	−0.07	−0.04	−0.07
Consumption of alcohol	−0.14	−0.13	−0.04	−0.08
Smoking	−0.04	−0.04	−0.06	−0.05
Contact with family and friends	−0.08	−0.08	−0.08	−0.09
Leisure-time activities	−0.19	−0.19	−0.11	−0.16

related, in the expected direction, to the health/illness indicators. Most of the correlations are of small to moderate magnitude. The relationship between NA and somatic complaints on the one hand, and frequency of exercise, consumption of alcohol, smoking and the social network indicators on the other, is also weak, several correlations approaching zero (but still significant, due to the large sample size). Interestingly, smoking and consumption of alcohol are inversely correlated with NA and somatic complaints.

In order to estimate the association between NA measures and somatic complaints when controlling for the list of extraneous variables, a multiple regression analysis was conducted (Table 4.4). A log transformation (natural logarithm) of the dependent variable was performed in order to transform the variable to the normal distribution. A forced entry of the

Table 4.3 Correlations between anxiety, depression, and total somatic complaints score on the one hand, and single symptoms comprising the somatic complaints scale on the other. All coefficients are significant at the 5% level (N = ca 7800)

	Anxiety	Depression	Somatic complaints: total score
Pain in shoulders, neck, arms, or hand	0.28	0.27	0.66
Back pain	0.22	0.23	0.61
Pain in hips or legs	0.21	0.27	0.60
Chest pain	0.23	0.27	0.45
Stomach pain	0.18	0.15	0.41
Heartburn, acid stomach	0.16	0.15	0.39
Diarrhoea	0.12	0.13	0.25
Constipation	0.18	0.20	0.41
Itching, allergy	0.14	0.13	0.34
Headache	0.26	0.21	0.49
Dizziness, weariness	0.40	0.43	0.57
Trembling	0.35	0.34	0.38
Heart-throbbing	0.39	0.34	0.48

variables was used, i.e. the variables were entered into the regression equation in a single step. Several regression diagnostics procedures (e.g. residuals analyses, assessment of collinearity) were employed to check the validity of the assumptions and estimates for a regression analysis (Kleinbaum, Kupper & Muller, 1988).

The regression model presented in Table 4.4 produced an acceptable fit to the data. As can be seen, the proportion of variance in the somatic complaints variable accounted for was 37%. The effects of anxiety as well as depression was highly significant.

In large regression analyses like these, the number of possible regression models and significant interaction terms comprising subsets of the independent variables are almost limitless. Several exploratory analyses were performed, varying both the set of independent variables to be included and the type of interaction terms. However, in all these analyses a clear main effect of NA facets on the dependent variables was evident. When interaction terms comprising combinations of anxiety or depression on the one hand, and sex, age, and presence of chronic illness on the other were included in the regression model analyzed above (Table 4.4), none of the interaction effects were significant

A multiple regression analysis was then performed with satisfaction with own health as dependent variable and the variables depicted in Table 4.4, plus somatic complaints, as independent variables. Somatic complaints and depression, but not anxiety, were significantly related to the dependent variable (T = 28.7, p < 0.001 and T = 10.7, p < 0.001, respectively).

Table 4.4 Predictors of somatic complaints (log-transformed), by multiple regression coefficients (standardized and unstandardized). All regression coefficients, with the exception of Contacts with family and friends, are significant at the 5 % level

Variable	B (unstandardized)	Beta (standardized)	SE B	T
Anxiety	0.145	0.234	0.008	18.5
Depression	0.122	0.164	0.009	12.6
Sex	0.032	0.088	0.004	8.9
Age	0.0007	0.074	0.0001	6.7
Family income	−0.004	−0.042	0.001	−4.0
Chronic disease	−0.051	−0.130	0.004	−13.6
Physical disability	−0.060	−0.090	0.006	−9.5
Reduced activity/partly in bed	0.009	0.202	0.0005	19.4
Number of contacts with health services	0.011	0.083	0.001	8.3
Alcohol	−0.006	−0.050	0.001	−4.8
Smoking	−0.011	−0.052	0.002	−5.1
Exercise	−0.005	−0.046	0.001	−4.8
Contacts with family and friends	0.001	0.005	0.002	0.5
Leisure-time activities	−0.005	−0.039	0.001	−3.7

$R^2 = 0.37$, $F(14, 7021) = 299.7$, $P < 0.001$.

The total amount of variation due to regression was 41% ($F(15, 7005) = 325.2$, $p < 0.001$). In models with interaction terms, significant effects of depression × chronic disease and depression × sex were found ($T = 2.9$, $p < 0.01$, and $T = 2.4$, $p < 0.05$, respectively). Additional analyses indicated that the interaction between anxiety and chronic disorder ($T = 3.9$, $p < 0.001$) as well as anxiety and sex ($T = 3.0$, $p < 0.01$) was significant.

When number of contacts with the health services was entered as dependent variable and the same independent variables as in the previous analysis were employed, it was found that somatic complaints and anxiety had significant beta coefficients ($T = 8.4$, $p < 0.001$, and $T = 4.1$, $p < 0.001$, respectively). The total amount of variance due to regression was 13% ($F(14, 7021) = 74.7$, $p < 0.001$). Significant interaction effects between depression and chronic disease ($T = 3.5$, $p < 0.001$) and depression and sex ($T = 2.5$, $p < 0.01$) were demonstrated.

STUDY 2

Method

Sample

A total of 312 persons (163 women and 149 men) from an industrialized area of Southern Norway participated in the investigation. Initially, 800 persons drawn randomly from the Central Bureau of Statistics' population registers were asked to participate. The primary reason for refusal was the time-consuming nature of the project. The subjects were asked to complete symptom check lists at regular intervals. In addition, several medical examinations and laboratory tests were required. However, comparison of the sample with the target population (available in official statistics) on variables such as age, sex, education level, and type of occupation, revealed no serious discrepancies.

In addition to the sample drawn from the general population, a sample comprising patients with chronic obstructive pulmonary disease (60 with asthma and 12 with other obstructive pulmonary disease) was studied. Initially, 111 patients with respiratory disease registered at the central hospital in the geographic region, were asked to participate.

The investigation was originally designed as a comprehensive multidisciplinary study. A selection of psychosocial and medical variables of particular relevance for the present study was therefore performed. Complete data sets were available for 224 individuals in the general population sample (101 men and 123 women, mean age 45 years), and 49 in the patient group (28 men and 21 women, mean age 49 years).

Medical variables and health behaviors

Of the large number of medical tests performed, the following measures, all obtained in the first medical examination, were selected:

1. Blood pressure (diastolic and systolic blood pressure (DBP and SBP) was measured by a physician, using a sphygmomanometer).
2. Peak expiratory flow rate (PEFR, a measure of lung/airways function, was recorded with a Wright Peak Flow Meter).
3. Hemoglobin level (HB, important because of its oxygen-binding capacity).
4. Blood sedimentation rate (SR, an indicator of several types of disease process, e.g. infections, rheumatic disease, and cancer).
5. Carbon monoxide level in blood (COHb). In the present study, the correlation between smoking (number of cigarettes per day) and COHb level was 0.83.

In addition, the subjects' height and weight were measured, and the height–weight ratio was calculated.

6. Physical exercise (rated on a 5-point scale ranging from 0, never exercise, to 4, exercise almost every day.
7. Consumption of alcohol. (This variable had 6 values, ranging from 0, less than once a month, to 5, daily consumption.)

Finally, the variables sex, age, and level of education were included in the analyses.

Somatic complaints and NA indicators

General psychological distress was assessed by the Symptom Checklist 90 (Derogatis, Lipman & Covi, 1973). The instrument was administered to the participants once, six to eight weeks after the initial medical examination. SCL-90 is scored on nine primary symptom dimensions, i.e. Somatization, Obsessive–Compulsive symptoms, Interpersonal Sensitivity, Depression, Anxiety, Hostility, Phobic Anxiety, Paranoid Ideation, and Psychoticism. The sub-scales Anxiety, Depression, and Hostility were chosen as the NA measures of most immediate interest, and the Somatization scale was selected as an indicator of somatic complaints level. The items comprising the Somatization scale are: (1) headaches; (2) faintness or dizziness; (3) pains in heart or chest; (4) pains in lower back; (5) nausea or upset stomach; (6) soreness of your muscles; (7) trouble getting your breath; (8) hot or cold spells; (9) numbness or tingling in parts of your body; (10) a lump in your throat; (11) feeling weak in parts of your body; and (12) heavy feelings in your arms or legs.

Results

Consistent with prior expectations, the somatization scale correlated significantly with depression ($r = 0.67$, $p < 0.001$) and anxiety ($r = 0.68$, $p < 0.001$), as well as hostility ($r = 0.33$, $p < 0.001$). In order to estimate the contribution of the NA indicators to the prediction of somatic complaints (log-transformed variable), when controlling for medical and demographic variables, as well as health behaviors, a multiple regression analysis (with forced entry of variables) was conducted. The results are presented in Table 4.5. Perhaps the most important result emerging from this analysis is the demonstration that anxiety, depression and hostility (but none of the other variables) contribute separately to the prediction of somatic complaints. Judged by conventional regression diagnostics, the fit of the regression model to the data was excellent.

Table 4.6 displays results from a multiple regression analysis where systolic blood pressure is included as the dependent variable. As can be seen, the variables age, height/weight ratio and physical exercise had significant effects on systolic blood pressure (the effect of sex approached significance). Surprisingly, frequency of physical exercise was positively related to systolic blood pressure. None of the NA variables or the other medical variables contributed significantly. Again, the model fit was very good.

Table 4.5. Predictors of somatic complaints (SCL-90 Somatization scale, log-transformed), by multiple regression coefficients

Variables	B (unstandardized)	Beta (standardized)	SE B	T
SCL-90 Anxiety	0.580	0.335	0.154	3.8*
SCL-90 Depression	0.365	0.220	0.154	2.4*
SCL-90 Hostility	0.357	0.141	0.162	2.2*
Age	0.005	0.079	0.005	1.0
Sex	0.005	0.003	0.136	0.04
Level of education	−0.026	−0.058	0.028	−0.9
Physical exercise	−0.005	−0.007	0.043	−0.1
Expiratory Peak Flow	−0.001	−0.078	0.001	−1.0
Blood sedimentation rate (SR)	0.001	0.068	0.001	1.2
Carbon monoxide (COHb)	−0.004	−0.007	0.031	−0.1
Hemoglobin (Hb)	0.019	0.062	0.019	1.0
Diastolic blood pressure (DBP)	0.003	0.037	0.006	0.5
Systolic blood pressure (SBP)	−0.006	−0.126	0.004	−1.4
Height/weight ratio	−0.141	−0.062	0.160	−0.9
Use of alcohol	−0.011	−0.017	0.040	−0.3

* $p < 0.05$.
$R^2 = 0.37$, $F(15, 193) = 7.4$, $p < 0.001$.

Table 4.6 Predictors of systolic blood pressure, by multiple regression coefficients.

Variables	B (unstandardized)	Beta (standardized)	SE B	T
SCL-90 Anxiety	2.863	0.777	3.586	0.8
SCL-90 Depression	2.045	0.058	3.496	0.6
SCL-90 Hostility	−0.302	−0.005	3.590	−0.1
SCL-90 Somatization	−3.471	−0.106	2.760	−1.3
Age	0.404	0.289	0.103	3.9*
Sex	5.023	0.138	2.993	1.7a
Level of education	−0.949	−0.101	0.601	−1.6
Physical exercise	2.344	0.158	0.910	2.6*
Expiratory Peak Flow	−0.009	−0.057	0.013	−0.7
Blood sedimentation rate (SR)	0.004	0.011	0.023	0.2
Carbon monoxide (COHb)	0.758	0.073	0.652	1.2
Hemoglobin (Hb)	0.187	0.028	0.427	0.4
Height/weight ratio	−8.613	−0.183	3.332	−2.6*
Use of alcohol	0.509	0.036	0.867	0.6

* $p < 0.01$.
a $p = 0.09$.
$R^2 = 0.28$, $F(14,211) = 5.7$, $p < 0.001$.

As in Study 1, additional regression analyses using interaction terms (comprising combinations of NA facets, sex and age) and different regression models, were performed. Again, the main effects of NA facets on somatic complaints turned out to be robust, and none of the regression terms tested were significant.

Differences regarding NA indicators and somatic complaints between the patient group and the general population sample are presented in Table 4.7. The two groups were significantly different only on the somatization scale, the patient group evincing a slightly higher complaint level. Further analysis (using t-tests) revealed that the groups were different only with respect to the symptoms Trouble getting your breath ($T(271) = 6.6$, $p < 0.001$), and Feeling weak in parts of your body ($T(271) = 1.9$, $p < 0.05$). The former symptom in particular is obviously related to having a chronic obstructive respiratory disease.

DISCUSSION

The results generally support our predictions, and are consistent with much previous research in this area. The data regarding NA are congruent with NA's conceptualization as a general dimension of somatopsychic distress: NA was consistently correlated with a broad range of somatic complaints and satisfaction with own health. Furthermore, facets of NA were significantly related to somatic complaints even after controlling for the

Table 4.7. SCL-90 scale values, standard deviations (SD), and intergroup t-tests for patients with chronic pulmonary disease ($n = 46$) and for the general population sample ($n = 225$).

Mean	Mean	SD	T
SCL-90 Somatization			
General population sample	0.59	0.52	1.72*
Patient group	0.74	0.60	
SCL-90 Depression			
General population sample	0.48	0.51	0.28
Patient group	0.50	0.45	
SCL-90 Anxiety			
General population sample	0.40	0.45	0.39
Patient group	0.42	0.39	
SCL-90 Hostility			
General population sample	0.28	0.33	0.52
Patient group	0.26	0.31	

* p < 0.05.

effects of demographic characteristics, as well as a number of health indicators and health behaviors. The use of extensive sets of control variables and samples drawn from the general population place the findings regarding NA facets, somatic complaints, and health behaviors on a more secure footing.

In exploratory analyses of possible interaction effects, none of the interaction terms in the models tested turned out to be significant. However, significant interaction effects of NA facets and chronic disorder on satisfaction with own health as well as number of contacts with the health services were found. Hence, the relationship between NA and these dependent variables cannot be considered indepently of presence/absence of chronic disorder. These results are of possible significance both theoretically and practically. Thus, interaction effects between NA measures and other relevant variables on different types of health indicators should be investigated more closely in future studies.

Some reports (e.g. Watson & Pennebaker's (1989) comprehensive studies) have concluded that NA is virtually unrelated to a diverse array of health indicators, including fitness and lifestyle variables, frequency of illness, health-related visits and absences, and objective biological measures. Thus, Watson and Pennebaker state:

> the data create a curious portrait of the high NA individuals. They complain of angina but show no evidence of greater coronary risk or pathology. They complain of headaches but do not report any increased use of aspirin. They report all kinds of physical problems but are not especially likely to visit their doctor, or to miss work or school. In general, they complain about their health but show no hard evidence of poorer health or increased mortality. (p. 244)

Results from Study 2 are consistent with previous research demonstrating low or zero correlations between NA and objective biological evidence of risk, dysfunction or pathology (e.g. elevated blood pressure). On the other hand, Study 1 demonstrated that NA facets correlated significantly (albeit weakly) with health-related behaviors. Both anxiety and somatic complaints contributed to the prediction of total number of contacts with the health services, even when number of days with reduced activity due to illness/injury in the study period and other relevant variables, were statistically controlled for. These discrepancies in findings may be due to differences between Norwegian and American health care systems, or to differences between the samples studied, i.e. college undergraduates and narrowly defined adult samples vs broader based, community samples, as was the case in the Norwegian studies. It should be emphasized, however, that the Norwegian studies also demonstrate weak associations between NA and health-related behaviors, much weaker than the relationship between NA and subjective somatic complaints. Somewhat higher correlations were demonstrated between satisfaction with own health and NA facets. Thus, some kind of connections between NA, subjective health eva-luation, and health behavior tendencies obviously exist.

Some weaknesses of the present study should be pointed out, however. First, it might be objected that the association between NA and somatic complaints may be inflated because it is based on the correlation of differ-ent parts of the same instrument (SCL-90 or selected questions from this instrument), administered at the same time and in the same response format. Certainly, there are grounds for the suspicion that shared response sets or situational factors might account for some of the observed relation. However, other research using different measurement instruments for NA and physical complaints (Vassend, 1989; Watson & Pennebaker, 1989), or measuring personality traits and complaints at a different time (Costa & McCrae, 1987), still demonstrates the association. Moreover, our own results showed that both NA and somatic complaints correlated with other indicators of health condition as well as health-related behaviors. Second, while the SCL-90 items undoubtedly tap dimensions of NA, it would have been desirable that inventories specifically constructed to measure trait-NA and other personality dimensions had been employed. As mentioned ear-lier, preliminary results from an ongoing study (Vassend et al., 1992) have shown that facets of the neuroticism dimension of the NEO Personality Inventory (Costa & McCrae, 1985b, 1989) correlates with the SCL-90R scales anxiety, depression, and hostility, as well as with somatic complaints scales.

Third, in Study 2 the SCL-90 was administered some weeks after the medical variables were measured. Studies have demonstrated high test–retest stability for the SCL-90 scales, however (Derogatis, 1983). Moreover, research on the SCL-90 and its precursors makes evident that the subscales are highly intercorrelated and are better interpreted as a measure of gen-eral distress (Cyr, McKenna-Foley & Peacock, 1985; Vassend et al., 1992). Thus, in addition to measuring momentary fluctuations in symptoms and mood, SCL-90 taps a more general tendency to experience negative affec-tivity. As accumulated research has demonstrated, this general NA trait is very stable in adulthood (Costa & McCrae, 1985b, 1989, see below).

The NA–somatic complaints correlation is open to various interpreta-tions, however (Watson & Pennebaker, 1989). One possibility—the classic psychosomatic hypothesis—is that NA, with its correspondingly elevated levels of anxiety, tension, hostility and depression, causes health problems. Conversely, according to an alternative interpretation—the disability hypothesis—presence of acute or chronic health problems may lead to heightened distress and therefore, high NA.

The low correlation between NA and presence of chronic disease/physi-cal disability demonstrated in Study 1, and the finding of no difference regarding NA between respiratory disease patients and the general popula-tion sample in Study 2, suggests that the NA–somatic complaints association cannot simply be understood as effects of somatic health problems. Studies have shown that, in adulthood at least, personality is extremely stable (e.g. Costa & McCrae, 1985b, 1989). Longitudinal studies covering 10 years or more have repeatedly shown retest correlations of about 0.70 for measures of neuroticism. Generally, there is little evidence that ill health leads to permanent change in personality (Brickman, Coates & Janoff-Bulman, 1978; Person & Sjøberg, 1987). Certainly, the presence of chronic illness and the uncertainty and threats it pose may affect state measures of anxiety and depression, but most individuals seem to adapt to even serious medical conditions (Costa & McCrae, 1985a).

The alternative interpretation, that NA leads to illness, has been a predominant viewpoint in psychosomatic medicine, but there are good reasons for also being sceptical of this position. Certainly, major components of the NA trait, e.g. anxiety and stress reactivity, are known to be associated with autonomic, endocrine, and even immunologic changes (Zahn, 1986; Kiecolt-Glaser & Glaser, 1991; Locke et al., 1984). However, anxiety, stress, and tension do not necessarily have long-term effects on somatic health, and the ultimate outcome will depend on a number of factors, such as biological vulnerability (Weiner, 1977), the employment of coping strategies (Ursin, 1980; Folkman et al., 1986), and (other) personality characteristics (Kobasa, 1979). In a thorough discussion of the evidence, Watson and Pennebaker (1989) maintain that virtually all prospective studies relating initial NA levels to later assessment of illness or mortality have reported results that either fail to support, or contradict the psychosomatic conception. Results from Study 2, showing a lack of relationship between NA and systolic blood pressure, are in agreement with accumulated evidence indicating that NA is unrelated to risk factors or objective indicators of cardiac pathology (Costa & McCrae, 1987; Denollet, 1991). In addition, results from Study 2 also indicate, again in line with much previous research, a lack of relationship between NA and other medical measures, i.e. lung function tests and serum indicators.

The question naturally arising at this point is: how should the NA–somatic complaints relationship be conceptualized given that psychosomatic factors ("stress") and chronic and acute illness effects are inadequate as general explanations? In recent years, variants of symptom perception theory have received increasing attention (Watson & Pennebaker, 1989; Barsky et al., 1988). In brief, the symptom perception hypothesis states that high-NA individuals are more likely to perceive, over-react to, and complain about physical problems and sensations. This hypothesis has received substantial support in several recent investigations. For example, in a study of patients with established coronary heart disease, Denollet (1991) demonstrated that high-NA individuals reported more negative mood states and health problems than both low-NA individuals and individuals characterized by repressive coping style. In contrast, no association was found between coping style and cardiovascular fitness as measured by exercise stress testing, a finding suggesting that high-NA individuals over-reacted to physical problems. Barsky et al. (1988) reported findings indicating that the general tendency to amplify bodily sensations was an important factor in predicting the reporting of and functioning with acute upper respiratory tract infection symptoms.

The symptom perception hypothesis is essentially a theory of coping style. As stated by Denollet (1991), NA is a *normal, generalized* and *emotion focused* (indicating how a stimulus is processed in an emotional fashion) coping style with pervasive behavioral and physiological correlates. Unfortunately, the physiological aspects of NA are the least studied, with the exception of the psychophysiological research on anxiety (Zahn, 1986). The psychophysiological tradition, however, has not emphasized the issue of symptom perception and symptom reporting and their relationship to NA.

The present studies and accumulated previous research have established beyond doubt the subjective and "autonomous" character of the NA–somatic complaints association. That is, the disposition to experience negative mood states and emotions is correlated with a tendency to perceive and report subjective physical symptoms and sensation, but this symptom sensitivity is, at it were, encapsulated from measurable biological/physical processes and events. On the other hand, objective measures of physiological functioning, such as blood pressure, are associated with variables reflecting biological characteristics, for example sex, age, and height/weight ratio, but *not* with NA.

As anticipated in the introductory section, this rather puzzling state of affairs is related to the problem of subjective and physiological correlates of state vs trait anxiety. Both trait and state NA measures are significantly related to health complaints, and elevated state NA is in addition associated—depending on, for example, the strength and duration of the affective state—with elevated autonomic activation and other biological changes. On the other hand, the general NA level, i.e. NA not linked to particular stressful situations, is correlated with somatic symptom reporting but not with general physiological functioning. Thus, one of the most important remaining questions concerns the role of state and trait NA in symptom perception and symptom reporting; that is, to what extent is the correlation a result of consistent and stable attributes of high NA individuals (characterized by a generalized tendency towards symptom amplification) as opposed to mechanisms associated with transient episodes of intense NA (occurring more often in high NA individuals). Certainly, even if trait NA does not have any large impact on objective health status, the plausible possibility exists that NA facets are related to transitory neuroendocrine activation changes and associated changes in subjective symptoms and sensations. When activation states are sustained for longer periods of time, a persistent low-grade biological dysfunction (e.g. elevated muscle tension or altered gastro-intestinal functions) may arise that serves as a generalized precursor to minor disorders (Depue & Monroe, 1986).

Thus, the seemingly autonomous NA-symptom perception mechanism should be studied in relation to psychophysiological activation; the link between mind and body should be re-established.

ACKNOWLEDGEMENT

I wish to thank Gunnar Bjerkness Haugen for collaboration and access to data on the "Grenland-project" on air pollution and health. I am also grateful to Linda Grytten for her help in improving my English.

REFERENCES

Barsky, A. J., Goodson, J. D., Lane, R. S. & Cleary, P. D. (1988). The amplification of somatic symptoms. *Psychosomatic Medicine*, 50, 510–519.

Bjørnøy, H. (1987). *The Norwegian Health Survey 1985*. Report No. 69. Bergen: Norsk samfunnsvitenskapelig datatjeneste.

Brett, J. F., Brief, A. P., Burke, M. J., George, J. M. & Webster, J. (1990). Negative affectivity and the reporting of stressful life events. *Health Psychology*, 9, 56–68.

Brickman, P., Coates, D. & Janoff-Bulman, R. (1978). Lottery winners and accident victims: Is happiness relative? *Journal of Personality and Social Psychology*, 36, 917–927.

Central Bureau of Statistics (1987). *The Norwegian Health Survey 1985*. Report No. B 692. Oslo.

Costa, P. T. & McCrae, R. R. (1985a). Hypochondriasis, neuroticism, and aging. When are somatic complaints unfounded? *American Psychologist*, 40, 19–28.

Costa, P. T. & McCrae, R. R. (1985b). *The NEO Personality Inventory manual*. Odessa, FL: Psychological Assessment Resources.

Costa, P. T. & McCrae, R. R. (1987). Neuroticism, somatic complaints, and disease: Is the bark worse than the bite? *Journal of Personality*, 55, 299–316.

Costa, P. T. & McCrae, R. R. (1989). *NEO PI/FFI manual supplement*. Odessa, FL: Psychological Assessment Resources.

Cyr, J. J., McKenna-Foley, J. M. & Peacock, E. (1985) Factor structure of the SCL-90-R: Is there one? *Journal of Personality Assessment*, 49, 13–28.

Denollet, J. (1991). Negative affectivity and repressive coping: pervasive influence on self-reported mood, health, and coronary-prone behavior. *Psychosomatic Medicine*, 53, 538–556.

Depue, R. A. & Monroe, S. M. (1986) Conceptualization and measurement of human disorder in life stress research: the problem of chronic disturbance. *Psychological Bulletin*, 99, 36–51.

Derogatis, L. R. (1983). *SCL-90-R. Manual-II*. Baltimore: Clinical Psychometric Research.

Derogatis, L. R., Lipman, R. S. & Covi, L. (1973). SCL-90: an outpatient psychiatric rating scale—preliminary report. *Psychopharmacology Bulletin*, 9, 13–28.

Diederiks, J. P., Van Der Sluys, H. Weeda, H. W. & Schobre, M. G. (1983). Predictors of physical activity one year after myocardial infarction. *Scandinavian Journal of Rehabilitation Medicine*, 15, 103–107.

Folkman, S., Lazarus, R. S, Gruen, R. J. & DeLongis, A. (1986). Appraisal, coping, health status, and psychological symptoms. *Journal of Personality and Social Psychology*, 50, 571–579.

Kiecolt-Glaser, J. K. & Glaser, R. (1991). Stress and immune-function in humans. In R. Ader, D. L. Felten, & N. Cohen (Eds), *Psychoneuroimmunology, 2nd edn* (pp. 849–867). New York: Academic Press.

Kleinbaum, D. G., Kupper, L. L. & Muller, E. M. (1988). *Applied regression and other multivariable methods*. Boston: PWS-KENT Publishing Company.

Kobasa, S. C. (1979). Stressful life events, personality, and health: an inquiry into hardiness. *Journal of Personality and Social Psychology*, 37, 1–11

Lavik, N. J. & Uhde, A. (1988). *Livsstil og samfunnsøkonomi* (Life style and social economy). Oslo: Medlex Norsk helseinformasjon.

Locke, S. E., Kraus, L., Leserman, J., Hurst, M. W., Heisel, E. J. S. & Williams, R. M. (1984). Life change stress, psychiatric symptoms, and natural killer cell activity. *Psychosomatic Medicine*, 46, 441–453.

Mechanic, D. (1980). The experience and reporting of common physical complaints. *Journal of Health and Social Behavior*, 21, 146–155.

Moum, T., Falkum, E., Tambs, K. & Vaglum, P. (1991). Sosiale bagrunnsfaktorer og psykiske plager (Social background variables and psychological complaints). In: T. Moum (Ed.) *Helse i Norge: Sykdom, livsstil og bruk av helsetjenester* (Health in Norway: Illness, life style, and use of the health services). Oslo: Gyldendal.

Persson, L.-O. & Sjøberg, L. (1987). Mood and somatic symptoms. *Journal of Psychosomatic Research*, 31, 499–511.

Russek, L. G., King, S. H., Russek, S. H. & Russek, H. I. (1990). The Harvard mastery of stress study 35-year follow-up: Prognostic significance of patterns of psychophysiological arousal and adaptation. *Psychosomatic Medicine*, 52, 271–285.

Sarafino, E.P. (1990). *Health psychology. Biopsychosocial interactions*. New York: Wiley.

Sarason, I.G., Sarason, B.R. & Pierce, G.R. (1988). Social support, personality, and health. In: S. Maes, C.D. Spielberger, P.B. Defares, & I.G. Sarason (Eds.). *Topics in health psychology* (pp. 245–256). Chichester:

Schroeder, D.H. & Costa, P.T., Jr. (1984). Influence of life event stress on physical illness: substantive effects or methodological flaws? *Journal of Personality and Social Psychology*, 46, 853–863.

Shaw, R.E., Cohen, F., Fishman-Rosen, J., Murphy, M.C. Stertzer, S.H., Clark, D.A. & Myler, R.K. (1986). Psychologic predictors of psychosocial and medical outcomes in patients undergoing coronary angioplasty. *Psychosomatic Medicine*, 48, 582–597.

Stein, M., Miller, A.H. & Trestman, R.L. (1991). Depression and the immune system. In: R. Ader, D.L. Felten & N. Cohen (Eds) *Psychoneuroimmunology*, 2nd edn (pp. 897–930). New York: Academic Press.

Tellegen, A. (1985). Structures of mood and personality and their relevance to assessing anxiety, with an emphasis on self-report. In A. H. Tuma & J.D. Maser (Eds), *Anxiety and the anxiety disorders* (pp. 681–706). Hillsdale, NJ: Erlbaum.

Tessler, R., Mechanic, D. & Dimond, M. (1976). The effect of psychological distress on physician utilization: a prospective study. *Journal of Health and Social Behavior*, 17, 353–364.

Ursin, H. (1980). Personality, activation and somatic health. A new psychosomatic theory. In S. Levine & H. Ursin (Eds), *Coping and Health* New York: Plenum Press.

Vassend, O. (1989). Dimensions of negative affectivity, self-reported somatic symptoms, and health-related behaviors. *Social Science and Medicine*, 28, 29–36.

Vassend, O., Lian, L. & Andersen, H. (1992). The Norwegian version of the NEO Personality Inventory, Symptom Checklist 90 Revised, and Giessen Subjective complaints list. Part I. *Journal of the Norwegian Psychological Association*, 29, 1150–1160.

Watson, D. & Clark, L. A. (1984). Negative affectivity: the disposition to experience aversive emotional states. *Psychological Bulletin*, 96, 465–490.

Watson, D., Clark, L. A. & Carey, G. (1988). Positive and negative affectivity and their relation to anxiety and depressive disorders. *Journal of Abnormal Psychology*, 97, 346–353.

Watson, D. & Pennebaker, J. W. (1989). Health complaints, stress, and distress. Exploring the central role of negative affectivity. *Psychological Review*, 96, 234–254.

Watson, D. & Tellegen, A. (1985). Toward a consensual structure of mood. *Psychological Bulletin*, 98, 219–235.

Weiner, H. (1977). *Psychobiology and human disease*. New York: Elsevier.

Zahn, T. P. (1986). Psychophysiological approaches to psychopathology. In: M. G. H. Coles, E. Donchin & S. W. Porges (Eds), *Psychophysiology. Systems, processes, and applications*. Oxford: Elsevier.

Zuckerman, M. (1991). *Psychobiology of Personality*. Cambridge: Cambridge University Press.

Part II

HEALTH BEHAVIOUR AND HEALTH PROMOTION

5 Promotion of Health: Integrating the Clinical and Public Health Approaches

BRIAN OLDENBURG

Department of Public Health, A27, University of Sydney, NSW, Australia 2006

BACKGROUND AND HISTORICAL PERSPECTIVE

A marked change in disease patterns has occurred in Western industrialised countries over the past 100 years. There has been a steady decline in the proportion of deaths due to infectious, respiratory and genito-urinary diseases, while in the second half of the twentieth century the major causes of premature death have become the circulatory diseases (mainly, coronary heart disease and stroke), a variety of neoplasms or cancers, accidents, suicide and injuries, and diabetes (Hetzel & McMichael, 1987). Analysis of those diseases causing years of life lost up to 65 years, reveals however, that while cardiovascular disease and cancer are the most common cause of death overall, accidents and injuries, and more recently in a number of countries, AIDS, contribute substantially to loss of years of life because they predominantly affect younger people.

An impressive amount of epidemiological evidence over the past 30 years has identified the association between a number of alterable lifestyle factors (such as cigarette smoking, physical inactivity and diet) and diseases such as cancer and cardiovascular disease. This began in the first half of the 1960s with the publication of three key research reports: the landmark Doll and Peto study which investigated the relationship between doctors' smoking habits and disease (Doll & Hill, 1964); the first reports emanating from the Framingham study which identified a number of "risk factors" for cardiovascular disease (Kannel & Gordon, 1968); and the first United States Surgeon General's Report on Smoking and Health (1964). Indeed the (United States) Centers for Disease Control (1980) estimated that 50% of mortality from the 10 leading causes of death in the United States can be traced to lifestyle (Centers for Disease Control, 1980).

International Review of Health Psychology, Volume 3. Edited by S. Maes, H. Leventhal and M. Johnston
© 1994 John Wiley & Sons Ltd

THE CHALLENGE OF HEALTH PROMOTION

Recommended goals and targets for disease prevention and health promotion have recently emanated from a variety of industrialised countries, including the United States of America (US Department of Health and Human Services, 1990), the United Kingdom (Department of Health, 1992), Canada (Ontario Premiers' Council on Health, 1987) and Australia (Nutbeam et al., 1993). These documents emphasise the importance of influencing lifestyle and related risk factors associated with preventable causes of death. Priority lifestyle areas which have been identified and to which a variety of actions have been proposed, include physical activity, diet and nutrition, smoking, alcohol and other drug use, safety behaviours, sun protective behaviours, appropriate use of medicines, immunisation, sexuality and reproductive health, oral hygiene and mental health.

A crucial element in efforts to prevent disease and promote health is lifestyle change. A range of approaches have been used to modify risk factors and influence behaviours associated with a variety of diseases. These approaches are many and varied and have included: community-wide approaches utilising the media and legislation; programmes targeting individuals or groups of individuals in a variety of community settings such as the worksite and schools; and efforts which have targeted the high-risk individual in clinical settings, such as hospitals, community centres and the physician's office. Community-wide or population-based strategies aim to reduce average levels of risk in the whole community by environmental and legislative changes, while the more clinical approaches aim to reduce the risk of select individuals or groups with elevated risk (WHO Expert Committee, 1982). However, health professionals, particularly family physicians have the opportunity to impact on both the risk of disease in the "high risk" individual, as well as the average levels of risk in the general population. Health professionals can achieve the latter by screening for and reducing disease risk in a large proportion of clients or patients whose levels of risk range from moderate to very high. In a disease such as cardiovascular disease where there is a synergistic effect of various risk factors, the effect of change in any individual risk factor is related to the entire constellation of risk factors present (Gordon & Kannel, 1975). Hence the benefits to be derived from lifestyle change vary, with greater benefits accruing to those individuals who are at elevated risk, even if only moderately so, from a number of risk factors, rather than being at elevated risk on only one risk factor.

However, since the landmark Lalonde (1974) report on the health of Canadians and the Alameda County study (Belloc and Breslow, 1972), it has become increasingly clear that in order to prevent disease and promote health, it is not sufficient to only address lifestyle change at an individual level. The wider environment and the context in which change is being addressed are also very important; in particular, social support, social networks and socioeconomic class are all very important. The Ottawa Charter (World Health Organization, 1986) his recognised the importance of this by stressing that health promotion in order to be effective, must incorporate the following elements: the development of personal skills; the creation of environments which are supportive of health; the refocusing of health and related services; an increase in community participation; and finally, the development of public policy which is health-enhancing.

It is clear therefore, that understanding the context of behaviour and what Raymond calls "risk contexts" (Raymond, 1989), rather than just the behavioural risk factors themselves, is a major challenge for epidemiological research. Furthermore, Raymond argues that the challenge is to establish an epidemiology of health, not just disease. In recent years, behavioural scientists and other researchers have contributed to an exponential growth in behavioural epidemiological research directed at understanding the many social, cultural and attitudinal factors which are important determinants of some of the major behavioural risk factors, in particular, smoking, physical inactivity and dietary behaviours. For example, Sallis and Nader (1988) argue for the critical role of the family in the development and alteration of smoking, dietary and exercise behaviours. Bruhn (1988) in the same textbook (Gochman, 1988) provides an overview of the range of environmental, cultural, family and personal factors which have been shown to shape lifestyle and health behaviours.

With the identification of the importance of behavioural, cultural, social and economic factors as determinants of disease, there is a need for all intervention strategies and approaches, particularly those focusing on lifestyle change, to take account of these. Stokols (1992) points out that to date, most health promotion programmes implemented in community, corporate and clinical settings, have focused on change within individuals rather than the environment; and such programs have been designed primarily to influence change in individuals' health habits and lifestyles such as smoking and exercise. Yet, there is an increasing body of research which suggests the value of environmental interventions in addition to the more traditional, behaviourally focused lifestyle interventions (e.g. Archea, 1985; Green & Kreuter, 1990; Karasek & Theorell, 1990). Stokols argues that this requires a more ecological view of health and health promotion, one which emphasizes linking individually focused, small-group, organisational, and community approaches.

Since the mid-1970s there has been some increase in the use of alternative service delivery methods for promoting lifestyle change and preventing disease. As a consequence, the distinction between population-based approaches and those focusing on the individual, particularly the "high risk" individual, is not as clear as it once was. This change is best exemplified by some of the community-based cardiovascular disease prevention programmes which have combined the use of a variety of strategies, including the media, legislation and other restrictive policies, and the involvement of schools, health professionals and other key groups in the community. The first generation of such programmes was implemented in North Karelia, Finland (Puska et al., 1985) and in three communities near Stanford, California (Farquhar & Maccoby, 1977). The first of these programmes was associated with a 24% reduction in coronary heart disease mortality among middle-aged males over a ten-year period and the second showed positive effects for saturated fat intake and plasma cholesterol level, cigarette smoking and systolic blood pressure. The next generation of community-based programmes has included the Minnesota Heart Health Program (Mittelmark et al., 1986), the Pawtucket Heart Health Program (Lefebvre et al., 1987) and the Stanford Five-City Project (Farquhar et al., 1990). These three programmes commenced in the United States in the early 1980s and the preliminary results for the latter programmes at least, have been quite encouraging (Farquhar et al., 1990).

INTEGRATION OF LIFESTYLE CHANGE APPROACHES WITH A PUBLIC HEALTH APPROACH

To date, a key challenge in much lifestyle change research in areas such as smoking cessation and dietary change, has been to develop intensive, efficacious interventions which maximise change within the individual. However, it has been argued in this paper so far, that the key public health challenge in terms of the health of the whole population, is how best to promote lifestyle change within the wider community as a precursor to preventing disease and promoting health. This challenge requires the identification and development of lifestyle change strategies which can be implemented and used effectively within a variety of health care and other settings in the community.

Implicit in this redefining of the nature of lifestyle change, is a shift away from viewing lifestyle change from a purely clinical perspective, towards that of a more public health orientation. Within this broader orientation, intervening with individuals to change lifestyle is only one part of a more all encompassing and comprehensive population-based approach.

In order to influence the myriad of personal and environmental factors which are associated with an increased risk of disease, a multilevel approach is required; that is, one that intervenes at all levels including the individual, the local community and at regional, national and even the international level. Different schema (e.g. Winrett, King & Altman, 1989; Stokols, 1992) have been proposed for conceptualising such a multilevel approach.

For example, the traditional clinical approach to the problem of smoking has focused on developing and delivering relatively intensive, but often, very effective help, usually delivered under reasonably "ideal" conditions to highly motivated individuals. i.e. intensive or high exposure programmes with limited programme reach. When these conditions have been achieved, programmes have been shown to achieve quit rates of greater than 20% (e.g. Richmond, Austin & Webster, 1986). Wider dissemination of such programme under more realistic conditions, that is, by increasing the reach of the programme, usually leads to much poorer results (Copeman et al. 1989). In the Copeman study, for example, those physicians who took up the Smokescreen programme developed by Richmond and her colleagues, which had previously been shown to be highly efficacious under research conditions, found it extremely difficult to recruit smokers and follow them up. An alternative and more public health-oriented approach to smoking addresses the problem at a population level, often focusing on "high risk" groups in their natural environment, including the worksite and primary health care settings. The aim of this latter approach is to provide as many individuals as possible with brief interventions at low cost, albeit generally, with "quit" rates of less than 5 or 10%. Such a public health approach should also take account of the environmental and contextual determinants of smoking which can arise in families, schools, from one's peers, and the work environment.

Table 5.1 contrasts the more traditional clinical approach to smoking with that of a more public health approach. The public health model demonstrates that a comprehensive approach to smoking cessation should include all smokers, including those seeking help, those not currently motivated to stop, as well as those who might make quite attempts if aware of programmes which could help (Glynn, Boyd & Gruman, 1990).

It is not being suggested here that a clinical approach to the problem of smoking and other health behaviours such as smoking and other health behaviours, is ineffective or irrelevant. In fact in the health care provider's office, clinical and public health perspectives come together. In most Western countries the great majority of citizens have some contact with the health care system and health professionals each year. Patients' health concerns provide a "teachable moment" (Vogt et al., 1989) and this can provide an opportunity for health professionals to deliver personalised and targeted lifestyle change assistance to large sections of the population. The public health approach can incorporate a whole range of more community-wide and environmental strategies, which can act to strengthen, support and maintain the health gains that health professionals have achieved with individuals in clinical and other settings. So, rather than clinical approaches being used in isolation, it is important that they be integrated with other strategies being pursued at at a local, regional and national level.

The importance of this more integrated approach to improving the health of whole communities has been recognised for instance, in the design and implementation of the United States National Heart, Lung, and

Table 5.1   Clinical versus public health perspectives on smoking cessation

Characteristic	Clinical perspective	Public Health perspective
Goal	To provide services for individual smokers who want help in quitting	To promote nonsmoking as a cultural norm
Definition of problem	Individual lifestyle	Community, wider environment
Focus	Individual smoker	The entire population of smokers
Target	Self-referred or identified individuals	Populations or high-risk groups
Setting	Clinical settings, smokers' clinics	"Natural" settings (primary care, worksites, schools)
Provider	Especially trained professionals	All health professionals, lay and automated
Intervention	Intensive, multisession, expensive, tailored to the individual	Brief, low-cost, self-instructional, menu of intervention options
Outcomes	Higher quit rates (20–40% over 1 year)	Lower quit rates (5–15% over 1 year)
Evaluation	Successful quit rates among smokers enrolled in programmes	Changes in population prevalence over time
Cost-effectiveness	Lower	Higher

Adapted from Lichtenstein and Glasgow (1992) and Glynn et al. (1990).

Blood Institute's National Cholesterol Education Program (NCEP) which is aimed at intervening in the risk factor of hypercholesterolaemia (The Expert Panel, 1988). The NCEP consists of two approaches which are integrated with and are supportive of one another: (1) a clinical or patient-based approach for those with hypercholesterolaemia; and (2) a population-based or public health approach to promote a lowering of the blood cholesterol distribution of the entire population (The Expert Panel, 1989).

The remainder of this paper reviews recent evidence concerning ways in which lifestyle change approaches, particularly those used in more clinical settings, can be used to increase the reach of programmes and individuals' exposure to these programmes, and hence increase the overall effectiveness of such programs. The following issues will be considered in detail:

1. an understanding of the change process and the steps involved, particularly as change occurs under "naturalistic" conditions;
2. identification of some of the key principles underlying effective lifestyle change programmes;
3. matching strategies to the stages of change.

THE CHANGE PROCESS UNDER NATURALISTIC CONDITIONS

The notion that lifestyle change occurs in a number of steps is not a particularly new concept; it has its origins in the writings of Horn and Waingrow (1966). Cashdan (1973), and Egan (1975). However, perhaps more than any other researchers, the work of Prochaska and DiClemente (1992) and summarized by Prochaska, DiClemente and Norcross (1992), has formally identified the dynamics and structure of change that underlie both self-mediated and treatment-facilitated modification of addictive and other health behaviour. Alternative versions to their stage model can be found, however, in the recent writings of Beitman (1986), Brownell et al. (1986), Dryden (1986), and Marlatt and Gordon (1985).

Prochaska, DiClemente and Norcross (1992) argue that, although there is now substantial evidence demonstrating that people can modify behaviours as diverse as alcohol abuse, obesity, smoking and opiate use (e.g. Cohen et al., 1989; Orford, 1985; Roizen, Cahaland & Shanks, 1978; Schachter, 1982; Tuchfeld, 1981), without formalised help, we have little understanding of the steps and processes involved. Understanding this is clearly an important prerequisite for developing and using minimal intervention strategies more widely, both in clinical settings and elsewhere in the community.

Prochaska, DiClemente and their colleagues (1992) have indentified five overlapping and interactive stages that individuals move through when initiating an attempt to modify some aspect(s) of their lifestyle:

- *Precontemplation stage.* This is the earlisest stage in the change process. At this point, lifestyle issues are not high on an individual's "personal agenda" and s/he is not considering the benefits of lifestyle change. Precontemplators are not convinced that the negative aspects of the problem behaviour outweigh the positive. Moving ahead to the next stage appears to be dependent on three factors: taking "ownership" of the problem, increasing awareness of the negative aspects of the problem and accurately evaluating one's ability and capacity to change (DiClemente & Prochaska, 1985).
- *Contemplation stage.* At this point, an individual begins to consider actively the benefits of lifestyle change, and maybe even intends to take some action to change, but s/he has not yet acted upon this intention. Contemplators are evaluating options. There is now evidence that smokers and individuals with alcohol problems, who are in this stage, are more concerned and upset about their problems, than are Precontemplators (Prochaska & DiClemente, 1992). Additionally, they have started to evaluate the losses and rewards that successful change would bring. However, such individuals are still at the stage of evaluating options and they have not made a firm decision to move on to the next stage.

- *Preparation stage.* Individuals in this stage are ready to change and are keen to take action and they need to set goals and priorities. Often, such individuals have already engaged in processes which have increased their ability to identify factors which influence their lifestyle and the relevant health behaviours, and to initiate behaviour change.
- *Action stage.* During this stage, the individual begins to engage in active attempt(s) to change or modify some aspect of his/her life. Action individuals require the skills to use the key strategies in order to change habitual patterns of behaviour and adopt a healthier lifestyle. Prochaska and DiClemente (1986) have examined the time frame for this stage; and for the addictive behaviours at least, six months appears to have received the greatest support from both the maintenance and relapse literature.
- *Maintenance stage.* If individuals makes it to this stage, then they have done so, by continuing to actively make changes to their behaviour and lifestyle. As noted by Prochaska and DiClemente (1992) and many other commentators, relapse is more the norm than the exception. Even after six months of active attempts to make change, setbacks and reversals are common.

Prochaska and DiClemente developed this model, initially in response to research they were carrying out with smokers and ex-smokers in the general community (DiClemente et al., 1991). Accumulating research over the past 10 years indicates that these stages of change are common to a number of groups of individuals, including outpatient psychotherapy clients, outpatient alcoholism patients, weight control clients and head-injury rehabilitation patients (Oldenburg & Pope, 1990). Overall, health behaviours are generally very resistant to long-term modification; and most people taking action to change some aspect of their lives do not succeed on the first occasion. Smokers for example, take an average of three to four attempts at action before becoming self-changers (Schachter, 1982). Brownell et al., (1986) and Donovan and Marlatt (1988) and many others have researched separately the phenomenon of relapse. Up to 80% of smokers who quit smoking will relapse over a 12-month follow-up period (Hunt & Bespalec, 1974). More generally, most reviews of the field have found that at least one-third of all patients fail to comply with any recommended regimen (Blackwell, 1973; Davis, 1968; Stimson, 1974); and these rates are usually well over 50% where the recommendations relate to changing lifestyle (Becker, 1985), such as exercise (Carmody et al., 1980) and diet (Dunbar and Stunkard, 1979), in asymptomatic individuals.

In order to account for the resilience of health behaviours and the high relapse rates associated with change, the original stage model has been modified in recent years. The most recent account of their model represents the cycle of change by a spiral pattern, which accounts for movement back and forth between the various stages, for example, recycling from action back to the precontemplation stage, or more commonly, from action back to the contemplation or action stages.

An increasing body of research into the behavioural epidemiology of health behaviours indicates that most people at any one time are not in the action stage or indeed, even the preparation stage. There is now compelling data to this effect with smokers, where aggregated data from a variety of studies and populations from developed countries, indicate that at any moment in time, approximately 10–15% of smokers are prepared for action, approximately 30–40% are in the contemplation stage, and the remainder are in the pre contemplation stage (Prochaska, DiClemente & Norcross, 1992). Although other health behaviours are less well researched, there are some comparable data emerging on physical activity (Booth et al., in press) and Southard et al., (1992) have noted the same phenomenon with respect to dietary change. If indeed, as appears likely, most individuals are not in the action stage, then action-oriented programmes are likely to be inappropriate for many individuals, particularly when those individuals are being targeted by relatively "low exposure" programs in non-clinical settings, such as the workplace and schools, and in the wider community.

THE PRINCIPLES UNDERLYING EFFECTIVE LIFESTYLE CHANGE PROGRAMS

Although over the past 25 years, there has been an exponential growth in research examining the efficacy of a variety of strategies for achieving lifestyle change in clinical and some other settings, such as the workplace, many health behaviours remain under-researched. For example, a meta-analytic study of 64 controlled trials in clinical settings, carried out by Simons-Morton et al. (1992), revealed an acceptable number of controlled trials in smoking cessation, nutrition and weight control, but a scarcity of such trials in most other areas of health, including injury prevention, exercise, stress, drug and alcohol problems and STD prevention. In fact, the authors were only able to find relevant and acceptable studies in 14 of the 21 prevention areas selected; although they did exclude any studies conducted in nonclinical settings, such as schools and worksites. Nevertheless, the health behaviours which have been well-researched, such as smoking and dietary behaviours, provide some clear pointers regarding how the reach and effectiveness of lifestyle change programmes might be improved.

There is little doubt now that health professionals can effect changes in individuals' risk of disease through promoting lifestyle changes such as smoking cessation, dietary change and increased physical activity. However, this has really only been shown convincingly for highly motivated clients attending specialised clinics with programmes conducted by health professionals who have been trained in some fashion. As indicated earlier in this paper, there is also evidence supporting the effectiveness of community-wide interventions, but to date it is not at all clear exactly what to attribute such changes to. There are many key questions which remain unanswered concerning the relative effectiveness of different types of interventions, of varying ways of delivering interventions and of delivering interventions in different settings.

A recent review of the smoking cessation literature by Lichtenstein and Glasgow (1992) and a meta-analysis of the same literature by Baille, Mattick and Webster (1990), indicated a lack of differential effectiveness for a variety intervention strategies. The latter showed, for example, that with the exception of nicotine gum, none of the effect-size estimates related to specific interventions were significant. Indeed, Kottke et al. (1988, p. 2888) in their concluding comments regarding the findings of a meta-analysis of 39 controlled trials characterised the situation as follows:

> Success was not associated with novel or unusual interventions. It was the product of personalized smoking cessation advice and assistance, repeated in different forms by several sources over the longest feasible period. The meta-analysis reported herein offers little reason for confidence in the scientific validity of claims that any particular intervention strategy is uniformly more effective than firm, consistent, and repeated help and advice to stop smoking ... it is reinforcement—by increasing the number of contacts, and the number of people making the contacts—not a specific intervention or delivery system for the smoking cessations message that produces result.

Hence, it would seem that a key element underpinning the potential effectiveness of any lifestyle change attempts, particularly with less than well-motivated individuals in the community, is that of programme reinforcement. The challenge that follows from this is how to maximise any given individual's exposure to a programme. In the context of primary care and the physician's office, it is often extremely difficult to achieve anything other than quite minimal contact between patients and health professionals. Conducting programmes which are mediated and implemented by a health professional, in conjunction with the use of high-quality printed and/or audio-visual self-help materials is one way of potentially extending the programme into the patient's family and social situation (Graham-Clarke et al., submitted). This issue of maximising program exposure has also been discussed recently, in relation to the nationwide implementation of the United States National Cholesterol Education Program (Southard et al., 1992). In addition to their specific suggestions regarding the importance of using strategies which are integrated with a stages of change approach which is to be discussed in more detail in the next section of this paper, they also stress the importance of using a variety of media through supermarkets and other settings and providing continuing opportunities for education and social networking outside of the clinical setting.

Not unrelated to the principle of programme exposure is that of programme reach. Within the public health model, as proposed already in this paper, there is a need to develop innovative ways of delivering programmes to larger numbers of individuals, not just through traditional clinical settings, but through the media, the workplace and elsewhere in the community. Improving programme reach will invariably tend to lead however, to a reduction in the average level of programme exposure.

One obvious way of increasing the reach of any programme is through the increased use of so-called minimal interventions strategies based on self-instructional materials. This approach has been best characterised with respect to smoking by Glynn, Boyd and Gruman (1990) in their summary of the findings of an US Expert Advisory Panel which addressed the question "What are the essential elements of self-help/minimal interventions for smoking cessation?". They have been able to base their recommendations on seven large US-based trials which have used self-help materials. They define self-help/minimal interventions as efforts to stop smoking on one's own, without the continued assistance of health professionals, by (1) devising one's own way to quitting; (2) receiving brief instructions or advice on how to stop and then doing it; (3) utilizing self-help materials or another aid to quitting. They argue that not only is there compelling evidence that such strategies may be the preferred means by which smokers can quit, but also that this is the only approach which has the potential to deliver programmes to all of the appropriate target groups in the population.

It is appropriate, however, to sound a note of caution regarding the use of minimal intervention strategies, particularly when they are used in isolation and not as part of, a more integrated approach. For example, Gritz et al. (1992) found that an unsolicited self-help smoking cessation programme consisting of six "staged" booklets mailed by a United States Health Maintenance Organization in weekly instalments to a randomly selected sample of female smokers, was ineffective. These results replicated the findings of a number of self-help studies for a variety of health behaviours and problem behaviours which were reviewed by Glasgow and Rosen (1978); distribution of self-help materials without any personal contact produces little behaviour change beyond what occurs in the environment without them (Ockene, 1992). Ockene (p. 278, 1992) argues strongly that based on this evidence, interpersonal influences and favourable environmental circumstances are required to facilitate the effectiveness of any self-help programme: "Without ensuring a motivating connection with the targeted smoker, we push the limits of the public health model when we expect self-help materials alone to have an effect beyond what already occurs from present public health approaches".

It also goes without saying that effective lifestyle change programmes need to be based, not only on demonstrably effective strategies which are relevant to the particular health behaviour(s) being influenced, but also on theories or models which are relevant to the health problem being addressed (Glanz, Lewis & Rimer, 1990; Hockbaum, Soreson & Lorig, 1992; Green & Kreuter, 1991). Some of the theoretical formulations which are relevant to intervening within a stages of change framework are discussed in the next section. Health psychologists and other behavioural scientists have given considerable attention to models of individual health behaviour such as the Health Belief Model and the Theory of Reasoned Action and more recently, to models of interpersonal behaviour such as Social Learning Theory. Much less attention has been given to models which attempt to understand health behaviour change within groups, or even within whole communities. To design programmes to reach populations, not merely individuals, which after all, is a fundamental aim of the public health approach, requires an understanding of how social systems operate, how change occurs within and among systems, and how large-scale changes influence people's health behaviour and health more generally (Glanz Lewis & Rimer, 1990). Diffusion of innovations theory and a number of other models discussed in detail in Glanz Lewis and Rimer, (1990) have added immeasurably to our potential to understand how to translate effective interventions into more widespread change, but to date there has been relatively little research which has addressed these issues, other than in a few key settings such as schools and the workplace.

Based on many years of health education research and some theories of behaviour change, there have been various attempts to define the key underlying principles required of any program attempting to promote change. Most recently, Simons-Morton et al. (1992), based on their meta-analysis of 64 studies, have identified five key educational principles: programme relevance, individualisation of the programme, and appropriate use of feedback, reinforcement and materials to facilitate the programme. In a report of the US Preventive Services Task Force (1989) which makes recommendations regarding the effectiveness of 169 interventions to be used as part of clinical preventive practice, the authors list those principles which empirical research and clinical experience have shown to enhance the effectiveness of physician counselling. These include: developing a therapeutic alliance; counselling all patients; ensuring that patients understand the relationship between behaviour and health; working with patients to assess barriers to behaviour change; gaining commitment from patients to change; involving patients in selecting risk factors to change; using a combination of strategies; design a behaviour modification plan; monitoring progress through follow-up contact; and involving other office staff.

While these principles have their most obvious application in clinical settings, they can also be adapted to and incorporated into programmes in other settings. Nevertheless, two settings where there is great potential for delivering brief, but nevertheless, personalised programmes, supported by self-help materials focused on a range of health behaviours, are the primary health care setting (Oldenburg, Gomel & Graham-Clarke, 1992) and the workplace (Gomel et al., 1993). In both these settings it is possible to not only intervene in a systematic fashion with individuals and groups, but also to use environmental approaches to support, encourage and maintain change. The worksite, in particular, offers exciting opportunities with respect to linking smoking policies and restrictions with cessation programs (e.g. Borland et al., 1990).

MATCHING STRATEGIES TO THE STAGES OF CHANGE

There is increasing evidence that matching an individual's or target group's stage of change with particular intervention strategies can lead to improved results (Oldenburg and Pope, 1990). For example, Ockene, Ockene and Kristellar (1988) showed that an intensive action- and maintenance-oriented programme directed at helping cardiac patients to quit smoking was very successful for those patients who were either in action or preparing for action; however, the programme was ineffective with those individuals who were at the earlier stages of precontemplation and contemplation. The same result was found when pregnant women attending a United States Health Maintenance Organization who were offered a self-help smoking cessation programme (Ershoff, Mullen & Quinn, 1987).

Based on Prochaska and DiClemente's stages of change formulation and other similar models of change, Brownell et al., (1986) have suggested that an individual's achievement of long-term lifestyle change is accomplished in three basic stages. Stage I involves motivating, preparing and advising the person to change (the Preparation stage). Stage II (the Action stage) involves the initial lifestyle change efforts. Stage III (the Maintenance stage) is characterised by attempts to help the person consolidate initial changes and build upon these in the longer term. There have been several attempts in recent years to formulate programmes according to these three stages. For example, Gomel et al. (submitted) have reported on the successful development and implementation of such a three-stage program for intervening in cardiovascular disease risk factors with emergency services workers. Southard et al., (1992) have proposed the use of such a model for increasing the effectiveness of the US National Cholesterol Education Program. Graham-Clarke, et al. (submitted) have developed and evaluated such a programme to be used by physicians in primary health care settings for assisting their patients to quit smoking, change dietary behaviours and increase physical activity.

The following discussion highlights the types of strategies and approaches which are likely to be most useful in moving individuals through the stages of change.

The Preparation stage

Aside from assuring a proper diagnosis and course of treatment, if that is necessary, health professionals can enhance the movement of individuals through this first stage into the Action stage. As already suggested, there is evidence that self-instructional materials and even the mass media, can help shift individuals along this continuum; the evidence for smoking cessation is compelling (e.g. Pierce, Macaskill & Hill, 1989) and for physical activity, the evidence is accumulating (e.g. Booth et al. 1992).

It goes without saying that there is no completely validated model of the factors which influence behaviour, and more particularly, lifestyle change. However, the Health Belief Model as originally proposed by Rosenstock and modified by Becker and Maiman (1975), provides a very useful framework for conceptualising the preparatory stage of lifestyle change. According to this model, individuals' perceptions of their susceptibility or vulnerability to an illness such as cardiovascular disease, the perceived consequences of not taking any action and their weighing up of the potential benefits and risks associated with taking action, are all important elements which will determine individuals' motivation and preparedness to take action. Health professionals are often able to influence the decision-making process and help people weigh up the "pros" and "cons" of making significant lifestyle change. It is important to bear in mind, however, that this is much more complex than merely considering the likely reduction in disease risk that would occur following a significant lifestyle change, such as stopping smoking. This discussion should be personalised and relevant to the group being targeted, bearing in mind that the more salient benefits, for example, for a young woman stopping smoking, are likely to be short-term ones, such as increased social approval and more money to spend on other valued activities, rather than the longer-term benefits, such as a reduced risk of having a heart attack. On the other hand, for such an individual attempting to quit smoking, there will undoubtedly be some "costs"; for example, many women will be concerned about gaining weight following smoking cessation. Ockene et al. (1988) discuss this issue in detail and Oldenburg et al., (1992) summarize the benefits and costs associated with smoking and weight loss.

Of course, a person's motivation to change is influenced by many other factors, including what Becker and Maiman (1980) have called "cues to action". These can be many and varied, but in the clinical setting, might include, other concurrent symptoms a person has, illness in other family members or friends, information being disseminated through the media, social influences and so on. Moreover, there are many other models of behaviour and influencing behaviour, in addition to those which have been discussed in this paper, which can be used to guide the development of effective intervention approaches and strategies (e.g. McGuire, 1991; Weinstein, 1980); most of these are discussed and reviewed in Glanz, Lewis and Rimer (1990).

Health professionals often have contact with people during times when they are most amenable to shifting from the Precontemplation to Contemplation stages and also, from the Contemplation to Action stages. These factors are relevant, not just simply as "cues for action", but in a much more general way. It is hardly very surprising that the complex interrelationships between people's behaviour and their social environment, can act as both enhancers and impediments to changing lifestyle. Social Learning Theory, as articulated by Bandura (1977), provides one model for characterising these interactions.

This model posits that behaviour is regulated by the consequences of behaviour, as these are interpreted by the individual. More than this, however, this theory poses that behaviour is also determined by "expectancies", which are influenced, in turn, by beliefs about the relationship between behaviour and the environment, beliefs about how actions affect particular outcomes, and whether we believe that we are competent to perform the behaviour required to achieve a given outcome. Bandura has labelled this latter construct as an individual's "self-efficacy". Social learning theory can help us understand, not only the habitual component of behaviour and why it can be so very difficult for people to change ingrained patterns of behaviour, but also that self-efficacy is a very important prerequisite for change.

It follows from this discussion of factors which have a bearing on this first stage of the lifestyle change process, that strategies which are directed at increasing a target group's or individual's level of motivation and self-efficacy, are are likely to be important. While ensuring that a person's knowledge base is adequate and that the attitude to change is positive, it is clear from almost 30 years' research in health education, that these are necessary, but not sufficient, for change to occur (Bettinghaus, 1986). Nevertheless, helping more people to understand the importance of lifestyle change by providing some high-quality educational materials, encouraging individuals to monitor their lifestyle or part of it, so they can gain a greater understanding of the lifestyle issues to be addressed, identifying barriers and enhancers to change, are all strategies which will all increase the likelihood that more individuals will move from Precontemplation to Contemplation and beyond.

The challenge in the Action stage of any lifestyle change programme to provide individuals with the skills and the resources that they require to initiate changes and then maintain and build upon these in the longer term.

The Action stage

Health professionals' efforts at lifestyle change are probably best directed at helping those individuals who are already motivated to increase their ability to change. Conversely, the mass media and other community-wide approaches can be effective in shifting large sections of the population into the Action stage and beyond. Perceived ability to change, or self-efficacy, has been shown to be a very good predictor of achieving success in many different lifestyle areas, including smoking cessation, weight control and becoming physically active (Strecher et al. 1986). The principles underlying effective action during this stage have already been outlined and the range of strategies available have been outlined recently by Oldenburg, Gomel and Graham-Clarke (1992) and Southard et al. (1992), and in numerous health psychology and behavioural textbooks (Ockene and Ockene, 1992, Taylor, 1991).

In summary, these self-management strategies can include goal-setting, a whole range of strategies aimed at modifying the environment and strategies at providing people with skills which they can then use to develop a new lifestyle. Most importantly, a host of other cognitive and social elements can influence whether an individual can move beyond this stage of change. A healthier lifestyle for most people is a means to an end and not an end in itself. People often initiate a lifestyle change attempt for quite idiosyncratic reasons and with these reasons can go a large number of unrealistic or irrational beliefs. These can include beliefs about how quickly success is likely to occur and that any setback will inevitably lead to total failure. It is appropriate for health professionals to discuss and challenge these beliefs, as it is often these distorted perceptions of behaviour which, in turn, lead to failure.

As is clear from the earlier discussion regarding the relative effectiveness of different approaches for smoking cessation, most studies of lifestyle change programme in clinical settings have utilized multicomponent interventions. However, greater gains may be made, in both programme the reach and exposure, by examining how various media and the use of technology can enhance those, oven where health professionals are having direct contact with individuals, not all of these contacts have to involve face-to-face sessions. Innovative use of well-produced and targeted printed and audio-visual materials, use of the telephone and, perhaps in the future, use of computers, can all be employed.

The Maintenance stage

So far, this article has conceptualised the lifestyle change process and outlined some of the steps involved in getting the change process under way and some of the strategies which are likely to help people experience some initial success. Long-term maintenance is the most difficult and often the most neglected aspect of the lifestyle change process. Although many lifestyle intervention studies show short-term changes, recidivism is a problem which afflicts the majority of lifestyle change programme.

Farquhar (1978) suggested a number of years ago that maintenance of lifestyle change simply involves ongoing use of the same motivation-enhancing and behaviour change strategies which are used during the Preparation and Action phases. This requires therefore, the ongoing use of self-management strategies and periodic review of the original goals and targets of the programme. These can then be modified and further developed accordingly. We now know that, while in some instances, this approach as outlined by Farquhar might be sufficient, most people will experience more difficulties than are assumed by this approach.

In recent years, we have come to understand more clearly, the distinction between the Action and Maintenance stages of change. While we now have a variety of lifestyle change programmes which address a broad range of health-related behaviours that result in short-term changes in areas as diverse as smoking cessation, dietary change and increasing physical activity, very few programmes have demonstrated consistent long-term changes.

The work of Marlatt and Gordon (1985) has demonstrated the downward spiral into relapse and eventual programme failure which often follows on from a minor "slip" or relapse episode. Marlatt and Gordon have gone on to develop a method of promoting maintenance, called relapse prevention training, during which individuals are taught to distinguish between a "slip" and a "relapse". Individuals are also taught to preempt such slips and to develop coping and other strategies for dealing with them before they arise; and indeed, such strategies can be built into the Action phase of the programme. Unfortunately, the enthusiasm with which this model was met in the literature by many, including Glasgow and Lichtenstein (1987), has not been supported by the research evidence. Studies by Curry et al., (1988) and others have typically produced no differences between conditions. In any case, such approaches, although of great interest from a research perspective, can be very time-intensive and expensive and are probably never likely to be shown to be cost-effective in clinical, worksite and other community settings (Lichtenstein and Glasgow, 1992).

So the challenge again becomes one of identifying other strategies or approaches which can be used to maintain contact with people over time and maintain programme exposure. Ongoing contact with a health professional, but probably at a reduced frequency, over a long period of time, for monitoring, feedback and revision is one possibility, but this is also difficult to achieve in practice. Peer-directed or professionally directed support groups can provide continuing opportunities for education and social networking outside of the clinical setting; there is evidence, for example, that such groups can take over and conduct smoking cessation programmes quite successfully (Lando, McGovern & Sipfle, 1989). And again, the media has a very important role to play in supporting and maintaining a climate of change as part of a community-wide or national attempt to encourage change (Redman, Spencer & Sanson-Fisher, 1990).

CONCLUDING COMMENTS

As is clear from many of the issues discussed in this paper, developing and implementing effective lifestyle strategies in key clinical settings, let alone the wider community, is no easy task. Although most of the discussion so far, has focused on the difficulties associated with engaging individuals in the change process and continuing to prompt them to move through the stages of change, it is also difficult to engage health professionals in the process. There are substantial barriers within the system and confronting health professionals that make the task of health promotion and disease prevention problematic. Nevertheless, it is important to bear in mind the conclusions reached by Green, Wilson and Lovato (1986) following their examination of the means by which health education, together with related organisational, economic and environmental supports and interventions, have resulted in improved health. They argued that changes in health-related behaviours such as smoking, diet, exercise and some safety practices, which have resulted, at least in part, from "the health promotion movement" as indicated by changed practices of health professionals, increased public and private sector investment and so on, are more durable than first appears and that experimental studies present an overly negative view of the real state of affairs.

This article has emphasized a public health perspective in order to increase the reach of health psychology. The clinical paradigm which has been used in the past to develop efficacious intensive, practitioner-delivered lifestyle change interventions, needs to be integrated within a broader public health approach. This integrated approach involves consideration of the whole spectrum of environmental factors which influence the development and changing of health behaviours. This social ecological view of health considers the lifestyle of individuals in the context of the dynamic interrelationships between individuals and their social and physical environment. Such a view emphasises the linkages between the whole range of individually focused, small-group, organisational, and community-wide approaches.

Stokols (1992) argues that multifaceted interventions that incorporate complementary behavioural and environmental components, spanning a variety of settings and at multiple levels, are more likely to be effective in promoting both personal and public health than more traditional approaches. However, it has also been argued that change strategies also need to take account of the stages of change and an individual's or target group's preparedness to change. In the coming years, many of the lessons which have been derived from research into smoking cessation and dietary change, will undoubtedly also be applied to nationally and regionally coordinated attempts to influence changes in other health behaviours which are very prevalent in Western countries, such as a sedentary lifestyle, unsafe sexual practices, a lack of safety behaviours and a lack of sun protective behaviours.

ACKNOWLEDGEMENTS

The author is grateful to both Peita Graham-Clarke and Penny Mitchell for their contribution to earlier drafts of this manuscript.

REFERENCES

Archea, J. C. (1985). Environmental factors associated with staircase accidents by the elderly. *Clinics in Geriatric Medicine*, 1, 555–569.

Baille, A., Mattick, R.P. & Webster, P. (1990). Review of published outcome literature on smoking cessation: preparatory readings for the Quality Assurance Project Smoking Cessation Expert Committee. National Campaign against Drug Abuse, National Drug and Alcohol Research Centre, Working Paper No. 1. Sydney, Australia: University of NSW.

Bandura, A. (1977). Self efficacy: toward a unifying theory of behavior change. *Psychological Review*, 84, 191–215.

Becker, M. H. (1985). Patient adherence to prescribed therapy. *Medical Care*, 23, 539–555.

Becker, M. H. & Maiman, L. A. (1975). Socio-behavioural determinants of compliance with health and medical care: recommendations. *Medical Care*, 13, 10–24

Becker, M. H. & Maiman, L. A. (1980). Strategies for enhancing patient compliance. *Journal of Community Health*, 6, 113–135.

Beitman, B. D. (1986). *The stucture of individual psychotherapy*. New York: Guilford Press.

Belloc, N. B. & Breslow, L. (1972). Relationship of physical health status and health practices. *Preventive Medicine*, 1, 409–412.

Bettinghaus, E. P. (1986). Health promotion and the knowledge–attitude–behavior continuum. *Preventive Medicine*, 15, 475–491.

Blackwell, B. (1973). Patient compliance. *New England Journal of Medicine*, 289, 249–253.

Booth, M. L., Bauman, A., Oldenburg, B., Owen, N. & Magnus, P. (1992). Effects of a national mass media campaign on physical activity participation. *Health Promotion International*, 7, 241–247.

Booth, M. L., Macaskill, P., Owen, N., Oldenburg, B., Marcus, B. H. & Bauman, A. (in press). Population prevalence and correlates of stages of change in physical activity. *Health Education Quarterly*.

Borland, R., Chapman, S., Owen, N. & Hill, D. J. (1990). Effects of workplace smoking bans on cigarette consumption. *American Journal of Public Health*, 80, 178–180.

Brown, L., Marlatt, G. A., Lichtenstein, E. & Wilson, G. T. (1986). Understanding and preventing relapse. *American Psychologist*, 41, 765–782.

Brownell, K. D., Marlatt, G. A., Lichtenstein, E. R. & Wilson, G. T. (1986). Understanding and preventing relapse. *American Psychologist*, 41, 765–782.

Bruhn, J. G. (1988). Life-style and health behavior. In: Gochman, D. F. (Ed), *Health Behavior: Emerging research perspectives* (pp. 71–84). New York: Plenum Press.

Carmody, T., Senner, J., Mailinow, M. & Matarazzo, J. (1980). Physical exercise for rehabilitation: Long-term dropout rate in cardiac patients. *Journal Behavioral Medicine*, 3, 163–168.

Cashdan, S. (1973). *Interactional psychotherapy: stages and strategies in behavioural change*. New York: Grune & Stratton.

Centres for Disease Control (1980). *Ten leading causes of death in the United States, 1977*. Washington, DC: US Government Printing Office.

Cohen, S., Lichenstein, E., Prochaska, J. O., Rossi, J. S., Gritz, C. R., & Carr, C. R. (1989). Debunking myths about self-quitting: evidence from ten prospective studies of persons quitting smoking by themselves. *American Psychologist*, 44, 1355–1365.

Copeman, R. C., Swannell, R. J., Pincus, D. F. & Woodland, K. A. (1989). Utilisation of the "Smokescreen" smoking-cessation program by general practitioners and their patients. *Medical Journal of Australia*, 151, 83–87.

Curry, S., Marlatt, G. A., Gordon, J. & Baer, S. (1988). A comparison of alternative theoretical approaches to smoking cessation and relapse. *Health Psychology*, 7, 545–556.

Davis, M. S., (1968). Physiologic, psychological and demographic factors in patients' compliance of doctors orders. *Medical Care*, 6, 115–122.

Department of Health (1992). *The health of the nation: a strategy for health in England*. London: Her Majesty's Stationery Office.

DiClemence, C. C. & Prochaska, J. O. (1985). Processes and stages of change: coping and competence in smoking behavior change. In: S. Shiffman & T. A. Wills (Eds), *Coping and substance abuse* (pp. 319–343). San Diego, CA: Academic Press.

DiClemente, C. C., Prochaska, J. O., Fairhurst, S. K., Velicer, W. F., Velasquez, M. M. & Rossi, J. S. (1991). The process of smoking cessation: An analysis of pre-contemplation, contemplation and preparation stages of change. *Journals of Consulting and Clinical Psychology*, 59, 295–304.

Doll, R. & Hill, A. B. (1964). Mortality in relation to smoking: 10 years' observations of British doctors. *British Medical Journal*, i, 1399–1410; 1460–1462.

Donovan, D. M. & Marlatt, J. A. (Ed) (1988). *Assessment of addictive behaviors: behavioral, cognitive and physiological procedures*. New York: Guilford Press.

Dunbar, J. & Stunkard, A. J. (1979). Adherence to diet and drug regimen. In: Levi, R., Rifkind, B., 000.

Dryden, W. (1986). Electric psychotherapies: a critique of leading approaches. In: J. C. Norcross (Ed), *Handbook of electric psychostherapy*. New York: Brunner/Mazel.

Egan, G. (1975). *The skilled helper: a model for systematic helping and interpersonal relating*. CA: Brooks/Cole.

Ershoff, D. H., Mullen, B. D. & Quinn, V. (1987). **Self-help interventions for smoking cessation with pregnant women.** Paper presented at the Self-help Intervention Workshop of the National Cancer Institute, Rockville, MD.

Farquhar, J. W. (1978). *The American way of life need not be hazardous to your health*. New York: W. W. Norton.

Farquhar, J. W. & Maccoby, N. (1977). Community education for cardiovascular health, *Lancet*, 1, 192–195.

Farquhar, J. W., Fortmann, S. P., Flora, J. A., et al. (1990). Effects of community-wide education on cardiovascular risk factors: the Stanford Five-City Project. *Journal of the American Medical Association*, 264, 359–365.

Glanz, K, Lewis, F. M & Rimer, B. K. (Eds). (1990) *Health behavior and health education: theory, research and practice*. San Francisco: Jossey-Bass.

Glasgow, R. E. & Lichtenstein, E. (1987), Long-term efects of behavioural smoking cessation interventions, **Behaviour Therapy**, 18, 297–324.

Glasgow, R. E. & Rosen, G. M. (1978). Behavioural bibliotherapy: a review of self-help behavior therapy manuals. *Psychological Bulletin*, 8, 1–23.

Glynn, T. J., Boyd, G. N. & Gruman, J. C. (1990). Essential elements of self-help/

minimal intervention strategies for smoking cessation. *Health Education Quarterly*, 17, 329–345.

Gochman, D. F. (1988). *Health behavior; emerging research perspectives*. New York: Plenum Press.

Gomel, M, Oldenburg, B. Simpson, J. & Owen, N. (1993). Worksite cardiovascular risk reduction: randomised trial of health risk assessment, risk factor education, behavioral counseling and incentive strategies. *American Journal of Public Health*, 83, 1231–1238.

Gordon, T. & Kannel, W. B. (1975). Multiple contributors to coronary risk implications for screening and prevention. *Journal of Chronic Diseases*, 25, 561–565.

Graham-Clarke, P., Walker, S., Oldenburg, B., Lee, A., Mills, A. & Shaw, J. (submitted) A process evaluation of General Practioner use of a program for the management of CVD risk factors.

Green, L. W. & Kreuter, M. W. (1990). Health promotion as a public health strategy for the 1990s. *Annual Review of Public Health*, 11, 319–334.

Green, L. W. & Kreuter, M. W. (1991). *Health promotion planning: an educational and environmental approach*. London: Mayfield.

Green, L. W. Wilson, A. L. & Lovato, C. Y. (1986). What changes can health promotion achieve and how long do these changes last? The trade-offs between expediency and durability. *Preventive Medicine*, 15, 508–521.

Gritz, E. R., Berman, B. A., Bastani, R. & Wa, M. (1992). A randomized trial of a self-help smoking cessation intervention in a non-volunteer female population: testing the limits of the Public Health Model. *Health Psychology*, 11, 280–289.

Hetzel, B. & McMichael, T. (1987). *The LS factor: lifestyle and health*. New York: Penguin.

Hockbaum, G. M., Sorenson, J. R. & Lorig, K. (1992). Theory in health education practice. *Health Education Quarterly*, 19, 295–313.

Horn, D. & Waingrow, S. (1966). Some dimensions of a model for smoking behaviour change. *American Journal of Public Health*, 56, 21–26.

Hunt, W. A. & Bespalec, D. A. (1974). An evaluation of current methods of identifying smoking behaviour. *Journal of Clinical Psychology*, 34, 431–438.

Kannel, W. B. & Gordon, T. (1968). *An epidemiological investigation of cardiovascular disease: the Franmingham Study*. Washington DC: US Department of Health Education and Welfare.

Karasek, R. & Theorell, T. (1990) *Healthy work: stress productivity, and the reconstruction of working life*. New York: Basic Books.

Kottke, T. E., Battista, R. N. DeFriese, G. H. & Brekke, M. L. (1988). Attributes of successful smoking cessation interventions in medical practice: a meta-analysis of 39 controlled trials. *Journal of the American Medical Association*, 259, 2883–2889.

Lado, H. A., McGovern, P. G. & Sifle, C. (1989). Public service application of an effective clinic approach to smoking cessation. *Health Education Research*, 4, 103–109.

Lalonde, M. (1974). *A new perspective on the health of Canadians: a working document*. Ottawa: Government of Canada.

Lefebvre, R. C., Lasater, T. M., Carleton, R. A. & Peterson, G. (1987). Theory and delivery of health programming in the community: the Pawtucket Health Health Program. *Preventive Medicine*, 16, 95.

Lichtenstein, E. R. & Glasgow, R. E. (1992). Smoking cessation: What have we learned over the past decade? *Journal of Consulting and Clinical Psychology*, 65, 518–527.

McGuire, W. J. (1991). Using guiding-idea theories of the person to develop educational campaigns against drug abuse and health related behavior. *Health Education Research*, 6, 173–184.

Marlatt, G. A. & Gordon, J. R. (1985). *Relapse prevention: a self-control strategy for the maintenance of behaviour change.* New York: Guilford Press.

Mittelmark, M. B., Luepker, R. V. & Jacobs, D. R. (1986), Community-wide prevention: education strategies of the Minnesota Heart Health Program. *Preventive Medicine,* 15, 1–17.

Nutbeam, D., Wise, M. Bauman, A., Harris, E. & Leeder, S. (1993). *Goals and targets for Australia's health in the year 2000 and beyond.* Sydney: Department of Public Health, University of Sydney.

Ockene, J. K. (1992). Are we pushing the limits of public health interventions for smoking cessation? *Health Psychology,* 11, 277–279.

Ockene, J. & Ockene, I. (Eds) (1992). *Preventing Coronary Heart Disease.* New York: Little, Brown.

Ockene, J. K. Sorensen, G., Kabat-Zinn, J., Ockene, I. S. et al. (1988). Benefits and costs of lifestyle change to reduce risk of chronic disease. *Preventive Medicine,* 17, 224–234.

Ockene, J., Ockene, I., & Kristella, J. (1988). *The Coronary Artery Smoking Intervention Study,* Worcester, MA: National Heart Lung Blood Institute.

Odenburg, B. & Pope, J. (1990). A critical review of determinants of smoking cessation. *Behaviour Change,* 7, 101–109.

Oldenburg, B. Gomel, M. & Grahame-Clarke, P. (1992). Cardiovascular risk reduction risk reduction through lifestyle change in clinical settings. *Annals, Academy of Medicine,* 21, 114–120.

Oldenburg, B. Owen, N. Gomel, M. & Grahame-Clarke, P. (1992). Lifestyle change and cardiovascular disease: evidence and issues. *Australian Family Physician,* 21, 1137–1144.

Ontarion Premier's Council on Health: Panel on health goals for Ontario (1987). *Health for all Ontarians: Report of the Panel on Health Goals for Ontario.* Ottawa: Ottawa Government Printing.

Orford, J. (1985). *Excessive appetites: a psychological view of addictions.* New York: Wiley.

Pierce, J. P., Macaskill, P. & Hill, D. (1989). Long-term effectiveness of mass media led Anti-smoking campaigns in Australia. *American Journal of Public Health,* 80, 565–569.

Prochaska, J. O. & DiClemente, C. C. (1986). Toward a comprehensive model of change. In: W. R. Miller & N. Heather (Eds), *Treating addictive behaviors: Processes of change* (pp. 3–27). New York: Plenum Press.

Prochaska, J.O. & DiClemente, C. C. (1992). Stages of change and the modification of problem behaviors. In: M. Hersen, R. M. Eisler & P. M. Miller (Eds), *Progress in Behaviour Modification.* Sycamore: Sycamore Press.

Prochaska, J. O. DiClemente, C. C. & Norcross, J. C. (1992). In search of how people change: applications to addictive behaviors. *American psychologist,* 47, 1102–1114.

Puska, P., Nissinen, A., Tuomilehto, J. et al. (1985). The community-based strategy to prevent coronary heart disease: conclusions from the ten years of the North Karelia Project. *Annual Review of Public Health,* 6, 147–193.

Raymond, J. F. (1989). Behavioural epidemiology: the science of health promotion. *Health Promotion,* 4, 281–286.

Redman, S., Spencer, E. A. & Sanson-Fisher, R. W. (1990). The role of mass media in changing health-related behaviour: a critical appraisal of two methods. *Health Promotion International,* 5, 85–101.

Richmond, R., Austin, A. & Webster, I. (1986). Three year evaluation of a program by general practitioners to help patients to stop smoking, *British Medical Journal,* 292, 803–806.

Roizen, R., Cahaland, D. & Shanks, R. (1978). Spontaneous remission among untreated problem drinkers. In: D. Randell (Ed), *Longitudinal research on drug use: empirical findings and methodological* issues. Washington, DC: Hemisphere.

Sallis, J. F. & Nader, P. R. (1988). Family determinants of health behaviours. In: Gochman, D. S. (ed). *Health Behaviour: Emerging Research Perspectives* (pp. 107–119). New York: Plenum Press.

Schachter, S. (1982). Recidivisim and self-cure of smoking and obesity. *American Psychologist*, 37, 436–444.

Simmons-Morton, D. J. Mullen, P. D. Mains, D. A. Tabak, E. R. & Green, L. W. (1992). Characteristics of controlled studies of patient education and counselling for preventive health behaviours. *Patient Education and Counselling*, 19, 175–204.

Southard, D. R Winett, R. A, Walberg-Rankin, J. L., Neubauer, T. E., Donckers-Roseveare, K. D, Burkett, P. A, et al. (1992). Increasing the effectiveness of the National Cholesterol Education Program: dietary and behavioral interventions for clinical settings. *Annals of Behavioral Medecine*, 14, 21–30.

Stimson, G. V., (1974). Obeying doctors orders: a view from the other side. *Social Science and Medicine*, 47, 6–22.

Stokols, D. (1992). Establishing and maintaining healthy environments: toward a social ecology of health promotion. *American Psychologist*, 47, 6–22.

Strecher, V. J., De Vellis, B. E., Becker, M. H. & Rosenstock, I. M. (1986) the role of self-efficacy in achieving health behaviour change. *Health Education Quarterly*, 13, 73–91.

Taylor, S. (1991). *Health psychology*: New York: McGraw-Hill.

The Expert Panel (1988). Report of the National Cholesterol Education Program Expert Panel on detection, evaluation and treatment of high blood cholesterol in adults. *Archives of Internal Medicine*, 148, 36–39.

The Expert Panel (1989). *Report of the Expert Panel on Detection, Evaluation and Treatment of Blood Cholesterol in Adults*. Washington, D C: US Government Printing Office.

Tuchfeld, B. (1981). Spontaneous remission in alcoholics: empirical observations and theoretical implications. *Journal of Studies on Alcohol*, 42, 626–641.

United States Surgeon General's Advisory Committee (1964). *Smoking and Health*. Washington: US Department of Health.

US Department of Health and Human Services (1990). *Healthy People 2000*. Washington D C: Office of Disease Prevention and Health Promotion, US Department of Health and Human Services.

US Preventive Services Task Force. (1989) *Guide to Clinical Preventive Services. An assessment of the effectiveness of 169 interventions*. London: Williams & Wilkins.

Vogt, T. M, Lichtenstein, E., Ary, D., Briglan, A., Danielson, R., Glasgow, R. E. et al. (1989). Integrating tobacco intervention into a health maintenance organisation: the TRACC Program. *Health Education Research*, 4, 125–135.

Weinstein, N. D. (1980). Unrealistic optimism about susceptibility to health problems. *Journal of Behavioral Medicine*, 5, 441–460.

WHO Expert Committee (1982). **Prevention of coronary heart disease**. World Health Organization Technical Report Series 678. Geneva: World Health Organization.

Winett, R. A., King, A. C. & Altman, D. G. (1989). *Health psychology and public health: an integrated approach*. New York: Pergamon Press.

World Health Organization (1986). The Ottawa Charter for Health Promotion. *Health Promotion International*, 1(4), iii–v.

6 The Prevention of Suicidal Behaviour: A Review of Effectiveness

RENÉ F. W. DIEKSTRA, AD J. F. M. KERKHOF
Department of Clinical and Health Psychology University of Leiden, Postbus 9555, 2300 RB Leiden, The Netherlands

INTRODUCTION

Suicidal behaviour constitutes a serious social and health problem. It puts a considerable drain on resources in both primary and secondary health care. Suicide is in many countries of the world among the eight leading causes of death for the general population, and among the three leading causes of death for young people aged 15 to 24 (World Health Organization, 1989). Suicide concerns 1 to 3% of all deaths in countries reporting to the World Health Organization. The number of suicide attempts treated in medical settings has increased considerably in the last decades (Diekstra, 1989; Platt et al., 1992). Any large inner city hospital in the Western world is likely to treat hundreds of suicide attempters a year, especially in emergency wards. The mean suicide attempt rate in 14 European centres was found to be 167 per 100 000 males and 222 per 100 000 females aged 15 years and over (Platt et al., 1992). The economic resources that are involved in health care are clearly enormous.

One would have expected the development of programmes for intervention and prevention of suicidal behaviour to have been assigned an important public health priority. This, however, is not the case. There is probably only one country in the world with a national suicide prevention programme: Finland. There are only a few countries in which there is an active interest in suicide prevention on the part of governments. However, there is variety of programmes on regional and local community levels in many countries. Traditionally these activities rely heavily on volunteer organizations, cooperating with health professionals and human services personnel (teachers, police). Some of those programmes date back to the beginning of this century when social concern for the "victims of the industrial society" was growing. It was some sixty years before federal and national governments hesitantly came to take an interest in the suicide problem and started to provide funds for preventive activities.

International Review of Health Psychology, Volume 3. Edited by S. Maes, H. Leventhal and M. Johnston
© 1994 John Wiley & Sons Ltd

Consequently, although there is a rich and scholarly uliterature on sociological, psychological and biological aspects of suicide, there is a scarcity of studies on the development and evaluation of programmes for treatment and prevention. As will become clear from the remainder of this paper, from a scientific point of view the prevention of suicidal behaviour is still in its infancy.

PREVENTION, INTERVENTION AND AFTERCARE

Prevention of suicide at the primary level is aimed at persons who are currently not feeling or manifesting any suicidal tendency, with a view to decreasing the risk that such a tendency will afflict them in the future. This could be accomplished by eliminating or alleviating circumstances that may promote distress and suicidal behaviour, such as mental disorder, unemployment, prejudice, and isolation. Prevention at this level is slow to take effect because it demands societal changes, or changes in behaviour of large social groups, a notoriously gradual occurrence at best. As far as we know, there is not one single study in the literature describing and evaluating a primary prevention programme that deals specifically with suicidal behaviour. The only possible exception can be made for so-called school-based suicide prevention programmes. Some of these programmes address the whole school community, but others are exclusively geared towards the detection and management of students with severe emotional problems or suicidal crises. We will describe and discuss school-based programmes as a separate category.

Most preventive efforts have been aimed at the secondary or intervention level, after suicidal tendencies or conditions that carry a high risk for such tendencies have become apparent. One often-employed method is the crisis intervention centre or suicide prevention centre telephone service or 24-hour "lifelines" or "hotlines" for those who are suicidal or in despair. Once suicidal tendencies have become manifest as ideation, depressive symptomatology or a non-fatal suicide attempt, medical, psychological and social interventions may be employed followed by some form of therapy to alleviate the circumstances and problems leading to the suicidal crisis. Over the last 30 years a considerable number of studies have been published in which such interventions and their effects on subsequent suicidal behaviour are described.

Another type of preventive measure includes the restriction of easy access to lethal methods for suicide, such as the switch from coal gas to natural gas, gun control, and restriction of dosage and type of medication. Most of these measures, however, have occurred for reasons other than preventing suicide.

Aftercare or "after the fact" prevention refers to efforts to aid those who remain following the suicide of a family member, partner or friend and who are often deeply affected by the death. Preventive measures at this level have only recently received attention and no systematic studies evaluating such measures are available.

SCHOOL-BASED PROGRAMMES

A new approach to suicide prevention that has received a great deal of attention involves curriculum-based prevention or education programmes. This approach has recently been critically reviewed by Garland and Zigler (1993). According to these authors the number of such programmes introduced into schools in the USA after 1984 continues to grow (Garland et al., 1989). Outside the USA there are only a few other countries where such programmes have been developed, such as the Netherlands (Mulder et al., 1989) and Canada (Dyck, in press). These programmes have been described in detail elsewhere (Diekstra & Hawton, 1987; Garland & Shaffer, 1990; Ross, 1980; Shaffer et al., 1988). The main goals (see Garland & Zigler, 1993) are:

- To raise awareness of the problem of adolescent suicide;
- To train participants to identify adolescents at risk for suicide;
- To educate participants about community mental health resources and referral techniques; and
- To prevent suicidal behaviour later in the lifespan.

The programmes are presented by mental health professionals or educators and are most commonly aimed at secondary school students, their parents, and teachers.

The contents of a typical suicide prevention programme for students include:

- A review of epidemiology of (adolescent) suicide;
- A list of "warning signs" of suicide, usually emphasizing symptoms of depression;
- A list of community mental health resources and how to access them;
- A discussion of skills for referring a student or peer to counselling, stressing concerns about confidentiality; and
- Training in contact-making and referral skills.

A number of programmes also include a training in communication skills, problem-solving skills and/or stress management.

While specific methods and contents vary across programmes, the theoretical model guiding them is consistent. Virtually all of the suicide prevention programmes employ a stress model of suicide, as opposed to a mental illness model (Garland et al., 1989). Suicide is presented as a reaction to extreme psychosocial or interpersonal stress and the link to mental illness is strongly denied, or at least underemphasized. The curricula often explicitly state that people who commit suicide are not mentally ill and that everyone is vulnerable to suicidal behaviour. The rationale behind this approach is that the de-stigmatization of suicide will encourage students who are feeling suicidal to identify themselves and to seek help.

In reviewing over 300 prevention programmes of various types (not just suicide prevention), Price et al. (1989) concluded that the most effective programmes are based on a sound foundation of empirical knowledge. That knowledge should include a clear understanding of the risks and problems confronting the target population. Another essential element is the collection of data to inform planners how well the programme achieves its goals or how it can be modified to do so. Unfortunately, many suicide prevention programmes have fallen short on one or both of these requirements.

Some curriculum-based programmes are not founded on current empirical knowledge of the risk factors of adolescent suicide. By de-emphasizing or denying the fact that many adolescents who commit suicide are mentally ill, these programmes misrepresent the facts. As we have discussed earlier, a considerable number of youth suicides have diagnosable psychiatric illnesses (see also Pardes & Blumenthal, 1990).

In their attempt to "destigmatize" suicide some school-based suicide prevention programmes may be, in fact, normalizing the behaviour and reducing potentially protective taboos. Suicide is sometimes portrayed as a reaction to common stresses of adolescence, namely problems with parents and teachers, problems with relationships, performance anxiety, and peer pressure. The emphasis on the role of stressful experiences, however, is more appropriate with regard to parasuicide than to suicide. Many curriculum-based programmes, therefore, are actually more geared towards non-fatal suicidal behaviour and less or even hardly towards fatal suicidal behaviour.

Also, the incidence of adolescent suicide is sometimes exaggerated in suicide prevention programmes since one of their goals is to increase awareness and concern about the problem. This exaggeration seems unnecessary in that surveys of teenagers indicate that they are certainly aware of the problem (The Gallup Organization, Inc., 1991; Kalafat & Elias, 1992). The danger of exaggeration is that students may perceive suicide as a more common and, therefore, more acceptable act. They may also become unnecessarily anxious about the possibility of suicide in their immediate peer group.

Another problem is the common use of print or visual media to present case histories of adolescents who have attempted or committed suicide. The purpose is to teach students how to identify friends who may be at risk for suicidal behaviour. However, as we have outlined in the paragraph on correlates of adolescent suicidal behaviour, this may have a paradoxical effect. Students may closely identify with the problems portrayed by the case examples and may come to see suicide as the logical solution to their own problems. A documentary on the suicide of an adolescent broadcast twice (1981 and 1982) on television in Germany, and which was meant to educate about suicide, turned out to inspire more suicides than it prevented (Schmidtke & Haffner, 1989). In the periods following the broadcasts, the model behaviour, jumping in front of a train, was imitated in excess of what might be expected on the basis of control periods. The modelling effect was greater for young viewers than for old viewers. This study, the best empirical evidence regarding the imitation effect, shows the importance of restraint in using fictional models.

A related important observation, with regard to the effect suicide education programmes might have, is reported by Mulder (in press). This researcher shows such a programme to have a moderate effect on the attitudes towards suicide among participants, the direction of this effect being that their attitude to suicide becomes more permissive, implying that they better understand and more readily accept suicidal behaviour in others as well as themselves. This might, in fact, mean a lowering of their "suicidal threshold", at least at the cognitive level.

Finally, at the practical level, suicide prevention programmes may, as Garland & Zigler (1993) state, never reach their target population, i.e. adolescents most at risk for suicide. Incarcerated and runaway youths have extremely high rates of suicide, as do drug abusers (Memory, 1989; Stiffman, 1989). They will not be in the audience, and, even if they were, it would not be surprising if awareness programmes alone did not affect them positively. Some reports suggest that suicide victims are likely to have been absent from school prior to their suicidal act (Hawton, 1986). They also show that a substantial percentage of those who make a parasuicidal act never return to school afterwards (Diekstra et al., 1991).

Therefore, students who are regularly attending school are not the highest risk group. Programme developers might argue that the programmes are not primarily intended to address the suicidal child, but rather to encourage peers to identify and seek help for someone who may need it, including themselves in the (near) future. Nevertheless, a programme aimed at a general audience of adolescents who are not at highest risk may be inefficient.

As to effectiveness (see also Garland & Zigler, 1993), although many curriculum-based suicide prevention programmes have been operating since 1981 (Garland et al., 1989), there are only a few published evaluation studies using a control group (Nelson, 1987; Ross, 1980). Spirito et al.'s (1988) evaluation of a suicide awareness programme for ninth graders is one of the exceptions. Approximately 300 students who attended the programme were compared with about 200 students in a geographically matched control group. All students completed a battery of exercises covering suicide, hopelessness, helping behaviours, and coping skills prior to, and ten weeks after, the implementation of a six-week curriculum in their health classes.

The results indicated that the programme was minimally effective in imparting knowledge, and was ineffective in changing attitudes. Slight increases in knowledge among girls were associated with programme attendance. In another similar study by the same research group (Overholser et al., 1989) boys changed in the undesirable direction, i.e. increased hopelessness and maladaptive coping responses.

In another large, well-controlled study in New Jersey, Shaffer et al. (1991) found few positive effects of three suicide prevention curriculum programmes and some possible negative effects. A minority of students before and after expressed unfavourable attitudes such as the belief that suicide can be a good solution to problems, or that suicidal confidences from friends should never be disclosed. Programme attendance did not effect a significant change in these students' attitudes. Programme attendance was associated with a small, but significant, increase in the number of students who responded that suicide could be a possible solution to problems, a finding that converges with the one reported above from Mulder's study (Mulder, in press). Most importantly, however, there was no significant increase or reduction in self-reported suicidal ideation or suicide attempts following programme implementation.

Summarizing, there is little evidence that the programmes have the desired effect on knowledge and attitudes towards suicidal behaviour (see also Garland & Zigler, 1993) and there is some suggestive evidence that programmes may increase the percentage of students that see suicide as a possible solution to problems. There is no clear-cut evidence, whatsoever, on effects of programmes on the suicidal or help-seeking behaviour of participants.

SUICIDE PREVENTION CENTRES

Virtually all metropolitan areas, as well as many urban areas, in European countries, the United States and Canada now have at least one crisis intervention or suicide prevention centre. These centres typically provide a 24-hour hotline plus referrals to other mental health or social work agencies. In some cases they have a walk-in centre and trained volunteers who can act as "befrienders" or confidants to persons in crisis. There are also innumerable telephone emergency or crisis lines in operation that deal with problems of living in general and are therefore not specifically geared to suicidal individuals.

Shneidman and Farberow (1957, 1965) originally outlined the rationale for suicide crisis centres as follows: suicidal behaviour is often associated with a crisis situation, and the victim often experiences ambivalence about living and dying. People have a basic need for interpersonal communication which will often be expressed in a last minute "cry for help." Although crisis or suicide prevention centres may employ mental health consultants, such as trained psychiatrists, psychologists and psychotherapists as external consultants or as staff members, the actual work is usually carried out by lay persons with varying degrees of training and expertise. Traditionally the clergy has played an important role in the foundation and operation of crisis centres and this is still the case in many centres.

Although crisis or suicide hotlines were already present in several large European and Northern American cities before World War II, the spread of such services really began in the early nineteen-sixties, stimulated by the establishment of The Samaritans in London and the first Suicide Prevention Center in Los Angeles.

Suicide prevention centres are essentially equipped for secondary prevention, that is to say for early intervention with persons who carry an elevated risk for suicidal behaviour. Generally such centres do not have an active outreach; they do not systematically seek out and try to establish contact with groups in the community who can be considered high risk. It is essentially the suicidal person who has to contact the centre.

It is for that reason that studies on the efficacy of such centres have addressed two major facets of their functioning: whether centres attract persons with an elevated risk for suicidal behaviour; and whether they prevent these individuals' suicide or suicide attempt (Lester, 1974; Bridge et al., 1977; Dew et al., 1987). These facets are closely entangled, for if centres do not attract high-risk individuals, it goes without saying that they will not exert any major reducing influence on suicide rates.

In a review of studies addressing these two questions, and the only one thus far using meta-analysis as the method of reviewing, Dew and her colleagues (1987) draw the following general conclusions. First of all, centres indeed seem to attract a high-risk population: centre clients were more likely to commit suicide than were members of the general population (seven studies analysed). The average client-suicide rate ranges from 2 times higher to almost 109 times higher than the general population rate. Individuals who committed suicide were more likely to have been clients of a suicide prevention centre than were members of the general population (six studies analysed). The average annual client rate among suicides ranges from 2.5 times higher to almost 10 times higher than the client rate in the general population.

Next, the verdict on the question whether the suicide rate decreases more in communities with a suicide prevention centre than in communities without such a centre, has to remain "undetermined". Of the five studies analysed three show an effect in favour of centre effectiveness, whereas the other two do not. Combined, however, there was virtually no effect, suggesting that the centre establishment has neither a positive nor a negative overall effect on community suicide rates.

Given the fact that centres are at least somewhat successful in attracting the population they are designed to help, the question arises whether centre effectiveness should not be established within specific cohorts rather than simply across the entire population of a community. Miller, Coomts & Leeper (1984) reported data on specific cohorts. They compared 28 centre communities with 48 control communities over the period 1968–1973 and found no significant difference in the overall suicide rate change between those two groups of communities. However, the suicide rate for white women and girls under age 25 showed a large and significant decrease in communities with a centre as compared to control communities. This finding is especially important because in the United States, as well as in many other countries, young white women are the most frequent users of prevention centres and telephone emergency services.

Since this group is also characterized by a relatively very high rate of attempted suicide, the question arises whether prevention centre evaluations should focus on outcomes other than suicide, such as attempted suicide. Unfortunately, there are no studies available yet that have examined other kinds of outcome in a scientifically sound way.

In addition, suicide rates are influenced by a multitude of factors and their interactions (such as unemployment rate, divorce rate, drug/alcohol (ab)use, prevalence of mental disorders, changes in age and sex composition of populations) that can obscure an effect of a suicide prevention centre in a community. None of the studies carried out thus far on the effectiveness of centres has been able to control adequately for the possible influences of those factors, one of the reasons being that it is extremely difficult, if not impossible, to obtain the necessary data on them. Furthermore there are always other agencies in the community that contribute to suicide prevention, such as psychiatric outpatient departments, privately operating psychiatrists and psychologists. This makes it difficult to filter out the effects of only one of them.

In sum, it is not possible to conclude that suicide prevention centres do prevent suicide, while at the same time it is safe to conclude that these centres indeed deal with persons who are at greater risk for suicidal behaviour. Even though the actual percentage of clients who commit suicide annually remains a small percentage of all clients seen, the corresponding suicide rates indicate that the potential for prevention of suicidal deaths by these centres is substantial.

The literature on client characteristics and effects of prevention centres is exclusively in the English Language, the only exception being the Danish study by Nielsen and Videbech (1973). It therefore remains to be seen whether the potential role with regard to suicide prevention applies to other parts of the world as well.

Finally, it is important to mention the strong conviction among the organizations that suicide prevention centres do prevent suicides. Volunteers and staff may think that they prevented someone from committing suicide. Also there are statements from individuals who say they are being prevented from suicide solely by the efforts of the centre. That does not, however, count as empirical evidence for the efficacy of these centres on the community level.

AFTERCARE PROGRAMMES FOR HOSPITAL-TREATED SUICIDE ATTEMPTERS

In the past 30 years the numbers of people treated in hospitals following a suicide attempt or parasuicidal act have increased dramatically in most countries (Diekstra, 1989). In recent times, attempted suicide and para-suicide are being defined as follows: "an act with nonfatal outcome, in which an individual deliberately initiates a non-habitual behaviour that, without intervention from others, will cause self-harm, or deliberately ingests a substance in excess of the prescribed or generally recognized therapeutic dosage, and which is aimed at realizing changes which the subject desired via the actual or expected physical consequences" (Platt et al., 1992, p. 99).

A considerable percentage of those treated in hospital after a suicidal act are "repeaters", i.e. have received hospital treatment before for the same reason. Estimates of the percentage of attempters that have made earlier attempts vary between 20% and 60%. Follow-up studies show that the risk of repetition is particularly high in the first few months after discharge from treatment or hospital: approximately 10% make another attempt within the first three months. This percentage rises to 15% after one year and to 30–40% after 10 to 15 years (Kerkhof, Diekstra & Koster, 1982; Kerkhof, 1985).

As to the outcome of subsequent attempts, there is a remarkable difference between studies published before and after 1982. From the first group of studies it emerges that approximately 1% of suicide attempters dies from the consequences of a subsequent attempt within one year after discharge. After 2 years this percentage rises to 2%, after 3 years to 3% and so forth, until it reaches approximately 10% after 10 years. Thereafter the percentage remains stable at this level.

Since 1982 a growing number of studies has been published indicating that the percentage of repeaters dying from a suicide attempt can be as high as 8 to 10% within two years after a previous attempt followed by treatment or admission in hospital (Kerkhof, Wal & Hengeveld, 1988). It remains to be seen whether this is an "acceleration" phenomenon or a reflection of a true increase in risk for suicide among suicide attempters, or an artefact caused by the use of better research methods.

Anyway, suicide attempters constitute a group with a very high risk for suicide—a rate 50 to 100 times the overall population rate—and therewith a pool from which many of the future suicides will be drawn. This raises the issue as to the possibilities for prevention of suicide by interventions specifically geared towards reducing the risk of subsequent attempts among suicide attempters in contact with medical services.

Screening of the literature reveals 18 publications reporting a systematic evaluation of the effects of special aftercare programmes for suicide attempters.

In terms of design these studies can be divided into two categories: those using a retrospective and those using a prospective design. Studies in the first category retrospectively collected data on the treatment history of suicide attempters after an index attempt and related those data to incidence of further attempts, either with a fatal or with a non-fatal outcome.

Greer and Bagley (1971) followed patients presenting at a casualty department with deliberate self-poisoning or self-injury. 204 out of 211 patients were traced after 18 months. They found that subsequent suicide attempts occurred significantly more among patients untreated than among patients treated by a psychiatrist, prolonged treatment being associated with the best prognosis. Unfortunately, the patients were not randomly allocated to the treatment or no treatment conditions, so that this finding is not truly validated.

Kennedy (1972) likewise compared three aftercare groups (admitted to the Edinburgh Regional Poisoning Treatment Centre, referred to psychiatrists elsewhere, or not referred at all). He found significant differences in further suicidal behaviour: those that were treated in the RPTC had the lowest number of subsequent attempted suicides in a follow-up period of one year (12% versus 38% and 37% in the referral and no-referral groups). But, as Kennedy himself noted, the only way of properly evaluating the effectiveness of the RPTC would be a controlled experiment with patients randomly allocated to treatment conditions, an experiment which he, and many researchers after him, considered ethically unjustified.

While retrospective studies report a relationship between more specialized psychiatric or more intensive psychosocial treatment on the one hand and lower incidence of suicidal acts on the other, suggesting a reducing effect of such treatments (Greer & Bagley, 1971; Kennedy, 1972), such results have to be taken with great caution owing to poor matching of comparison groups with regard to factors like motivation for treatment and reasons for offering treatment.

The design used in most prospective studies can be described as follows. When a patient has been admitted or treated in a hospital for the physical consequences of a suicide attempt, he or she is seen as soon as possible by a psychiatrist, a psychologist or another member of the treatment or research team in order to assess the social and mental health status as well as the suicide risk. Consequently the patient is more or less randomly assigned to one of several treatment conditions or to a control group (Chowdhury, Hicks & Kreitman, 1973; Welu & Pickard, 1974; Ettlinger, 1975; Termansen & Bywater, 1975; Oast & Zitrin, 1975; Litman & Wold, 1976; Motto, 1976; Gardner et al., 1977; Welu, 1977; Wullemier, Kremer & Bovet, 1978; Gibbons et al., 1979; Liberman & Eckman, 1981; Hawton et al., 1981, 1987; Moller, 1989; Allard, Marshall & Plante, 1992). Sometimes the control group consists of all suicide attempters seen in the year previous to the start of the experimental treatment (see Ettlinger, 1975; Wullemier, Kremer & Bovet, 1978).

Experimental conditions in most studies are either the usual minimum procedure (one or a few interviews with a psychiatrist, psychologist or social worker during admission and referral to family physician or other health care professional after discharge) or a treatment programme specially designed for suicide attempters (including regular individual or group sessions, usually on a once-a-week basis for a period of 3 to 6 months). The individual or group sessions focus mainly on helping the patients in alleviating or solving social and practical problems in their everyday lives.

After termination of the treatment there are one or several follow-up meetings, in which changes in social conditions, psychological well-being and behaviour problems are assessed, including subsequent suicidal acts.

A typical problem in this kind of study is presented by Oast and Zitrin (1975). They selected 495 patients admitted to a psychiatric ward due to suicide attempts or gestures, and randomly allocated 265 persons to the experimental treatment condition. The treatment consisted of extra after-care check-ups, intensified personal guidance, and possibly even outreach contacts in the patients' homes. It turned out that at the start, nearly half of the experimental group (48%) could not be contacted for participation in the study (15% were institutionalized at the time of the first reaching out contacts, 6% were traced to the point that they left New York City, 14% were untraceable (no address, no address of friends or relatives), in 11% of the cases it seemed appropriate to respect the patient's resistance and to discontinue active follow-up). Furthermore, of those persons that could be contacted, only 69 (= 26% of the selected patients) were willing to start the experimental condition (refused prolonged treatment, did not show up at appointments, no continuing problem, hospitalization was a mistake, etc.). In an appreciable number of cases the major obstacle was the patient's crisis orientation to medical attention: they contacted the services only at times of crisis, and when the crisis subsided they broke off contact and resisted referral for continuing help (Oast & Zitrin, 1975, p. 145). It goes without saying that such a state of affairs is not beneficial for reaching scientifically based conclusions.

These kinds of problems do show up regularly, even in the better designed studies that claim positive results. Welu and Picard, for instance, state that "nearly half of the suicide attempters in the comparison group were not contacted by the end of the four-month follow-up period and presumably were lost because of inadequate follow-up mechanism" (Welu & Picard, 1974, p. 450). The claim that the experimental group showed less further suicidal behaviour than the (remaining) controls is therefore not substantiated.

Almost all studies report on projects that were in operation for a limited number of years after which they were terminated, often owing to lack of further funding. Unfortunately, most of the prospective studies have not used a proper controlled design in which patients have been randomly assigned to either a treatment or non-treatment group, also because of practical considerations (Streiner & Adam; 1987).

Not surprisingly, the overall picture with regard to efficacy of special aftercare programmes that emerges from the studies reviewed contains a number of contradictions. Only four studies report a reduction in suicidal behaviour in the special aftercare condition, compared to fourteen studies where no differences were found (Liberman & Eckman, 1981; Wulliemier et al. 1978; Termansen & Bywater, 1975; Welu, 1977). When scrutinized carefully, on the methodological points mentioned above, the results of these four studies may be questioned.

No effect was found for a programme offering antidepressant medication (Montgomery, Roy & Montgomery, 1983). In one study (Litman & Wold, 1976) that focused exclusively on chronic suicidal persons with a high risk for repetition, no effect was found of a special aftercare programme with regard to suicides and suicide attempts in comparison with a control condition.

The most recent study in this series, using a methodologically well-structured design, found—convincingly—no effect at all (Allard et al., 1992). 224 subjects were offered participation in a study; 150 actually enrolled (others did not meet inclusion criteria, were already under treatment elsewhere, were incapable of consenting, language barriers, would not be able to keep appointments). 76 patients were randomized to the experimental group, 74 to the comparison group (no differences regarding sex and age). The intensive intervention programme consisted of: "an explicit treatment plan for each patient, a schedule of visits, at least one home visit, written or telephone reminders, or home visits in case of missed appointments, referral to usual psychiatric resources after the experimental treatment, if applicable. The treatment plan could include any combination of support or psychoanalytically oriented psychotherapy, psychosocial, drug, or behavioral therapy, according to the needs of the patient and the training of the therapist. Free use was made of outside resources such as Alcoholics Anonymous, when needed" (Allard et al., 1992, p. 306).

A positive characteristic of this study is that only 24 subjects dropped out of the study in the follow-up period, equally distributed between the experimental and the control group (13 versus 11). Results showed that 22 subjects (35%) in the experimental group and 19 subjects (30%) in the comparison group made at least one suicide attempt in the two years following randomization (not significant). Three completed suicides occurred among experimental subjects and one among the comparison subjects. Clearly the intensive intervention did not have the intended effect.

In sum, the identification of effective methods for the prevention of further episodes of suicidal behaviour continues to be a problem. It is noteworthy, however, that some of the studies reviewed have found that the special or intense forms of treatment have a positive effect on other outcomes such as psychological and social functioning of patients. For our understanding of such findings, some explanations may be offered. Most of the special treatment programmes focus on the alleviation of the immediate emotional and social problems of the patient. Consequently it is not at all certain whether the patient indeed learns different ways of coping with identical or similar problems whenever they recur.

In the majority of the studies no data have been collected on the sequential relationship between psychiatric diagnosis and risk of repetition. It might well be that new episodes of acute psychiatric disturbance are an important factor of suicidal recidivism. Most special aftercare programmes do not seem to be particularly tailored to deal with such conditions.

No studies control for the effect of treatment history on subsequent suicide attempts. Many suicidal patients have previously been in contact with helping agencies and health care professionals. Their experiences in this respect may rather be negative and may give rise to negative expectations of further help after the index attempt and therewith to rather low compliance (Moller, 1989).

Finally, selecting patients for a specific treatment method on the basis of the fact that they have attempted suicide might in itself be a questionable procedure. Suicidal behaviour can be reached via different roads and it might be more appropriate to select treatment modalities on the basis of "how the patient got there", i.e. using the underlying social and psychological problems as the criterion, instead of on the basis of one particular symptomatic behaviour. The available literature testifies to the fact that selecting a specific treatment for a specific subgroup of suicidal persons, such as suicidal persons suffering from a depressive disorder, might be preferable.

THERAPIES FOR AFFECTIVE DISORDERS

The evidence for a close relationship between mental illness and suicidal behaviour is convincing. Although the percentages may differ, most studies on the topic concur in the conclusion that the majority of persons dying through their own hand suffer from an ascertainable mental disorder at the time of their death. Of the suicides suffering from a mental illness, most are diagnosed as having depressive disorders.

About 15% of patients suffering from major depression finally die by their own hand, while 50 to 60% of persons committing or attempting suicide suffer from depressive disturbances (Sainsbury, 1986). It is therefore necessary to investigate the question whether effective methods for the treatment and/or prevention of depressive disorders will also have an effect on the prevention of suicidal behaviour.

Within contemporary psychiatry three modalities for the treatment of depressive disorders are psychotherapy (ranging from classical psychoanalysis via interpersonal approaches to behaviour therapy), antidepressant drug therapy and electroconvulsive therapy (ECT). Literature reviews indicate that all three modalities are effective in diminishing, reducing and preventing depressive disorders and that the differences in efficacy between them are relatively small for unipolar depressive disturbances, while drug treatment and ECT seem to be considerably more effective in bipolar depression (Tanney, 1986).

If all three modalities are effective in depressive disorders where suicidal behaviour is a recognized complication, the question arises as to the available evidence for their efficacy in diminishing, reducing and preventing suicidal behaviour.

With regard to psychotherapeutic treatment modalities, the conclusion is that psychotherapy deserves its place among the therapies for depression and has a symptom-reducing effect, including reduction of suicidal ideation, but it is not possible to state anything definite with regard to its effect on the incidence of suicidal behaviour. The reason for this is that among the controlled studies in this area studies that use subsequent suicidal behaviour as an outcome criterion are virtually non-existent.

With regard to antidepressant drug therapy, the situation is not much different. Several studies (Montgomery Roy & Montgomery, 1983) indicate that antidepressant medication, if prescribed and used appropriately, may have an effect on suicidal ideation and possibly on suicidal behaviour, but at the same time such medication might also be a risk factor since many suicidal patients overdose with their antidepressant medication.

Remarkably, we know most about the effectiveness of ECT in preventing suicidal behaviour. In his review Tanney (1986) used several methods to evaluate the impact of ECT on the frequency of suicidal behaviours in affective disorders. On the one hand one can compare the number of suicidal deaths in different treatment periods (pre-ECT versus ECT and post-ECT). Although Tanney suggests that the available studies warrant the conclusion that introduction of ECT had a reducing effect, careful examination of their designs indicate that these are all retrospective and do not accurately specify the distribution of the patients included in the studies over the diagnostic categories. Therefore, any definite conclusion with regard to the effects of ECT on suicidal behaviour on the basis of this set of studies is premature.

However, when we on the other hand look at the set of published controlled studies on the role of ECT in reducing suicidal behaviour in depressed patients, the picture that emerges is somewhat clearer. Five out of six studies (Tanney, 1986) show a preventive effect of ECT. The one exception (Babigian & Guttmacher, 1984) found no advantage to ECT in preventing suicide within five years of the first psychiatric hospitalization for depression. Since the number of patients in this latter study is larger than the total sum of patients included in the other five studies, a meta-analytic review would probably conclude that the verdict on the preventive effect of ECT is still "undetermined". However, the control group used in Babigian and Guttmacher's study presumably included many patients who received antidepressant and other psychotropic drug therapy as well as continuation and maintenance therapies.

This raises the question as to the differential effects of ECT versus drug therapy and other treatment modalities in reducing suicidal behaviour in patients suffering from affective disorders. Again there is a scarcity of information. The only controlled study that reported on differential out-come of ECT versus antidepressant drug therapy (Avery & Winokur, 1978) suggests an advantage to ECT when suicide attempts, not suicides, are used as outcome criterion. Several other studies using retrospective designs failed to show such a difference between ECT and antidepressant drug therapy (Tanney, 1986). Our conclusion is a cautious one: the available evidence for a preventive effect of ECT is at most suggestive, but certainly not convincing.

RESTRICTION OF EASY ACCESS TO LETHAL METHODS

The oldest method of preventing suicide is the removal or obstruction of means to commit suicide. Admitting patients to a closed ward with intensive supervision and removal of knives, razorblades and ropes and locking away medication inevitably reduces the possibility of giving in to a suicidal impulse. Locating such a closed ward on the ground floor, and using non-flammable materials may add to the feelings of security of patients and staff. The effectiveness of such measures seems to be undisputed, at least in the short run. Of course in this way many suicides have been prevented, or at least postponed. There is, however, no way of measuring the effectiveness of such methods because there is no experimental design that could be applied ethically. The application of such restrictions to suicidal behaviour may have suicide-promoting effects as well. The concentration of highly suicidal patients in one place may have unwanted effects such as stigmatization and imitation. It appears that making a closed ward completely "suicide-proof", if that were possible at all, would obstruct ordinary daily living, would complicate treatment and would in the end violate basic human rights. There is no empirical evidence whatsoever that the policy of (involuntary) admission to a psychiatric hospital would prevent suicides on a national or regional level. In fact many suicides take place within the boundaries of psychiatric hospitals. But that is to be expected with such a high density of suicidal patients. The question remains, how many of these patients would have committed suicide if they had not been admitted. This is a question that cannot be answered. There is empirical evidence however that quite a number of recently discharged patients commit suicide, especially among those patients that were admitted because of suicide risk (Kerkhof, 1985). All this only testifies that many highly suicidal patients are identified as having such a risk, that they are being concentrated in places where specialized treatment is available, and that the transfer from the psychiatric hospital to the outside world is a rather critical period.

A similar situation can be found in prisons and police lock-ups. Strict measures to prevent suicide temporarily reduce the risk of actual suicidal behaviour. Yet the incidence of suicide is ten times higher in jails and prisons than in the population (Kerkhof and Bernasco, 1990). What this means for the assessment of the effectiveness of these preventive measures is unclear. Given the characteristics of incarcerated persons one might even claim that these suicide rates in jails and prisons are extremely low.

Because many suicides are made impulsively, some people claim that the removal of means that are easily accessible would reduce the number of impulsive acts (Lester, 1988, 1992). One might think of preventing people from reaching the roofs of high buildings, restrict the possiblity of opening windows, etc. Barbiturates are notably dangerous in overdoses. The shift from barbiturates to other medication (such as benzodiazepines) during the nineteenth-seventies, however, has not been accompanied by a substantial decrease in suicides. Gun control legislation, especially gun ownership, seems to be related to differences in regional suicide rates, as well as homicide rates (Lester, 1988). Whether this finding opens possibilities for suicide prevention is questionable.

The switch from coal gas to natural gas in the United Kingdom in the nineteenth-sixties showed a marked decline in suicide due to domestic gas, while suicide due to non-gas methods increased at the same time, but not in all age–sex subgroups (Kreitman, 1976). Whether this reflected a causal relationship is still questionable (Crombie, 1990). Note that this switch was economically driven, and not with a view of suicide prevention (Lester, 1992). Car emission control may have an incidental impact on suicide

(Lester, 1992). But none of these methods seem to offer possibilities for effective suicide prevention on a large scale.

DISCUSSION AND CONCLUSIONS

From this review of the literature on suicide prevention programmes or methods it can be concluded that there is no empirical evidence whatsoever that any of the measures designed to reduce suicides has a substantial effect. This is not to say that no suicides and attempted suicides are being prevented by the approaches and methods that are currently in operation. What it does mean is that no data, sufficiently hard and replicated, are available that testify to such an effect.

There are methodological shortcomings in many effectiveness studies, there are ethical objections against experimental designs, and there are doubts about the representativeness of the populations being studied. But there are more substantial shortcomings in many of the programmes being studied, in the sense that there may often be a problem in the match between treatment and problem, between programme goals and participants' lack of resources. Essentially there is a complexity of causation of suicidal behaviour. There are societal, psychological and biological variables involved in each and every case of suicide and attempted suicide. It might well be that we have not yet sufficiently defined distinct subgroups of suicidal persons. The tendencies to self-destruction are not yet fully understood. Even the definitions of attempted suicide, deliberate self-harm and self-injurious behaviour are not yet fixed: we might in fact be studying different forms of behaviour with different psychodynamics under a rather vague concept such as attempted suicide. Suicide and attempted suicide—in all its diversity—are behaviours that can be reached via several pathways. And every pathway has numerous outcomes other than suicide. Maybe we should concentrate more on these pathways. For example, there is evidence that sexual and physical abuse in childhood increases the likelihood that suicidal tendencies will appear later in life (van Egmond & Jonker, 1988; van Egmond et al., 1993). One suicide prevention strategy would be to "work for the reduction in the incidence of sexual and physical abuse of children and to provide good psychotherapy for those so abused" (Lester, 1992, p. 46). Similarly, the improvement of psychotropic medication might not only improve the mental health of people, but might also prevent suicide. The prevention of loneliness and depression in the elderly might also have some effect on suicidal behaviour. All of these pathways to suicide deserve attention and should be incorporated into national suicide prevention programmes. Whether the effects of such programmes on incidence rates of suicide and attempted suicide will ever be detectable, remains to be demonstrated.

REFERENCES

Allard, R., Marshall, M. & Plante, M. C. (1992). Intensive follow-up does not decrease the risk of repeat suicide attempts. *Suicide and Life Threatening Behavior*, **22**, 303–314.

Avery, D. & Winokur, G. (1978). Suicide, attempted suicide, and relapse rates in depression. *Archives of General Psychiatry*, **35**, 749–753.

Babigian, H. M. & Guttmacher, L. B. (1984). Epidemiologic considerations in electroconvulsive therapy. *Archives of General Psychiatry*, **41**, 246–253.

Brent, D. A. & Kolko, D. J. (1990). The assessment and treatment of children and adolescents at risk for suicide. In: S. J. Blumenthal & D. J. Kupfer (Eds). *Suicide over the life circle*. Washington: American Psychiatric Press.

Bridge, T. P., Potkin, S. G., Zung, W.W.K. & Soldo, B. J. (1977). Suicide prevention centers: ecological study of effectiveness. *The Journal of Nervous and Mental Disease*, **164**, 1, 18–24.

Chowdhury, N., Hicks, R. C. & Kreitman, N. (1973). Evaluation of an after-care service for parasuicide (attempted suicide) patients. *Social Psychiatry*, **8**, 67–81.

Cohen-Sandler, R., Berman, A. & King, R. (1982). Life stress and symptomatology: determinants of suicidal behavior in children. *Journal of the American Academy of Child Psychiatry*, **21**, 178–186.

Crombie, I. K. (1990). Suicide in England and Wales and in Scotland: an examination of divergent trends. *British Journal of Psychiatry*, **157**, 529–532.

Dew, M. A., Bromet, E. J., Brent, D. & Greenhouse, J. B. (1987). A quantitative literature review of the effectiveness of suicide prevention centers. *Journal of Consulting and Clinical Psychology*, **55**, 239–244.

Diekstra, R.F.W. (1989). Suicide and attempted suicide: an international perspective. *Acta Psychiatrica Scandinavica (suppl. 354)*, **80**, 1–24.

Diekstra, R.F.W. & Hawton, K. (1987). *Suicide in adolescence*. Dordrecht/New York: Kluwer Academic Publishers.

Dyck, R. J. (in press). Guidelines for the development and organization of suicide prevention programs. In: R.F.W. Diekstra & W. Culbinot (Eds). *Preventive strategies for suicide*. Leiden/Cathena: Brill. Geneva: World health organization (co-publication).

Egmond, M. van & Jonker, D. (1988). Seksueel misbruik en lichamelijke mishandeling: risicofactoren voor (recidiverend) suicidaal gedrag bij vrouwen? *Tijdschrift voor Psychiatrie*, **30**, 21–38.

Egmond, M. van, Garnefski, N., Jonker, D. & Kerkhof, A. (1993). The relationship between sexual abuse and female suicidal behavior. *Crisis, The Journal of Crisis Intervention and Suicide Prevention*, **3**, 129–139.

Ettlinger, R. W. (1975). Evaluation of suicide prevention after attempted suicide. *Acta Psychiatrica Scandinavica (suppl.)*, **260**, 1–135.

Gallup Organization, Inc. (1991). *Teenage suicide study: executive summary*. (Available from the Gallup Organization, Inc.)

Gardner, R., Hanka, R., O'Brien, V. C., Page, A.J.F. & Rees, R. (1977). Psychological and social evaluation in cases of deliberate self-poisoning admitted to a general hospital. *British Medical Journal*, **2**, 1567–1570.

Garland, A. & Shaffer, D. (1990). School-based adolescent suicide prevention programmes. In: M. J. Rotheram, J. Bradley & N. Obolensky (Eds), *Planning to live: evaluating and treating suicidal teens in community settings*. Tulsa: University of Oklahoma Press.

Garland, A. Shaffer, D. & Whittle, B. (1989). A national survey of adolescent suicide prevention programs. *Journal of the American Academy of Child and Adolescent Psychiatry*, **28**, 931–934.

Garland, A. & Zigler, E. (1993). Adolescent suicide prevention: current reasearch and social policy implications. *American Psychologist*, 48(2), 169–182.

Gibbons, J.S., Butler, J., Urwin, P. & Gibbons, J.L. (1979). Evaluation of a social work for service for self-poisoning patients. *British Journal of Psychiatry*, 133, 111–118.

Greer, S. & Bagley, C. (1971). Effect of psychiatry intervention in attempted suicide. A controlled study. *British Medical Journal*, 1, 310–312.

Hawton, K. (1986). *Suicide and attempted suicide among children and adolescents.* Beverly Hills, CA: Sage.

Hawton, K., Brancroft, J., Catalan, J., Kingston, B., Stedeford, A. & Welch, N. (1981). Domiciliary and out-patient treatment of self-poisoning patients by medical and non-medical staff. *Psychological Medicine*, 11, 169–177.

Hawton, K., McKeown, S., Day, A., Martin, P., O'Connor, M. & Yule, J. (1987). Evaluation of out-patient counselling compared with general practitioner care following overdoses. *Psychological Medicine*, 17, 751–761.

Hoberman, H.M. & Garfinkel, B.D. (1988). Completed suicide in children and adolescents. *Journal of the American Academy of Child and Adolescent Psychiatry*, 27, 689–695.

Holding, T.A. (1974). The BBC "Befrienders" series and its effects. *British Journal of Psychiatry*, 124, 470–472.

Kalafat, J. & Elias, M. (1992). Adolescents' experience with and response to suicidal peers. *Suicide and Life Threatening Behavior*, 22, 3, 315–321.

Kennedy, P. (1972). Efficacy of a regional poisoning treatment centre in preventing further suicidal behaviour. *British Medical Journal*, 4, 255–257.

Kerkhof, A.J.F.M. (1985). *Suicide en de Geestelijke Gezondheidszorg.* Lisse: Swets & Zeitlinger.

Kerkhof, A.J.F.M. & Bernasco, W. (1990). Suicidal behavior in jails and prisons in The Netherlands. *Suicide and Life Threatening Behavior*, 20, 123–137.

Kerkhof, A.J.F.M., Diekstra, R.F.W. & Koster, A.M. (1982). *Over de effectiviteit van nazorgprogramma's voor suicidepogers; een literatuuroverzicht.* Rijksuniversiteit Leiden, Vakgroep Klinische Psychologie.

Kerkhof, A.J.F.M., Wal, J. van der & Hengeveld, M.W. (1988). A typology of persons who attempted suicide with predictive value for repetition: a prospective cohort study. In: H.J. Möller, A. Schmidtke & R. Welz (Eds), *Current issues of suicidology* (pp. 193–203). Berlin: Springer Verlag.

Kienhorst, C. W. M., De Wilde, E. J., Diekstra, R. F. W. & Wolters, W. H. G. (1992). Differences between adolescent suicide attempters and depressed adolescents. *Acta Psychiatrica Scandinavica*, 85, 222–228.

Kreitman, N. (1976). The coal gas story: United Kingdom suicide rates 1960–1971. *British Journal of Preventive Social Medicine*, 30, 86–93.

Lester, D. (1976). Effect of suicide prevention centers on suicide rates in the United States. *Health Services Reports*, 89, 37–39.

Lester, D. (1988). Gun control, gun ownership and suicide prevention. *Suicide and Life Threatening Behavior*, 18, 176–180.

Lester, D. (1992). Is there a need for suicide prevention? *Crisis, The Journal of Crisis Intervention and Suicide Prevention*, 2, 94.

Liberman, R. P. & Eckman, T. (1981). Behavior therapy vs. insight-oriented therapy for repeated suicide attempters. *Archives of General Psychiatry*, 38, 1126–1130.

Litman, R. E. & Wold, C. I. (1976). Beyond crisis intervention. In: E. S. Shneidman (Ed), *Suicidology: contemporary developments* (pp. 525–546). New York: Grune & Stratton.

Miller, H. L., Coombs, D. W. & Leeper, J. D. (1984). An analysis of the effects of suicide prevention facilities on suicide rates in the United States. *American Journal of Public Health*, **74**, 340–343.

Memory, J. M. (1989). Juvenile suicides in secure detention facilities: correction of published rates. *Death Studies*, **13**, 455–463.

Möller, H. J. (1989). Efficacy of different strategies of aftercare for patients who have attempted suicide. *Journal of the Royal Society of Medicine*, **82**, 643–647.

Montgomery, S. A., Roy, D. & Montgomery, D. B. (1983). The prevention of recurrent suicidal acts. *British Journal of Clinical Pharmacology (suppl.)*, **15**, 183–188.

Motto, J. A. (1976). Suicide prevention for high risk persons who refuse treatment. *Suicide and Life Threatening Behavior*, **6**, 223–230.

Mulder, A., Methorst, G. & Diekstra, R. (1989). Prevention of suicidal behavior in adolescents: the role and training of teachers. *Crisis*, **10**, 36–51.

Mulder, A. (in press). Prevention of suicidal behaviour in adolescents: the development and evaluation of a teachers education programme. Leiden: University of Leiden, Doctoral Dissertation.

Nelson, F. L. (1987). Evaluation of a youth suicide prevention school program. *Adolescence*, **38**, 813–825.

Nielsen, J. & Videbech, T. (1973). Suicide frequency before and after introduction of community psychiatry in a Danish island. *British Journal of Psychiatry*, **123**, 35–39.

Oast, S. P. & Zitrin, A. (1975). A public health approach to suicide prevention. *American Journal of Public Health*, **65**, 144–147.

Overholser, J., Hemstreet, A. H., Spirito, A. & Vyse, S. (1989). Suicide awareness programmes in the schools: effects of gender and personal experience. *Journal of the American Academy of Child and Adolescent Psychiatry*, **28**, 925–930.

Pardes, H., & Blumenthal, S. J. (1990). Youth suicide: public policy and research issues. In: S. J. Blumenthal, & D. J. Kupfer (Eds). *Suicide over the life circle*. Washington: American Psychiatric Press.

Platt, S., Bille Brahe, U., Kerkhof, A. J. F. M., Schmidtke, A. et al. (1992). Parasuicide in Europe: the WHO/EURO multicentre study on parasuicide. I. Introduction and preliminary analysis for 1989. *Acta Psychiatrica Scandinavica*, **85**, 97–104.

Price, R. H., Cowen, E. L., Lorion, R. P. & Ramos-McKay, J. (1989). The search for effective prevention programmes: what we learned along the way. *American Journal of Orthopsychiatry*, **59**, 49–58.

Ross, C. P. (1980). Mobilizing schools for suicide prevention. *Suicide and Life Threatening Behavior*, **10**, 239–243.

Sainsbury, P. (1986). Depression, suicide and suicide prevention. In: A. Roy (Ed), *Suicide*. Baltimore: Williams & Wilkins.

Schmidtke, A. & Haffner, H. (1988). The Werther effect after television films: new evidence for an old hypothesis. *Psychological Medicine*, **18**, 665–676.

Shafii, M., Steltz-Lenarsky, J., McCue Derrick, A. et al. (1988). Comorbidity of mental disorders in the post-mortem diagnosis of completed suicide in children and adolescents. *Journal of Affective Disorders*, **15**, 227–233.

Shneidman, E. S. & Farberow, N. L. (1957). *Clues to suicide*. New York: McGraw-Hill.

Shneidman, E. S. & Farberow, N. L. (1965). The Los Angeles suicide prevention center: a demonstration of public health feasibilities. *American Journal of Public Health*, **55**, 21–26.

Shaffer, D., Garland, A. Gould, M. Fisher, P. & Trautman, P. (1988). Preventing teenage suicide: a critical review. *Journal of the American Academy of Child and Adolescent Psychiatry*, **27**, 675–687.

Shaffer, D., Vieland, V., Garland, A., Rojas, M., Underwood, M. & Busner, C. (1990).

Adolescent suicide attempters: Response to suicide prevention programmes. *Journal of the American Medical Association*, **264**, 3151–3155.

Shaffer, D., Garland, A., Vieland, V., Underwood, M. & Busner, C. (1991). The impact of curriculum based suicide prevention programmes for teenagers. *Journal of the American Academy of Child and Adolescent Psychiatry*, **30**, 588–596.

Spirito, A., Overholser, J., Ashworth, S., Morgan, J. & Benedict, D. C. (1988). Evaluation of a suicide awareness curriculum for high school students. *Journal of the American Academy of Child and Adolescent Psychiatry*, **27**, 705–711.

Spirito, A., Brown, C., Overholser, J. & Fritz, G. (1989a). Attempted suicide in adolescence: a review and critique of the literature. *Clinical Psychology Review*, **9**, 335–363.

Spirito, A., Overholser, J. & Stark, L. (1989b). Common problems and coping strategies. II: Findings with adolescent suicide attempters. *Journal of Abnormal Child Psychology*, **17**, 213–221.

Stiffman, A. R. (1989). Suicide attempts in runaway youths. *Suicide and Life Threatening Behaviour*, **19**, 147–159.

Streiner, D. L. & Adam, K. S. (1987). Evaluation of the effectiveness of suicide prevention programmes: a methodological perspective. *Suicide and Life Threatening Behaviour*, **17**, 93–106.

Tanney, B. L. (1986). Electroconvulsive therapy and suicide, In: R. Maris (Ed), *Biology of suicide* (pp. 116–140). New York: Guilford Press.

Termansen. P. E. & Bywater, C. (1975). S.A.F.E.R.: a follow-up service for attempted suicide in Vancouver. *Canadian Psychiatric Association Journal*, **20**, 29–34.

Welu, T. C. (1977). A follow-up programme for suicide attempters: evaluation of effectiveness. *Suicide and Life Treatening Behavior*, **7**, 17–30.

Welu, T. C., & Picard, K. M. (1974). Evaluating the effectiveness of a special follow-up programme for suicide attempters: a two year study. In: N. Speijer & R.F.W. Diekstra (Eds) *Proceedings 7th International Congress on Suicide Prevention*. Amsterdam: Swets & Zeitlinger.

World Health Organization (1989). *World Health Statistics Annual*. Geneva: World Health Organization.

Wullemier, F. Kremer, P. & Bovet, J. (1978). Comparative study of two intervention modes on suicide attempters hospitalized in the genral hospital. In *Proceedings 9th IASP Congress*, Helsinki 1977. Oy-Lansi-Savo: Mikkeli.

7 Regulatory Innovations, Behavior and Health: Implications of Research on Workplace Smoking Bans

RON BORLAND
Centre for Behavioural Research in Cancer, 1 Rathdowne Street, Carlton South, Australia 3053

NEVILLE OWEN
Department of Community Medicine, University of Adelaide, PO Box 498, Adelaide, Australia 5801

DAVID HILL
Centre for Behavioural Research in Cancer, 1 Rathdowne Street, Carlton South, Australia 3053

SIMON CHAPMAN
Department of Community Medicine, University of Sydney, Westmead Hospital, Westmead, New South Wales 2145, Australia

INTRODUCTION

Psychological research on behaviour change in relation to preventive-health matters has paid considerable attention to individual learning processes and self-regulation, but has paid relatively less attention to the role of institutional regulation of human actions and habits. Rules and regulations are potent influences on human behaviour, even though the imposition of rules may not produce the behaviour change they are designed to, or theoretically should, produce. In this paper we explore some of what psychology can offer in understanding and improving regulatory approaches to behaviour change. In doing so, we focus on work we have done on the effects of the imposition of workplace smoking bans. The issues we canvass potentially have relevance to health psychology, and beyond that to much wider concerns—for example, in encouraging people to behave in ways which may promote social goals related to environmental protection. We begin by raising a number of issues which we believe are central to an

International Review of Health Psychology, Volume 3. Edited by S. Maes, H. Leventhal and M. Johnston
© 1994 John Wiley & Sons Ltd

understanding of the role of regulation as a modifier of behaviour, and suggest areas where psychological research might contribute.

Environmental changes and regulations which constrain individual freedoms in favour of a common good can occur to promote public health, public order, protection of the environment, and the preservation of social equity. Many of these constraints are accepted unthinkingly—for example, the side of the road on which we drive. We tend to become aware of and concerned about constraints when they are new, or when they discourage or make more difficult behaviours which we value or in which we habitually engage. Where desired behaviours are constrained, those who wish to engage in the behaviours may make a case for easing the constraints, or may argue for new social arrangements to facilitate what is desired—for example, lobbying for reduced penalties or decriminalization in relation to the possession of small amounts of marijuana. However, where engaging in a particular behaviour is incompatible with other behaviours, or is seen to conflict with broader social values, potential for social conflict exists. The case of marijuana is a good example of conflicting values, in this case between the predominant values of the community and of some subgroups.

REGULATORY INNOVATIONS AND BEHAVIOR CHANGE

Large-scale public-policy innovations to reduce risks to health are becoming more frequently used, particularly as persuasive communication campaigns and other activities place health promotion and disease prevention more strongly on the public agenda. In the prevention of cardiovascular disease and cancer, there is now a range of public-policy oriented initiatives which use social and environmental change strategies for the promotion of health (Milio, 1986; Williams, 1982). In most industrialized countries, governmental and charitable bodies continue to use public-education programs, but are also pursuing specific policy initiatives in the attempt to reduce the prevalence of unhealthy behaviors, for example smoking (Hill, 1988b) and fatty foods (Winikoff, 1977), or to promote healthy behaviours, for example, exercise (Owen & Lee, 1989). In the case of smoking, there is now good evidence that mass campaigns have had some impact (Flay, 1987; Pierce, Macaskill & Hill, 1990). Restrictive legislation and financial disincentives have also been used to reduce the prevalence of cigarette smoking (Chapman & Richardson, 1990; Warner, 1986; World Health Organization, 1986). Regulatory innovations to promote health are now being introduced to residents of developed countries, who have already been exposed to persuasive communication and educational health campaigns, have had the opportunity to take part in various types of community-health programs, or have at least been made aware of them, but where public education and individual behavior change strategies have been slow or inadequate to overcome the identified problems (Winett,

King & Altman, 1989).

In pluralistic democracies, initiatives to promote health which involve the imposition of restrictions on individual freedoms may be resisted if there is not adequate public support for such restrictions. The discipline of psychology potentially can enhance the understanding of factors which may, or may not, make such restrictions acceptable. But the impact of such public-policy innovations on health-related behaviors, beliefs and attitudes has not been studied extensively by psychologists, except where they have had a role in implementing such changes in small-scale systems. Such work has, for example, involved research on institution-wide behavior management programmes (Winkler, 1973) or on experimental studies of systems to regulate household energy and water consumption (Winkler & Winett, 1982).

Contemporary public-health campaigns use persuasive communication, education and mass-media social-modeling strategies in an effort to promote behavioral change (see Farquhar, Maccoby & Wood, 1985; Taylor & Owen, 1989). The direction of influence on health-related behaviors in much of this work is intended to be through an approximate sequence of changes to knowledge, then attitudes, motivation, intention to change and increased confidence that change is possible (Farquhar, Maccoby & Wood, 1985). The initiation of behavioral changes (and, hopefully, the maintenance of change) is then facilitated through the provision of personal advice or therapy, group programs, community events, and the provision of self-help materials.

Figure 7.1 suggests some of the ways in which regulatory innovations to promote health may interact with public-health campaigns, and with individuals' behavior, knowledge and attitudes. Individuals' attitudes and

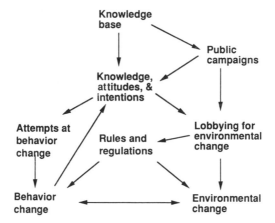

Figure 7.1   A schematic diagram of the major links between attitudes and behavioral and environmental changes

intentions may not only influence attempts to change behavior, but they may also lead to the creation of a climate in which regulatory innovations are more likely to be initiated and accepted. Hill (1988b) has documented the use of public opinion polls as a means of reassuring politicians about community support for increasing government regulation and taxing of cigarette smoking—thus facilitating the passage of important public health legislation. Regulatory changes, once in place may affect behaviour, the effects of which feed back to influence attitudes. Positive attitudes to regulatory or other environmental changes are critical if such changes are to be accepted.

The sequence of changes in attitudes and behaviour may differ, depending on the extent to which they require the activation of the personal initiatives and self-regulatory capacities of individuals, or are influenced more by regulatory or environmental controls which may be imposed on behaviours. Figure 7.2 describes the different potential paths of influence on behaviours. Where the relevant behaviours are mainly under self-regulated control (as may result from health-education campaigns or more specific behavior-change interventions) behaviour change may precede environmental change. By contrast, where the relevant behaviours are mainly under externally regulated control, environmental changes (such as taxes or bans or restrictions on behaviours) may be necessary preconditions for widespread behaviour change. Such an analysis is consistent with the reciprocal determinism postulated by Bandura (1986) in his social cognitive theory.

Under conditions where attitudes to possible change are negative, people are likely to actively resist change, thus reducing the chances of it occurring. Or, if change has occurred, they may be likely to revolt against it,

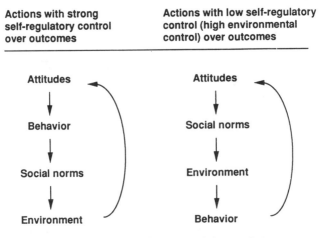

Figure 7.2   Sequences of events in behavioral change

thus further reducing the chance of it achieving its desired ends and also increasing the likelihood of it being abandoned, or of being replaced by measures less effective than were the original set of conditions.

WHEN IS A PRIMARY FOCUS ON INDIVIDUAL BEHAVIOR CHANGE INADEQUATE?

In democracies individual freedom is prized. Unnecessary and unwanted regulation or other environmental constraints on behaviour are likely to be resisted both at the individual and at the political level. At the same time, societies have an obligation to facilitate the behaviors that are valued by a majority of their members. We suggest that regulation may be necessary in situations where any of the following apply: where consistency of behaviour is required (for example, the side of the road on which to drive); where there maybe limits on the resource base required for the behaviour (for example, excessive consumption of fossil fuels); where the behavior can or does produce adverse consequences on others (for example, spitting in public, and pollution of the environment by toxic chemicals, including tobacco smoke); where the behaviour is addictive and it results in social cost, either because of health or other effects (for example, smoking and narcotic use) and, more generally, where the conditions supporting socially undesirable behavior have a net effect of discouraging or otherwise making more difficult alternative socially desirable behaviour. In addition, as we have argued elsewhere (Owen, Borland & Hill, 1991), there needs to be social support for such regulations and there is also the need for the rights of minority groups to be protected. The level and kind of regulation required will depend on the societal goals and on the nature of the behaviour to be regulated.

In the case of cigarette smoking there is now strong evidence that it is addictive (United States Department of Health & Human Services, 1988) and is dangerous to the health of smokers (United States Department of Health & Human Services, 1989), and also that nonsmokers' health can be affected by exposure to environmental tobacco smoke (National Health and Medical Research Council, 1986; United States Department of Health & Human Services, 1986; Glantz & Parmley, 1991). Individual behaviours which meet only some of these criteria have been regulated, for example, spitting in public (Chapman et al., 1990). We argue that the current situation with regard to cigarette smoking is one where many smokers are not able to control their smoking in the way that they may desire, and are not able or willing to refrain from smoking in situations where their sidestream smoke may affect others. Currently in Australia, the majority of smokers acknowledge that sidestream smoke is dangerous, and community support for increased regulation of smoking is strong (Borland & Naccarella, 1990). Smokers also express a desire to stop, but lack adequate control over their smoking habit: in Australia about 40% of current smokers claim that there is at least an even chance of them attempting to quit smoking in the next three months; about 30% claim that they very much want to give up smoking; and about 40% claim to have made a serious quit attempt in the previous year, but to have failed in the attempt (Borland, Nacarella & Hill 1990). Permanently stopping smoking can be extremely difficult, at least in the social context of past years. The most successful treatment programs achieve about a 30% long-term success rate, and many achieve less (Schwartz, 1987). This and other evidence suggests that many smokers are unable to gain control over their smoking behavior.

A greater degree of social regulation of smoking may help smokers to increase their level of control of their smoking behaviour. Marks (1990) argues that optimum control of addictive behaviours is achieved at some intermediate level of regulation between complete prohibition and total availability. According to Marks, some behaviors—most notably smoking and alcohol consumption—are under-regulated, in that individuals are expected to control their habits in a social context that encourages excess. When a behavior is socially acceptable in virtually all social contexts, is easy to engage in with high frequency, and when it is addictive, it may be difficult for many individuals to regulate consumption to either socially of individually defined optimums. By contrast, where people desire a behavior or product where its availability is overconstrained (for example, pro-hibited), alternative methods may be developed to ensure access. The sophisticated distribution networks of international drug barons in this generation, or of the alcohol bootleggers in the USA of the 1920s bears graphic testimony to this assertion. According to Marks's (1990) perspec-tive, increased regulation of smoking behavior should reduce net consump-tion with few if any attendant social problems, because smoking is currently underregulated.

Drug use in some form or another is common in most societies. Some drugs which English-speaking societies now see as socially reprehensible have long histories of controlled use in other societies, and in earlier his-torical periods in our own societies. Typically, consumption is controlled by restricting use to special ritual or religious occasions, and forbidding use outside of these contexts. A small proportion of the population is sus-ceptible to addiction, even where social control regulates use for the majority, but widespread epidemics of abuse are probably not likely to be seen unless social controls begin to break down (Brecher et al. 1972).

The current moves towards the social regulation of tobacco use can be seen as creating circumstances which will help individuals gain control over their tobacco usage, to be more likely to be able to stop altogether if they desire (that is what medical and public health authorities advise), or to regulate their usage to levels at which the perceived benefits (from the smoker's perspective) outweigh the costs. When smoking is restricted to few places or occasions, it will be much easier for smokers to smoke less. Workplaces are where most people spend the largest proportion of the time outside of the home, either in the role of worker or of client or customer. Perhaps the most effective social restriction on smoking behaviour is to prevent it in workplace settings.

WORKPLACE SMOKING BANS

Bans on cigarette smoking in enclosed work environments have recently begun to be implemented by many organizations in a number of industrialized countries (e.g., Beiner et al., 1989; Borland et al. 1989; Martin & Silverman, 1986; Martin, Fehrenbach & Rosner, 1986; Petersen, et al., 1988), and are widespread in Australia (Borland, 1990). Because of potential risks to the health of non smokers associated with exposure to environmental tobacco smoke, the imposition of workplace smoking restrictions is increasingly seen to be part of employers' duties to protect the health of all workers (Woodward & McMichael, 1987). Also, at least in Australia, the public is now more aware of the risks of passive exposure to tobacco smoke Hill, 1988a), and is increasingly accepting of restrictions on smoking in public places Hill, 1986; Borland & Hill, 1989; Borland & Naccarella, 1990).

Published studies have shown majority employee support for workplace smoking bans, although not always among smokers, and total bans have typically been less popular than lesser restrictions (Andrews, 1983; Rosenstock, Stergachis & Heaney, 1986; Petersen et al, 1988; Biener et al. 1989; Borland et al. 1989). Our work in Australia has shown that total bans become increasingly accepted once implemented, and in both of our major workplace smoking-ban studies we have found majority support from smokers at some time after implementation (Borland et al. 1990a; Hocking et al. 1991). In these studies, compliance with the bans was generally high. However, in one organization, a small number of areas reported significant levels of violations. These were associated with high levels of staff tension. The violations seemed to be related to poor managerial practice, rather than to any particular characteristics of the staff involved (Hocking et al. 1991).

The major concern which has motivated the introduction of workplace smoking bans has been the protection of the health of non smokers, and the extent to which this is achieved is of some interest (Woodward & McMichael, 1987). But the introduction of workplace smoking bans also provides a unique opportunity for understanding another matter of considerable public-health importance: what the impact might be of these major regulatory innovations on the behaviour, attitudes and perceptions of smokers themselves. If smoking bans produce reductions in cigarette consumption, then they are likely to result in health benefits for the smokers who are influenced by them. The introduction of these restrictions thus provides an opportunity to study the ways in which a regulatory innovation may influence a health-related behaviour. This is in contrast to the types of behaviour change which health psychologists most often study: those associated with voluntary participation in face-to-face education and behavior-change programs (Glasgow & Lichtenstein, 1987), or those associated with exposure to persuasive communications in mass-media health campaigns (Farquhar, Maccoby & Wood, 1985)

As we noted above, smokers become increasingly accepting of bans following their implementation (Borland et al. 1990a: Hocking et al. 1991). As might be expected, the increase in acceptance appears to be inversely related to the extent to which their smoking habit is disrupted (Borland et al. 1993). There is also considerable evidence that workplace smoking bans lead to reductions in daily smoking rates, although the size of the reported reductions have varied. Studies of partial bans (some smoking allowed in the workplace) have reported a reduction of from two to four cigarettes a day (Peterson et al. 1988; Biener et al. 1989; Millar, 1988). while the studies of total bans have reported reductions of between three and six cigarettes a day (Rosenstock, Stergachis & Henney, 1986; Borland et al., 1990b: Borland, Owen & Hocking, 1991; Stillman et al. 1990).

Developing an accurate perspective on the effects of bans on cigarette consumption on the basis of published studies is difficult for four reasons. First, there can be differing levels of pre-existing restrictions on smoking; second, data on compliance with the bans is generally poor; third, different methods of estimating consumption and consumption change have been used; and finally, the characteristics of the populations studied have varied. In our studies of a prospective cohort, we calculated separate estimates of reductions in consumption following the implementation of total bans in smokers previously subject to strong versus weaker or non-existent restrictions on their smoking. For the latter group we found reductions of 5.2 cigarettes a day in one study (Borland et al., 1990b) and 3.7 in the other (Borland, Owen & Hocking, 1991). The discrepancy is partly due to greater outdoor consumption in the latter study, but also to somewhat greater compensatory smoking among this group. It may also be due to characteristics of the workforce. The difference is unlikely to be due to differential compliance, as in both studies reported compliance was high and reported indoor work consumption was low. All studies of total bans found evidence that the reduction in cigarette consumption was greatest among heavier smokers. The greater reduction in consumption among heavier smokers means that the potential health benefit is likely to be largest in this group. This is of particular importance for smoking control, as heavier smokers face the greatest health risks and generally have been found to be less likely to quit successfully (Pomerleau, Adkins & Pertschuck, 1978).

The reductions in consumption that occur are in those settings in which not smoking is strongly mandated by the ban. In our study of the Australian Public Service (Borland et al., 1990b), we found a mean reduction of 7.0 cigarettes a day while working indoors. The net reduction in daily consumption was 5.2 cigarettes a day, this means that 1.8 extra cigarettes were smoked in periods or places where smoking was allowed. Analyses of this compensatory smoking indicated that most of it occurred before work, while working outside, and in the hour after work. There was no evidence of compensatory smoking during coffee breaks, during lunch and in the evening following the hour after work. The lack of compensatory smoking during work breaks may be because staff did not always leave the building during these times, and therefore were not able to smoke. The finding of no reported compensatory smoking in the evening suggests that any compensation probably occurs close to the periods of enforced abstinence. We did not examine smoking topography (puff frequency, depth of inhalation, amount of the cigarette that is smoked), but argued that variations in topography were unlikely to completely eliminate the effect of reduced consumption, as the extra smoking only took place at circumscribed times and this only accounts for a small proportion of total consumption. These conclusions do not necessarily apply to the results of our other smaller study (Borland, Owen & Hocking, 1991), in which the compensatory smoking was half the reduction due to the ban and where it was more evenly spread across non-work periods.

We also have some evidence from our 18-month prospective study of one organization that about 20 % of smokers had changed non-workday consumption. These smokers had average workday reductions of six cigarettes a day: consumption on non-work days was also reduced by an average of six cigarettes per day (Borland, Owen & Hocking, 1991). No such effect was evident at the earlier six months follow-up, so the non-workday reduction may represent a longer-term effect of the bans.

While smokers have reduced consumption due to the bans, it is not so clear as to whether bans have increased the incidence of smoking cessation. While several published studies have reported reductions in smoking prevalence (Andrews, 1983; Petersen et al. 1988; Millar, 1988; Stillman et al., 1990; Borland et al., 1990b; Borland, Owen & Hocking, 1991), others have not found such effects (Biener et al., 1989). Where effects have been found, no proper control conditions have been available to determine whether those rates of cessation are greater than for a comparison group.

In our studies we found reductions of about twice what would be expected from estimates of cessation in the community. In one study (Borland Owen & Hocking, 1991), we found retrospective evidence of cessation before the bans, little net activity over the first six months following implementation, and then evidence of increased cessation. Stillman et al. (1990) have suggested that the time between the announcement that there will be a ban and its formal introduction is a time when cessation may be common. The above data support this. We also have some evidence that the change to a ban does result in increased cessation activity in the months immediately after a ban is imposed. In one of our studies (Borland et al., 1991), many smokers were subject to extensive restrictions before the mandated ban, so this study provided the opportunity to explore whether the change to a ban led to greater cessation activity. The shift from quite limited restrictions to a full ban did result in a greater number of quit attempts than when the shift was from more extensive restrictions to a full ban. Among smokers who tried to quit, there was no effect of prior restrictions on the outcome of their attempts. This is expected, as all of these smokers were by then subjected to the same total ban. This is evidence that either the change to a total ban, the existence of extensive restrictions on smoking, or both of these factors can stimulate greater cessation activity.

By contrast, the evidence from our study in Telecom Australia (Hocking et al., 1991) was of no reduction in smoking prevalence in the six months after a ban, but then a fall in prevalence. It is difficult to reconcile the results from the two studies. The pattern of cessation may be a function of organizational dynamics. For instance, in Telecom Australia extensive assistance was provided to smokers to help them quit before the bans were implemented, but there was at least a perception following implementation that management lost interest in helping smokers cope. It is possible that this perceived lack of support could have acted to discourage cessation initiatives.

The findings summarized above suggest that workplace smoking bans are having an effect on smoking behavior. The enforced reduction on smoking within the workplace is leading to a small amount of compensatory smoking at other times, although the extent of compensation is only partial, meaning that continuing smokers are smoking less on workdays. There is also some evidence that some smokers may be reducing consumption on non-work days. Finally, there may be a facilitative effect on smoking cessation. Taken together, this evidence suggests that the smoking bans are helping some smokers to have increased levels of personal control over their habits. If the greatest possible health benefits to smokers of workplace smoking bans are to be realized, it is important to maximize cessation, and among those who choose to continue to smoke or are unable to quit, to minimize compensatory smoking and maximize generalization of reductions in consumption. Understanding the conditions in which such effects can be obtained and developing interventions to achieve them represents a challenge for health psychologists.

The high level of support for the workplace bans, and the behavioral change which have followed from them, need to be understood in the context of high levels of support for such restrictions among the public at large (Borland & Nacarella, 1990). We believe that new social norms about where it is, and is not, appropriate to smoke are unlikely yet to have stabilized, and that further changes may occur to what are seen by the public to be acceptable settings and circumstances for smoking behavior. We might expect further changes in the behavior of smokers as a result.

IMPLICATIONS FOR UNDERSTANDING THE CHANGE AND MAINTENANCE OF SMOKING BEHAVIOR

Although the broad patterns of change in behavior and attitudes associated with the smoking bans are informative, we were most interested in understanding in a more precise manner the nature of the behavioral and attitudinal changes produced by regulatory innovations affecting cigarette smoking. The smoking-cessation literature provides some guidelines which may be useful in studying more closely the impact of workplace smoking bans.

There is evidence available regarding the characteristics of smokers which are related systematically to success or failure with cessation. Best (1978), concluded, somewhat pessimistically, that studies examining the tailoring of smoking-cessation methods to personality and motivational differences did not help to identify characteristics related to success or failure in smoking cessation. But follow-up studies of smokers taking part in formal cessation programmes have identified some relevant smoker characteristics. For example, Pomerleau et al., (1978) found that smokers most likely to stop successfully were characterized by lower smoking rates, higher levels of motivation to stop and being less likely to smoke in response to negative emotional states. In a large-scale study using mass media, Best (1980) found that smokers most likely to quit successfully using self-help materials were those who had the highest initial levels of motivation and confidence, lower smoking rates, and more previous attempts at stopping. Other studies have found that initial confidence of success at quitting (self-efficacy) was related to achieving abstinence (e.g., Baer, Holt & Lichtenstein, 1986). Other variables which potentially may be useful in making sense of successes and failures at smoking cessation include social support, perceptions of the costs and benefits of smoking, and stated intentions to stop (Glasgow & Lichtenstein, 1987; Pierce et al., 1987).

A major challenge for smoking-cessation research is in understanding the determinants of maintenance of non-smoking following cessation attempts (Glasgow & Lichtenstein, 1987). We, like other smoking-cessation researchers (Prochaska et al., 1988), have found that the factors which predict maintenance are generally quite different to those which predict the success of cessation attempts. For example, in our study, having made a previous cessation attempt was related to an increased probability of attempting to stop after the smoking bans had been introduced, but bore a negative relationship to the success of the attempt (Borland et al., 1991).

It has been argued that there may be incremental-learning processes associated with attempts to stop, so that the possibility of the success of future attempts increases with each quit attempt (Brownell et al., 1986). On the other hand, failed attempts at cessation may also act to undermine confidence in being able to stop smoking, and this may decrease the likelihood of future success (Owen & Brown, 1991). Cohen et al., (1989) were not able to provide a definitive answer to this question: in their studies, neither a clearly positive nor a clearly negative relationship emerged between having made or not made a previous cessation attempt, or between the number of previous cessation attempts, and the future maintenance of non-smoking.

In our study of predictors of attempts and sustained cessation (Borland et al., 1991) motivation to quit and being confident about doing so were related to attempting to quit, while being better educated, wanting to quit, having lower habit strength, having social support and not having tried to quit before were predictive of maintaining non-smoking. These variables may be categorized as either relating to stable and difficult-to-change personal characteristics (for example, education), aspects of the social environment (for example, social support), or smoking history (previous cessation attempts). These two latter categories are potentially changeable, and an understanding of them may be incorporated into public-health cessation strategies.

While the preceding argument is speculative, it does relate to some potentially important research questions in the public-health aspects of smoking-cessation: to what extent is the probability of long-term smoking cessation increased or decreased by multiple attempts to stop? Environmental restrictions on smoking do significantly reduce consumption, but the present evidence, in the absence of enough studies with adequate control or comparison groups, cannot conclusively show whether or not workplace smoking bans actually result in increased numbers of cessation attempts, and whether such cessation activity promotes sustained cessation. Controlled studies on such changes in smoking behavior associated with environmental restrictions would be very informative.

Research on changes in smoking behavior associated with regulatory changes like workplace smoking bans might usefully address three concerns which our study has identified. The first relates to how the personal and social characteristics (age, education, social support) of smokers influences success with cessation. The second relates to more proximal aspects of smoking behavior: to what extent is the probability of sustained non-smoking related to number of previous cessation attempts, feeling dependent or addicted, smoking rate, or the duration of previous periods of abstinence? The third relates to the influence of environmental characteristics and environmental change: how, for example, does the introduction of workplace (and other) smoking bans influence quit attempts? What are their short- and long-term effects on maintenance of non-smoking?

These workplace smoking-ban studies have begun to provide some data which bear on these questions. Understanding the relationships between social and environmental innovations and the stability and change of health-related behaviors and attitudes is a major challenge to health-psychology researchers. One specific line of research which is needed is to better understand the factors which can affect the stages of readiness of individuals to change health-related behaviors (Prochaska et al., 1988), in contexts where there are increased external controls on those behaviors. This perspective potentially allows some of the more subtle aspects of the processes of behavior change associated with social and environmental health innovations to be assessed.

Behavior-change programs usually deal with those who are already involved in some form of action to change. But in a public-health context, a key issue is encouraging large numbers of people to contemplate change, and to choose to take action. In this context, it is helpful to consider, from the perspective of the individual, the circumstances under which a person will, or will not, accept regulatory influences on their personal behavior. Changes in behavior induced by regulation may emerge, in part, as a consequence of the active or passive support of the individuals they affect— not simply through being imposed from above by authorities. At a more personal level, individuals are also involved in regulatory influences on their own behavior. A smoker might avoid visiting bars with her drinking friends (thus changing her proximal social environment), in order to increase her chances of quitting by minimizing temptations to smoke. At another level, she may lobby for restrictions on smoking at work to further enhance the chances of successfully quitting. But unlike personal efforts to change smoking behavior, regulatory innovations which may influence smoking can occur as the result of the actions of others, rather than as the result of personal action. Here, passive support, or even a failure to act on opposing beliefs, can increase the likelihood of such regulatory influences being implemented. It may be the case that this occurs at an earlier stage in the change process than do the factors which are necessary for permanent change based only on individual initiative. Figure 7.1 highlights how paths of influence like these may interact, particularly at a broader social level.

IMPLICATIONS FOR OTHER REGULATORY STRATEGIES AND POLICY ISSUES

Our analyses and discussion of the smoking ban studies have so far focused largely on behavior and attitude change in the context of a major regulatory innovation. But these findings need to be examined critically, and also to be considered in the context of broader psychological and social issues related to the regulation of tobacco use. Of considerable importance in this context is the use of pricing policy to restrict usage. Studies of the price elasticity of tobacco consumption show that consumption is affected by price, particularly among younger and economically less well-off members of the community (Chapman & Richardson, 1990). Evidence also suggests that price affects the incidence of new smokers (Warner, 1986). In terms of achieving stable control over smoking it is probably desirable that control be exercised in a variety of ways, regulated both by external authorities and by focusing on beliefs and social mores. Where there is social and or individual acceptance of the desirability of constraining use, individual and social forces will operate to maximize the effects of the constraints rather than being directed at ways of circumventing them.

But it cannot be assumed that rules and regulations will automatically have the effects that a simple compliance model would predict. One factor determining the optimal level of regulation is the beliefs about the value of the activity that are held by the community in general and by, in this case, smokers in particular. Furthermore, it is not enough for the belief to be that the behavior is undesirable; it needs to be seen as one where there is a high priority for it being regulated to or beyond the level of regulation that exists. As we have seen in the case of workplace smoking bans, there is now evidence that at least in some circumstances, the bans can facilitate further chances in behavior (smoking less out of working hours and on non-working days), as well as those directly induced by the ban. This suggests that some smokers may be taking the opportunity to build increased internal regulation onto the external regulation.

Individually oriented theories of behavior change suggest that attitudes lead to behavior change. While this can be an important route to behavior change, we hope we have demonstrated that environmental change can be a potent factor. According to the model outlined in Figure 7.1, personal attitudes contribute not only to attempts to change behavior, but also to attempts to change the environment, either directly or through the imposition of rules and regulations. Changing the environmental context can facilitate behavior change, as we have shown above. Environmental changes are not all at the societal level, for example, individual smokers trying to quit can avoid high-risk situations, thus changing their personal environments so as to support the maintenance of non-smoking (Marlatt & Gordon, 1985).

Accepting that environmental change is one route to behavior change, the next question that arises is: when is it the desired route for change. We would answer, in part, that this is when volitional control over the behavior in question is limited. The choice not to smoke and the act of not doing so involves a set of behaviors which need to be sustained and which is difficult to sustain because of forces, both internal and external, pressing towards a resumption of smoking (Marlatt & Gordon, 1985). Attempts to help people to quit smoking which focus on individual change are generally only moderately successful, at best (Schwartz, 1987). Thus, environmental control may be a necessary part of any effective public smoking control strategy. For increased environmental control to be feasible, there needs to be broad social support for such innovations. We would argue that studies of the effects of workplace smoking bans, and the evidence from Australian community surveys show that there is broad societal support for environmental changes as part of the strategy to control smoking. The support for workplace bans is high, and has been boosted by an increased level of concern about passive smoking. These concerns are real and will continue.

We need to consider carefully what social and environmental innovations may be helpful in helping smokers to assume greater control over their habits, enough control to quit if they want to, or at least to consume less dangerous quantities of cigarettes. Deciding what levels of control are acceptable will require, among other things, a dialogue between health experts and the public, to arrive at plans for the future that have broad support and which will not induce counter-reaction when implemented. Psychological studies like those we have discussed are needed to inform, and also to examine the outcomes of, such activities.

CONCLUSIONS

Our research on workplace smoking bans has found that a majority of nonsmokers had positive attitudes to these restrictions before they were implemented, and that a significant minority of smokers also had positive attitudes to them. Following the implementation of the bans, attitudes to them became more positive among both smokers and nonsmokers. The bans resulted in significant reductions in reported smoking rates, with heavier smokers reducing their workday consumption by more than lighter smokers. Our initial findings on predictors of attempts to quit and sustained cessation are beginning to identify variables related to changes in smoking behavior. Overall, it appears that these regulatory innovations are acceptable to those affected by them, and that they produce reductions in smoking rates which are of potential health benefit to smokers.

Research in health psychology which examines the impact of regulatory innovations such as workplace smoking bans may help to provide a base of knowledge from which individuals and social groups may work to create environments that make it easier for them to conduct aspects of their lives in ways that they and their society value. Studies of workplace smoking bans show that the public is prepared to accept increased regulation when it produces desirable outcomes. The studies also show that smoking bans do provide desirable outcomes, and for this reason are an effective method of smoking control.

There is a range of other areas where environmental regulation needs to play a role alongside individual action. Some of the most important of these are regulation of other public health domains—for example, other addictive behaviors and road safety, as well as in other areas such as industrial and domestic waste recycling, chemical pollution control and other activities necessary to promote environmental protection. The study of the implementation and the impact of workplace bans on cigarette smoking is an example of how behavioral and attitudinal research in health psychology can extend its boundaries into some socially important and theoretically interesting new territories.

ACKNOWLEDGEMENTS

The studies described in this paper were funded by the Anti-Cancer Council of Victoria, Telecom Australia, and the Anti-Cancer Foundation of the Universities of South Australia. The support of these bodies is gratefully acknowledged.

REFERENCES

Andrews, J. L. (1983). Reducing smoking in hospital: an effective model program. *Chest*, 84, 206–209.
Baer, J. S., Holt, C. S. & Lichtenstein, E. (1986). Self-efficacy and smoking re-examined: construct validity and clinical utility. *Journal of Consulting and Clinical Psychology*, 54, 846–852.
Bandura, A. (1986). *Social foundations of thought and action: a social cognitive theory.* Englewood Cliffs. NJ: Prentice Hall.
Beiner. L., Abrams D. B., Follick, M. J., & Dean, L. (1989). A comparative evaluation of a restrictive smoking policy in a general hospital. *American Journal of Public Health*, 79, 192–195.
Best, J. A. (1978). Targeting and self-selection of smoking modification methods. In J. L. Schwartz (Ed). *Progress in smoking cessation* (pp. 105–118). New York: American Cancer Society.
Best, J. A. (1980). Mass media, self-management and smoking modification. In: P. O. Davidson & S. M. Davidson (Eds), *Behavioral medicine: changing health lifestyles* (pp. 371–390). New York: Brunner/Mazel.
Borland, R. (1990). The extent of restrictions on smoking in the workplace. *Journal of Occupational Health and Safety: Australia and New Zealand*, 6, 93–96.
Borland, R. and Hill, D. (1989). Public attitudes to smoke-free zones in restaurants. *Medical Journal of Australia*, 150, 407.
Borland, R. & Naccarella, L. (1990). Public attitudes to restrictions on both smoking and the promotion of smoking in Victorian Smoking and Health Program. *Quit: Evaluation Studies No. 4.* Carlton: VSHP.
Borland, R. Nacarrella, L. & Hill, D. (1990). Reactions of smokers to the 1989 Quit campaign in Victorian Smoking and Health Program. *Quit: Evaluation Studies No. 4*, Carlton VSHP.

Borland, R. Owen, N. & Hocking, B. (1991). Changes in smoking behavior following the implementation of a total workplace smoking ban. *Australian Journal of Public Health*, 15, 130–134.

Borland, R., Owen, N., Hill, D. & Chapman, S. (1989). Staff acceptance of the introduction of workplace smoking bans on smoking in the Australian Public Service. *Medical Journal of Australia*, 151, 525–528.

Borland, R. Owen, N., Hill, D. & Chapman, S. (1990a). Changes in acceptance of workplace smoking following their implementation: a prospective study. *Preventive Medicine*, 19, 314–322.

Borland, R. Chapman, S., Owen, N. & Hill, D. J. (1990b). Effects of workplace smoking bans on cigarette consumption. *American Journal of Public Health*, 80, 178–180.

Borland, R. Owen, N., Hill, D. & Schofield, P. (1991). Predicting attempts and sustained cessation of smoking following the introduction of a workplace smoking ban. *Health Psychology*, 10, 336–342.

Borland, R, Owen, N., Schofield, P. & Hill, D.J. (1993). Predictors of smokers' attitude change associated with a workplace smoking ban. Unpublished manuscript, Centre for Behavioural Research in Cancer, Melbourne, Australia.

Brecher, E.M., & the Editors of Consumer Reports (1972). *Licit and illicit drugs.* Boston: Little, Brown.

Brownell, K.D., Marlatt, G.A. Lichtenstein, E. & Wilson, G.T. (1986). Understanding and preventing relapse. *American Psychologist*, 41, 765–782

Chapman, S., & Richardson, T. (1990). Tobacco excise and declining tobacco consumption: the case of Papua New Guinea. *American Journal of Public Health*, 80, 537–540

Chapman, S., Borland, R., Hill, D.J., Owen, N., & Woodward, S. (1990). Why the tobacco industry fears the passive smoking issue. *International Journal of Health Services*, 20, 417–427.

Cohen, S., Lichtenstein, E., Prochaska, J.O., Rossi, J.S., Gritz, E.R., Orleans, C.T., Schoenbach, V.J., Biener, L., Abrams, D., DiClemente, C., Curry, S., Marlatt, G.A., Cummings, K.M., Eamont, S.L., Giovino, G. & Ossip-Klein, D. (1989). Debunking myths about self-quitting: evidence from 10 prospective studies of persons who attempt to quit smoking by themselves. *American Psychologist*, 44, 1355–1365.

Farquhar, J.W., Maccoby, N. & Wood, P. (1985). Education and communication studies. In: W.W. Holland, R. Detels & G. Knox (Eds), *Oxford textbook of public health* Vol 3, pp. 207–221). London: Oxford University Press.

Flay, B.R. (1987). Mass media and smoking cessation: a critical review. *American Journal of Public Health*, 77, 153–160.

Glantz., S.A. & Parmley, W.W. (1991). Passive smoking and heart disease: epidemiology, physiology, and biochemistry. *Circulation* 83 (1), 1–12.

Glasgow, R.E. & Lichtenstein, E. (1987). Long term effects of behavioral smoking cessation intervention. *Behavior Therapy*, 18, 297–324.

Hill, D.J. (1986). Public opinion about smoking in restaurants and at work. *Medical Journal of Australia*, 145, 657–658.

Hill D (1988a) Letter to the editor on public attitudes to passive smoking. *Medical Journal of Australia*, 148, 153–154.

Hill, D. (1988b). Public opinion on tobacco advertising, sports sponsorship and taxation prior to the Victorian Tobacco Act, 1987. *Community Health Studies*, 12, 282–288.

Hocking, B., Borland, R., Owen, N. & Kemp, G, (1991). A total ban on workplace smoking is acceptable and effective. *Journal of Occupational Medicine*, 33, 163–167.

Marks, J. (1990). Opium: religion of the people. Invited address, *5th International Conference on the Treatment of Addictive Behaviors*, Sydney, Australia, February 1990.

Marlatt, G.A. & Gordon, J.R. (Eds) (1985). *Relapse prevention: maintenance strategies in the treatment of addictive behaviors*. New York: Guilford Press.

Martin, M. J., Fehrenbach, A. & Rosner, R. (1986). Ban on smoking in industry. *The New England Journal of Medicine*, 315, 647–648.

Martin, M. J. & Silverman, M. F. (1986). The San Francisco experience with regulation of smoking in the workplace: The first twelve months *American Journal of Public Health*, 76, 585–586.

Milio, N. (1986). *Promoting health through public policy*. Ottawa: Canadian Public Health Association.

Millar, W. J. (1988). Evaluation of the impact of smoking restrictions in a government work setting. *Canadian Journal of Public Health*, 79, 379–382.

National Health and Medical Research Council (1987). *Effects of passive smoking on health*. Report of NH&MRC working party of the effects of passive smoking on health. Canberra, Australia: Australian Government Publishing Service.

Owen, N., Borland, R. & Hill, D. (1991). Regulatory influences on health-related behaviours: the case of workplace smoking bans. *Australian Psychologist*, 26, 188–191.

Owen, N. & Brown, S. (1991), Smokers unlikely to quit. *Journal of Behavioral Medicine*, 14, 627–636.

Owen, N. & Lee, C. (1989). Development of behaviorally-based policy guidelines for the promotion of exercise. *Journal of Public Health Policy*, 10, 43–61.

Petersen, L. R., Helgerson, S. D., Gibbons, C. M., Calhoun, C. R. Ciacco, K. H. & Pitchford, K. C. (1988). Employee smoking behavior changes and attitudes following a restrictive policy on worksite smoking in a large company. *Public Health Reports*, 103, 115–120.

Pierce, J. P., Dwyer, T., Chamberlain, A., Aldrich, R. N. & Shelley, J. (1987). Targetting the smoker in an antismoking campaign. *Preventive Medicine*, 16, 816–824.

Pierce, J. P., Macaskill, P. & Hill, D. (1990). Long terms effectiveness of mass media led anti-smoking campaigns in Australia. *American Journal of Public Health*, 80, 565–569.

Pomerleau, O. F., Adkins, D. & Pertschuck, M. (1978). Predictors of outcome and recidivism in smoking cessation treatment. *Addictive Behaviors*, 1, 193–202.

Prochaska, J. O., Velicer, W. F., Di Clemente, C. C. & Fava, J. (1988). Measuring processes of change: applications to cessation of smoking. *Journal of Consulting and Clinical Psychology*, 56, 520–538.

Rosenstock, I. M., Stergachis, A. & Heaney, C. (1986). Evaluation of smoking prohibition policy in a health maintenance organization. *American Journal of Public Health*, 76, 1014–1015.

Schwartz, J. L. (1987). *Review and evaluation of smoking cessation methods: the United States and Canada, 1978–1985*. Washington, DC: Division of Cancer Prevention and Control, National Cancer Institute.

Stillman, F. A., Becker, D. M., Swank, R. T., Hantula, D., Moses, N., Glantz, S. & Waranch, H. R. (1990). Ending smoking at the John Hopkins Medical Institutions: an evaluation of smoking prevalence and indoor air pollution. *Journal of American Medical Association*, 264, 1565–1569.

Taylor, C. B. & Owen, N. (1989). Behavioural medicine: research and development in disease prevention. *Behavior Change*, 6, 3–11.

United States Department of Health & Human Services (1986). The health consequences of involuntary smoking: a report of the Surgeon General. US Department of Health and Human Services.

United States Department of Health & Human Services (1988). The health consequences of smoking: nicotine addiction: a report of the Surgeon General. US Department of Health and Human Services.

United States Department of Health & Human Services (1989). Reducing the health consequences of smoking: 25 years of progress: a report of the Surgeon General. US Department of Health and Human Services.

Warner, K. E. (1986). Smoking and health implications of a change in the Federal Cigarette Excise Tax. *Journal of the American Medical Association*, 255, 1028–1032.

Williams, A. F. (1982). Passive and active measures for controlling disease and injury: the role of health psychologists. *Health Psychology*, 1, 399–409.

Winett, R. A., King, A. C. & Altman, D. G. (1989) *Health psychology and public health: an integrative approach*. New York: Pergamon, 1989.

Winikoff, B. (1977). Nutrition and food policy: the approaches of Norway and the United States. *American Journal of Public Health*, 67, 552–557.

Winkler, R. C. (1973). An experimental investigation of economic balance, savings, and amount of reinforcement in a token economy. *Behavior Therapy*, 4, 22–40.

Winkler, R. C. & Winett, R. A. (1982). Behavioral interventions in resource conservation: a systems approach based on behavioral economics. *American Psychologist*, 37, 421–435.

Woodward, A. & McMichael, A. J. (1987). Smoking at work. *Journal of Occupational Health and Safety—Australia and New Zealand*, 3, 578–583.

World Health Organization (1986). A discussion document on the concepts and principles of health promotion. *Health Promotion*, 1, 73–76.

Part III

ILLNESS BEHAVIOUR AND HEALTH CARE

8 Self-regulation and Control of Rheumatic Disorders

DENISE C. PARK

Department of Psychology, University of Georgia, Athens, Georgia 30602, USA

Rheumatic disorders encompass a range of diseases of the musculo-skeletal structures. Among the most common rheumatic disorders are osteoarthritis, rheumatoid arthritis, and systemic lupus erythematosus. In order to present a behavioral perspective with respect to treatment and course of disease, it is important to distinguish osteoarthritis from most other rheumatic disorders. Osteoarthritis (OA) is by far the most common rheumatic disorder, affecting about 12% of the population over the age of 25 (Brandt & Flusser, 1991). It is the single greatest cause of disability in the elderly with 53% of adults over age 65 reporting arthritis to be a significant health problem (Controller General, 1979). Osteoarthritis involves progressive deterioration of cartilage and the growth of bone and cartilage into joints, resulting in pain. Its prevalence increases dramatically with age. The effects of osteoarthritis are localized and specific to affected joints. Treatment involves rest, judicious exercise, and the use of nonsteroidal antiinflammatory drugs (NSAIDs) to alleviate pain. There are no drug treatments to stop the disease or even to slow its progression. Its etiology is poorly understood.

In contrast to the localized effects of osteoathritis, most other rheumatic diseases (e.g., rheumatoid arthritis, systemic lupus erythematosus, scleroderma, and polymyositis) are classified as autoimmune diseases wherein an overly active immune system attacks healthy tissue including joints (rheumatoid arthritis), connective tissue (lupus), muscle (polymyositis), or skin (scleroderma). These systemic diseases have diffuse symptoms and differ from one another, but all are characterized by multiple target sites in the body that can compromise pulmonary, kidney, and cardiovascular function, and by multiple arthralgias, as well as fatigue. Treatment for these disorders typically includes the prescription of NSAIDs to reduce pain and inflammation, as well as the use of steroids (primarily pred-

International Review of Health Psychology, Volume 3. Edited by S. Maes, H. Leventhal and M. Johnston
© 1994 John Wiley & Sons Ltd

nisone) and immunosuppressants to decrease function of the overly aggressive immune system.

Despite their differences, all rheumatic diseases have characteristics that make them particularly suited to behavioral study and intervention—they are incurable, progressive, unpredictable, and painful. The affected individual must cope with these disorders for many years, although given the variable course of these disorders, the prognosis is frequently unclear. A disease like systemic lupus erythematosus (SLE) or rheumatoid arthritis (RA) can present as a minor and occasional inconvenience or as an immobilizing disorder which results in permanent disability that dramatically affects personal and professional function of the affected individual. These disorders can even lead to death.

Treatment for most rheumatic disorders may alleviate distressing symptoms such as pain but often creates other health problems such as gastrointestinal disturbances and liver dysfunction (from NSAIDs) or compromised immune function (from steroids or immunosuppressants). Thus, it is virtually certain that the election of any sustained treatment for rheumatic disorders will lead to additional health problems. Given the chronic and incurable nature of rheumatic disorders, the focus of this chapter will be on control and adaptation to disease, rather than on prevention. Behavioral approaches to rheumatic disorders appear to have great potential for management of these diseases as reports of pain and distress of affected individuals are highly variable and appear not necessarily to be well-predicted by objective measures of disease, such as radiographic representations of joint damage or biochemical markers of autoimmune activity (Dekker et al., 1992).

In acknowledgment of the importance of psychosocial aspects of these diseases and behavioral interventions for them, Fries and Bellamy (1991) in a recent medical text on prognosis of rheumatic diseases note the "disturbingly multivariate world of chronic illness" (p. 7). They go on to state,

> Nonbiologic inputs clearly affect outcome. Yet, our medical system teaches biologic mechanism almost exclusively. In the rheumatic diseases, patient motivation and compliance, educational level, socioeconomic status, availability of community resources, payment mechanisms, public and patient education, family support, level of depression, and other factors may be more important determinants of disability than the biologic activity of the disease or the effect of medication. These multiple influences on patient outcome require a broader model of health. (P. 7)

The present chapter is an attempt to provide the behavioral framework for understanding rheumatic disorders to which Fries and Bellamy (1991) allude, with the goal of developing interventions that result in enhanced physical and psychosocial functioning for affected individuals. In an effort to organize the behavioral work done on rheumatic disorders, a strong theoretical approach will be adopted. The approach taken in this chapter will be based on the seminal work of Leventhal and colleagues on illness representation and self-regulation of illness. The self-regulatory model of illness was initially proposed by Leventhal, Meyer and Nerenz (1980) and has been revised and expanded in recent publications (Leventhal & Diefenbach, 1991; Leventhal, Leventhal & Schaefer, 1992).

The focus of this chapter will be on understanding the cognitive representation of rheumatic illness by the individual and then isolating mechanisms which underlie effective representations which lead to adaptive self-regulation of the rheumatic disorder. Initially, I will present an overview of the self-regulatory model in the context of rheumatic disorders. This will be followed by a review of instruments used to assess key constructs when the self-regulatory model is adopted for the study of rheumatic diseases. Following this overview, a review of the psychosocial literature on rheumatic diseases will be presented within the framework of the self-regulatory model. First, literature will be presented which provides insight into how individuals with rheumatic disorders construct or represent their illness. Then, a review of the processes which are used to self-regulate rheumatic disorders will occur, with an emphasis on coping responses and medication adherence behaviors. Finally, behavioral interventions which result in more effective self-regulation of coping and adherence will be discussed. Throughout the chapter, unresolved issues and hypotheses which require exploration will be presented.

THE SELF-REGULATORY MODEL OF ILLNESS APPLIED TO RHEUMATIC DISEASES

The key constructs in Leventhal, Leventhal and Schaefer's (1992) model are illness representation, coping, and appraisal. Leventhal, Leventhal and Schaefer (1992) postulate that an individual develops an implicit cognitive representation of his or her illness that is based on stored knowledge about disease, as well as on information that he/she receives from physician, friends, and family. Key components of a representation include a name for the disorder or symptoms, beliefs about the time course, controllability, and consequences of the disease, as well as causes of the disease. It is essential to note that the representation of the disease by the individual may be flawed or inaccurate, but it is this representation which drives attempts to cope with the disease. Coping responses can be instrumental and focused on attempts to mitigate symptoms or to rid oneself of the disease (e.g., rest, take medicine, seek more information), or they can be focused on dealing with the distress and affect (e.g., anger or depression) generated by the disease representation. After coping attempts have occurred, Leventhal, Leventhal and Schaefer (1992) postulate that appraisal of these efforts will occur. Based on this appraisal, an adjustment in both the disease representation as well as in continued coping responses will take place.

The self-regulatory model of illness is a dynamic model that is particularly well-suited as a heuristic to help understand the complex behavioral sequelae associated with rheumatic disorders. With respect to rheumatic diseases, the objective reality is that they are incurable, progressive, and unpredictable in course, and may lead to permanent disability. Thus, a newly diagnosed patient with rheumatoid arthritis might experience considerable emotional distress, with degree of distress related to symptoms but also to the subjective representation of illness and the patient's beliefs about how severe and controllable his/her particular case of this unpredictable disease is likely to be. The nature of initial representations and coping responses to such a diagnosis are likely to be highly related to what information a patient receives from a diagnosing physician, as well as how much pain and symptomatology a patient is experiencing at the time of diagnosis. Changes in illness representation and attempts at regulation will be related to how successful an individual perceives initial attempts at coping with pain and distress are.

An insightful point presented by Kiyak and Borson (1992) that is highly compatible with self-regulatory views of rheumatic disease is that the nature of coping responses changes over the temporal course of an illness. They suggest that initial coping attempts may be focused on dealing with emotions and distress associated with diagnosis, but that over time, coping efforts should shift to more behaviorally based attempts which will help control discomfort and functional disability. Thus, it seems essential that an effective behavioral understanding of rheumatic disorders includes a documentation of changes in behaviors across the temporal course of the disease, a dimension that is almost entirely missing from the literature on the psychosocial aspects of rheumatic disorders (Zautra & Manne, 1992).

Another important point to consider, which is indeed reflected as an emphasis in the current literature, is that because a primary symptom of rheumatic diseases is chronic pain, a great deal of energy on the part of patients is likely to be directed towards management strategies for pain. A challenge that remains is to integrate conceptually the instrumental aspects of coping with pain with strategies patients use for managing the affect associated with the disability and other consequences of chronic pain. A final point is that it seems likely that patients develop elaborate self-regulatory strategies for rheumatic disorders partially because the course of the disease is unpredictable and remissions may occur at any time. Regulatory strategies of dubious value that the patient is testing at the time of a remission (e.g., copper bracelets, bee pollen therapy) are likely to be evaluated favorably as effective and thus become integrated into the patient's regulation of illness. The unpredictable course of rheumatic diseases is likely the basis for much of the quackery in treatment that has been associated with these disorders.

INSTRUMENTS FOR MEASUREMENT OF KEY CONSTRUCTS

There are a number of instruments that have typically been used in the rheumatic literature for measurement of many constructs relevant to the self-regulatory model. Most of these instruments are specific to arthritis— both rheumatoid and osteoarthritis, but could readily be adapted for use with another rheumatic disorder. Because these instruments will be discussed repeatedly and in order to provide the interested reader with a concise summary and sources for these instruments, they will be briefly reviewed here.

Illness representation

Although the construct of illness representation is well-developed theoretically within the Leventhal, Leventhal and Schaefer (1992) model, this construct has not been highly researched at the empirical level. Representation of perceived symptoms can be obtained from many different symptoms checklists such as the Medical History Checklist (American Rheumatism Association, 1987). There are no published instruments available to measure belief about time course of the disease, although we have recently developed such an instrument in our own lab and its psychometric properties are currently under investigation (Park et al., 1993a). The most well-developed construct with respect to illness representation is belief about controllability of the rheumatic disorder, measured by the Arthritis Helplessness Index (Nicassio et al., 1985) which has subscales for internality and helplessness (Stein, Wallston & Nicassio, 1988). Related to the helplessness construct, the multidimensional Health Locus of Control instrument (MHLC) (Wallston, Wallston & DeVellis, 1978) focuses on perceived causes of disease. It includes subscales about illness in general where causes of illness are attributed to be internal, due to chance, or caused by others. Knowledge about disease has been measured in a number of studies (Lorig et al., 1985; Parker et al., 1984), but knowledge has typically been used as outcome measure rather than as a predictor of self-regulatory behavior. With respect to knowledge of illness, it should be noted that it is more important to understand what an individual believes to be true of the illness (as in the MHLC), rather than how much factual information they have available, because it is the individual's beliefs about what is true rather than the objective reality that will drive illness behaviors.

Self-regulation: coping with rheumatic disorders

Because of the centrality of pain to rheumatic disorders, there are a number of measures in the arthritis literature that focus primarily on strategies for coping with pain. The most widely used is the Coping Strategies Questionnaire (CSQ) developed by Rosenstiel and Keefe (1983) which they reported to have three major factors (cognitive coping and suppression, helplessness, and diverting attention or praying) as major factors with additional associated subscales. The Vanderbilt Pain Management Inventory (Brown & Nicassio, 1987) has two major factors—active and passive ways of coping with pain, each with associated subscales. Some researchers have adopted a more general stress and coping framework based on the work of Folkman and Lazarus (1980) in the study of rheumatic diseases. The Ways of Coping Checklist has a five-factor structure as described by Vitaliano et al. (1985) that includes problem-focused strategies, seeking of social support, blaming self, wishful thinking, and avoidance. Zautra and Manne (1992) provide a thorough review of this literature as it applies to rheumatoid arthritis and note that the different questionnaires address very different aspects of coping, with little known about how the various factors and constructs interrelate across instruments.

Appraisal of self-regulatory strategies

One instrument which would appear to measure perceived success of attempts at self-regulation has been developed by Lorig et al. (1989a). The Arthritis Self-Efficacy Scale contains subscales which measure the individual's perception that they have strategies available to them to control pain, to control other symptoms of the disease such as fatigue and depression, and to perform daily physical activities. The Park et al. (1993a) group is currently evaluating an instrument designed to measure appraisal of self-regulatory strategies.

Adaptation to illness and functional status

Three major categories of outcome measures have been used in the rheumatic literature: pain, functional disability and health, and depression. Presumably, the individual's self-regulatory illness behavior should be focused on achieving lower levels of pain, higher levels of physical function, and higher levels of psychological well-being (which has typically been defined in the arthritis literature as the absence of depression). All of these constructs have been well-developed in the rheumatic literature and instruments have been developed with known psychometric properties. Depression associated with rheumatic disease has been most commonly measured by the Center for Epidemiologic Studies Depression Subscale

(CES-D), (Radloff, 1977) and by the mood subscale of the Arthritis Impact Measurement Scale (AIMS) which was initially developed by Meenan, Gertman & Mason (1980) and recently revised as the AIMS-2 (Meenan et al., 1992). Pain indices are typically measured by the McGill Pain Inventory (Melzack, 1975), the pain subscale of the AIMS-2 (Meenan et al., 1992), and the Visual Analog Scale (Downie et al., 1978). Finally, functional status and disability are measured by a number of subscales of the AIMS-2 (Meenan et al., 1992), and by the Health Assessment Questionnaire (HAQ), (Fries et al., 1980). It should be noted that Kaplan, Coons and Anderson (1992) have argued against the use of paper and pencil measures of functional mobility, suggesting that they underestimate levels of dysfunction, and recommend interviews questions followed by probes. They also suggest disease-specific instruments do not permit comparison across diseases and also do not assess the magnitude of dysfunction due to treatments for rheumatic disorders (e.g., more illness due to decreased immune function from the use of immunosuppressants). These are all legitimate points. The measurement of treatment-related disability has been virtually ignored in the literature to date, and is an area of concern that requires instrument development in order to accurately assess functional status.

ILLNESS REPRESENTATION IN RHEUMATIC DISORDERS

The cognitive representation of illness plays a central role in the self regulation of disease. Leventhal and Diefenbach (1991) suggest important dimensions of illness representation are the symptoms and associated label for the disorder, whether the disease is acute or chronic, and fatal or nonfatal. Bishop (1991) suggests a similar mental organization for illness, but substitutes the perceived time course of the disorder for the chronic/acute distinction, and also suggests that perceived causes and cures are important in the initial representation of an illness. Bishop (1991) presents data suggesting that specific illnesses have prototypical characteristics and are wellorganized mental schemas. He notes that healthy subjects, when given random but serious symptoms to label as a disease for which they clearly have no prototype, "go into overdrive" and report that they would have great anxiety and concern about these symptoms.

Bishop's observation may be highly relevant to the prediagnosis phase of many of the autoimmune rheumatic disorders. Patients presenting with lupus, polymyositis, and even rheumatoid arthritis may experience a confusing range of serious and seemingly unrelated symptoms (e.g., numbness, weakness, fatigue, joint pain, chest pain, light sensitivity are all symptoms of lupus), that are not typical of any common illness schema. Many patients have frequently seen a number of physicians prior to a correct diagnosis and have been told that there is no somatic basis for their symptoms. Thus, the affected individual may go into the state of cognitive overdrive so aptly described by Bishop (1991). It would appear that a major source of initial distress in the experience of autoimmune rheumatic diseases may be due to the inability of the individual to form a stable illness representation that accounts for observed symptoms. The search for an illness representation is a frequent and ongoing theme in the popular literature on rheumatic and other chronic diseases like multiple sclerosis (Permut, 1989; Register, 1987), but the search process has not been investigated in the scientific literature. In fact, an important difference between osteoarthritis and many of the autoimmune rheumatic disorders may relate to the amount of time and effort expended to achieve a diagnosis, as individuals afflicted with osteoarthritis likely undergo a relatively brief search. It seems plausible that a lengthy initial search for illness representation could subsequently affect the self-regulatory process, possibly creating a sense of helplessness and perceived lack of self-efficacy.

Although the construct of illness representation is theoretically central to the Leventhal and Schaefer (1992) model, there are no studies which have used this construct to guide research on rheumatic diseases. At the same time, a review of existing literature yields considerable information about the illness representation of individual affected with rheumatic disorders. In a qualitative study of adult women with chronic illness, most of whom had arthritis, Belgrave (1990) categorized conceptualizations of illness. Some women viewed themselves as ill individuals who faced coping with disease as a major life task, whereas others considered themselves to be basically healthy individuals who had occasional bad times. One might expect that individuals with these contrasting frames of reference might adopt different self-regulatory strategies with the "ill" individuals having more complex and elaborate strategies. Moreover, one might hypothesize that individuals with autoimmune rheumatic disorders would be more likely to conceptualize themselves as ill, given the diffuse, systemic nature of their symptoms and disorder. In contrast, OA patients might view themselves as basically healthy individuals with problems, because of the focused, mechanical nature of their illness.

Given the role that physicians play in the transmission of diagnoses and information about rheumatic orders, it is likely important that there be some congruency between the illness representations of patients and physicians. As Skelton (1991) notes, the illness representations between lay and professionals cannot be too different, or the social foundation for medical care could not be maintained. Nevertheless, it appears that there are some differences in illness representations as a function of lay/professional status as well as a function of ethnic group. Lorig et al., (1984) asked Anglo-Americans, Hispanics, and a group of physicians the first five things that came to mind upon hearing the term "arthritis". The lay people were primarily diagnosed with osteoarthritis but some RA patients were included. Both groups rated pain and disability as the two most important constructs, providing evidence for a shared representation. Physicians, however, rated deformity and psychosocial problems as more salient than did lay persons. Moreover, Hispanics reported inflammation as a key construct, something not mentioned by the other two groups. With respect to treatment, both patients and physicians rated exercise and conventional treatment highly. Patients believed more in heat and diet than did physicians. Perhaps of most interest, physicians incorrectly predicted patients' beliefs with respect to every single dimension of treatment, suggesting that physicians' perceptions of their patients' illness representations are erroneous—that patients and physicians have more congruent representations than physicians recognize. The same findings emerged when physicians and patients reported what made arthritis worse—physicians judgments about what the patients believed were strikingly incorrect and there was a surprising congruence in beliefs between patients and physicians. More work is required to compare representations between patients and physicians, as this may be an important construct underlying illness behavior and treatment decisions.

There is limited evidence in the literature that OA patients construct their illness differently from RA patients. Andersson and Ekdahl (1992) reported that RA patients' self-appraisal of disease was more strongly related to functional abilities and length of time since diagnosis than OA patients. More acceptance of disease was observed in RA patients with longer periods of diagnosis, suggesting the dynamic nature of illness representation does change over time, as Leventhal and Diefenbach (1991) suggest. In addition, although both groups reported experiencing equivalent amounts of pain, OA patients used minimization of disease and avoidance strategies more than RA patients in coping with pain. Although the study does not provide direct measures of disease representation, the fact that different coping strategies were reported by different patient groups suggests that the initial representation of illness was likely different.

It appears that an important component of adaptation to rheumatic disorders may be how one conceptualizes disease status relative to others. There is evidence that RA patients who compare their own disease status favorably relative to other patients (downward comparison) show better psychological adjustment (Affleck et al., 1988, 1987), and that this is true even after actual disease status is controlled. These studies also indicated that downward comparisons were more common early in the course of the illness, again suggesting the importance of time course in understanding, adjustment to, and regulation of arthritis. The work of Blalock and colleagues provides more specificity about the nature and role of downward comparisons in illness representation and adjustment. Blalock, Devellis & Devellis (1989) noted that the majority of comparisons that RA patients make of their own performance are downward, and that such comparisons are associated with better adjustment and well-being. Nevertheless, when making judgments about desired performance, RA patients use the behavior of nonarthritis patients as the comparison standard. This pattern of findings suggests patients' recognition of their own disability, as they use nonarthritic adults as the desired standard, but that adjustment, nevertheless, is characterized by an illness representation that includes acceptance of limitations. Congruent with this interpretation, satisfaction with ability was more important than perceived ability in predicting adjustment. In later research, Blalock and colleagues found that the relationship between satisfaction with ability and well-being was mediated by how important the ability was to the RA patient (Blalock et al., 1992). Satisfaction was predictive of well-being only for patients who rated the abilities as important.

Despite a considerable body of existing research, there nevertheless appears to be major gaps in our knowledge of illness representation with respect to rheumatic disease. Important areas for future investigation include changes in illness representation across the course of rheumatic disorders, how representation is related to adjustment and well-being, and the highly inaccurate views physicians hold regarding patients' disease representations. Perhaps most important, little is known about how illness representations of either physicians or patients relate to evaluation and treatment decisions. Development of these areas of research will likely result in more complete explanations for the regulatory behaviors of coping and medical adherence, key aspects in the self-regulation of disease.

SELF-REGULATION OF RHEUMATIC DISORDERS

The central construct in the Leventhal, Leventhal and Schaefer (1992) model of illness relates to the dynamic process of disease regulation in which the affected individual engages. These self-regulatory behaviors are governed by the individual's construction of his/her illness. Two major categories of self-regulatory behaviors with respect to rheumatic diseases are coping and medication adherence. Each will be discussed in turn.

Coping with rheumatic disorders

Coping can be viewed as strategies developed for dealing with problems created by rheumatic disorders. Coping has two components: (a) regulation of emotion and negative affect associated with disease representation and appraisal, and (b) strategies for addressing concrete instrumental problems associated with the disorder, such as pain, disability, and fatigue. There is a voluminous literature on coping with rheumatic disorders (reviewed by Manne and Zautra (1992) and Zautra and Manne (1992). Zautra and Manne (1992) note that this literature emerges from two traditions: a general model of coping proposed by Folkman and Lazarus (1980) and models for coping with chronic pain. The Folkman and Lazarus (1980) approach is perhaps most compatible with the self-regulatory model of disease. Folkman and Lazarus suggest that the individual appraises the stressful situation and then makes an attempt to cope with the stressor based on the appraisal. Coping is viewed as a dynamic, contextual behavior rather than as a stable, individual trait. Folkman and Lazarus (1980) presented individuals with a range of daily problems and reported that appraisal played a central role in the coping strategy subjects reported that they would adopt. When individuals appraised a stressful situation as one where something could be done, coping attempts tended to be problem-focused. When appraisal of the situation suggested that the individual should hold back a response, the coping strategies subjects reported using were focused primarily on regulating negative emotions associated with the situation. Thus, when applied to illness, the Folkman and Lazarus model would suggest that the appraisal of how effective instrumental actions might be in regulating disease will play a critical role in the nature of coping attempts adopted.

Despite the importance that illness representation and appraisal appear to occupy in understanding illness coping strategies, the focus of the coping literature on rheumatic diseases has been primarily to categorize strategies used by individuals to deal with problems resulting from rheumatic disorders. These strategies have then been related to subsequent psychological adjustment and physical disability. Little effort has been focused on identifying the mechanisms underlying the coping strategies adopted, and there have been few studies that differentiate attempts to regulate emotional affect from attempts to regulate more concrete problems associated with the disorder.

Research done within the Folkman and Lazarus (1980) model has typically involved administering the Ways of Coping Checklist which was adapted for use with arthritis patients by Felton and Revenson (1984). Subjects are instructed to consider how frequently they would use each strategy listed to cope with problems associated with their illness, with the problems remaining unspecified. Given that situational determinants and appraisal appear to be primary determinants of coping, this context-free approach presents obvious problems. The items on the Ways of Coping Checklist factor into six subscales: information-seeking, cognitive restructuring, emotional expression, wish-fulfilling fantasy, threat minimization, and self-blame. Revenson and Felton (1989) indicated that RA patients most commonly used wish-fulfilling fantasies, threat minimization, and cognitive restructuring to cope with their illness. A higher reported use of any strategy was related to heightened positive affect six months later. It is not clear what components of the illness the subjects are addressing in their coping attempts, given the vague instructions accompanying the instrument. It would be useful to present specific, standardized scenarios, as Folkman and Lazarus (1980) did, that included separate vignettes relating to depressed affect, pain, and disability and determine if different coping responses are associated with each, an approach used successfully to distinguish coping responses to different diseases (Felton, Revenson & Hinrichsen, 1984) and to different situations (Mattlin, Wethington & Kessler, 1990). Evidence that this may be a productive approach is provided by Cohen et al. (1986) who reported that strategies that RA patients use to cope with pain differ substantially from strategies used to cope with threats to self-esteem. Direct actions were frequently used to cope with pain but almost never used to cope with threats to self-esteem. Such a finding supports the importance of the distinction between self-regulation of pain and self-regulation of illness-generated affect.

One study that provided insight into the dynamic nature of coping behavior was reported by Manne and Zautra (1989). They administered the Ways of Coping Checklist to female RA patients, and also measured the number of critical remarks spouses made about the RA patient in an interview. They found spouses' critical remarks predicted wishful thinking in RA patients, a maladaptive coping strategy. This study is notable in that it attempted to determine the contextual basis and potential mechanisms underlying coping responses. The findings suggest that a spouse may be important in shaping illness representation and appraisal, although the Manne and Zautra (1989) study does not provide a direct linkage, and it is even possible that the use of maladaptive coping strategy by the patient served as the basis for the spouse's critical remarks. In any case, studies of this sort point to the dynamic nature of coping as a self-regulatory process and suggest the highly contextual nature of coping responses.

Although studies that focus specifically on coping with pain in rheumatic disorders have less generality than those that use the Ways of Coping Checklist, this specificity of focus has resulted in a relatively good understanding of the relationship between pain and coping. The most commonly used instrument for assessing coping with pain is the Coping Strategies Questionnaire initially developed by Rosenstiel and Keefe (1983). The CSQ has been used extensively to study RA and OA patients and has been used primarily as a predictor of functional status and depression. The most striking finding from work with the CSQ is not so much that there are coping strategies that lead to excellent self-regulation of pain and dysfunction, but rather that there do appear to be coping strategies that are maladaptive. Rosenstiel and Keefe (1983) initially reported such a finding when they studied patients with low back pain. They found that a helplessness factor appeared to be related to depression and anxiety. The helplessness factor measured patients' belief in their ability to control and decrease pain, as well as their tendency to catastrophize or expect the worst with respect to future outcomes of their disorder.

In a later study of OA patients with knee pain, Keefe et al. (1987)

reported that two factors from the CSQ accounted for 60% of the variance in responding. One factor was labeled Coping Attempts and the second was labeled Pain Control and Rational Thinking (PCRT). These constructs have been used in many additional studies. The Coping Attempts Factor can be viewed as a measure of the effort subjects invest in self-regulation of disease and includes diverse strategies such as praying and hoping, increasing activity, ignoring pain, diverting attention, and making coping self-statements. The Pain Control and Rational Thinking Factor included the same three items earlier labeled helplessness by Rosenstiel and Keefe (1983), and measures the tendency to catastrophize as well as the patient's beliefs about pain controllability. Keefe et al. (1987) found that the PCRT was a significant factor in predicting both physical and psychological disability, even after initial levels of reported pain was controlled. This finding suggests that the perception that one has the ability to self-regulate pain and also that one does not tend to catastrophize about future events may be more important than specific types or amounts of coping efforts. Keefe et al. (1987) hypothesize that training OA patients not to catastrophize and to restructure beliefs about disease controllability may be an important mechanism underlying pain control.

There are several studies that examine the relationship of the PCRT factor to disability and adjustment in RA patients prospectively. These studies address the important question of whether a high score on the PCRT predicts later disability, pain, and poor adjustment, after controlling for initial levels of these variables. Parker et al. (1989) studied male RA patients in a VA hospital with a one-year follow-up measure. They reported that PCRT scores did not correlate with scores on the Beck Depression Inventory or AIMS scores of physical functioning over a one-year interval. Changes in the PCRT, however, were correlated with changes in pain and physical functioning. Parker et al. (1989) note the similarity of their findings to Keefe et al. (1987), and suggest that patients' belief in self-efficacy with respect to pain and the absence of catastrophizing is a construct of major importance in the treatment of RA

The Parker et al. finding was replicated and extended by Keefe et al. (1989). They measured catastrophizing in RA patients using a six-item scale from the CSQ, and also collected measures of functional disability from the AIMS, measures of depression (CES-D) and measures of pain with the Visual Analog Scale (Downie et al., 1978). They reported that catastrophizing was a stable behavior, and after controlling for autoregressive effects at time one, they reported that catastrophizing continued to predict pain, disability, and depression. Similarly, Beckham et al. (1991) found that the PCRT explained significant variance in physical disability, pain, psychological disability, depression, and hassles in RA patients, after controlling for disease status. The consistent findings with respect to the PCRT do suggest that it is a dysfunctional self-regulatory strategy and that it may be a general and important construct in understanding and managing both pain and affect associated with rheumatic disorders. Dekker et al. (1992) make the suggestion that catastrophizing effects on pain and disability may be mediated through avoidance of exercise, resulting in muscle weakness. Thus, they suggest that catastrophizing results in a decrease in appropriate self-regulatory activities.

From a self-regulatory perspective, it appears that catastrophizing represents an appraisal that self-regulation of the rheumatic disorder is not possible—the patient's belief that coping attempts will not be successful and that disease activity cannot be modified. An important issue that must be addressed is understanding the conditions under which such an illness representation can be modified, and whether or not modifications lead to improvements in pain and physical function. It is also important to understand the temporal course of catastrophizing—whether it is a stable response within the individual to the disease or if it is more contextual and occurs as a result of a history of unsuccessful attempts to modify disease activity.

An important prospective study by Brown (1990) on depression and pain suggests that the latter may be the case, at least for a subset of individuals. He collected six waves of data at six-month intervals from RA patients, measuring pain, disability, and depression. He reported that LISREL models indicated that pain prospectively predicted depression in the last 12 months of data collection, but that depression did not predict pain for any interval. In other words, the data suggest that it is the perception of pain that causes depression, not depression that heightens the experience of pain. Unfortunately, no data are available regarding changes in number of attempts at coping and changes in coping strategies over time. If parallel results were found for catastrophizing, that is, that pain predicts catastrophizing but catastrophizing does not predict pain, it would suggest that modifying catastrophizing might not lessen the experience of pain, and that possibly catastrophizing occurs in response to pain. More use of the powerful, prospective, longitudinal studies like those conducted by Brown (1990) would result in the ability to disentangle these issues.

There are a few studies which relate patient beliefs about illness to catastrophizing. According to the self-regulatory model, patients' belief that they are helpless or powerless regarding management of their arthritis should be predictive of catastrophizing. The Arthritis Helplessness Index (AHI) developed by Nicassio et al. (1985) provides a measure of perceived helplessness with respect to control of disease. Stein, Wallston and Nicassio (1988) provided evidence that a high score for RA patients on the helplessness subscale was positively related to measures of passive coping on the Vanderbilt Pain Management Inventory (Brown & Nicassio, 1987), suggesting that perceptions about disease controllability influenced coping style. Brown and Nicassio (1987) report a similar finding. Parker et al.

(1989) related helplessness and catastrophizing and found that the PCRT (catastrophizing factor) predicted a significant amount of variance on the AHI, using a hierarchical regression model. This finding does not directly address the self-regulatory model of illness because Parker et al. (1989) used catastrophizing to predict beliefs. The self-regulatory model, however, would suggest that beliefs should be used to predict coping, so that the AHI, which measures beliefs, should be used in a hierarchical regression to predict the coping strategy of catastrophizing. This work remains to be done but could be accomplished with existing data.

Finally, the coping literature has largely neglected how rheumatic patients cope with disease-generated affect. One instrument that shows promise that has not yet been widely used was developed by Lorig et al. (1989a). The instrument measures patients' perceived self-efficacy to manage pain, physical function, as well as fatigue and depression associated with arthritis. Although the factor structure of this instrument does not map directly onto constructs for self-regulation of emotion, physical function, and disease, this instrument appears to be a promising start towards measuring patients' beliefs about ability to manage both the physical and emotional consequences of disease. Data relating beliefs in these different domains to coping strategies and to adherence are badly needed in order to understand the mechanisms underlying adaptive self-regulatory strategies.

In summary, there is a vast literature on coping with rheumatic disorders that has been aptly reviewed by Manne and Zautra (1992) and Zautra and Manne (1992). It appears that catastrophizing about pain is a maladaptive coping strategy for management of pain associated with rheumatic disorders. Catastrophizing may represent an appraisal that self-regulation of disease is not possible. Prospective studies of the development of catastrophizing strategies are needed, and the contextual factors that contribute to such a strategy must be examined. Also, little is known about self-regulation of negative affect and coping with instrumental problems associated with rheumatic diseases, as well as shifts in the focus of coping across disease course.

Medication adherence and rheumatic disorders

In addition to coping with pain, affect, and disease-related problems, a key component of self-regulation of rheumatic disorders for patients relates to the patient's adherence to medical treatments. Adherence can include the correct use of medications, following a prescribed exercise regimen, splint-wearing or attending physical therapy as prescribed, as well as keeping medical appointments. Leventhal and Cameron (1987) specifically apply the self-regulatory model of illness to adherence behaviors. The patient is viewed as a problem solver, choosing and adhering to treatment regimens as a function of illness representation and appraisal of the results of adherence behaviors.

Medication adherence is a behavior of particular interest with respect to rheumatic disorders because the implications of adherence behaviors vary as a function of type of rheumatic disorder. Perhaps the most striking comparison is one between osteoarthritis and rheumatoid arthritis. For osteoarthritis, medications are prescribed solely to relieve pain. Thus the only gain available to an OA patient from taking medications (usually NSAIDs) is relief of pain, as there are no improvements in disease status or prevention of disease progression as a function of medication usage. For an RA patient, NSAIDs and corticosteroids are prescribed to reduce inflammation as well as to alleviate pain, and immunosuppressants are frequently prescribed to reduce disease activity. It is widely believed that the use of corticosteroids and powerful immunosuppressants may prevent disease progression and help minimize or slow disability and deformity, although well-controlled studies are not available that demonstrate this (Wolfe, 1991). Thus, objectively, it is likely of more importance for long-term outcome that RA patients adhere to a medication regimen to prevent future pain and disability, whereas adherence has little effect on long-term outcome for OA patients. Indeed, one might argue that a desirable self-regulatory goal for OA patients would be to take as little medication as possible, given the adverse side effects associated with NSAIDs. A "failure to comply" for an OA patient may represent the success of other pain management techniques over less desirable medication therapies.

Little is known about adherence behaviors in osteoarthritis patients, whereas a more substantial literature has emerged with respect to RA patients. Most of the literature has focused on the role of disease and medication variables in predicting adherence. There is little research which examines patients' cognitions about medications and disease, and the appraisal of the results of using or not using medications. In recognition of this point, Deyo (1982) notes that an understanding of lay models of rheumatic diseases may play an important role in understanding adherence. In addition, Jette (1982) makes the important point that nonadherence may also be related to cognitive failures or dysfunction, due to difficulties understanding and remembering medication and other treatment regimens, a point echoed by Park (1991). Thus, a complete understanding of adherence behaviors with respect to rheumatic disorders must take into account representations about illness and treatments, as well as the important role that memory, comprehension, and overall cognitive function may play in adhering to a complex regimen.

Variables which have been hypothesized to affect adherence and likely play a role in representation of treatment regimen and appraisal of results include doctor–patient interactions (Geertsen, Gray & Ward, 1973; Feinberg, 1988), patient beliefs (Ferguson & Bole, 1979), and medication side effects (Deyo, 1982). Most adherence studies have been atheoretical, focusing on the relationship between a subset of these variables and adherence to a regimen without examining illness representation as a construct mediating the relationship. Also, despite the close relationship between medication usage as a coping strategy to regulate illness, little work has been done to integrate the construct of coping with adherence conceptually or empirically. One notable exception is work by Folkman, Bernstein and Lazarus (1987) where they related coping strategies to medication usage in an elderly sample. They found coping strategies to be unrelated to medication usage, but because they did not measure illness coping behaviors in particular and the patient group was heterogeneous, this is not surprising.

There are a few studies that examine patients' beliefs and relate these representations to adherence. Ferguson and Bole (1979) found that adherence to aspirin therapy (measured by salicylate levels in the bloodstream) was related to patients' beliefs in the medication's efficacy. In contrast, Beck et al. (1988) reported that RA patients who perceived adverse side effects associated with NSAID use were just as likely to be adherent as those not perceiving side effects. Because NSAIDs are an analgesic, it may be that patients continue to take them, despite perceived adverse side effects, but this hypothesis has not been tested in the literature. It is important to understand more about arthritis patients' beliefs about their medication and the relationship of these beliefs to adherence. When do patients maintain medication-taking behaviors despite side effects and under what conditions do they discontinue medications? Much more work is needed in this important area, as it may be possible to present patients with information that will result in beliefs about the medication that are critical to maintenance of adherence.

Another area of potential importance in medication adherence is the physician–patient relationship. Geertsen, Gray and Ward (1973) reported that patients' satisfaction with the amount of time a physician spent with them as well as a low perceived waiting time predicted adherence. Adherence, however, was measured by physician estimates which are notably unreliable (Mushlin & Appel, 1977; Norell, 1981), and the positive relationship observed may have merely reflected the good opinion the physician generally had of patients deemed to be adherent and his/her willingness to spend more time with such patients. Geertsen, Gray and Ward (1973) also reported that adherence was related to the belief that arthritis is not inevitably crippling. There is little research that systematically relates physician–patient relationships to adherence behaviors in rheumatic patients, despite the fact that this relationship may play an important role in illness representation and self-regulatory strategies adopted.

With respect to disease variables, it is generally believed that OA patients are less adherent than RA patients (Lorig, Konkol & Gonzalez,

1987), but there are no systematic comparisons available. Given the fact that OA patients can regulate only pain, but not disease activity, with medication, such an observation would appear to be consonant with a self-regulatory view of illness. Hulka (1979) has noted that disease severity and length of illness does not appear to be systematically related to adherence in diabetics and this also appears to be true for arthritis (Ferguson & Bole, 1979; Lee & Tan, 1979), a finding counter intuitive to a self-regulatory view. The compatibility of such findings for a self-regulatory view of illness, however, cannot be evaluated in the absence of data regarding patients' cognitions about their illness and beliefs about their medications.

With respect to medication variables, there is some evidence that adherence is not a stable individual behavior but is related to the category of drug prescribed (Deyo, Inui & Sullivan, 1981; Park et al., in press, 1993b), consonant with a self-regulatory view of adherence behavior. This notion of selective nonadherence to certain medications but not others may be of particular importance for autoimmune rheumatic diseases. Some medications prescribed for autoimmune rheumatic disease are slow-acting (e.g. immunosuppressants), and may have noticeable adverse side effects without improvement in disease status for a period of weeks, whereas others such as NSAIDs provide immediate symptomatic relief from pain. Such differences in outcome likely affect patients' beliefs about medications, unless they have appropriate instructions and representations about the relationships of these medications to symptoms. Instructions and information about treatments may play a critical role in adherence with respect to rheumatic disease, an issue considered more fully later. Based on the different temporal course of medication efficacy, it would be worthwhile to investigate the hypothesis that RA patients are more likely to fail to adhere to immunosuppressants than NSAIDs, and that failure to adhere is likely related to beliefs that the medication is not producing positive gains, that is, contributing to modulation of disease.

Complexity of regimen may also affect adherence. Wasner et al. (1981) reported that adherence in arthritis was best predicted by complexity of drug regimen and number of doses required per day, although Deyo (1982) suggests complexity of drug regimen may be confounded with disease severity. Lochead et al. (1985) showed better adherence with an aspirin regimen prescribed once rather than four times a day. The self-regulatory model does not make strong predictions about complexity, and it is likely that the effects of complexity are mediated through cognitive function, an issue considered more fully later.

The psychosocial and functional/behavioral outcomes of adherence is an issue of critical importance. Given Wolfe's (1991) contention that little systematic research exists providing controlled comparisons of long-term outcomes for specific medications for RA patients, and the limited gains to be had from adherence for OA patients, it is surprising that, the consequences of adherence have largely been ignored (Belcon, Haynes & Tugwell, 1984). Deyo (1982) explicitly questions the emphasis on adherence when little is known about its contribution to well-being, particularly for the OA patient. Because the medications taken by OA patients, and many other rheumatic patients do not cure disease, perhaps the most critical question regarding adherence, after initial disease severity is controlled, is how it relates to quality of life. Prospective outcome studies using measures of adherence as a predictor variable and psychological well-being, and functional ability as outcomes are urgently needed, particularly when one considers the chronic, incurable nature of rheumatic disorders (Lorig, Konkol & Gonzalez 1987).

Cognitive function may also be an important aspect of adherence with respect to rheumatic disease. Although the notion that cognitive function plays an important role in adherence behaviors in arthritis patients is frequently stated (Haynes, Wang & Gomes, 1987; Blechman, 1984), there is little if any data on the topic. Park (1991) has suggested that there are four cognitive components to adherence: the patient must (a) understand the individual instructions for each medication; (b) integrate the instructions across medications and develop a daily plan for medication-taking behavior; (c) remember or write the plan down; and (d) remember to perform the prospective action of taking the medication at the appropriate time. Because rheumatic patients tend to be older adults, there is particular concern about the role of cognitive factors in adherence behavior. Morrell, Park and Poon (1989, 1990) have demonstrated that older adults show poorer memory and comprehension for medication information than young adults. In addition, Park et al. (1992) measured adherence behaviors with precise electronic monitors and found that oldest-old adults had the highest rate of nonadherence, and were also most helped by a cognitive prosthesis which reduced comprehension and memory burden by organizing medications according to day and time. Such findings suggest that the role of cognitive factors may play an important role in the self-regulation of disease, and that with increased age, an appropriate illness representation may not be sufficient for the individual to engage in self-regulatory adherence behaviors.

The finding that social support appears to be an important factor in adherence behaviors of arthritis patients (Oakes et al., 1970) and in chronically ill elderly (Schwartz et al., 1962) also implicates cognitive factors. The presence of others may act as cognitive prosthesis to remind the older adult to take medications and may also ensure that medications are taken correctly.

One problem that has plagued adherence research has been obtaining accurate measures of adherence. Deyo, Inni and Sullivan (1981) note the absence of a "gold standard" (Rudd, 1979) for measuring adherence in rheumatic patients. The most commonly relied upon measure for studying adherence in rheumatic disease has been verbal report, which likely results in the under-reporting of nonadherence behavior. Pill counts have been used with somewhat more success (Deyo, Inni & Sullivan 1981), as have salicylate levels (Beck et al., 1988). More recent techniques which allow microelectronic monitoring of adherence behaviors (Park et al., 1992; Dunbar, Dunning & Dwyer, 1989) hold great promise for more accurate and comprehensive measures of adherence behavior than has been the case in the past. Electronic monitoring permits testing of precise hypotheses about categories of medication to be tested, as well as permits patterns of nonadherence to be recorded over prolonged intervals. Studies which measure psychosocial variables along with adherence behaviors using microelectronic techniques are certainly needed. Such research would integrate the use of beliefs and coping strategies, as well as adherence behaviors, in determining the self-regulatory processes that characterize rheumatic disorders, providing a more integrated view of the complex illness behaviors associated with these diseases, as well as an evaluation of what illness representations and behaviors are particularly adaptive.

To summarize, there are a number of important issues that remain to be addressed with respect to adherence behaviors in rheumatic disorders. First, little is known about the effects of adherence on quality of life or prevention of disability. Work must proceed in this area. Second, the role of cognitive function in adherence behaviors should be integrated into the self-regulatory model, particularly given the large number of older adults who comprise the population of rheumatic patients. Third, an empirical integration of illness representation with adherence behaviors needs to be developed for the rheumatic disorders.

PSYCHOLOGICAL INTERVENTIONS FOR SELF-REGULATION OF RHEUMATIC DISORDERS

Regulation of pain and distress

There is an extensive literature on the effects of patient education as well as cognitive behavior therapy on pain, disability, and distress associated with rheumatic disorders. The literature on patient education clearly points to the need to restructure an illness representation effectively if an educational intervention is to be useful. A study by Parker et al. (1984) illustrates this point. They presented RA patients at a VA hospital with a seven-hour educational program about RA. Although patients' knowledge about the disease increased, there was evidence for greater pain and disability in the intervention group relative to a control group. The authors concluded that the extensive presentations patients received on the disease process may have highlighted the salience of pain and increased ptients' sense of vulnerability. They suggest a cognitive explanation for the finding of increased dysfunction with education, noting that "patients place their own cognitive interpretations on the education process, and that such interpretations are not always those which are intended by educators" (p. 774). Thus, this study suggests that it is of great importance to consider the illness representation that may result from any educational program, and how such a representation might be related to an improvement in regulatory capabilities.

This point is also made by the work of Lorig and colleagues. Lorig et al. (1985) developed a complex patient Arthritis Self-Management Program (ASMP) that involved education about arthritis as well as training in self-management techniques. The course was presented in six sessions over a four-month period. Subjects were tested at four, eight, and 20 months. Subjects (OA and RA patients) in the ASMP condition showed a reduction in pain and an increase in knowledge about arthritis relative to a control group, suggesting that the ASMP was an effective technique. In later research, however, Lorig et al. (1989b) reported a curious finding. Although the ASMP course had a positive effect for both OA and RA patients across four months in terms of pain, disability, knowledge, and appropriate arthritis behaviors, specific changes in health behaviors were not related to changes in health status. For example, an increase in exercise was not related to a decrease in pain, disability, or depression, as would be expected. The authors concluded that the ASMP training was effective, but that the variable mediating improvement was not known.

In follow-up research, Lorig and Gonzalez (1992) suggested that the mechanism underlying improvement was an increase in self-efficacy and the patient's belief that the rheumatic disorder was controllable. In other words, the ASMP's primary effect appeared to be mediated by modification of illness representation. Based on this hypothesis, Lorig and Gonzalez redesigned the ASMP to heighten improvements in patients' beliefs that they had techniques available to them to modify pain and cope with depression. They reported that this revised course was particularly effective, and that significant, positive changes in self-efficacy were noted. Thus, it appears that self-efficacy, the patient's belief that the disease can be regulated, may be a critical component of an adaptive illness representation with respect to rheumatic disorders. Lorig, Konkol and Gonzalez (1987), provide support for this view, as they concluded after reviewing the literature that although arthritis education may be effective in reducing pain and disability, the effect is not based on behavior change. Studies remain to be done which examine the configuration of patient beliefs about disease and how they relate to outcomes, as well as whether modifications in beliefs and self-efficacy scores produce changes in pain, disability, and depression.

Another intervention related to self-regulation views of illness involves treatment of rheumatic patients with cognitive/behavioral therapy (CBT). Parker et al. (1988) presented RA patients with CBT that involved patient education as well as training in various strategies that included coping, problem-solving, distraction and stress management. A control group received group therapy that focused on education and social support, and a no treatment control group was also included. Although both treatment groups rated the intervention they received effective, only the CBT group showed significant behavior change. At a 12-month interval, the CBT group catastrophized significantly less and reported increased perception of control over pain. Nevertheless, the CBT group reported pain and depression equivalent to the control group, suggesting that interventions which decrease catastrophizing may not decrease experienced pain or depression.

Bradley et al. (1987) provided RA patients with CBT therapy or group therapy that emphasized social support. Subjects were assessed at the end of treatment and six months later. Although subjects in both groups were equally confident about the positive effects of the treatment they received, CBT subjects showed lower displays of pain behavior and also showed lower disease activity scores, although ratings of pain did not differ from controls and depression increased at six months in all subjects. The most exciting finding was that disease activity appeared to be somewhat modified by treatment, but the failure to demonstrate improvement in depression and reported pain is problematic.

Overall, the data on the role of cognitive/behavior therapy is promising but sufficiently limited that more research needs to be done to determine the effectiveness of this intervention. The CBT approach does not adopt an explicit self-regulatory framework, but is certainly consistent with the notion of the patient as a dynamic problem-solver attempting to develop strategies to regulate and modify disease.

Interventions to improve adherence behaviors

Lorig, Kankol and Gonzalez (1987) note that the goals of arthritis education should be to help the patient make appropriate decisions about their disease and that "compliance is not always of prime importance" (p. 208). This is particularly true, as noted earlier, for OA patients where medication adherence may not be desirable. It may be of considerably more importance that patients with autoimmune disorders adhere to a treatment regimen to prevent systemic damage and disability. For these patients, little is known about how to improve adherence. The focus of most intervention research has been to improve understanding of the need to take medications and follow other medical instructions including physical therapy, wearing of splints, and exercise. Little research has been focused on the role of cognitive interventions to improve medication adherence. This is a particular concern for rheumatic patients who tend to be older, as there is compelling evidence suggesting that cognitive function does decline with advanced age (Salthouse, 1991).

Medication adherence may be a particular concern for patients with autoimmune disorders, many of whom take eight or more prescriptions medications. Frequently medications are prescribed to offset or control damage done to various organs by the disease, as well as to regulate the disease itself. Every local drugstore in the USA provides a complex array of adherence devices in the form of various pill containers and medication organizers designed to partition and organize medication regimens along temporal dimensions. Presumably, these devices are designed to serve as cognitive prostheses to improve adherence behaviors, yet little is known as to their actual efficacy with respect to improving adherence. Park et al. (1991) examined the ability of arthritis patients to load three such prototypical medication organizers correctly. OA patients were asked to load their medications into one of three different types of organizers. Park et al. (1991) reported the highest error rate for an organizer that simply had a large compartment for each day of the week. Once the medication was dropped into the daily compartment, all information about when it was to be taken as well as the identity of the medication was lost. Given the high number of errors made in simply placing the medication into the container, it seems likely that the use of such an organizer by an arthritis patient might contribute to nonadherence behaviors rather than facilitate adherence Park et al. (1991) reported that the organizer that arthritis patients were able to load with the highest degree of accuracy was a seven-day organizer that had four partitions divided according to time associated with each day of the week. OA patients made few errors loading this organizer, and although identity of the medication was lost once it was placed in the organizer, detailed scheduling information was now available to the patient as to when and how much medication should be taken at a particular time.

In a later study, Park et al. (1992) loaded older adults' medications into such an organizer and also provided subjects with an organizational chart for medication taking. Oldest-old subjects made the most errors in a control condition but were significantly facilitated by the organizational aids. These findings suggest cognitive aids may play a significant role in improving adherence, but much more research is required to understand the most effective prostheses. Moreover, studies must be conducted that relate improved adherence to improvements in physical function, depression, and quality of life.

In attempting interventions, it is important to determine what aspects of behavior require change for adaptation to the rheumatic disorder. If an individual has an appropriate illness representation, but due to age-related changes in cognitive function, can no longer manage medications effectively, a psychosocial intervention will not likely improve the targeted behavior of medication adherence. Similarly, providing an individual who perceives that his/her medications are not useful with a cognitive intervention to improve adherence will not facilitate behavior, and in this case a psychosocial intervention might be more appropriate.

CONCLUSION

Although much remains to be learned about the role psychosocial and cognitive factors may play in the regulation of rheumatic disorders, there is a solid foundation of existing research upon which to build. Much of the recent research on coping and interventions has been developed from a solid theoretical focus which provides integration and unity for future work. There are a large number of instruments available with known psychometric properties which measure important constructs. The use of sophisticated prospective designs to determine causal relationships between predictors and outcomes is a strength. Much work, however, remains to be done and there are a number of areas where more work needs to be focused. First, there needs to be an integration of illness representation with styles of coping, in order to understand the mechanisms which underlie different styles of coping. Second, there needs to be more work on regulation and control of disease-generated affect, as well as documentation of how the focus of coping efforts may evolve and change across the course of the disease. Third, the importance of adherence behaviors as a self-regulatory strategy requires urgent investigation, as does their relationship to illness representations. To the extent that these questions are addressed, mechanisms for interventions which effectively minimize pain and enhance function and well-being will be isolated.

ACKNOWLEDGMENTS AND AUTHOR'S NOTE

Preparation of this manuscript was supported by a research grant (R01 AG09868) to the author from the National Institute on Aging. The author thanks Lisa Howard, Katherine Echt and Christy Gaines for assistance with library work and references. Correspondence may be addressed to the author at the Department of Psychology, University of Georgia, Athens, GA 30602, USA.

REFERENCES

Affleck, G., Tennen, H., Pfeiffer, C., Fifield, J. & Rowe, J. (1987). Downward comparison and coping with serious medical problems. *American Journal of Orthopsychiatry*, 57, 570–578.

Affleck, G., Tennen, H., Pfeiffer, C. & Fifield, J. (1988). Social comparisons in rheumatoid arthritis: accuracy and adaptational significance. *Journal of Social and Clinical Psychology*, 6, 219–234.

American Rheumatism Association (1987). *Medical History Checklist*. Atlanta, GA: American Rheumatism Association.

Andersson, S. I. & Ekdahl, C. (1992). Self-appraisal and coping in out-patients with chronic disease. *Scandinavian Journal of Psychology*, 33, 289–300.

Beck, N. C, Parker, J. C., Frank, R. G. et al. (1988). Patients with rheumatoid arthritis at high risk for noncompliance with salicylate treatment regimens. *Journal of Rheumatology*, 15, 1081–1084.

Beckham, J. D., Keefe, F. J., Caldwell, D. S. & Roodman, A. A. (1991). Pain coping strategies in rheumatoid arthritis: relationships to pain, disability, depression, and daily hassles. *Behavior Therapy*, 22, 113–124.

Belcon, M. C., Haynes, R. B. & Tugwell, P. (1984). A critical review of compliance studies in rheumatoid arthritis. *Arthritis and Rheumatism*, 27, 1227–1233.

Belgrave, L. L. (1990). The relevance of chronic illness in the everyday lives of elderly women. *Journal of Aging and Health*, 2, 475–500.

Bishop, G. D. (1991). Understanding the understanding of illness: lay disease representations. In: J. A. Skelton & R. T. Croyle (Eds), *Mental representation in health and illness* (pp. 32–59). New York: Springer Verlag.

Blalock, S. J., DeVellis, B. M. & DeVellis, R. F. (1989). Social comparison among individuals with rheumatoid arthritis. *Journal of Applied Social Psychology*, 19, 665–680.

Blalock, S. J., DeVellis, B. M., DeVellis, R. F., Giorgino, K. B., van H. Sauter, S., Jordan, J. M., Keefe, F. J. & Mutran, E. J. (1992). Psychological well-being among people with recently diagnosed rheumatoid arthritis. *Arthritis and Rheumatism*, 35, 1267–1272.

Blechman, W. (1984). Managing the older arthritic: can the family help? *Geriatrics*, 39, 131–132.

Bradley, L. A., Young, L. D., Anderson, K. O., Turner, R. A., Agudelo, C. A., McDaniel, L. K., Pisko, E. J., Semble, E. L. & Morgan, T. M. (1987). Effects of psychological therapy on pain behavior of rheumatoid arthritis patients: treatment outcome and six month follow-up. *Arthritis and Rheumatism*, 30, 1105–1114.

Brandt, K. D. & Flusser, D. (1991). Osteoarthritis. In: N. Bellamy (Ed), *Prognosis in the Rheumatic Diseases* (pp. 11–36). London: Kluwer.

Brown, G. K. (1990). A causal analysis of chronic pain and depression. *Journal of Abnormal Psychology*, 99, 127–137.

Brown, G. K. & Nicassio, P. M. (1987). Development of a questionnaire for the assessment of active and passive coping strategies in chronic pain patients. *Pain*, 31, 53–64.

Brown, G. K., Nicassio, P. M. & Wallston, K. A. (1989). Pain coping strategies and depression in rheumatoid arthritis. *Journal of Consulting and Clinical Psychology*, 57, 652–657.

Cohen, F., Reese, L. B., Kaplan, G. A. & Riggio, R. E. (1986). Coping with the stresses of arthritis. In: R. W. Moskowitz & M. R. Haug (Eds), *Arthritis and the elderly* (pp. 47–56). New York: Springer.

Controller General (1979). *Entering a nursing home—Costly implications for Medicaid and the elderly* (PAD 80–12). Washington, DC: General Accounting Office.

Dekker, J., Boot, B., van der Woude, L. H. V. & Bijlsma, J. W. J. (1992). Pain and disability in osteoarthritis: a review of biobehavioral mechanisms. *Journal of Behavioral Medicine*, 15, 189–214.

Deyo, R. A. (1982). Compliance with therapeutic regimens in arthritis: issues, current status, and a future agenda. *Seminars in Arthritis and Rheumatism*, 12, 233–244.

Deyo, R. A., Inui, T. S. & Sullivan, B. (1981). Noncompliance with arthritis drugs: magnitude, correlates, and clinical implications. *Journal of Rheumatology*, 8, 931–936.

Downie, W. W., Leatham, P. A., Rhind, V. M., Wright, V., Branco, J. A. & Anderson, J. A. (1978). Studies with pain rating scales. *Annals of Rheumatoid Disease*, 37, 378–381.

Dunbar, J., Dunning, E. J. & Dwyer, K. (1989). Compliance measurement with arthritis regimen. *Arthritis Care and Research*, 2, S8–S16.

Feinberg, J. (1988). The effect of patient-practitioner interaction on compliance: a review of the literature and application in rheumatoid arthritis. *Patient Education and Counseling*, 11, 171–187.

Felton, B. J. & Revenson, T. A. (1984) Coping with chronic illness: a study of illness controllability and the influence of coping strategies on psychosocial adjustment. *Journal of Consulting and Clinical Psychology*, 52, 343–353.

Felton, B. J., Revenson, T. A. & Hinrichsen, G. A. (1984). Stress and coping in the explanation of psychological adjustment among chronically ill adults. *Social Science and Medicine*, 18, 889–898.

Ferguson, K. & Bole, G. G., (1979). Family support, health benefits, and therapeutic compliance in patients with rheumatoid arthritis. *Patient Counseling and Health Education*, 1, 101–105.

Folkman, S., Bernstein, L. & Lazarus, R. S. (1987). Stress processes and the misuse of drugs in older adults. *Psychology and Aging*, 2, 366–374.

Folkman, S. & Lazarus, R. S. (1980). An analysis of coping in a middle-aged community sample. *Journal of Health and Social Behavior*, 21, 219–239.

Fries, J. F. & Bellamy, N. (1991). Introduction. In: N. Bellamy (Ed), *Prognosis in the Rheumatic Diseases* (pp. 1–10). London: Kluwer.

Fries, J. F., Spitz, R., Kraines, R. G. & Holman, H. R. (1980). Measurement of patient outcome in arthritis. *Arthritis and Rheumatism*, 23, 137–145.

Geertsen, H. R., Gray, R. M. & Ward, J. R. (1973). Patient non-compliance within the context of seeking medical care for arthritis. *Journal of Chronic Diseases*, 26, 689–698.

Haynes, R. B., Wang, E. & Gomes, M. D. M. (1987). A critical review of interventions to improve compliance with prescribed medications. *Patient Education and Counseling*, 10, 155–166.

Hulka, B. S. (1979). Patient-clinician interactions and compliance. In: R. B. Haynes, D. W. Taylor & D. L. Sackett (Eds), *Compliance in Health Care* (pp. 63–77). Baltimore: Johns Hopkins University Press.

Jette, A. M. (1982). Improving patient cooperation with arthritis treatment regimens. *Arthritis and Rheumatism*, 25, 447–453.

Kaplan, H. M., Coons, S. J. & Anderson, J. P. (1992). Quality of life and policy analysis in arthritis. *Arthritis Care and Research*, 5, 173–183.

Keefe, F. J., Caldwell, D. S., Queen, K. T., Gil, K. M., Martinez, S., Crisson, J. E., Ogden, W. & Nunley, J. (1987). Pain coping strategies in osteoarthritis patients. *Journal of Consulting and Clinical Psychology*, 55 208–212.

Keefe, F. J., Brown, G. K., Wallston, K. A. & Caldwell, D. S. (1989). Coping with rheumatoid arthritis pain: catastrophizing as a maladaptive strategy. *Pain*, 51–56.

Kiyak, H. A. & Borson, S. (1992). Coping with chronic illness and disability. In M. G. Ory, R. P. Abeles & P. D. Lipman (Eds), *Aging, health, and behavior* (pp. 141–173). Newbury Park: Sage.

Lee, P. & Tan, L. J. P. (1979). Drug compliance in outpatients with rheumatoid arthritis. *Australian and New Zealand Journal of Medicine*, 89, 165–167.

Leventhal, H. & Cameron, L. (1987). Behavioral theories and the problem of compliance. *Patient Education and Counseling*, 10, 117–138.

Leventhal, H. & Diefenbakh, M. (1991). The active side of cognition. In: J. A. Skelton & R. T. Croyle (Eds), *Mental representation in health and illness* (pp. 247–272). New York: Springer Verlag.

Leventhal, H., Leventhal, E. A & Schaefer, P. M. (1992). Vigilant coping and health behavior. In: M. G. Ory, R. P. Abeles & P. D. Lipman (Eds), *Aging, health, and behavior* (pp. 109–140). Newbury Park: Sage.

Leventhal, H., Meyer, D. & Nerenz, D. (1980). The common sense representation of illness danger. In: S. Rachman (Ed), *Contributions to Medical Psychology* (Vol. 2, pp. 7–30). New York: Pergamon Press.

Lochead, J. A., Baragar, F. D., Tetreault, L. L. et al. (1985). A double blind comparison of piroxicam and enteric coated ASA in rheumatoid arthritis. *The Journal of Rheumatology*, 12, 68–77.

Lorig, K. & Gonzales, V. (1992). The integration of theory with practice: a 12-year case study. *Health Education Quarterly*, 19, 355–368.

Lorig, K., Konkol, L. & Gonzalez, V. (1987). Arthritis patient education: a review of the literature. *Patient Education and Counseling*, 10, 207–252.

Lorig, K., Cox, T., Cuevas, Y., Kraines, R. G. & Britton, M. C. (1984). Converging and diverging beliefs about arthritis: Caucasian patients, Spanish speaking patients, and physicians. *The Journal of Rheumatology*, 11, 76–79.

Lorig, K., Lubeck, D., Kraines, R. G., Seleznick, M. & Holman, H. R. (1985). Outcomes of self-help education for patients with arthritis. *Arthritis and Rheumatism*, 28, 680–685.

Lorig, K., Chastain, R. L., Ung, E., Shoor, S. & Holman, H. R. (1989a). Development and evaluation of a scale to measure perceived self-efficacy in people with arthritis. *Arthritis and Rheumatism*, 32, 37–44.

Lorig, K., Seleznick, M., Lubeck, D., Ung, E., Chastain, R. L. & Holman, H. R. (1989b). The beneficial outcomes of the arthritis self-management course are not adequately explained by behavior change. *Arthritis and Rheumatism*, 32, 91–95.

Manne, S. L. & Zautra, A. J. (1989). Spouse criticism and support: their association with coping and psychological adjustment among women with rheumatoid arthritis. *Journal of Personality and Social Psychology*, 56, 608–617.

Manne, S. L. & Zautra, A. J. (1992). Coping with arthritis: current status and critique. *Arthritis and Rheumatism*, 35, 1273–1280.

Mattlin, J. A., Wethington, E. & Kessler, R. C. (1990). Situational determinants of coping and coping effectiveness. *Journal of Health and Social Behavior*, 31, 103–122.

Meenan, R. F., Gertman, P. M. & Mason, J. H. (1980). Measuring health status in arthritis: the arthritis impact measurement scales. *Arthritis and Rheumatism*, 23, 146–152.

Meenan, R. F., Mason, J. H., Anderson, J. J., Guccione, A. A & Kazis, L. E. (1992). AIMS2: the content and properties of a revised and expanded arthritis impact measurement scales health status questionnaire. *Arthritis & Rheumatism*, 35, 1–10.

Melzack, R. (1975). The McGill pain questionnaire: major properties and scoring methods. *Pain*, 1, 277–299.

Morrell, R. W., Park, D. C. & Poon, L. W. (1989). Quality of instruction on prescription drug labels: effects on memory and comprehension in young and old adults. *The Gerontologist*, 29, 345–353.

Morrell, R. W., Park, D. C. & Poon, L. W. (1990). Effects of labeling techniques on memory and comprehension of prescription information in young and old adults. *Journal of Gerontology: Psychological Sciences, Special Issue*, 45, 166–172.

Mushlin, A. M. & Appel, F. A. (1977). Diagnosing potential noncompliance. *Archives of Internal Medicine*, 137, 318–321.

Nicassio, P. M., Wallston, K. A., Callahan, L. F., Herbert, M. & Pincus, T. (1985). The measurement of helplessness in rheumatoid arthritis. The development of the arthritis helplessness index. *Journal of Rheumatology*, 12, 462–467.

Norell, S. E. (1981). Accuracy of patient interviews and estimates by clinical staff in determining medication compliance. *Social Science Medicine*, 15, 57–61.

Oakes, T. W., Ward, J. R., Gray, R. M., Klauber, M. R. & Moody, P. M. (1970). Family expectations and arthritis patient compliance to a hand resting splint regimen. *Journal of Chronic Diseases*, 22, 757–764.

Park, D. C. (1991). Applied cognitive aging research. In: F. I. M. Craik & T. A. Salthouse (Eds). *Handbook of Cognition and Aging* (pp. 449–493). Hillsdale, NJ: Erlbaum.

Park, D. C., Morrell, R. W., Frieske, D., Blackburn, B. & Birchmore, D. (1991). Cognitive factors and the use of over-the-counter medication organizers by arthritis patients. *Human Factors*, 33, 57–67.

Park, D. C., Morrell, R. W., Frieske, D. & Kincaid, D. (1992). Medication adherence behaviours in older adults: effects of external cognitive supports. *Psychology and Aging*, 7, 252–256.

Park, D. C., Leventhal, H., Morrell, R. W., Hertzog, C., Birchmore, D. & Leventhal, E. (1993a). Psychosocial instrument package for the assessment of osteoarthritis and rheumatoid arthritis patients. Unpublished.

Park, D. C., Morrell, R. W., Gaines, C. & Lautenschlager, G. (1993b). Measurement techniques and level of analysis of medication adherence behaviors across the life span. *Proceedings of the Human Factors and Ergonomics Society: Designing for Diversity*, 1, 188–192.

Park, D. C., Willis, S. L., Morrow, D., Diehl, M. & Gaines, C. L. (in press). Cognitive function and medication usage in older adults, *Journal of Applied Gerontology*.

Parker, J. C., Singsen, B. H., Hewett, J. E., Walker, S. E., Hazelwood, S. E., Hall, P. J., Holsten, D. J. & Rodon, C. M. (1984). Educating patients with rheumatoid arthritis: a prospective analysis. *Archives of Physical Medicine Rehabilitation*, 65, 771–774.

Parker, J. C., Frank, R. G., Beck, N. C., Smarr, K. L., Buescher, K. L., Phillips, L. R., Smith, E. I., Anderson, S. K. & Walker, S. E. (1988). Pain management in rheumatoid arthritis patients: a cognitive-behavioral approach. *Arthritis and Rheumatism*, 31, 593–601.

Parker, J. C., Smarr, K. L., Buescher, K. L., Phillips, L. R., Frank, R. G., Beck, N. C., Anderson, S. K. & Walker, S. E. (1989). Pain control and rational thinking. *Arthritis and Rheumatism*, 32, 984–990.

Permut, J. B. (1989). *Embracing the wolf: a lupus victim and her family learn to live with chronic disease*. Atlanta: Cherokee.

Radloff, L. S. (1977). The Ces-D scale: a self-report depression scale for research in general populations. *Applied Psychological Measurement*, 1, 385–401.

Register, C. (1987). *Living with chronic illness: days of patience and passion*. New York: Macmillan.

Revenson, T. A. & Felton, B. J., (1989). Disability and coping as predictors of psychological adjustment to rheumatoid arthritis. *Journal of Consulting and Clinical Psychology*, 57, 344–348.

Rosenstiel, A. K. & Keefe, F. J. (1983). The use of coping strategies in chronic low back pain patients: relationship to patient characteristics and current adjustment. *Pain*, 17, 33–44.

Rudd, P. (1979). In search of the gold standard for compliance measurement. *Archives of Internal Medicine*, 139, 627–628.

Salthouse, T. A. (1991). *Theoretical Perspectives on Cognitive Aging*. Hillsdale, NJ: Erlbaum.

Schwartz, D., Wand, M., Zeitz, L. & Goss, M. E. (1962). Medication errors made by elderly chronically ill patients. *American Journal of Public Health*, 52, 2018–2029.

Skelton, J. A. (1991). Laypersons' judgments of patient credibility and the study of illness representations. In: J. A. Skelton & R. T. Croyle (Eds), *Mental representation in health and illness* (pp. 108–131). New York: Springer Verlag.

Stein, M. J., Wallston, K. A. & Nicassio, P. M. (1988). Factor structure of the Arthritis Helplessness Index. *The Journal of Rheumatology*, 15, 427–432.

Vitaliano, P. P., Russo, J., Carr, J. E., Maiuro, R. D. & Becker, J. (1985). The ways of coping checklist: revision and psychometric properties. *Multivariate Behavioral Research*, **20**, 3–26.

Wallston, K. A., Wallston, B. S. & DeVellis, R. (1978). Development of the multi-dimensional health locus of control (MHLC) scales. *Health Education Monographs*, **6**, 160–170.

Wasner, C., Britton, M. C., Kraines, R. G. et al. (1981). Nonsteroidal antiinflammatory agents in rheumatoid arthritis and ankylosing spondylitis. *Journal of the American Medical Association*, **246**, 2168–2172.

Wolfe, F. (1991). Rheumatoid arthritis. In: N. Bellamy (Ed), *Prognosis in the Rheumatic Diseases* (pp. 37–82). London: Kluwer.

Zautra, A. J. & Manne, S. L. (1992). Coping with rheumatoid arthritis: a review of a decade of research. *Annals of Behavioral Medicine*, **14**, 31–39.

9 Psychological Preparation For Surgery: Marshalling Individual and Social Resources to Optimize Self-regulation

RICHARD J. CONTRADA
Tillett Hall, Livingston Campus, Rutgers University, New Brunswick, New Jersey 08903, USA

ELAINE A. LEVENTHAL
University of Medicine and Dentistry, Robert Wood Johnson Medical School, New Brunswick, New Jersey 08903, USA

JUDITH R. ANDERSON
Tillett Hall, Livingston Campus, Rutgers University, New Brunswick, New Jersey 08903, USA

Surgery has become the treatment of choice for a variety of physical disorders, including a number of highly prevalent conditions. For many patients, surgery is life-saving. In addition, it can substantially reduce or even eliminate incapacitating pain, and improve quality of life by enabling the person to carry out physical and social activities. However, notwithstanding the high probability of a positive outcome and the magnitude of the resulting benefits, impending surgery is a major life stressor. Procedures for repairing, removing, or replacing diseased or damaged bodily organs can have negative psychological and material effects, and these effects may be severe and wide-ranging. In the individual case, negative physical, emotional, and economic outcomes are not only experienced by the patient, but may also affect family, friends, and work associates. In the aggregate, costs associated with surgery have a significant impact on the health-care system and on the national economy. As a consequence, we all share costs generated by surgery performed on individuals external to our social networks, and most of us at some time will either undergo surgery ourselves or will be affected by surgery experienced by someone with whom we have a personal relationship.

International Review of Health Psychology, Volume 3. Edited by S. Maes, H. Leventhal and M. Johnston
© 1994 John Wiley & Sons Ltd

Following passage of the 1983 Omnibus Health Act, in response to escalating costs and governmental regulations involving reimbursement, many surgeries and other invasive medical procedures are now performed with a shorter hospital stay or on an outpatient basis. This has been made possible by technological advances that allow many surgeries to be performed through natural openings in the body (i.e., endosurgery), through small incisions with fiber optic directed instruments (e.g., laparoscopy), with greater use of regional rather than general anesthesia, and/or with less pain medication. In traditional hospitals, outpatient surgeries increased from 6.95 million procedures in 1985 to 11.07 million procedures in 1990. During the same period, surgical procedures performed annually in non-hospital, free-standing surgical centers increased from 0.71 million to 2.32 million (Burke, 1992). It is predicted that by 1995, laparoscopy performed on an outpatient basis could account for 70% to 90% of many high-volume surgeries, including gallbladder removals, various cancer stagings, select lung procedures, kidney removals, hernia repairs, hysterectomies, and certain vagotomies and bowel procedures (Burke, 1992).

These changes create a context in which psychological interventions may play an important role in maximizing the cost-effectiveness of health-care delivery. Because there may be little or no opportunity to provide care for patients following surgery, pre-surgical interventions may become essential as a means of preparing patients for the physical and psychological difficulties they are likely to face during the post-operative period. By enhancing the patient's capacity to understand and to cope with surgery and its sequelae, relatively low-cost efforts at psychological preparation may reduce psychological stress and improve physical recovery. If so, effective psychological intervention may make it possible to ensure that patients experience an acceptable level of mental and physical well-being in the face of hospital understaffing and trends toward shorter hospital stays and greater reliance on outpatient procedures.

Patterns of change in the way surgery is performed and the magnitude of the potential benefits of psychological intervention increase the need for theoretical analysis and hypothesis-testing research in this area. Work conducted in the last thirty years indicates that psychological preparation for surgery is associated with improved recovery. However, much of this work predates the trends toward shorter hospital stay and outpatient surgery. Moreover, available findings provide only suggestions regarding the modes of intervention that are most likely to be effective, the psychological processes that may mediate those effects, patient characteristics that may define groups more or less responsive to surgical preparation, principles that would make it possible to tailor interventions to suit the individual patient, and outcome domains in which effects are more or less likely to be detected. Answers to these questions will provide a deeper theoretical understanding of psychological ramifications of major surgery and other health threats, and serve as a guide for improving surgical intervention programs.

The purpose of this chapter is to provide a critical overview of substantive and methodological issues associated with research concerned with the evaluation of surgical preparation programs. Our main thesis involves two conceptual domains, which we will refer to as *individual self-regulation* and *social self-regulation*. Individual self-regulation involves cognitive and behavioral activity whereby the patient influences the course of surgical recovery. Social self-regulation involves exchanges between the patient and members of his or her close social network that also may affect recovery. We propose that an integration of individual and interpersonal self-regulation constructs provides a conceptual framework that will facilitate the understanding and improvement of surgical outcomes.

The chapter begins with an overview of the available empirical literature examining the effects of surgical preparation. The next section presents a general conceptual framework describing the individual and interpersonal processes whereby the patient understands and copes with the adaptive demands posed by impending surgery. The following section provides an analysis of the major elements of psychological interventions designed to enhance recovery from surgery. The chapter concludes with a comment on practical, methodological, and data-analytic issues relevant to conducting theory-driven research in this area.

THE CURRENT STATE OF KNOWLEDGE: AN OVERVIEW OF EMPIRICAL FINDINGS

Over the past few decades, numerous studies have been conducted in which the effects of psychological interventions were evaluated with respect to one or more outcomes representing some aspect of psychological and/or physical recovery from surgery. Analytic sophistication and methodological rigor have been highly variable. Many studies have employed vaguely specified psychological treatments, have lacked appropriate comparison groups, and have utilized outcome measures of questionable reliability or validity. By contrast, others have employed fully randomized experimental designs and have provided controlled tests of the effects of clearly defined forms of intervention on well-specified outcomes.

One of the earliest examinations of a surgical preparation intervention was conducted by Egbert et al. (1964). Patients undergoing abdominal surgery either received routine treatment or were given special care, prior to and following surgery. Special care involved encouragement, information about physical sensations, and instructions regarding the use of deep-breathing relaxation techniques. Results indicated that patients receiving special care required less pain medication and a shorter hospital stay than routine care controls. Another early study, by Layne and Yudofsky (1971), sought to reduce the incidence of "post-perative psychosis", a syndrome of confusion and delirium that often occurs immediately following major surgery. The intervention involved pre- and post-surgical delivery of information about surgical procedures and provided an opportunity for patients to express their fears regarding surgery. The treatment group experienced a lower rate of post-perative psychosis than a routine-care control group. A third study was conducted by Schmitt and Wooldridge (1973). Patients undergoing a variety of surgeries attended group discussions led by a nurse in which they received orienting information and instruction in physical activities to be performed post-operatively. Compared with patients receiving routine care, patients participating in the discussion groups required less pain medication, experienced less urinary retention, and had shorter hospital stays.

These and other early studies generated results suggesting that psychological interventions might improve adaptation to major surgery. They also identified three key components of surgical preparation: information, coping strategies, and emotional support. Thus the stage was set for more recent work which has sought to characterize the overall value of psychological preparation for surgery and to evaluate the relative effectiveness of specific intervention components.

Is surgical preparation associated with positive outcomes?

Following publication of studies conducted in the 1960s and early 1970s, research on the effects of psychological preparation for surgery burgeoned. As noted earlier, the evidence indicates that psychological interventions can improve surgical recovery. This conclusion is supported by a number of meta-analyses. For example, Mumford, Schlesinger and Glass (1981) reviewed 34 studies in which surgical patients or patients suffering a myocardial infarction underwent some form of psychological intervention that was designed to improve recovery. The average effect size (ES) across diverse types of psychological intervention and a variety of outcome measures was $+0.49$, which indicates that treatment groups did better than control groups by about one-half a standard deviation. Devine and Cook (1983) conducted a meta-analysis of 49 studies of surgical patients and focused on length of hospital stay as an outcome measure. They reported a mean ES of $+0.39$. Hathaway (1986) examined 68 studies in which the effects of surgical preparation were evaluated with respect to a variety of outcomes. The overall ES across all outcomes was $+0.44$. Heater, Becker and Olson (1988) reviewed 84 studies which were conducted by nurses and reported an overall ES of 0.59 across various dependent measures.

Although the foregoing effect-size estimates appear to reflect statistically significant associations, the nature and strength of support for this conclusion varies across the meta-analyses. Mumford, Schlesinger and Glass (1982) conducted a formal statistical test of the effect sizes obtained for a subset of 13 studies that examined length of hospital stay as a dependent variable. They found that hospital stays for subjects receiving psychological treatment averaged about two days shorter than those of control subjects, and that this difference was significantly greater than zero. A two-day reduction in length of hospital stay represents an enormous cost saving if it is followed by uncomplicated recovery and rehabilitation. Devine and Cook (1983) did not conduct significance tests. Instead, they provided an indirect and somewhat questionable argument based on a characterization of the degree of methodological rigor with which individual studies were carried out. It was concluded that the association between receipt of surgical preparation and more favorable outcomes was likely to be real because it was obtained in subgroups of studies with features that would be expected to minimize the operation of biases favoring positive results, e.g., studies in which physicians were blind with respect to group assignment, in which subjects were randomly assigned to treatment, and/or in which subject attrition was low and comparable across subject groups. Neither Hathaway (1986) nor Heater, Becker and Olson (1988) tested the overall ESs they obtained against the null hypothesis of no effect. However, Heater, Becker and Olson (1988) obtained a significantly larger mean effect for nursing interventions involving randomization to treatment (ES = +0.69) as compared to those that did not involve a randomized design (ES = +0.32), which would suggest that the effect obtained in randomized studies differed significantly from zero.

The potential practical import of the association between surgical preparation and surgical outcome can be gauged by utilizing indices for characterizing the magnitude of effect size in clinical terms. For example, using an index (U_3) described by J. Cohen (1988), Heater, Becker and Olson (1988) showed that the mean ES of +0.59 they obtained for studies involving nursing interventions indicates that the average subject in a treatment group had better outcomes than 72% of patients in control groups. Alternatively, this effect may be expressed using the effect size display presented by Rosenthal and Rubin (1982), which indicates that patients receiving surgical preparation experienced a 28% improvement in outcome. Similar calculations reported by Hathaway (1986) indicate that the average ES of +0.44 they obtained represents an effect in which 67% of the patients receiving psychological treatment experience a 20% improvement in outcome. Note that although these estimates indicate that psychological intervention can produce a substantial improvement in outcome, they are mean values that represent the average difference associated with psychological treatment in the research reviewed. Therefore, variability in treatment outcome both across and within the individual studies reviewed in a given meta-analysis is not reflected in the summary statistics. Nonetheless, there is a clear indication that, on average, psychological intervention produces meaningful improvements in outcome.

What theoretical principles account for the empirical findings?

Information and coping

Early efforts to provide a theoretical account of the effects of surgical interventions were framed in terms of Janis's (1958) notion of the "work of worry". According to this model, it is the level of the patient's worry that plays a critical role in determining outcomes: adaptation to surgery is optimized under conditions in which the patient experiences a moderate level of anticipatory fear. It is assumed that moderate fear stimulates productive worrying, that is, adaptive, problem-focused thought. As a consequence, the patient can comprehend, and later recall and utilize, information delivered by hospital staff that provided suggestions to facilitate coping. By contrast, too little fear fails to motivate productive worrying, whereas a very high level of fear generates neurotic, i.e., nonproductive worrying. Although Janis's (1958) observations stimulated interest in psychological aspects of adaptation to surgery, correlational analysis of the relationship between pre-surgical fear on surgical outcome (e.g., Johnson, Leventhal & Dabbs, 1971; Sime, 1976; Wolfer & Davis, 1970), and a direct experimental test (Vernon & Bigelow, 1974), failed to confirm the Janis (1958) model. As will be discussed in the next section, the role of emotion-related processes in adaptation to illness threats may require a more complex model which explicitly distinguishes between the patient's subjective-emotional reactions to surgery and his or her perception of objective aspects of the underlying medical condition and its surgical treatment.

More recent theoretical analyses have focused on the role of information, training in coping strategies, and emotional support. These three factors have often been pitted against each other in individual studies of surgical preparation, or in meta-analyses comparing groups of studies involving delivery of either information or training in coping activity. In attempting to derive general theoretical principles from these comparisons, several authors (e.g., Johnson, 1984; MacDonald & Kuiper, 1983) have stressed the value of interventions that include presentation of specific coping strategies. However, they have also noted that coping effects have generally not been obtained independently of information, and that information appears to be a necessary component of interventions emphasizing coping procedures. Moreover, information content appears to play a significant role in determining outcome, with interventions involving a description of specific sensory experiences associated with medical procedures found to be most effective (Johnson & Leventhal, 1974; Johnson, Morrissey & Leventhal, 1973). In addition to accommodating data indicating interactions between information content and the provision of specific coping strategies, theoretical analysis must account for findings suggesting that emotionally supportive counseling, by itself, has produced positive results (e.g., Felton et al., 1976). The implication is that effective treatment has multiple components that may interact in complex ways.

This observation appears to have been borne out by additional findings of the Devine and Cook (1983) meta-analysis described earlier. Intervention studies were characterized in terms of the types of content they conveyed. The content categories were information, coping skills training, and psychosocial support. Effect sizes for studies in which the intervention involved two or three of these content areas were consistently larger than those for studies involving just one type of content (evidently, there were too few studies to determine whether any two of the three intervention components formed a particularly effective combination). Although other explanations are possible, this finding is consistent with the notion that maximizing the effectiveness of surgical preparation requires a multi component strategy. It is of interest to note, however, that effect sizes for studies combining all three types of content, although consistently larger than those for studies involving a single type, were slightly smaller than those for studies involving two types of content. This may suggest that multi-component interventions reach a point of diminishing returns, possibly because patients have difficulty assimilating and integrating diverse types of information. We will return to the issue of helping the patient to integrate components of complex treatment programs later in this chapter.

Social-psychological processes

Although interventions that target intrapersonal processes by delivering information and coping skills to the patient have received continued empirical attention, increasing emphasis has been given to the potential utility of health-promoting interventions that involve interpersonal processes (Gottlieb, 1988). An illustrative study involving cancer patients was conducted by Ward et al. (1991). In an initial correlational study, it was found that whereas cancer patients undergoing chemotherapy generally had high levels of social support, the more patients spoke with others about their condition, the *lower* their self-esteem. An experimental trial was then conducted in which patients were randomized into a usual care (control) condition, an information condition designed to improve self-esteem, and a shared information condition in which the patient and a significant other participated together. In the usual care group, the inverse correlation between communication and self-esteem was replicated, and the corresponding correlation in the information condition did not differ significantly from zero. However, among patients in the shared information group, there was a *positive* correlation between amount of communication and patients' self-esteem. This research provides preliminary support for hypotheses concerning the role of patient–partner communication in determining how well subjects cope with unpleasant medical procedures, a topic we will examine in detail in the following section.

Summary and implications

A brief overview of the available findings suggests that psychological preparation can improve patients' ability to recover from major surgery. This conclusion appears to be statistically real and reflects positive outcomes on clinically and economically important measures such as psychological distress and length of hospital stay. These findings do not appear amenable to explanations involving a single-factor such as worry, information, coping, or social support. Instead, positive outcomes may reflect a complex set of processes whereby the patient acquires information about surgical procedures and their likely effects, learns to perform specific behaviors as a means of coping with the prospect and consequences of surgery, and experiences supportive interpersonal contact with a health care professional, relative, or friend. However, the available meta-analyses cast little or no light on precisely how preparation works and/or on the specific components or combinations of components that are essential for efficacy. In the following section a theoretical framework is proposed as a means of addressing these issues.

INDIVIDUAL AND SOCIAL SELF-REGULATION: A FRAMEWORK FOR CONCEPTUALIZING THE PROCESS OF ADAPTING TO HEALTH THREATS

The investigation of psychological stress (Lazarus, 1966; Lazarus & Folkman, 1984), illness cognition (H. Leventhal & Johnson, 1983; H. Leventhal, Meyer & Nerenz, 1980), and social support (S. Cohen, 1988; S. Cohen & Hoberman, 1983) has generated two interrelated sets of theoretical principles that provide a conceptual framework for understanding how psychological intervention can improve surgical recovery and rehabilitation. Principles of individual self-regulation describe intrapersonal processes, such as cognitive appraisal and coping, that may enable the patient to adapt to the threat of surgery. Principles of social self-regulation specify interpersonal processes whereby the patient draws upon health-care workers, family, and friends to enhance coping efficacy. The following section describes the process of individual self-regulation as it relates to the patient confronting major surgery. Subsequently, the process of social self-regulation is described, and interactions between the two levels of analysis are discussed.

Individual self-regulation

The main elements of the intrapersonal component of the self-regulation framework are depicted in Figure 9.1. A major stressor such as impending surgery initiates a set of processes that may be described in terms of three phases: problem representation, coping, and outcome appraisal. Each phase entails two parallel processes, one reflecting the person's perception of the objective situation, and one involving emotional and other subjective responses to that perception. The three phases are conceived as over-lapping, rather than sharply demarcated, and although the depiction of the three phases is sequential, they are in constant interaction and affect one-another bidirectionally. Whereas the cognitive and emotional branches are partially independent, they, too, are in constant interaction, though the

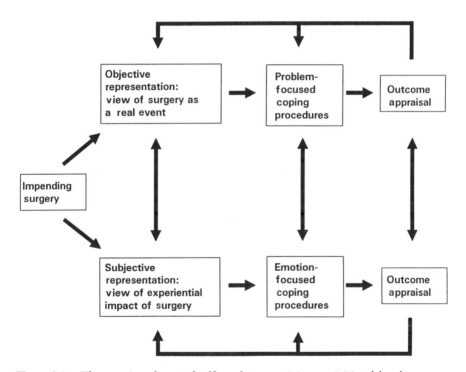

Figure 9.1. Three major phases of self-regulatory activity are initiated by the percep-tion of stressful events such as major surgery. A mental representation is formed con-sisting of objective and subjective elements of the threat. The mental representation guides the selection and performance of problem-focused and emotion-focused coping procedures. Appraisal of the outcome of coping efforts provides updates which may lead to minor modifications in coping activity or to a major transformation of the mental representation. The objective and subjective limbs reflect parallel but interacting modes of activity

conditions under which their effects are bidirectional remain to be specified. In addition, the model is nonrecursive in the sense that there are many opportunities for feedback and feedforward, especially as time unfolds and the individual takes in, processes, and acts upon new information.

The mental representation of major surgery

Being informed of the need for surgery and apprised of its ramifications constitute a major life stressor whose immediate effect on the person is to initiate the process of problem representation (H. Leventhal, Meyer & Nerenz, 1980). Problem representation involves the construction of an internal model of the stressor. The person actively creates a mental problem space that defines the dimensions, features, and implications of the threat of impending surgery. One fundamental postulate of the self-regulation model is that it is the patient's construal of health threats, not that of the researcher or health-care practitioner, that must be understood and modified in order to effect optimization of outcome. Another is that an accurate mental representation of disease and treatment provides the patient with a reality-based framework to guide self-regulation (H. Leventhal, Diefenbach & Leventhal, 1992; E. Leventhal et al., 1989). The active process of taking in information from external sources, and coordinating it with internal cues such as bodily sensations, allows the patient to construct a base of knowledge about surgery that gives meaning to the experience, reduces distress, and organizes efforts to gather new information and to plan, evaluate, and modify coping strategies (H. Leventhal & Diefenbach, 1991).

The following generalizations describe the process of problem representation and convey an appreciation of the difficulties entailed by the patient as he or she attempts to form a coherent mental model of the experience of undergoing major surgery: (1) surgery is a high-stakes stressor, (2) it involves a changing series of adaptive goals, (3) it has features that make it difficult to construct a complete and accurate mental representation, and (4) its representation involves both objective and subjective elements.

Major surgery is a high-stakes stressor In a phrase used by Lazarus to characterize adaptive threats (Lazarus & Folkman, 1984), there is much at stake for the surgical patient. The risks are both severe and multifaceted. They include consequences such as death, pain, disfigurement, loss of function, economic loss, loss of social roles, an uncertain time-line, i.e., how long one will take to recover and how long it will take to resume activities, the threat of recurrence due to uncertainty as to the cause of the condition, the uncontrollability of these causes, and uncertainty as to one's ability to perform the necessary coping responses.

As features of the disease and its surgical treatment are elaborated over time, their combined representation will have implications of potential danger to the patient's physical and psychological well-being. Appraisals of these danger implications results in a sense of threat. The level of threat will be proportional to the potential magnitude of these danger implications, i.e., to the level of physical and psychological changes that disease and treatment can generate. However, the amount of threat experienced is buffered by the perceived availability of personal and social resources to mitigate these dangers. When appraisals of danger are greater than appraisals of buffering resources, the result is a stress response, which may involve negative emotional reactions, activation of autonomic, neuroendocrine, and other physiologic systems, and reduced capacity to perform cognitive and behavioral tasks.

An event is perceived to be significant for well-being and generates a threat appraisal when it signals potential or actual harm to that which is valued by the person. Terms such as *commitments* (Lazarus & Folkman, 1984) and *resources* (Hobfoll, 1989) have been used to refer to material and psychological "assets" that may be threatened by a stressful life event. These may include objects, conditions, personal characteristics, and energies (Hobfoll, 1989). Impending surgery is threatening, therefore, because there is a potential for loss of assets, such as physical health and functional capacity, that are valued both intrinsically and for their instrumental value for attaining other assets. At the same time, surgery often represents a potential for improvement in physical and psychological well-being, for example, the prospect of reduced pain, increased physical capacity, and greater longevity. However, even where the greater likelihood is for a positive outcome, major surgery is psychologically threatening because it represents the sudden emergence of a high-stakes event. It demands that the patient make an immediate investment of valued resources, with at least the possibility that this investment will result in a net loss before the situation is resolved, in the sense that anticipated benefits of surgery may not be forthcoming.

Thus, the process of threat appraisal mediates the patient's initial emotional response to the prospect of major surgery, and subsequent reappraisals produced by changes in the mental representation of the surgical episode mediate changes in the patient's emotional state. Reduction of emotional distress, particularly during the period prior to surgery, is a major goal of surgical preparation interventions. In addition to humanitarian considerations, there are data that demonstrate that by reducing presurgical anxiety it is possible to lower the risk of general anesthesia, reduce pain and the need for pain medications and sedatives, and lower the incidence of complications (Anderson, 1987). According to the self-regulation model, threat appraisal and the emotional distress it generates can be reduced by providing the patient with information that fosters an accurate representation of surgical procedures and their effects, as well as information describing cognitive and behavioral strategies for coping with the surgical episode.

Different phases of the surgical experience are associated with a changing series of adaptive goals How the foregoing threats will be organized in the mind of a particular patient will depend upon a host of factors reflecting the patient's psychosocial and demographic attributes, life situation, medical status, and the surgical procedure to be performed. However, for most patients, adaptation to major surgery is likely to involve four general issues: (1) the immediate physical danger represented by surgery itself, that is, the threat of general anesthesia, incision, grafting, resection, amputation, reconstruction, catheterization, and so forth; (2) after-effects of undergoing the foregoing procedures, that is, pain, discomfort, disorientation, fatigue, and reduced capacity for physical activity and ambulation; (3) inability to resume valued social roles, that is, to engage in occupational,

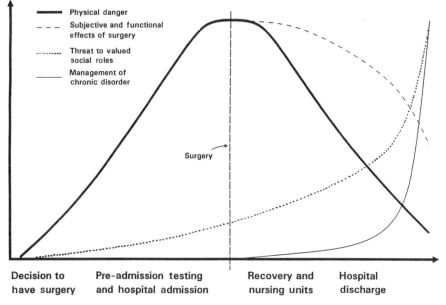

Figure 9.2. The patient about to undergo major surgery faces a multidimensional stressor. Although the specifics will vary from patient to patient, four major themes are likely to be represented: (1) physical danger associated with surgery, (2) subjective and functional effects of surgery, (3) potential inability to enact valued social roles, and (4) long-term management of the underlying physical condition. The relative salience of these four themes varies over time, with physical danger and subjective and functional effects dominating during the period immediately surrounding surgery, and social role-related and disease-management issues assuming increasing importance following discharge

family-related, and leisure activities; (4) long-term management of a chronic medical condition, that is, the need to diet, exercise, take medication, monitor symptoms and signs of disease, and/or undergo follow-up procedures (e.g., radiotherapy).

The salience in consciousness of any one of the foregoing themes will vary over time. Figure 9.2 depicts one possible pattern of changes as a function of the temporal phases comprising the surgical episode, i.e., the anticipatory surgical phase (the time from committing oneself to surgery until the time of admission to a surgical unit), the encounter phase (the time from admission until anesthesia), the intensive care phase (the time spent in the recovery unit), and the rehabilitation phase (the time from transfer to a nursing unit through discharge and physical, behavioral, and psychosocial recovery). Thus, during the anticipatory surgical and encounter phases, the most salient adaptive problems will likely be the immediate physical danger posed by surgical procedures. Assuming that surgery is successful, this concern diminishes rapidly during the intensive care and rehabilitative phases. In its wake the patient is confronted by the after-effects of surgery. In the case of an uneventful recovery from those after-effects and timely discharge, the patient's ability to enact social roles may be compromised by cardiac, neoplastic, orthopedic, and other diseases for which surgery has only palliative or partially curative effects. In addition, the rehabilitative phase is marked by the need to engage in long-term management of the patient's chronic medical condition.

Note that increased salience of social role-related and disease-management themes during the post-discharge period may or may not represent areas of concern that are new to the patient. Consider the patient who has been living with the angina of symptomatic ischemic heart disease. Successful coronary bypass surgery and consequent reductions in chest pain and improved capacity for physical activity mark the return to the task of managing coronary atherosclerosis, possibly coping with limitations on social behavior, workload, and the like, and possibly working to reduce alcohol intake and/or to quit smoking cigarettes. By contrast, in the case of surgical removal of recently diagnosed colon cancer, the patient is confronted for the first time with the need to cope with the experience of cancer and its treatment (e.g., follow-up radiotherapy or chemotherapy) and their potential effects on social activity and quality of life. Thus, in some instances the surgical episode is experienced as having resolved a crisis, and the effects and implications of underlying disease may lose salience in the mind of the patient. In other cases, the experience of resolution is marred by the presence of visible damage, modified and/or disrupted function, and the need for additional invasive treatment.

The nature of major surgery is such that there is considerable opportunity for the patient to come to an inaccurate or incomplete understanding of the adaptive goals that are at stake   The threat of having one's body physically invaded and manipulated may arouse vivid but not necessarily realistic images of actual surgical procedures and of their subjective impact. For example, the person may overestimate the degree to which resection of relatively insensitive internal organs can produce pain, and underestimate the subjective impact of other aspects of surgery, such as incisional pain or prolonged physical immobility. Where impending surgery does not cause the individual to form clear albeit inaccurate expectations, the result may instead be a state of uncertainty. Many events associated with surgery, such as regaining consciousness after undergoing general anesthesia, may be difficult to relate to naive previous experience, and therefore are not easily comprehended before the fact. The patient's efforts to arrive at an overall evaluation of the stakes involved in undergoing major surgery are further complicated by the need to take into account the temporal dimension discussed earlier. The short-term, low-probability risks associated with general anesthesia and surgery must somehow be weighed, combined with the demands of physical recovery that will unfold following surgery, and balanced against long-term benefits that may seem remote, at best, during the period prior to surgery.

The need to work toward adaptive goals that differ with respect to clarity and time-course can make it very difficult for the patient to organize coping efforts and evaluate progress. Consider a coronary-bypass patient at the early post-surgical phase of recovery. Two relevant adaptive concerns are the immediate experience of pain and the need to engage in rehabilitative exercises that are essential to eventual recovery of mobility and of the capacity for physical activity. It is quite likely that efforts to engage in rehabilitative exercises may be disrupted by the experience of severe wound pain. As a consequence, the desire to minimize chest pain, an immediate, perceptually motivated goal, may conflict with the execution of responses such as coughing and ambulating that are necessary for the also desired, though more abstract and distant goal of physical rehabilitation.

The mental representation of health threats involves both objective and subjective elements   Over time, the patient's mental representation of major surgery, i.e., his or her representation of the *objective features* of the disease and impending treatment threat, may become quite elaborate. It will likely include features that characterize: (1) the underlying physical disorder or condition, its identity, label, symptomatic manifestation, causes, consequences, and time-course, (2) the recommended surgical procedure, represented by features that parallel those describing the underlying disease, e.g., the nature of the surgical procedure, its effects on the patient, the likelihood of positive versus negative outcomes, and the time-course of those outcomes, and (3) available coping options, cognitive and behavioral strategies that may facilitate the process of adapting to the surgical episode. The generation and elaboration of these three major facets of the objective representation will be paralleled by the unfolding of a varied set of *subjective* experiences. The subjective representation includes the anxiety produced by a high-risk situation and anticipated experiential consequences of surgical procedures such as emotional distress, pain, and discomfort. It also includes bodily sensations and symptoms stemming from the patient's physical condition and from treatment of that condition.

The distinction between objective and subjective elements of problem representation is of fundamental importance in understanding how individuals respond to health threats such as major surgery. Both components must be considered in efforts to understand and modify the patient's perceptions of surgery, because the patient may simultaneously hold what appear to be contradictory objective and subjective beliefs (Bauman & Leventhal, 1985). For example, a patient may endorse objective statements pertaining to people in general (e.g., "fatigue following surgery often is due to the after-effects of general anesthesia"), while at the same time expressing different beliefs regarding their own condition (e.g., "I am exhausted because my medical condition is worsening"). As will be discussed shortly, coping behavior and the process of evaluating coping activity also entail objective and subjective components, which can result in situations of conflict between the goals of managing negative emotional states and facilitating physical recovery. Moreover, because subjective states cannot be directly shared by two individuals, the existence of subjective as well as objective representational features introduces communication problems between patient and health-care provider, and between the patient and members of his or her close social network.

Coping: the patient's efforts to optimize adaptive goals

Coping activity is shaped by features of the problem space constructed by the person in forming a mental representation of the threat (H. Leventhal & Nerenz, 1983). Thus, coping involves two parallel modes of self-regulation that correspond to the objective and subjective components of the mental representations of the stressor (Lazarus & Folkman, 1984; E. Leventhal, Suls & Leventhal, in press). *Problem-focused* coping consists of efforts to deal directly with objective elements of the problem representation. *Emotion-focused* coping refers to the reduction of distress and other subjective responses. Immediately following surgery, problem-focused coping includes patient behaviors that may facilitate physical recovery and reduce the probability of post-operative complications, such as the performance of deep-breathing, coughing, and range-of-motion exercises. Later on, the emphasis may shift to the task of becoming ambulatory and regaining the capacity to perform daily living activities. Later still, resumption of social roles and management of chronic disease become the goals of coping efforts. Examples of emotion-focused coping procedures include requests for pain medication, the cognitive construal of symptoms as useful indicators of recovery rather than merely as unpleasant and upsetting sensations, and emotional acceptance of temporary diminished physical capacity or of the need to curtail valued social involvements and take on others.

Understanding and coping with chronic disease and its treatment

The model of treatment (H. Leventhal, Diefenbach & Leventhal, 1992) refers to the patient's understanding of the effects of surgery on the underlying physical disorder or condition. Because the medical condition and the surgical procedure are represented in terms of similar features (e.g., tissue injury, symptoms, impaired function), there is potential for confusion and distress during the post-operative period in which effects of surgery (e.g., incision pain, fatigue) may be misinterpreted as indicating a worsening of the physical disorder. The process whereby the patient models the role of surgery in treating the disorder is particularly important once the surgical episode has been resolved, that is, when the patient has recovered from the immediate impact of surgery, is discharged, and begins to become re-engaged in daily activities and family- and work-related roles. At this stage, modifying the patient's treatment model to optimize self-management of chronic medical conditions for which surgery is only a short-term control may be a useful component of interventions. For example, the patient who inaccurately views surgery as a permanent cure for a chronic condition such as coronary atherosclerosis may fail to adhere to medication prescriptions or to modify diet and exercise regularly. An inaccurate treatment model also may undermine long-term recovery in cases where the patient *under*estimates the curative benefits of surgery. A patient who fails to appreciate the degree to which surgery corrects an orthopedic problem may be overly cautious in performing rehabilitative exercises and attempting to increase mobility because of unrealistic fears about the efficacy of surgical repairs.

Outcome appraisal: the patient's evaluation of self-regulatory efforts

Execution of coping procedures is followed by an appraisal process in which outcomes are evaluated against criteria that represent the adaptive goals at which coping is directed (H. Leventhal, Diefenbach & Leventhal, 1992). Self-regulation is optimized by the availability of clear, appropriate, and realistic criteria for evaluating progress toward adaptive goals. Accurate appraisal of initial efforts to cope with surgery and its effects provides a means of guiding further coping efforts, whether by encouraging continuation or modification of strategy. Evidence of success is critical to the acquisition of a sense of efficacy (Bandura, 1982), maintenance of active engagement in the coping process (Carver & Scheier, 1981), and development of a coherent perspective on the process of self-regulation (H. Leventhal, Diefenbach & Leventhal, 1992; H. Leventhal & Nerenz, 1983). The development and maintenance of efficacy, engagement, and coherence, in turn, promote and sustain further adaptive coping activity.

A number of factors may cause the patient to view coping efforts as having failed: (1) the mental representation of the problem may be inaccurate, e.g., difficulty tolerating pain and discomfort that are to be expected after surgery may be appraised as a failure to cope; (2) coping goals and criteria used to evaluate coping efforts may be unrealistic or rigid, e.g., "I should be back at work by now", (3) the coping strategy may be counterproductive or inappropriate for the particular point in time of the recovery process, e.g., refusing narcotic-analgesics to "tough it out" or because of fear of addiction; (4) the evaluation of coping itself may be inaccurate, e.g., the patient fails to perceive that efforts to get up and move about actually have increased alertness and mobility.

Regardless of the actual source of negative appraisal, the individual may attribute failure to any number of factors, including the coping tactic itself, his/her personal inadequacy, the incompetence of his/her support system, or characteristics of the disease he/she is attempting to manage. Some patients who make unrealistically negative appraisals (e.g., "cardiac cripples") may fail to remain actively engaged in recovery and in life because of fear of recurrent angina and or fear of further weakening of a "weak heart". Unrealistic success appraisals may also be problematic. Some patients who make inappropriately positive evaluations of their coping efforts may lose sight of the seriousness of their medical condition and overlook the need for lifestyle management, for example diet and physical activity in the coronary patient following bypass surgery or in the diabetic patient following amputation.

The patient's evaluation of his or her progress will likely be strongly influenced by social comparison processes. Festinger's (1954) analysis would suggest that surgical patients will generally compare themselves with other patients who are recovering at a somewhat faster rate. Upward comparisons such as this might allow patients to learn to facilitate their own recovery by emulating the coping strategies employed by more successful models. However, as pointed out by Taylor (1983), it is also possible that patients will select unrealistically successful models for social comparison process, for example, patients who are much younger or who have a significantly less serious medical condition. Family members may do the same and set unrealistic goals for the patient or for their own caregiving efforts. This more extreme sort of upward comparison is one possible source of unrealistic criteria for evaluating coping efforts which, as discussed earlier, might generate emotional distress and impede recovery and rehabilitation.

In a study of women adjusting to breast cancer, Taylor and her colleagues found evidence of a third pattern of social comparison. Nearly all patients made *downward* comparisons, that is, they believed they were doing as well or better than other woman coping with the same condition. These findings suggest that surgical patients might be expected to engage in social comparisons that serve to enhance self-esteem and improve morale but do not necessarily provide accurate feedback regarding the efficacy of coping efforts. In addition to selecting models that allow downward comparisons, patients may choose evaluative dimensions that generate favorable appraisals (Taylor, 1983). For example, a cancer patient who suffers hair loss as a consequence of radiotherapy but is able to maintain active engagement in occupational activities may select for comparison another patient who has had to suspend work as a consequence of cancer treatment, rather than one for whom treatment has had a less negative effect on physical appearance. These findings suggest that patients may implicitly assign greater priority to emotion-focused as opposed to problem-focused coping, with the possible consequence of failure to optimize management of the disorder and its treatment.

Updating representations and modifying coping procedures

It should be clear from the foregoing discussion that transactions among the environment, coping procedures, and representations of illness threats lead to constant updating of the self-regulatory system. The representations are differentiated and refined, coping procedures elaborated upon, new criteria set to evaluate outcomes, and so forth. Surgery entails a complex progression of adaptive concerns. The pace and markers of change, e.g., diagnostic testing, admission, surgery, discharge, etc., are constrained by the health-care system. However, at the present time, the patient takes a much more active role in initiating these transitions than was the case in the past. Where once the patient was admitted two days prior to surgery for blood work, EKG, signing of release forms, and so forth, the patient is now responsible for scheduling such procedures prior to admission. Thus, there may be a greater need than ever to help the patient to identify and to characterize newly emerging facets of the overall task of navigating through a surgical episode, to make appropriate revisions in coping procedures, and to adopt changing criteria for outcome evaluation. The patient who successfully negotiates these tasks may be said to have achieved *coherence* in his/her self-regulatory activity. Coherence involves a continued state of congruence between the patient's mental representations of surgery and disease and his/her actual medical status, and a high degree of coordination among the components of self-regulation, that is, problem representation, coping, and outcome appraisal (H. Leventhal, Diefenbach & Leventhal, 1992). Enhancing the coherence of self-regulatory activity may be seen as an overarching goal of psychological interventions designed to enhance adaptation to major surgery.

Summary and implications

Several points arising from the self-regulation view of the patient's responses to impending surgery are worth emphasizing. The model stresses the adaptive value of developing a complete and accurate understanding of surgery, and calls attention to the different types of information that such an understanding entails. More specifically, the model specifies two distinct types of information, objective and subjective, which are processed in parallel and initiate distinct but interacting coping procedures. Coping activity is generated by specific features of the patient's mental representation of surgery. As the episode unfolds, that representation is updated by new information received from external sources, by perceived changes in physical and psychological well-being, and by evaluations of the effectiveness of coping procedures. It follows that surgical preparation should explicitly target the representation-coping-appraisal sequence, address both objective and subjective facets of the patient's understanding of surgery and associated problem-focused and emotion-focused modes of coping, and seek to increase the overall coherence self-regulatory activity.

Social self-regulation

The basic premise of the interpersonal component of the self-regulation model is that the social context in which the person is embedded plays a major role in shaping the impact of stressful life events. Findings indicating beneficial effects dominated the early literature on this topic (for reviews see S. Cohen and Syme, 1983), and social factors have been positively associated with measures of recovery from major surgery (Fontana, et al., 1989; Kulik & Mahler, 1987, 1989). However, there has been increasing awareness of the potential for social relationships to produce negative effects on health outcomes (e.g., Abbey, Abramis & Caplan, 1985; Fiore, Becker & Coppel, 1983; Rook, 1984; Sandler & Barrera, 1982; Thompson, Bundek & Sobolew-Schubin, 1990). An illustrative finding was reported by Manne and Zautra (1989), who found that women with rheumatoid arthritis who had highly critical husbands engaged in more maladaptive coping behaviors and reported poorer psychological adjustment than those with less critical husbands. This effect was independent of results indicating that patients who reported having a supportive husband were more likely to engage in adaptive coping behaviors. Thus, positive and negative aspects of the patient–spouse relationship had opposite effects on adaptation to disease, but negative effects would have gone undetected had only perceived support been measured. In addition to evidence of negative effects for the patient, a growing literature provides documentation of the potential for "care-giver stress" in the family members and friends of medical patients, setting the stage for vicious cycles in which care-giver stress may undermine the patient's health and well-being (Coyne & DeLongis, 1986; Coyne, Wortman & Lehnman, 1988; Pearlin et al. 1990).

Social-contextual factors influencing individual adaptation to stress are often described in terms of two broad concepts, *network* and *support* (Berkman, 1985). *Social network* refers to the structure of personal relationships in which the individual is embedded, for example, number, density, proximity, and frequency of contact. *Social support* involves interpersonal functions enacted by members of the person's social network, for example, delivery of emotional support, information, and tangible assistance. The latter approach, with its emphasis on process, is more compatible with the self-regulation view. Whatever the structure of the patient's network of social relationships, many of its effects on his/her ability to cope with major surgery presumably are mediated by social-psychological processes that take place in the context of specific interpersonal exchanges that occur following the decision to undergo surgery and throughout the hospital stay and post-discharge period. Accordingly, social aspects of self-regulation are described below with reference to the behavior of a close, cohabiting, primary support person, such as a spouse. Our analysis will consider the simple case of a dyad comprised of the patient and a single support person. However, the reader should recognize that processes unique to larger social groups such as the family may also be important, and that many surgical patients may have no support person to help them to prepare for and to recover from surgery.

The interpersonal portion of the self-regulation model has two main components. The *task*-focused component targets the surgical episode as the stressor and describes exchanges between patient and partner that center around the task of understanding and coping with surgery. The *role*-focused component addresses social roles enacted by the patient and the partner. Task- and role-focused social self-regulation represent two interacting levels of analysis, rather than independent processes. Efforts to cooperate in performing specific tasks entailed in adapting to surgery occur within the context of other aspects of the patient–partner relationship, and problems that may arise in that relationship do so partially in response to the challenge posed by the surgical episode. Nonetheless, for purposes of analysis and exposition, it is useful to consider each component of social self-regulation separately.

Task-focused social self-regulation: cooperating in order to understand and cope with surgery

As depicted in Figure 9.3, the task-focused component of social self-regulation involves social inputs to the processes of problem representation, coping, and outcome appraisal. These inputs occur in the context of patient–partner exchanges that are organized around interrelated but distinct sets of adaptive goals. Adaptive goals of patients have already been discussed. These include coming to an understanding about what will be done to them and why, how this will feel, what can be done to optimize the effects, and how to evaluate coping efforts. For the partner, there is the goal of helping the patient to cope with impending surgery, and the goal of managing his or her own psychological stress. Both partner goals differ from those guiding the patient's behavior, thereby raising the issue of goal coordination. Even though the goal of optimizing the patient's ability to cope with surgery is nominally shared by both individuals, the task takes a different shape for each member of the dyad because each has his or her own mental representation of the problem. In particular, the partner is not

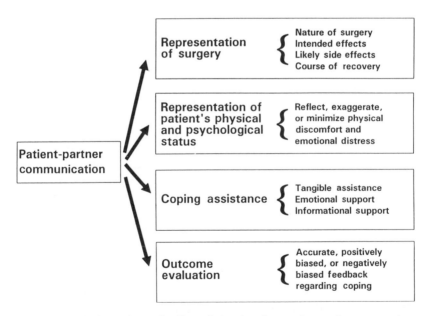

Figure 9.3. Task-focused social self-regulation involves exchanges between patient and partner that influence their respective representations of the surgical episode. Thus the partner will provide input to the patient's view of surgery and of his/her own physical and psychological state. The partner also may provide coping assistance in the form of tangible, emotional, and/or instrumental support, and may influence the patient's appraisal of coping efforts

directly privy to the patient's subjective state, that is, how much pain, fatigue, and discomfort the patient is experiencing and how the partner's advice and/or assistance affects those factors.

In considering the specific effects of patient–partner exchanges upon the task of coping with major surgery, it should be borne in mind that communication occurs at many levels. Apart from the partner's deliberate efforts to facilitate the process of surgical preparation and recovery, he or she may emit expressive reactions, not specifically intended to influence the patient, which may nonetheless be encoded as a reflection of the partner's view of the patient's physical status or coping efforts. Similarly, whether or not the patient deliberately solicits input and assistance, his or her communications of emotional distress, pain, and so forth may elicit or discourage supportive reactions from the partner. One of the authors (EAL) observed an extreme example of unintended communication. A woman who monitored her sleeping husband kept activating his medication delivery system because she believed that his movements indicated that he was in pain. The result was that he became delirious because of over-medication.

Partner's mental representation of surgery

A close, cohabiting, primary support person such as a spouse (hereafter "partner") is uniquely situated to enhance or to reduce the patient's ability to acquire an accurate mental representation of major surgery. A patient whose partner correctly views surgery as a treatment that produces pain and distress in the short run, but will reduce pain, increase longevity and/or enhance quality of life over time, is likely to develop such a view him/herself. By contrast, if the partner has an inaccurate view of surgery, for example, as a permanent cure for a chronic condition such as coronary atherosclerosis, or as a sign that the patient has entered a state of permanent invalidism and dependency when this is not, in fact, the case, the patient may come to acquire a similar, maladaptive view. Alternatively, a persistent difference in views may pose an obstacle to developing a cooperative approach to coping with recovery, and produce interpersonal conflict that spills over into other aspects of the patient–partner relationship.

Partner's assessment of the patient's physical/psychological status

The partner is likely to be highly motivated to acquire information regarding the patient's medical and psychological status. The accuracy of the partner's representation of that status may have a major impact on the patient's own assessment. In effect, the partner is a mirror in which the patient may see an image that exaggerates, minimizes, or more or less accurately reflects his/her medical status and emotional state. If these reflections bias the patient's self-appraisal in either direction, before surgery or at any stage of recovery, there is a risk of negative consequences including over/under-utilization of pain medication, too slow/rapid resumption of daily activities, and non-optimal timing in returning to work and other role activities.

Coping assistance offered by the partner

Analyses of social support functions indicate a number of ways that the surgical patient's partner may provide coping assistance (S. Cohen & Hoberman, 1983). Tangible assistance (or instrumental support) includes direct efforts to orient the patient in space and time when he/she first regains consciousness following surgery, and helping with daily living activities and household and work-related tasks. Emotional support includes efforts to reduce the patient's concerns and elevate his/her spirits. Informational support includes suggestions the partner may make regarding ways the patient can cope with a variety of recovery tasks, including the management of pain and discomfort through medication or distraction, the facilitation of ambulation by performing range-of-motion exercises, and the resumption of social roles by making phone calls and having visitors to the house. Numerous opportunities either to enhance or to inhibit recovery from surgery may arise depending on the degree to which the partner offers coping assistance, the type of assistance offered, the manner in which it is offered, and the way the patient responds. Because patient and partner do not have identical mental representations of recovery, there is considerable opportunity for lack of coordination between coping assistance offered by the partner and the patient's perceived coping needs. For example, the patient's expression of physical pain may solicit emotional support when the patient would prefer a more problem-focused response. Indeed, an empathetic reaction may be threatening to the patient if it has the effect of increasing the salience of his/her inability to tolerate discomfort.

Partner's evaluation of the patient's coping efforts

As in the case of other self-regulatory activities, the process of evaluating coping efforts may either be facilitated or undermined by members of the patient's close social network. The partner may or may not be actively involved in helping the patient to evaluate the results of coping activity and rate of recovery, and the impact of this involvement may either facilitate or hinder the patient's recovery, depending upon the effects of involvement on each of the elements of coping evaluation discussed earlier. For example, a partner who has come to see the patient as permanently disabled, or who is overly sensitized to the patient's pain and discomfort, may deliver feedback that encourages less than adequately vigorous efforts at physical recovery. Conversely, a partner who inaccurately sees surgery as a permanent cure for a chronic disease, or who is insufficiently sensitive to the patient's pain and discomfort, may deliver feedback that pushes the patient too fast too soon, and may possibly give the patient the impression that he/she is failing to cope adequately with the task of recovery. One possible source of maladaptive appraisals of the patient's coping efforts is the selection by the partner of inappropriate models for evaluating the patient's progress. By making comparisons with other patients, whether younger and healthier or older and less well, the partner may develop evaluative standards that are inappropriate for judging the adequacy of the patient's efforts to cope with recovery. These and other problems arising from the partner's expectations about the recovery process are best viewed in terms of social roles emerging from the surgical experience, a topic to which we now turn.

Role-focused social self-regulation: mutual regulation of social selves

Adaptation to major surgery entails a number of psychosocial adjustments for which the appropriate unit of analysis is the set of interrelated social roles enacted by patient and partner. This level of analysis elaborates upon what S. Cohen (1988) refers to as identity and self-esteem models of social support, and draws upon Coyne and DeLongis's (1986) and Pearlin et al.'s (1990) analyses of social relations and adaptation. As depicted in Figure 9.4, role-focused self-regulation involves efforts to cope with the threatened or actual loss of valued social roles and with the retention or acquisition of problematic roles.

	Valued roles threatened or lost	Problematic roles retained or gained
Patient	Occupational Parent/spouse Community Recreational Gender-identity Well person	Sick person
Partner	Occupational Parent/spouse Community Recreational	Caregiver

Figure 9.4. Role-focused social self-regulation is initiated when the patient and partner are confronted by threatened or actual loss of one or more valued social roles, and by the retention or acquisition of the problematic roles of sick person and caregive.

Role-loss

The surgical patient is likely to be faced with the prospect of at least temporary inability to work, and may also be forced to relinquish a number of other social and leisure activities. Although in some cases required by the patient's medical condition, abandonment of major role activities also may occur as a consequence of coping failures that are inaccurately attributed to basic deficiencies in coping efficacy or to a worsening and uncontrollable disease process. That is, the patient may fail to return to work or to resume fully the role of spouse or parent because of the belief that he or she is unable to manage even routine tasks owing to the direct debilitating effects of a medical condition or because efforts to cope with disease have exhausted physical and mental energy and/or are perceived to have failed. The resulting difficulty associated with engaging in role-related activity adds to the burden of coping with physical recovery because it requires attention and effort from a system (e.g., the individual, his/her family) whose coping resources have already been taxed (Hobfoll, 1989). In addition, inability to enact important roles may undermine life satisfaction (e.g., Ogilvie, 1987) and reduce self-esteem. Such a depressive response may further compromise efforts to facilitate recovery and may reduce motivation to maintain engagement in social, recreational, and work-related activities that are not actually threatened by the patient's medical condition. In some cases, the threat to identity stemming from the loss of valued social roles may loom larger than the health threat. The realization that one must curtail career-related activity, or that one has undergone removal of bodily organs or has lost physical functions that are integral to one's gender-identity (e.g., mastectomy) or sense of being an intact person (e.g, colostomy), may initiate self-regulatory activity in which the individual must cope with feelings of meaninglessness, helplessness, and diminished self-esteem (Taylor, 1983). Maladaptive reactions to role-loss may be especially likely among older patients who may perceive their recovery to progress more slowly than that of younger patients or by comparison with their own recovery from medical conditions experienced when they were younger.

The partner may also experience role-loss. He or she may have to reduce or suspend work-related, parenting, and/or leisure activity in order to care for the patient or to allow time and energy to take up responsibilities which the patient is no longer able to fulfill. To the degree that the patient has become less capable of enacting the role of spouse and/or parent, the partner may suffer a reduced capacity to experience satisfaction and fulfillment as husband, wife, son, or daughter. In severe cases, for example, those involving dementia, stroke, or other conditions that impair communication ability, the partner may experience an almost total loss of the patient as the person he/she once was. Partner's role loss, as with all losses, can lead to a sense of pain, depression, and even anger at the patient for causing the loss.

Role-retainment and role-gain

During the course of recovery, it is likely that the partner will come to see him/herself as a caregiver. This may amount to retention or minor elaboration of an existing role (e.g., for partners with experience caring for a chronically ill family member or who themselves have had some similar surgical or other invasive medical procedures), or it may be an entirely new feature of identity (e.g., for individuals without relevant experience). There is evidence to suggest that the responsibility of being a source of support for others is itself a major source of stress, particularly among women (e.g., Belle, 1982; Fischer, 1982; Gove & Hughes, 1979; Kessler & McLeod, 1985). Like the partner, the patient may undergo minor or major change in the degree to which he/she comes to view the partner as a source of support and caregiving, and to view him/herself as at least partially dependent on that support and care. Enhanced dependency may be very distressing to the patient (e.g., Palmer, Canzona & Wai, 1982; Williamson, 1985), forming part of a newly established "sick role" whose negative features (e.g., passivity, helplessness, a potential for permanent disability) may add to the identity threat stemming from lost social roles that have been supplanted by the sick role.

Features of the patient–partner role-relationship prior to surgery may have a major impact on the acquisition of new roles during the course of recovery. The patient and partner may or may not have had a history of interactions in which the partner has collaborated with the patient in coping with the patient's symptomatic condition (e.g., angina, rheumatoid arthritis), or with a chronic asymptomatic condition (e.g., essential hypertension, high coronary risk status). Where there is a relevant, pre-existing role-relationship, it may be easier for the patient and partner to develop congruent mental representations of surgery, to coordinate efforts to cope with both the immediate impact of surgery and the ensuing need for follow-up therapy and lifestyle management, and to manage with the reduction in the patient's contribution to domestic chores. Where this sort of collaboration is new, the need to develop one may itself become an added burden in the process of coping with the medical problem.

The caregiver role

In relinquishing other responsibilities and assuming the caregiver role, the partner must strike an optimal level of involvement in the patient's recovery. As depicted in Figures 9.5 and 9.6, either too little or too much involvement may have negative consequences (Coyne & DeLongis, 1986).

Partner under-involvement (Figure 9.5) may stem from a variety of factors that culminate in a set of relatively modest caregiver goals. These include: (1) assumptions regarding the patient's medical condition, e.g., the belief that the recovery process, whether or not it seems to be going well, cannot be facilitated or has no room for further progress; (2) assumptions regarding the patient's receptivity to caregiving, e.g., the belief that efforts to help will be rejected or criticized; (3) self-referent assumptions, e.g., the belief that caregiving efforts will be ineffectual; (4) role conflict and role strain, e.g., the partner's other major commitments are not compatible with taking an active role as caregiver or the total set of commitments exceed the partner's capacity to enact fully a caregiver role. Like beliefs about the patient's condition and coping efforts, beliefs about caregiving also may be influenced by social comparison processes involving other patients and their primary support persons. For example, a spouse who has observed the rapid, relatively unassisted recovery of a younger and/or healthier man may underestimate the importance of these age and/or health differences and set far too modest caregiver roles for her own caregiving activities.

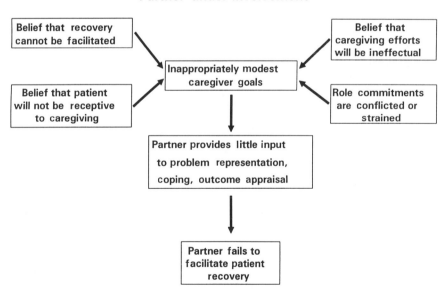

Partner under-involvement

Figure 9.5. Caregiver under-involvement reflects inappropriately modest caregiver goals, which may stem from a variety of sources but chiefly reflects the partner's beliefs about the patient's medical condition and receptivity to caregiving and self-referent beliefs concerning efficacy and the feasibility of integrating the caregiver role with other role commitments. The result is a low level of input to the patient's self-regulatory activity, which may or may not compromise recovery, depending upon the patient's ability to draw upon personal resources and other potential caregivers.

Whatever their source, modest caregiver goals will prevent the partner from attempting to facilitate the patient's recovery, causing the patient to draw upon others for support or to rely more heavily upon individual self-regulatory efforts. Therefore, whether the under-involved partner actually compromises the recovery process will depend upon the patient's ability to mobilize other resources, which may explain reported gender differences in recovery (Stanton et al., 1984; Zyzanski, Stanton & Jenkins, 1981; but see Sokol et al., 1987).

Partner *over*-involvement may reflect unrealistically *ambitious* caregiver goals (Figure 9.6). As in the case of under-involvement, these goals stem from the partner's beliefs about the patient's medical condition (e.g., recovery will suffer without considerable involvement from the partner), patient receptivity (e.g., the patient desires a high level of partner involvement or eventually will accept it despite initial resistance), self-referent assumptions

Partner over-involvement

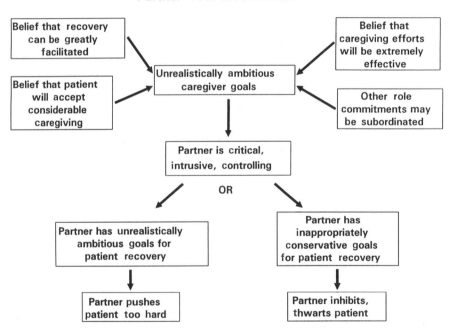

Figure 9.6. Caregiver over-involvement reflects unrealistically ambitious caregiver goals which also stem from the partner's view of the patient and the self. When combined with unrealistically ambitious goals for patient recovery, over-involvement may lead the partner to push the patient too hard. When combined with an inappropriately conservative view of recovery, the result may be efforts to inhibit and thwart the patient's efforts to speed recovery. Either pattern of over-involvement is likely to strain the patient–partner relationship and may impede recovery

(e.g., high self-efficacy as a caregiver), and other role commitments (e.g., other roles can be put aside for the time being). Although patients vary with respect to their preferred level of partner involvement in the recovery process, well-intended but over-zealous caregiving is likely to be perceived as intrusive, controlling, and critical, which may strain the patient–partner relationship (Bilodeau & Hackette, 1971; Wishnie et al., 1971).

As depicted in Figure 9.6, the specific consequences of caregiver over-involvement will depend up the caregiver's beliefs about the process of patient recovery. The over-involved partner who holds relatively ambitious goals regarding the pace at which the patient should progress may tend to push the patient too hard, whereas the over-involved partner with conservative recovery goals may inhibit the patient's efforts to resume normal activities. Over-reaction to the patient's emotional expressiveness may be an interesting and infrequently mentioned determinant of the partner's goals regarding the pace of recovery. As our model suggests, the stress of surgery and recovery will be associated with both objective, i.e., cognitive-representational, and emotional responses in the patient and partner. A partner who is closely tuned to and who over-reacts emotionally to the patient's expressive reactions may be far too ready to discourage the patient from engaging in pain-producing activities such as physical exercise that is essential for a speedy and full recovery. Conversely, communication of affect from patient to partner may be such that the partner encourages physical activity beyond the patient's ability to tolerate pain and discomfort.

Either form of caregiver over-involvement can prove self-defeating, for example, by undermining performance of coping tasks, inadvertently reinforcing the patient's feelings of dependence, or causing the patient to behave in a maladaptive manner as a means of asserting his/her autonomy (Coyne, Wortman & Lehnman, 1988). In addition to these effects on the patient, a partner with unrealistically high expectations regarding his/her ability to help the patient recover risks experiencing as a personal failure what may be a quite acceptable course recovery. When the patient also has unrealistic expectations regarding the partner's capacity for caregiving, the result may be even more damaging, since the patient may be failing to take a sufficiently active role in his/her own recovery while at the same time undermining the partner's motivation to provide support. Alternatively, the patient may reduce requests for assistance, in an effort to convey the false impression that the partner's efforts to provide support have been successful (Hilbert, 1984). This suggest the possibility of a negative cycle involving alternating periods of under- and over-involvement.

Coherence in the patient–caregiver relationship

Earlier it was suggested that the coherence of the patient's individual self-regulatory activities is key to successful adaptation to major surgery. This principle has a counterpart at the interpersonal level of analysis. Coherence in the patient–caregiver relationship is also integral to surgical recovery and rehabilitation. Here coherence refers to a continued state of congruence or compatibility between two (or more) individuals' mental representations of the same health threat, leading to coordinated behavioral efforts to deal with the threat and its effects on other aspects of the individuals' relationship. At the level of **task**-focused social self-regulation, congruence involves a shared view of: (1) objective and subjective aspects of the patient's medical condition, (2) objective and subjective aspects of the surgical procedure, (3) available coping procedures, and (4) criteria for evaluating coping outcomes. At the level of *role*-focused social self-regulation, congruence involves a shared view of: (1) the impact of surgery and illness on both the patient's and partner's mutual roles, (2) the appropriate level of caregiver involvement, and (3) criteria for evaluating the caregiver's efforts to facilitate patient recovery.

Discontinuities in the relationship   There are many factors that may contribute to divergences in the representations of the surgical experience held by the patient and the partner. As discussed earlier, only the patient has direct access to internal subjective states such as pain, discomfort, fatigue, and emotional distress that may be produced by surgery. Likewise, the patient may not fully appreciate the emotional toll that his or her medical situation exacts from the partner. Even in the case of directly observable events (e.g., progressive improvements in the patient's capacity for physical activity; the degree to which the partner assumes additional household responsibilities), patient and partner have different perspectives and may therefore come to different conclusions regarding the progress of patient recovery and effectiveness of partner caregiving. Actor–observer differences in attribution (Jones & Nisbett, 1972) may further undermine coherence by leading patient and partner to draw different conclusions regarding their roles in bringing about even agreed-up improvements or setbacks in recovery. Patient and partner may also take different perspectives in making social comparisons, e.g., choosing different models or evaluative dimensions in appraising recovery and caregiving. In addition, differences in value may lead to disagreement regarding the evaluation of adaptive gains. For example, the patient may place greater emphasis on the capacity to return to work, while the partner focuses on signs of physical discomfort and efforts at long-term management of the medical condition.

Coherence as a barrier to recovery   A common representation of disease and treatment is no assurance, however, of effective management of the stresses of surgery and recovery. A couple sharing an inaccurate representation of surgery can reinforce one another in inappropriate and maladaptive coping procedures, thereby slowing recovery and creating dangers to the patient's physical well-being. For example, in an elderly couple, patient and spouse may share an overly protective orientation toward the patient's condition, restricting participation in "overtaxing" activities involving ambulation and other forms of physical exertion in an effort to "conserve the patient's energy resources".

Summary and implications

A consideration of social aspects of the self-regulation process highlights the importance of distinguishing between issues that most directly involve the task of preparing the patient for surgery and its effects, and issues that arise from the impact of the surgical episode on the set of interrelated social roles in which the patient and partner are embedded. The first set of issues may be cast in terms of patient–partner exchanges that provide input to the representation–coping–appraisal sequence that describes the patient's intrapersonal response to impending surgery. A clear implication for intervention is that it may be possible to educate both the patient and the partner in a way that maximizes their ability to cooperate in coming to an accurate understanding of surgery, enhancing the efficacy of coping efforts, and facilitating the realistic appraisal of coping activity. There also may be opportunities for the partner to contribute directly to the patient's outcome, for example, through efforts to orient the patient to time and place in the period immediately following surgery, or through efforts to schedule family visits in a way that optimizes social stimulation without burdening the patient.

With respect to role-related issues, the matter is somewhat more complex. The inability to carry out valued roles may cause both patient and partner to experience a sense of loss that undermines long-term recovery from major surgery. Patient enactment of the "sick role" may impede recovery. The need to assume the role of caregiver may produce role-strain and role-conflict in the partner, among the possible consequences of which are feelings of inadequacy as a caregiver and patterns of under- or over-involvement in the patient's preparation for and recovery from surgery. The overarching goal of establishing coherence in the caregiver–patient relationship may be impeded by a variety of factors, including interpersonal issues that precede the need for surgery and those that arise from or are exacerbated by the surgical encounter. Although it may be difficult to develop interventions to address these problems thoroughly in a cost-effective way, it may be possible to draw the attention of patients and their partners to some of the more salient issues that might influence physical recovery. In cases where long-standing marital difficulties appear likely to undermine the recovery process, referral to a marriage counselor may be in order. Increased surveillance for interpersonal difficulties that may interfere with recovery and appropriate efforts to address the problem early in the surgical experience may in many cases lower long-term costs associated with avoidable complications and re-admission.

THE STRUCTURE AND CONTENT OF SURGICAL PREPARATION INTERVENTIONS

The following discussion of surgical preparation interventions draws upon both the self-regulation model and the many surgical preparation studies conducted to date. It also describes features of psychological interventions that have been employed to reduce distress and facilitate recovery in non-surgical populations, such as post-MI patients and individuals undergoing radiotherapy or noxious pharmacological regimens. It should be borne in mind that many of the suggestions made below have yet to be examined systematically and should be taken as intervention elements that may warrant empirical examination rather than as recommendations for clinical practice.

Intervention source

The intervention source refers to the individual or department responsible for creating and implementing the treatment, for example, nurses, physicians, anesthetists, psychologists and/or pastoral care workers. The requirements of an effective source of psychological intervention include training in the art and science of communication, knowledge of psychological theory, medical knowledge, and patient access. Unfortunately, the specialized language of the professions creates barriers to effective communication, and health care professionals may fail to translate medical concepts into comprehensible, lay language even when the concept is relatively simple. The communication task becomes increasingly complex when a single term or phrase refers to a complex set of procedures that may extend over minutes or hours, or in the case of procedures such as diagnostic angiography which, depending upon the results or as a consequence of accidental damage caused by the procedure itself, may need to be followed immediately by a second procedure. Communication in these instances may be of special importance as complex, multi-part procedures may be misinterpreted or perceived as multiple unannounced procedures, some of which may be seen as unnecessary.

Providing education to patients has always been an integral part of professional nursing practice (American Nurses Association, 1973; Joint Commission on Hospital Accreditation, 1981), and nursing curricula include patient education principles and teaching strategies. Typically, pre-operative delivery of information and coping techniques is given by the nurse. However, with the explosion of outpatient procedures, this preparation frequently must occur minutes or hours before surgery as the nurses perform routine baseline physical measures prior to surgery. Moreover, nurses often are inadequately trained in the psychological theory in which surgical preparation must be grounded. It is also possible that the nurse's concern for the patient's physical and emotional comfort will at times conflict with the need to provide the kind of information necessary to prepare the patient for surgery and its effects.

As specialized health services have developed, more individuals are available to educate patients and many have assumed this role, including pharmacists, dieticians, respiratory therapists, physical therapists, and others. Since not all hospitals have access to these specialized services, nurses often become the source of patient preparation. They are present in large numbers in all hospitals and uniquely available to patients twenty-four hours a day. As outpatient surgeries continue to grow in number, it may become necessary to provide pre-operative preparation in the patient's home. This may require greater use of audiotapes, videotapes, or written materials, as opposed to face-to-face instruction. Still, a nurse with appropriate training in surgical medicine, psychological theory, and patient communication may be in the best position to coordinate the intervention.

Intervention content

Intervention content refers to the substance of what is transmitted to recipients, and may generally be described in terms of the type of information that is conveyed by the treatment and its intended effects. Surgical preparation interventions have involved the following content areas.

Procedural information

Procedural information involves a description of what will be done to the patient. This typically involves temporal orienting information, i.e., when specific events will occur and how long they will last, as well as spatial orienting information, i.e., specific locations within the hospital where different events will occur (Johnson, 1984). Presentation of this information may be accompanied by a discussion of the purpose of each aspect of the procedure. Specific knowledge as to what will be done, when it will be done, and why it is being done is designed to reduce uncertainty, confusion, and distress by short-circuiting the process of threat appraisal. In addition to immediate effects on threat appraisal, the information adds to the patient's disease representation a schema or script within which to assimilate the surgical episode as it unfolds. The availability of such a script may continue to reduce distress by continuing to minimize uncertainty and by decreasing the amount of cognitive work the patient must perform in order to comprehend the surgical experience (Johnson, 1984).

Subjective information

Subjective information describes the phenomenology of undergoing surgery, that is, the somatic sensations produced by the operation, how these can be distinguished from those produced by disease, and the emotional reactions likely to be experienced in response to specific cues. Preparation in the subjective domain is of special importance as subjective experiences, particularly those of somatic sensations, are very likely to be perceived as indicators of one's somatic well-being. If these signs are noxious or unexpected, they will readily and understandably be seen as signs of serious danger, that is, as indicators of threats to life stemming from the surgery and/or from the exacerbation of disease.

Delivery of subjective information must be couched in probabilistic terms, because patients will differ in their reactions to surgery. Nonetheless, it is possible to prepare patients for many features of their subjective experiences prior to surgery and on regaining consciousness afterward. The key is to provide benign interpretations of these sensations, a task that may require accurate preparation regarding their time course as well as correct identification of their significance. For example, a coronary-bypass patient who recognizes that post-operative chest pain is produced by the incision, and is a sign of healing, will probably appraise the pain in a more benign way and be less distressed that one who mistakenly believes that the pain reflects damage to the heart or to coronary arteries or that the pain is from the incision area and indicates that the sutures may open with movement. Just as procedural information provides the patient with a script describing surgery as an objective series of events, subjective information provides a script describing the internal sequence of somato-sensory and emotional events. The availability of such a script should reduce uncertainty and worry.

Specific experiences for which to prepare the patient will depend upon the specific surgical procedure to be performed. In general, these are likely to involve pain, sensations, emotional reactions, and cognitive states. Pain may be produced in a number of locations, including the incision area, at the site where tissue may be harvested for grafting, and in the throat where tubes are inserted. It is probably best to decompose and explain pain into its components, e.g., "You might feel tightness as the wound heals and burning sensations from pain fibers in the skin that were cut and injured during surgery. Although it is natural that this pain might make you feel upset, it actually reflects the body's normal healing response". Various other sensations will be associated with specific procedures, e.g. catheter insertion, or with specific phases of the surgical episode, e.g., muscular stiffness associated with positioning on the operation room table or prolonged bed rest. Emotional reactions, which are common and to be expected, include increased anxiety as the day on which surgery is scheduled draws near, distress that accompanies severe pain, anergy during recovery from general anesthesia, and frustration with the slow pace of recovery. Cognitive states for which the patient and partner should be prepared include confusion and disorientation during the post-operative period.

Coping strategies

Coping strategies are specific cognitive and behavioral activities which the patient may perform in order to facilitate adaptation to surgery. Problem-focused strategies are directed at objective features of the task of undergoing and recovering from surgery. Examples include deep-breathing, coughing, range-of-motion, and ambulation exercises designed to reduce the incidence of complications and facilitate recovery of physical capabilities. Emotion-focused coping strategies are directed at subjective reactions such as pain and distress. Emotion-focused strategies are often criticized, incorrectly, as maladaptive. Although this characterization may be correct when such strategies are emphasized to the neglect of effective problem-focused strategies, many aspects of the surgical experience are not amenable to direct control by the patient, who in such cases must focus on subjective reactions. Examples of emotion-focused coping include: (1) appropriate requests for pain medication; (2) distraction to reduce distress during short-term procedures (e.g., injections) and monitoring of sensations followed by distraction for longer-term and repeated procedures (e.g., colonoscopy); (3) focusing on positive aspects of surgery (e.g., reduced post-operative pain, improved functional status); (4) repeating positive self-statements; (5) somatic procedures for reducing distress (e.g., deep-breathing, muscle-relaxation exercises).

There is a multifaceted theoretical rationale for providing the patient with coping strategies. Behavioral strategies such as coughing, deep-breathing, and walking exercises were introduced to post-surgical care as a means of reducing complications such as thrombophlebitis, pneumonia, and emboli (Johnson, 1984). In addition to this direct medical benefit, the availability of specific coping options may lower anxiety by reducing threat appraisal. Moreover, by facilitating ambulation and resumption of daily living activities, behavioral coping strategies may improve muscle conditioning and enhance self-esteem and feelings of autonomy and efficacy. Still another possible benefit of physical activity is the production of somatic sensations that may be incompatible with vegetative aspects of depression. Thus, it may be especially important for patients for whom the prospect of reduced social role activity and/or progressive physical deterioration brings a sense of loss, sadness, and helplessness. Emotion-focused strategies are designed to reduce distress which, as noted earlier, may lower the risk associated with general anesthesia, reduce pain and complications, and improve the patient's capacity to recall and engage in behavioral coping procedures.

Adaptive goals and evaluative criteria

In the self-regulation view of surgical preparation, the provision of coping strategies is more than skills training. Although certain techniques do involve procedures that must be mastered by the patient, it is essential that, in the mind of the patient, these procedures become embedded in the larger self-regulation process. This involves the formation of a mental representation in which enactment of coping strategies is linked to: (1) general adaptive goals that provide the rationale for performing the coping activity; (2) clear, specific evaluative criteria that represent concrete instantiations of adaptive goals and allow an assessment of the effectiveness of the coping strategy; (3) a clear, specific model of the coping procedure itself, to provide a guide for efforts to modify its behavioral enactment in response to feedback indicating that outcomes do not satisfy evaluative criteria; (4) an understanding that evaluative criteria associated with adaptive goals should be applied with flexibility and do not represent rigid, absolute standards. The tendency to focus on specific responses in many coping skills training programs may overlook the need to embed specific skills in the larger framework of representations and goals, and therefore may fail to suggest substitutes and/or ways of varying a specific response which may be needed when the focal strategy proves too difficult to perform or fails to produce positive outcomes.

Psychotherapeutic aspects of intervention

Many surgical preparation studies have used interventions with psychotherapeutic components ranging from specific techniques such as rational emotive therapy (Langer, Janis & Wolfer, 1975), systematic desensitization (Aiken & Hendricks, 1971), and hypnosis (Field, 1974), to somewhat less structured efforts to provide emotional support, encouragement, and reassurance (Finesilver, 1978; Wolfer & Visintainer, 1975). For the most part, these interventions are designed to reduce emotional distress, and therefore may be seen as a form of emotion-focused social support delivered by health care professionals.

In the self-regulation view, this component of intervention is best delivered in the context of presenting the patient with procedural and subjective information, coping strategies, and information concerning adaptive goals and associated evaluative criteria. The rationale is that the latter approach fosters the formation of an associative link between a realistic representation of the health threat, self-regulatory activity, and emotional assurance and support. As a consequence, each component of the overall mental representation should acquire the capacity to activate and reinforce others, a characteristic of a system in which moment-to-moment regulatory activity is coherent. Thus, the expectation of a favorable outcome and associated positive affect become grounded in an accurate sense of the probability of such an outcome and the availability of a set of coping strategies whose enactment should help bring it about. Conversely, enactment of coping strategies should come to evoke positive outcome expectations and improved morale. In this perspective, emotional support becomes self-generating and both facilitates and is facilitated by the process of self-regulation. Social exchanges with individuals who can provide expert information play an especially important role for patients experiencing surgery for the very first time. Expert information can help the patient to evaluate the meaning of his or her ongoing experience if the two sources of input (expert information and subjective experiences) become integrated within a coherent mental representation. In the incoherent representation, abstract information from experts may register but remain isolated from the many noxious and novel experiences occurring during surgery, in which case the patient acquires little understanding of his or her subjective reactions and is unlikely to benefit emotionally from the encounter.

Intervention Media

The intervention medium refers to the format or means of delivering the treatment, and may involve printed matter, audiotape, videotape, didactic presentation, and/or discussion groups. Selecting from among these alternatives involves a consideration of standardization, impact, individualization, and cost. An intervention that is delivered face-to-face by a health care professional, while costly, is likely to have greater impact on the patient than one involving printed matter. In addition to the attention the health care professional is likely to command by virtue of his or her status and expertise, a face-to-face encounter allows the patient to ask questions and to verbalize concerns, or to express confusion, uncertainty, and anxiety in a non-verbal manner. The health care professional may then repeat portions of the presentation, provide additional information, and/or engage in efforts to calm the patient and allay his/her concerns. Thus, although costly, face-to-face intervention maximizes impact and possesses the flexibility needed to permit individualization of treatment. Flexibility is a two-edged sword, however, if the intervention is being implemented as part of a controlled experimental trial, in which case lack of standardization poses a serious threat to internal validity.

Automated media such as videotapes and audiotapes have been used effectively as a less costly and more standardized alternative to face-to-face interventions (e.g., Anderson,. 1987; Johnson et al., 1978). In addition to issues of cost and standardization, the use of audiotapes and, to a greater extent, videotapes, makes it possible to take advantage of learning techniques that involve modeling and graphic presentation. For example, *Living Proof* (Keach, 1981), the film used in an intervention study reported by Anderson (1987), portrays interviews with a recovering cardiac surgery patient. The concrete, visual depiction of a real person with whom the patient can identify may facilitate the assimilation of procedural, subjective, and coping information through vicarious learning processes (cf.

Kulik & Mahler, 1987). In this regard, a major virtue of videotaped presentations is that they provide a direct model of coping behavior. This is especially valuable if the behavior is complex and/or if the behavior elicits pain or can generate other negative experiences, allowing the observer to acquire techniques for overcoming such barriers. With the increasing prevalence of outpatient surgery, it would be useful to evaluate the utility of videotaped preparation materials which the patient and partner can review at home prior to surgery.

During the period following hospital discharge, face-to-face intervention and/or psychological assessment is most feasible and cost-efficient on the occasion of hospital visits for medical follow-up. However, contact with patients and their partners on other occasions may be indicated as a means of maintaining lifestyle changes designed to manage chronic disease and to support efforts to cope with noxious follow-up regimens such as radiation and chemotherapy. Videotaped materials might prove a suitable means of addressing these concerns. Alternatively, telephone-based interventions, which have yielded promising findings in studies of cardiac patients, might have greater impact because they can provide direct contact with health care professionals (Beckie, 1989; Frazure-Smith & Price, 1989).

Intervention target

The intervention target is the social unit on which the intervention is carried out, for example, the individual patient, small groups of patients, patient–partner dyads, or small groups of patient–partner dyads. As has already been discussed, the self-regulation model provides a specific theoretical basis for designing interventions that target both the patient and a partner. It also provides guidance regarding intervention content that explicitly addresses the patient, the partner, and the patient–partner relationship. The self-regulatory view is also consistent with the use of interventions that target patient groups or groups of patient-partner dyads (e.g., Brown, Glazer & Higgins, 1984; Ibrahim et al., 1974; Meagher, Gregor & Stewart, 1987; Taylor et al., 1985). The latter approach should provide additional opportunities for each patient–partner dyad to acquire information to elaborate and refine their mental representations of surgery, to expand their repertoire of coping strategies, and to make use of social comparisons in evaluating both patient recovery and partner caregiving.

Individuals differ in a number of ways that may have implications for intervention. These include medical history, current medical condition, the specific surgical procedure to be carried out, age, gender, parameters of pre-surgical social support and social network, and personality. Research on these variables suggest a number of factors that may be associated with recovery and rehabilitation either directly or in interaction with psychological intervention. For example, the broad literature on personality and

health implicates a number of personality dispositions as potential contributors to surgical recovery because they appear related to individual differences in responses to psychological stress (Contrada, Leventhal &
O'Leary, 1990). Research focusing on personality and responses to surgical
procedures would appear to bear this out. Dispositional optimism is associated with better recovery from coronary bypass surgery as evidenced by
early ambulation and shorter hospital stay (Scheier et al., 1989). Individuals experiencing high levels of emotional distress or psychological symptoms prior to surgery show poor recovery (Bass, 1984; Mayou & Bryant,
1987). Intrapsychic coping or defensive styles such as denial may have
complex relationships with recovery (Folks et al., 1988; Freeman et al.,
1984; see also Levine et al., 1987).

A study reported by Miller and Mangan (1983) illustrates the potential
for interactions between personality and psychological preparation for
medical procedures. On undergoing a diagnostic procedure for detecting
uterine cancer, gynecological patients with a vigilant coping style
("monitors") showed more emotional arousal overall than those with an
avoidant style ("blunters"). However, both groups showed lowest levels of
arousal when their treatment condition matched their coping style. That is,
blunters showed reduced arousal when they received minimal information
about the procedure, whereas for monitors, arousal was lowest when they
received extensive information.

These selected findings on personality suggest that it may be important
to take psychosocial characteristics of the patient into account in designing,
implementing, and evaluating interventions aimed at improving surgical
recovery and rehabilitation. Unfortunately, practical limitations may make
it impossible to do much more than assess patients' medical status, gender,
and age, and perhaps one or two relevant personality dimensions or coping
styles. Pending further correlational research identifying predictors response
to psychological preparation, there remains the danger that certain patients
may actually be harmed psychologically by interventions that are incon-
gruent with their preferred mode of coping. Strategies for minimizing this
possibility include careful screening for psychiatric symptoms at the time of
recruitment or pre-surgical assessment, close monitoring of responses to the
intervention, and, at least at the pilot-testing stage, open-ended interviews
to determine how subjects respond to psychological preparation.

Intervention schedule and setting

The intervention schedule refers to the timing of the treatment, which may
involve one or more sessions occurring prior to surgery, during the post-
operative hospital stay, and/or following discharge. Because these events
occur in different locations, the intervention setting must be taken into
account in specifying an intervention schedule. The opportunities for and

obstacles to psychological intervention and assessment differ dramatically as the patient progresses to potential intervention settings that may include the surgeon's office, the pre-admission testing site, the surgical intensive care unit, the regular nursing unit, and the patient's home.

Analysis of the major temporal transitions of the surgical episode (see Figure 9.2) provides a rationale for scheduling intervention sessions so as to maximize their effectiveness in optimizing outcomes *vis-à-vis* the changing series of adaptive goals that arise following the decision to undergo surgery, through the post-operative hospital stay, discharge, and resumption of role activities. Pre-surgical preparation for *both* patient and partner is essential to reduce acute emotional distress and to begin to lay the groundwork for later components of the intervention. Preparation for the partner at about the time of surgery is worth considering in the case of procedures such as coronary bypass in which surgery may last many hours and may be followed by a period of a few days in which the patient's condition is critical or involves prolonged periods of sleep or a semiconscious state. An additional, in-hospital session for certain major surgeries, at a time close to discharge, may also be worth considering as a means of beginning to address psychosocial aspects of recovery (e.g., return to work, caregiver role-strain), lifestyle, and compliance issues (e.g., glycemic control in the diabetic amputee, physical reconditioning in the coronary-bypass patient). Post-discharge intervention, though costly, may be critical to cost-effective management of psychosocial and lifestyle adjustments and may serve to detect emotional problems that represent maladaptive responses to the surgical episode, possibly brought about by major changes in physical capacity or valued social roles.

Summary and implications

The foregoing discussion suggests that implementation of a comprehensive intervention program would run the risk of bombarding the patient (and co-participating spouse, etc.) with an overwhelming amount of information. Several steps might be taken to minimize the potential for information overload and resulting anxiety and confusion without sacrificing positive impact. The initial session might provide an overview of the overall program, in the form of a simple schematic diagram or brief videotape, including a printed or videotaped version that can be retained by the patient. Subsequent sessions would involve focused informational packages relevant to each stage of the surgical experience. This should allow the presentation of a substantial amount of information overall while minimizing the amount of information delivered at any single point in time, keeping the intervention understandable and memorable for the period of its use. Attention can be focused on current issues while minimizing worry and distress about future concerns. Organizing the intervention schedule in this manner also should help with cost-containment by minimizing the amount of time required of research staff at each session.

PRACTICAL, METHODOLOGICAL, AND ANALYTIC ISSUES: A FINAL COMMENT

A host of factors present a challenge to research aimed at understanding and improving psychological effects of major surgery. Organizational and economic factors make the hospital a difficult setting into which to introduce efforts to modify procedures for treating patients. This is particularly true of modifications that are to be individualized for different patients, that involve increasing the amount of time health care professionals spend with patients, and that may require the presence of patients' family members. When surgery is to be performed on an emergency basis, participation of the patient in a research project may be impossible. The urgency with which non-emergent surgeries must sometimes be performed may have the same effect, and even surgery that is clearly elective and non-urgent offers few windows of opportunity for introducing experimental treatments and collecting outcome measures, and may do so only for a subset of patients.

Thus, the hospital setting in which the study of surgical preparation may take place poses a number of obstacles for research. Difficulties in gaining access to subjects and time pressures that affect the health care professional who may be involved in implementing interventions argue for simple experimental designs that maximize statistical power for detected treatment effects by requiring a small number of comparison groups. The same set of pressures argue for limiting the scope of psychological assessment. Lengthy interviews and questionnaires present a burden that may cause patients to decline to participate or to drop out of the study prior to completion. In the busy and often unpredictable hospital environment, complex protocols for acquiring staff ratings of patient status may be difficult to carry out in a way that produces reliable and valid assessments. Acquiring data from medical charts and the notes of staff nurses offers an alternative but may present other difficulties related to accessing and coding hospital records.

Another set of obstacles encountered in the hospital setting involve treatment contamination. Care must be taken to ensure that patients assigned to "usual care" and other comparison groups do not experience elements of the experimental treatment as a consequence of cross-talk between individuals implementing treatment, hospital staff not involved in carrying out the study, or the patients themselves. A different variety of treatment contamination reflects systematic implementation of administrative policy. As a consequence of early demonstrations of the effectiveness of surgical preparation, routine hospital care now includes elements such as procedural and subjective information that facilitate psychological and physical recovery and therefore render usual care groups inappropriate as a baseline control group. Similarly, as noted earlier, cost considerations have led to discharge policies that have substantially reduced the average length of hospital stay. Both factors reduce the power of intervention studies aimed at demonstrating that further shortening of hospital stay and additional improvements in recovery can be effected by modifying routine care. Given the magnitude of the problem when viewed at a national level, efforts to demonstrate such effects are still valuable, but now require larger sample sizes and are, as a consequence, more costly to carry out.

Still other methodological problems are not a consequence of the hospital setting *per se* but stem from factors inherent in the study of stressful life events in chronically ill individuals (Contrada & Krantz, 1987). Pre-existing disease, previous surgical experiences, and the trauma of impending major surgery may influence psychosocial measurement in complex ways. It is therefore virtually impossible to conduct truly prospective research in this area. Baseline assessments that are prospective with respect to hospital admission and surgery may be influenced by parameters of disease, treatment, personality, and social relationships that are correlated with outcomes. These factors may not confound fully randomized experimental trials if treatment groups are adequately stratified with respect to important subject characteristics. However, given the constraints of hospital-based research, stratification may not be feasible. Even if it is, pre-existing medical and psychosocial factors may undermine the validity of pre-surgical assessments of emotional state, cognitive functioning, and social support, which, at a minimum, will reduce the ability of those measures to increase statistical power for detecting effects of psychological treatment on recovery and rehabilitation.

In view of the difficulties described above, it is clear that planning an experimental trial to evaluate a program of psychological preparation for surgery can be a daunting task. The particular mix of problems confronting an individual investigator will depend upon a number of factors, including features of the setting, surgical procedures, and patient characteristics. Although this makes it difficult to derive general guidelines for research in this area, one clear implication is that practical considerations will necessitate compromise with respect to the scope and complexity of theoretical yield. In our view, it would be unfortunate if researchers capitulate too readily and reduce the breadth of psychosocial assessment or the contents of intervention programs, to the point where it becomes impossible to learn something of the psychological processes that may account for treatment effects. We believe it remains possible to employ theory-based research designs to test hypotheses regarding the self-regulatory processes that mediate preparation effects at different points in the sequence of events that comprise the surgical episode. The "active ingredients" of psychological intervention may be isolated experimentally in the context of simple, two-group designs (prepared versus usual care) involving careful assessment of the patient's and partners' perceptions of surgery and post-surgical procedures, and the performance of coping behaviors. Multiple regression/correlation techniques may then be used to determine whether perceptions and coping activity mediated the effects of the interventions.

As should be clear from the body of this chapter, our perspective emphasizes the need for research designed to examine the interplay between individual and social self-regulation. Although there is more to be learned by treating intra-individual and interpersonal aspects of surgical recovery as different levels of analysis, the separation is artificial. Depending upon researcher's perspective, it can result in the neglect of basic cognitive-affective processes, such as problem representation, coping, and coping appraisal, or basic social-psychological processes, such as emotional communication, social comparison, and role-strain. Interactions between these two sets of processes are likely to be responsible for both between- and within-individual variation in surgical recovery and rehabilitation. They are therefore prime targets for psychological interventions aimed at improving those outcomes.

ACKNOWLEDGMENTS

Preparation of this chapter was supported by grants MH-46900 and AG-03501. We thank Michael Diefenbach and Howard Leventhal for their comments on earlier drafts of this chapter.

REFERENCES

Abbey, A., Abramis, D. J. & Caplan, R. D. (1985). Effects of different sources of social support and social conflict on emotional well-being. *Basic and Applied Social Psychology*, **6**, 111–130.

Aiken, I. & Hendricks, T. F. (1971). Systematic relaxation as a nursing intervention with open heart surgery patients. *Nursing Research*, **20**, 212–217.

Anderson, E. A. (1987). Preoperative preparation for cardiac surgery facilitates recovery, reduces psychological distress, and reduces the incidence od acute postoperative hypertension. *Journal of Consulting and Clinical Psychology*, **55**, 513–520.

American Nurses Association (1973). *Standards of nursing practice*. Kansas City, MO: The Association.

Bandura, A. (1982). Self-efficacy mechanism in human agency. *American Psychologist*, **37**, 122–147.

Bass, C. (1984). Psychological outcome after coronary artery bypass surgery. *British Journal of Psychiatry*, **145**, 526–532.

Bauman, L. J. & Leventhal, H. (1985). "I can tell when my blood pressure is up, can't I?". *Health Psychology*, **4**, 203–218.

Beckie, T. (1989). A supportive-educative telephone program: impact on knowledge and anxiety after coronary artery bypass surgery. *Heart and Lung*, **18**, 46–55.

Belle, D. (1982). Social ties and social support. In: D. Belle (Ed), *Lives in stress: Women and depression* (pp. 133–144). Beverly Hills, CA: Sage.

Berkman, L. F. (1985). Measures of social networks and social support: evidence and measurement. In: A. M. Ostfeld & E. D. Eaker (Eds), *Measuring psychosocial variables in epidemiologic studies of cardiovascular disease* (pp. 51–79). Bethesda, MA: Public Health Service, National Institutes of Health.

Bilodeau, C. B. & Hackette, T. P. (1971). Issues raised in a group setting by patients recovering from myocardial infarction. *American Journal of Psychiatry*, 128, 73–78.

Brown, D. G. Glazer, H. & Higgins, M. (1984). Group intervention: a psychological and educational approach to open heart surgery patients and their families. *Social Work in Health Care*, 9, 47–59.

Burke, M. (1992). New surgical technologies reshape hospital strategies. *Hospitals*, 66, 30–42.

Carver, C. S. & Scheier, M. F. (1981) *Attention and self-regulation: a control-theory approach to human behavior*. New York: Springer Verlag.

Cohen, J. (1988). *Statistical power analysis for the behavioral sciences*. Hillsdale, NJ: Erlbaum.

Cohen, S. (1988). Psychosocial models of the role of social support in the etiology of physical disease. *Health Psychology*, 7, 269–297.

Cohen, S. & Hoberman, H. M. (1983). Positive events and social supports as buffers of life change. *Journal of Applied Social Psychology*, 13, 99–125.

Cohen, S. & Syme, S. L. (1985). *Social support and health*. New York: Academic Press.

Contrada, R. J. and Krantz, D. S. (1987). Measurement biases in health psychology research designs. In C. Cooper and S. Kasl (Eds), *Stress and health: issues in research methodology* (pp. 57–78). London: Wiley.

Contrada, R. J. Leventhal. H. & O'Leary, A. (1990). Personality and health. In: L. A. Pervin (Ed), *Handbook of personality: theory and research* (pp. 638–669). New York: Wiley.

Coyne, J. C. & DeLongis, A. (1986). Going beyond social support: the role of social relationships in adaptation. *Journal of Consulting and Clinical Psychology*, 54, 454–460.

Coyne, J. C., Wortman, C. B. & Lehnman, D. R. (1988). The other side of support: emotional overinvolvement and miscarried helping. In: B. Gottlieb (Ed), *Marshalling social support: formats, processes, and effects* (pp. 305–330). Newbury, CA: Sage.

Devine, E. C. & Cook, T. D. (1983). A meta-analytic of effects of psychoeducational interventions on length of postsurgical hospital stay. *Nursing Research*, 32, 267–274.

Egbert, L. D., Battit, G. E., Welch, C. E. & Barlett, M. K. (1964). Reduction of postoperative pain by encouragement and instruction of patients. *New England Journal of Medicine*, 270, 825–827.

Felton, G., Huss., K., Payne, E. E. & Srsic, K. (1976). Preoperative nursing interventions with the patient for surgery: outcomes of three alternative approaches. *International Journal of Nursing Studies*, 13, 11–24.

Festinger, L. (1954). A theory of social comparison processes. *Human Relations*, 7, 117–140.

Field, P. (1974). Effects of tape-recorded hypnotic preparation for surgery. *International Journal of Clinical Hypnosis*, 22, 54–61.

Finesilver, C. (1978). Preparation of adult patients for cardiac catheterization and coronary cineangiography. *International Journal of Nursing Studies*, 15, 211–221.

Fiore, J., Becker, J. & Coppel, B. (1983). Social network interactions: a buffer or a stress? *American Journal of Community Psychology*, 11, 423–439.

Fischer, C. S. (1982). *To dwell among friends: personal networks in town and city*. Chicago: University of Chicago Press.

Folks, D. G., Freeman, A. M., Sokol, R. S. & Thurstin, A. H. (1988). Denial: predicator of outcome following coronary bypass surgery. *International Journal of Psychiatry in Medicine*, 18, 57–66.

Fontana, A. F., Kerns, R. D., Rosenberg, R. L. & Colonese, K. L. (1989). Support, stress, and recovery from coronary heart disease: a longitudinal causal model. *Health Psychology*, 8, 175–193.

Foreman, M. D. (1986). Acute confused states in hospitalized elderly: a research dilemma. *Nursing Research*, 35, 34–38.

Frazure-Smith, N. & Price, R. (1989). Long-term follow-up of the ischemic heart disease life stress monitoring program. *Psychosomatic Medicine*, 51, 485–513.

Freeman, A. M., Cohen-Cole, S., Fleece, L., Waldo, A. & Folks, D. (1984). Psychiatric symptoms, type A behavior, and arrhythmias following coronary bypass. *Psychosomatics*, 25, 586–589.

Gottlieb, B. H. (1988). *Marshalling social support: formats, processes, and effects.* Newbury Park, CA: Sage.

Gove, W. & Hughes, M. (1979). Possible causes of the apparent sex differences in mental health. *American Psychological Review*, 44, 59–81.

Hathaway, D. (1986). Effect of preoperative instruction on postoperative outcomes: a meta-analysis. *Nursing Research*, 35, 269–275.

Heater, B. S., Becker, A. M. & Olson, R. K. (1988). Nursing interventions and patient outcomes: a meta-analysis of studies. *Nursing Research*, 37, 303–307.

Hilbert, R. A. (1984). The acultural dimension of pain: flawed reality construction and the problem of meaning. *Social Problems*, 31, 365–378.

Hobfoll, S. E. (1989). Conservation of resources: a new attempt at conceptualizing stress. *American Psychologist*, 44, 513–524.

Ibrahim, M. A., Feldman, J. G., Sultz, H. A., Staiman, M. G., Young, L. J. & Dean, D. (1974). Management after myocardial infarction: a controlled trial of the effect of group psychotherapy. *International Journal of Psychiatry in Medicine*, 5, 253–268.

Janis, I. L. (1958). *Psychological stress.* New York: Wiley.

Johnson, J. E. (1984). Psychological interventions and coping with surgery. In: A. Baum, S. E. Taylor & J. E. Singer (Eds), *Handbook of psychology and health* (Vol. 4., pp. 167–187). Hillsdale, NJ: Erlbaum.

Johnson, J. E. & Leventhal, H. (1974). The effects of accurate expectations and behavioral instructions on reactions during a noxious medical examination. *Journal of Personality and Social Psychology*, 29, 710–718.

Johnson, J. E., Leventhal, H. & Dabbs, J. M. (1971). Contribution of emotional and instrumental response processes in adaptation to surgery. *Research in Nursing and Health*, 1, 4–17.

Johnson, J. E., Morrissey, J. F. & Leventhal, H. (1973). Psychological preparation for an endoscopic examination. *Gastrointestinal Endoscopy*, 19, 180–182.

Johnson, J. E., Fuller, S. S., Endress, M. P. & Rice, V. H. (1978). Altering patients' responses to surgery: an extension and replication. *Research in Nursing and Health*, 1, 111–121.

Joint Commission on Hospital Accreditation (1981). *Accreditation manual for hospitals 1981 edition.* Chicago: The Commission.

Jones, E. E. & Nisbett, R. E. (1972). The actor and the observer: divergent perceptions of the causes of behavior. In: E. E. Jones, D. E. Kanouse, H. H. Kelley, R. E. Nisbett, S. Valins & B. Weiner (Eds), *Attribution: perceiving the causes of behavior* (pp. 79–94). Morristown, NJ: General Learning Press.

Keach, S. (Producer and Director) (1981). *Living proof* [Videotape]. North Hollywood, CA: Stacey Keach Productions.

Kessler, R. C. & McLeod, J. D. (1985). Social support and mental health in community samples. In: S. Cohen & S. L. Syme (Eds), *Social support and health* (pp. 219–240). New York: Academic Press.

Kulik, J. A. & Mahler, H. I. M. (1987). Effects of preoperative roommate assignment on preoperative anxiety and recovery from coronary-bypass surgery. *Health Psychology*, 6, 525–543.

Kulik, J. A. & Mahler, M. I. M. (1989). Social support and recovery from surgery. *Health Psychology*, 8, 221–238.

Langer, E. J., Janis, I. L. & Wolfer, J. A. (1975). Reduction of psychological stress in surgical patients. *Journal of Experimental Social Psychology*, 11, 155–165.

Layne, O. L. & Yudofsky, S. C. (1971). Postoperative psychosis in cardiotomy patients. *New England Journal of Medicine*, 284, 518–520.

Lazarus, R. S. (1966). *Psychological stress and the coping process*. New York: McGraw-Hill.

Lazarus, R. S. & Folkman, S. (1984). *Stress, appraisal, and coping*. New York: Springer.

Levental, E., Suls, J. & Leventhal, H. (in press). Coping through the lifespan. In: H. Krohne (Ed), *Attention and avoidance: strategies in coping with aversiveness*.

Leventhal, E., Leventhal, H., Shacham, S. & Easterling, D. V. (1989). Active coping reduces reports of pain from childbirth. *Journal of Consulting and Clinical Psychology*, 57, 365–371.

Leventhal, H. & Diefenbach, M. (1991). The active side of illness cognition. In: J. A. Skelton & R. T. Croyle (Eds), *Mental representation in health and illness* (pp. 247–272). New York: Springer Verlag.

Leventhal, H., Diefenbach, M. & Leventhal, E. (1992). Illness cognition: using common sense to understand treatment adherence and affect-cognition interactions. *Cognitive Therapy and Research*, 16, 143–163.

Leventhal, H. & Johnson, J. (1983). Laboratory and field experimentation: development of a theory of self-regulation. In: P. J. Wooldridge, M. H. Schmitt, J. K. Skipper & R. C. Leonard (Eds), *Behavioral science and nursing theory* (pp. 189–262). St Louis: Mosby.

Leventhal, H., Meyer, D. & Nerenz, D. (1980). The common sense representation of illness danger, In: S. Rachman (Ed), *Medical psychology* (Vol. II., pp. 7–30). New York: Pergamon Press.

Leventhal, H. & Nerenz, D. R. (1983). A model for stress research with some implications for the control of stress disorders. In D. Meichenbaum & M. Jaremko (Eds), *Stress reduction and prevention* (pp. 5–38). New York: Plenum.

Levine, J., Warrenburg, S., Kerns, R., Schwartz, G., DeLaney, R., Fontana, A., Gradman, A., Smith, A., Allen, S. & Cascione, R. (1987). The role of denial in recovery from coronary heart disease. *Psychosomatic Medicine*, 49, 109–117.

MacDonald, M. R. & Kuiper, N. A. (1983). Cognitive-behavioral preparations for surgery: some theoretical and methodological concerns. *Clinical Psychology Reviews*, 3, 27–39.

Manne, S. L. & Zautra, A. J. (1989). Spouse criticism and support: their association with coping and psychological adjustment among women with rheumatoid arthritis. *Journal of Personality and Social Psychology*, 56, 608–617.

Mayou, R. & Bryant, B. (1987). Quality of life after coronary artery surgery. *Quarterly Journal of Medicine*, 62, 239–248.

Meagher, D. M., Gregor, F. & Stewart, M. (1987). Dyadic social-support for cardiac surgery patients—a Canadian approach. *Social Science in Medicine*, 25, 833–837.

Miller, S. M. & Mangan, C. E. (1983). The interacting effects of information and coping style in adapting to gynecological stress: should the doctor tell all? *Journal of Personality and Social Psychology*, 45, 223–236.

Mumford, E., Schlesinger, H. J. & Glass, G. V. (1982). The effects of psychological intervention on recovery from surgery and heart attacks: an analysis of the literature. *American Journal of Public Health*, 72, 141–151.

Ogilvie, D. M. (1987). Life satisfaction and identity structure in late middle-aged men and women. *Psychology and Aging*, 2, 217–224.

Palmer, S. E., Canzona, L. & Wai, L. (1982). Helping families respond effectively to chronic illness: home dialysis as a case example. *Works in Health Care*, 8, 1–14.

Pearlin, L. I., Mullan, J. T., Semple, S. J. & Skaff, M. M. (1990). Caregiving and the stress process: an overview of concepts and their measures. *The Gerontologist*, 30, 583–591.

Rook, K. S. (1984). The negative side of social interaction: impact on psychological well-being. *Journal of Personality and Social Psychology*, 46, 1097–1108.

Rosenthal, R. & Rubin, D. B. (1982). A simple, general purpose display of magnitude of experimental effect. *Journal of Educational Psychology*, 74, 166–169.

Sandler, I. M. & Barrera, M. (1982). Toward a multimethod approach to assessing the effects of social support. *American Journal of Community Psychology*, 10, 65–80.

Scheier, M. F., Matthews, K. A., Owens, J. F., Magovern, G. J., Lefebve, R. C., Abott, R. A. & Carver, C. S. (1989). Dispositional optimism and recovery from coronary artery bypass surgery: the beneficial effects on physical and psychological well-being. *Journal of Personality and Social Psychology*, 57, 1024–1040.

Schmitt, F. E. & Wooldridge, P. J. (1973). Psychological preparation of surgical patients. *Nursing Research*, 22, 108–116.

Seeman, M. & Syme, S. L. (1987). Social networks and coronary artery disease: a comparison of the structure and function of social relations as predictors of disease. *Psychosomatic Medicine*, 49, 340–353.

Seaman, T. (1984). Social networks and coronary artery disease. Unpublished Doctoral Dissertation, University of California, Berkeley.

Sime, A. M. (1976). Relationship of preoperative fear, type of coping, and information received about surgery to recovery from surgery. *Journal of Personality and Social Psychology*, 34, 716–724.

Sokol, R. S., Folks, D. G., Herrick, R. W. & Freeman, A. M. (1987). Psychiatric outcome in men and women after coronary bypass surgery. *Psychosomatics*, 28, 11–16.

Stanton, B., Jenkins, C. D., Savageau, J. A. & Thurer, R. L. (1984). Functional benefits following coronary bypass graft surgery. *The Annals of Thoracic Surgery*, 37, 286–290.

Taylor, S. E. (1983). Adjustment to threatening events: a theory of cognitive adaptation. *American Psychologist*, 38, 1161–1173.

Taylor, G. B., Bandura, A., Ewart, C. K., Miller, N. H. & DeBusk, R. F. (1985). Exercise testing to enhance wives' confidence in their husbands' cardiac capability soon after clinically uncomplicated acute myocardial infarction. *American Journal of Cardiology*, 55, 635–638.

Thompson, S. C., Bundek, N. I. & Sobolew-Schubin, A. (1990). The caregivers of stroke patients: an investigation of factors associated with depression. *Journal of Applied Social Psychology*, 20, 115–129.

Vernon, T. A. & Bigelow, D. A. (1974). Effect of information about a potentially stressful situation on responses to stress impact. *Journal of Personality and Social Psychology*, 29, 50–59.

Ward, S., Leventhal, H., Easterling, D., Luchterhand, C. & Love, R. (1991). Social support, self-esteem, and communication in patients receiving chemotherapy. *Journal of Psychosocial Oncology*, 9, 95–116.

Williamson, P. S. (1985). Consequences for the family in chronic illness. *Journal of Family Practice*, 21, 23–32.

Wishnie, H. A., Hackette, T. P. & Cassem, N. H. (1971). Psychological hazards of convalescence following myocardial infarction. *Journal of the American Medical Association*, **215**, 1292–1296.

Wolfer, J. A. & Davis, C. E. (1970). Assessment of surgical patients' preoperative emotional condition and postoperative welfare. *Nursing Research*, **19**, 402–414.

Wolfer, J. & Visintainer, M. (1975). Pediatric surgical patients' stress responses and adjustment as a function of psychologic preparation and stress-point nursing care. *Nursing Research*, **24**, 244–255.

Zyzanski, S. J., Stanton, B. A. & Jenkins, C. D. (1981). Medical and psychosocial outcomes in survivors of major heart surgery. *Journal of Psychosomatic Research*, **23**, 213–221.

Index